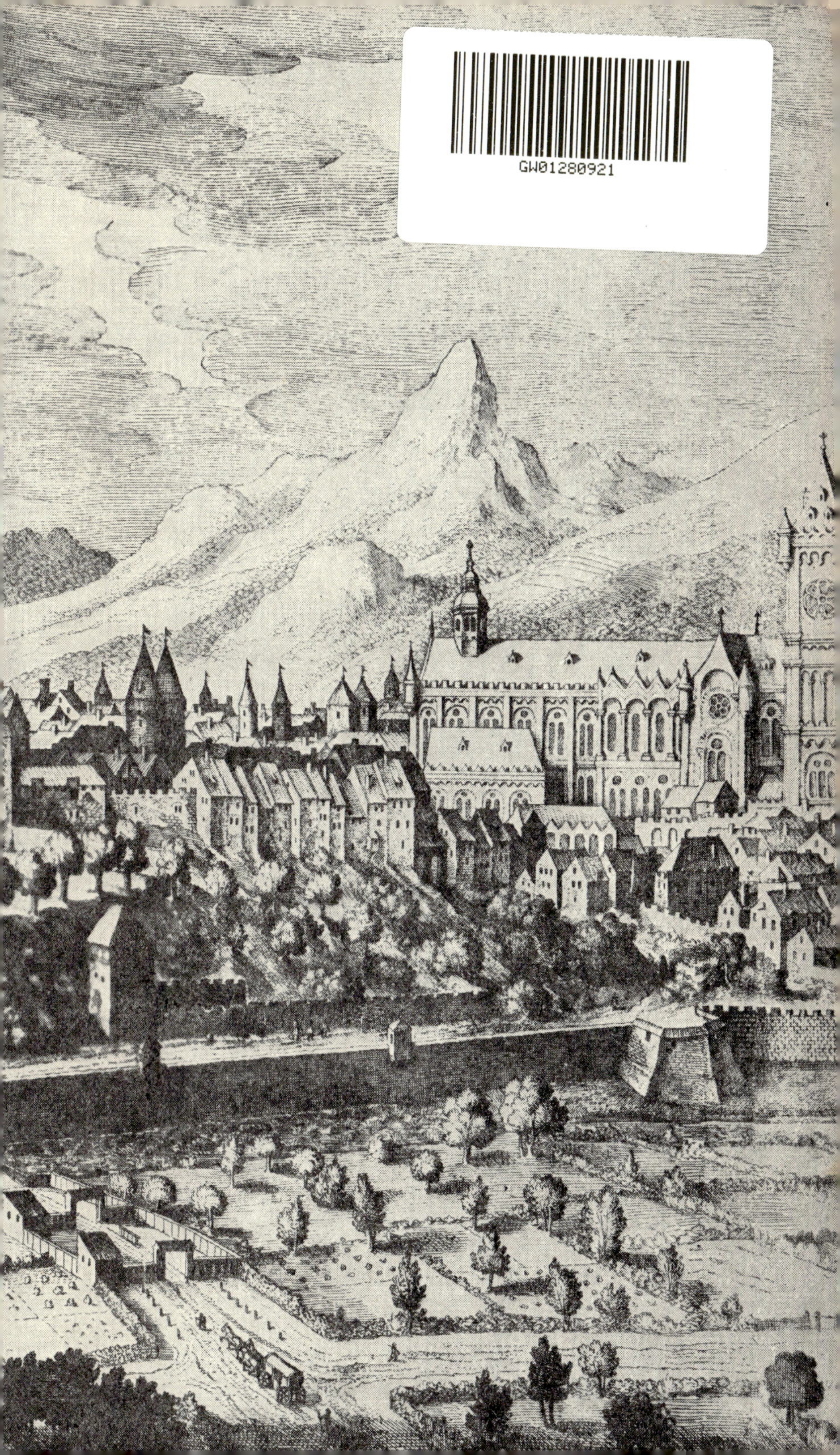

Catherine B Simpson
90 Whitselt Knowe
Forth

A
GENEVA
SERIES
COMMENTARY

REVELATION

THE BOOK OF
REVELATION

*An Exposition of the First Eleven Chapters
originally published under the title
'The Spiritual Kingdom'*

JAMES B. RAMSEY, D.D.

with an introduction by
CHARLES HODGE

THE BANNER OF TRUTH TRUST

THE BANNER OF TRUTH TRUST
3 Murrayfield Road, Edinburgh EH12 6EL
P.O. 621, Carlisle, Pennsylvania 17013, U.S.A.

First published 1873 by the Presbyterian
Committee of Publication, Richmond, Virginia

First Banner of Truth Trust edition
reprinted by photo litho 1977
© The Banner of Truth Trust, 1977

ISBN 0 85151 256 9

*Printed by offset lithography in Great Britain
by Robert MacLehose and Company Limited
Printers to the University of Glasgow*

JAMES BEVERLIN RAMSEY.

Dr. RAMSEY was born in Cecil county, Maryland, May the 20th, 1814. When only six years old, the death of his father, a godly man, consigned him to the sole care of his mother, a woman of uncommon sagacity, energy and piety. They were thenceforth never separated till the time of her death, which occurred at an extreme age, and not long before his own. His filial reverence and affection were beautiful to behold. At the age of fourteen years he made a public profession of faith in Christ. His own statement was that he never knew when he became a child of God. His mother thought he gave manifest evidence of being a christian from the time his father died. His academical education was completed at Lafayette College, Pa., of which the Rev. George Junkin, D. D., was then president. He entered the Theological Seminary at Princeton in 1836, where, after completing the full course, he remained a fourth year, in the study of theology and the original languages of the Scriptures. Dr. J. Addison Alexander, one of his teachers, who became intimately acquainted with him at that time, is known to have said that when Dr. Ramsey left the Seminary he was prepared to teach any class in the institution.

He was ordained a minister of the gospel in 1841, and installed pastor of the Presbyterian Church at West Farms, New York, where he continued till called, in 1846, to go as a missionary to the Choctaw Indians, and to be the Principal of Spencer Academy. After more than three years of arduous, useful labours, failing health compelled him to return.

During the next five years he was engaged in teaching, and, as far as health would permit, in preaching. The last two of these years were spent in the bounds of New Providence Church, Rockbridge county, Virginia, in the family of the Rev. James Morrison; a period to which he afterwards referred as one of the happiest of his life.

Under improved health he was installed pastor of New Monmouth Church, in that county, in 1854, where, during four years of devoted pastoral labour, and surrounded by an affectionate people, precious and abundant fruits were gathered unto eternal life. In 1858 he severed tender ties, under a sense of public duty, and became the pastor of the First Presbyterian Church in Lynchburg, Virginia. This relation continued till 1870, when, after repeated solicitations from himself, the session and church consented to unite with him in a request for its dissolution. This was caused by the feeble and hopeless condition of his health. Under great suffering he meekly and patiently awaited the hour of his departure, which came on the Sabbath day, July 23, 1871, when he rested from his labours and fell asleep in Jesus, entering upon that Sabbath which shall never end.

Dr. Ramsey was an eminently good man; of profound convictions of sin; of unfeigned humility; of deep-rooted faith; of ardent love to Christ and His Church. His whole life was in close communion with God, and full of a spirit truly apostolical. He was also a man "mighty in the Scriptures." His general scholarship was extensive and accurate. His fine attainments and discriminating judgment made him a wise instructor in sacred things; and few men of his age had secured in so high a degree the love and confidence of the Church wherever he was known. Had longer life and more comfortable health been granted, larger and richer fruits would no doubt have been gathered from his careful culture and ripe religious experience. This volume is the only production of any considerable extent which has been left. His name is worthy to be had " in everlasting remembrance."

CONTENTS.

I.

INTRODUCTORY.

LECTURE 1.—CHAPTER 1 : 3.
The Promised Blessing,.. 25

LECTURE 2.—CHAPTER 1 : 4–7.
The Gospel of the Kingdom,.. 40

LECTURE 3.—CHAPTER 1 : 17–18.
The Consolations of the Kingdom,............................... 59

II.

THE VISIBLE REPRESENTATION OF THE KINGDOM.

LECTURE 4.—CHAPTER 1 : 20.
The Golden Candlesticks. The Visible Church: its Mission,....... 73

LECTURE 5.—CHAPTER 1 : 20.
The Seven Stars. The Authority of Christ in the Visible Church,... 95

LECTURE 6.—CHAPTER 2 : 1–11.
Imperfections and Varieties of the Visible Church. Ephesus and Smyrna. Declining Love. Persecution,.............................. 121

LECTURE 7.—CHAPTER 2 : 12–29.
Imperfections and Varieties continued. Pergamos and Thyatira. Friendship of the World. Heresy, ... 141

LECTURE 8.—CHAPTER 3 : 1–22.
Imperfections and Varieties continued. Sardis. Philadelphia and Laodicea. Spiritual Deadness. Spiritual Power. Lukewarmness, ... 163

CONTENTS.

LECTURE 9.—CHAPTERS 2 AND 3.
Condition of the Promises. The Individual Conflict required,...... 190

LECTURE 10.—CHAPTERS 2 AND 3.
The Promises. The Glory of the Triumphant Church,............... 205

III.

THE TRUE CONCEPTION OF THE SPIRITUAL KINGDOM.

LECTURE 11.—CHAPTER 4 : 1-6.
Its Divine and Spiritual Nature and Privileges,........................... 223

LECTURE 12.—CHAPTER 4 : 6-8.
Its Spiritual Life,... 238

LECTURE 13.—CHAPTER 4 : 6-8.
The Glory, Claims, and Privileges of this Life,........................... 252

LECTURE 14.—CHAPTER 4 : 8-11.
The Worship of the Kingdom,.. 264

IV.

ITS MEDIATOR KING, AND HIS REIGN.

LECTURE 15.—CHAPTER 5 : 1-7.
The Administration of the Kingdom undertaken by the Slain Lamb, 283

LECTURE 16.—CHAPTER 5 : 8-14.
The Investiture and Praises of the Slain Lamb,........................... 296

LECTURE 17.—CHAPTER 6 : 1—8 : 1.
The Reign of the Lamb, and its Results,.................................... 311

LECTURE 18.—CHAPTER 6 : 12-17.
The Great Revolution Involved,.. 330

V.

ITS CONFLICTS AND TRIUMPH.

LECTURE 19.—CHAPTER 8 : 2-6.
The Prayers of the Saints,.. 353

CONTENTS.

LECTURE 20.—CHAPTER 8 : 7–12.
The Earthly Good Smitten,.. 367

LECTURE 21.—CHAPTER 9 : 1–12.
The Soul Smitten. The Curse of Error. Spiritual Despotism,...... 381

LECTURE 22.—CHAPTER 9 : 13–21.
The Reaction of the Worldly Power and Wisdom : completing the Course of Disciplinary Judgments,...................................... 399

LECTURE 23.—CHAPTER 10.
The Divine and Gracious Agency, and the Human Instrumentality which it provides,... 419

LECTURE 24.—CHAPTER 11 : 1, 2.
The True Church, and the Subjects of her Testimony,................... 435

LECTURE 25.—CHAPTER 11 : 2.
The Power of the World in and over the External Church,............ 453

LECTURE 26.—CHAPTER 11 : 3–10.
The Power of a Witnessing Church during these Abounding Corruptions, in her Worship and Government,............................ 469

LECTURE 27.—CHAPTER 11 : 10–13.
The Vitality and Triumph of a Pure Spiritual Testimony,.............. 488

LECTURE 28.—CHAPTER 11 : 14–18.
The Final Triumph,.. 504

SYNOPSIS OF LECTURES.

PART I.

INTRODUCTORY.

LECTURE I.

THE PROMISED BLESSING.

CHAP. 1: 3.

Neglect of this book guarded against. I. Reasons of this neglect: (1.) Its mysteriousness; (2.) A mistaken notion as to the design of prophecy; (3.) The too specific application of its symbols; (4.) An idea that great learning was necessary to get practical benefit from it. II. Its practical value shown: (1.) By the nearness of the times of which it treats; (2.) By its title; (3.) By its general scope and design; (4.) By its special discoveries of truth; (5.) By its very mystery; (6.) In the whole history of the church's experience.

LECTURE II.

THE GOSPEL OF THE KINGDOM.

CHAP. 1: 4–8.

The author of the book. To whom addressed. Its subject here announced. I. *The gospel message.* Grace and peace from the triune God. These blessings exhaustless and free. II. *The church's response.* (1.) Conscious dignity and privileges; (2.) Price of these blessings; (3.) Grateful ascription of glory. III. *The world's warning and the church's hope.* Christ's second coming. Consummation of salvation and damnation. Now coming in the progress of His mediatorial reign. All present judgments preparatory. Tremble and rejoice.

LECTURE III.

THE CONSOLATIONS OF THE KINGDOM.
CHAP. 1: 17, 18.

This the spirit and design of the whole book. Circumstances of the church when written. Still the same need of consolation. I. The believer's terrors are groundless. The whole previous vision one of grace. II. The Redeemer is divine, the First and the Last in creation, providence and redemption. III. His atonement and intercession perfectly remove guilt and secure life. IV. His dominion is universal, even over death and the unseen world. These four topics pervade all this book. All in Christ. No other consolation for sinners.

PART II.

THE VISIBLE MANIFESTATION OF THE KINGDOM.
CHAP. 1: 20.—CHAP. 3: 22.

LECTURE IV.

THE VISIBLE CHURCH; ITS MISSION.
CHAP. 1: 20.

Design of this section of the book. 1. The real kingdom invisible. 2. The visible church represents it, and is of divine origin. 3. Importance of definite distinctions between a true and a false representative. 4. The true here defined by symbols and examples.

The true church symbolized: *first*, in its mission, by the golden candlesticks. This the FIRST MARK of a true church. These represent her, (1.) As a light-bearer, not passively but actively, by witness-bearing in all her worship and government; (2.) In this dependant on Christ's presence; (3.) Identical in all ages; (4.) Her unity not visible but in Christ; (5.) Most precious; the central object of this book; attachment to her ordinances. Are you a true or a false witness for God?

LECTURE V.

THE AUTHORITY OF THE VISIBLE CHURCH.
CHAP. 1: 20.

The SECOND MARK of a true church: the authority by which it is ruled. The stars in Christ's right hand symbols of authority. I. Meaning of these star-angels. 1. Angels not a designation of any particular office. 2. Designates the nature of all church offices, as involving only the function of messengers of Christ. 3. Shown by the nature and position of these stars. 4. Shown by their relation to the other accompanying symbols. 5. Each church has its own, and but one. In connection with the candlesticks, this a decisive test of a true church. II. Application of these principles: 1. All authority in the church from Christ. 2. Responsibility of ordaining men to office, of receiving and accrediting men as Christ's messengers. 3. Church authority purely spiritual, and for edification. 4. Gives admonition and encouragement to church rulers. 5. Esteem and obedience due them.

LECTURE VI.

VARIETIES AND IMPERFECTIONS OF THE VISIBLE CHURCH; EPHESUS AND SMYRNA.

CHAP. 2: 1-11.

I. General character of all these epistles. A sevenfold picture of the church as it is. Defines the true church by actual examples. Their relation to the rest of the book. Observe, (1.) Their style; (2.) Christ's titles in them; (3.) Their common introduction, "I know thy works."

II. The sevenfold variety. 1. *Example* 1. *Ephesus*, or DECLINING LOVE. The city and church. (1.) Commendations. Orthodox in doctrine and pure in morals. (2.) Censures. First love forsaken. Danger in contending for truth. (3.) Lessons to all churches. Personal application. Admonitions. Remedy and preventive.

Example 2. *Smyrna*, or PERSECUTION. The church. Uncensured. Martyrdom of Polycarp. Consolations. Needed in all ages. Promise of grace to endure suffering, not of freedom from it. Outward wealth and prosperity no mark of a true church. The bitterest persecutions by apostate churches. Faithfulness.

LECTURE VII.

THE SAME SUBJECT CONTINUED; PERGAMOS AND THYATIRA.

CHAP. 2: 12-29.

Example 3. *Pergamos*, or the WORLD'S FRIENDSHIP. Balaamites and Nicolaitanes. Conformity to the world ever the same in principle, though different in form. Worldly alliances mark "Satan's dwelling-place."

Christ's rebukes severe. Discriminate between His faithful people and these polluters of His church.

The Balaamite doctrine now specially prevalent. Various ideas of what is worldly conformity. Bible definition clear. The church and the world confounded: 1st, By the variable and defective standard of separation; 2d, By the change wrought externally upon the world by the church. Christian civilization, so called, polishes, not purifies; intensifies earthliness by refining it. Increased danger from this cause. Christian social life pervaded by worldly conformity. Claims of Christ; a life of trust, how little shown.

Example 4. *Thyatira*, or HERESY. Toleration of a false teacher. Effects the same as in the church of Pergamos. Jezebel; why so named? "Depths of Satan," profundities of human wisdom. The judgments threatened.

This peculiar type of church character often realized. Grew to gigantic proportions in the church of Rome. Special promise to those who in such times are faithful. Dangers, warnings, and means of safety. Promise of victory over the world.

LECTURE VIII.

SAME SUBJECT CONTINUED; SARDIS, PHILADELPHIA, AND LAODICEA.

CHAP. 3: 1-22.

Example 5. *Sardis*, or SPIRITUAL DEADNESS. The city. The church in high reputation, yet dead. A galvanized corpse. Works not perfect. Garments defiled. Some things remaining. The charge and the warning. The sleeper's danger. Remember past mercies. The faithful remnant. Encouragement in the title Christ here uses, and the promise.

Example 6. *Philadelphia*, or SPIRITUAL POWER. This church uncensured. Commendations. Yet feeble. The peculiar promise to it of success, and of security under trial. The crowning promise of Christ's speedy coming, and the believer's crown.

Example 7. *Laodicea*, or LUKEWARMNESS. The worst of all. External prosperity, pride and loathsomeness. On the point of utter rejection. Christ's long-suffering and tenderness. Final promise.

Concluding inferences from this sevenfold view. (1.) Its completeness as a picture of the visible church. Warnings suited to all dangers.

Outward forms not once alluded to. (2.) Special application to the authorities of the churches. Importance of discipline. (3.) The full display of the divine attributes of Christ (4.) The personal presence of Christ now in His churches, and His present reign over them. Personal and visible often erroneously confounded. The spiritual presence a real one. (5.) Practical value of this whole picture of the visible church, as a test of a true church.

LECTURE IX.

AN INDIVIDUAL CONFLICT AND VICTORY, THE DESIGN OF THE VISIBLE, AND THE NECESSARY MEANS OF ATTAINING THE GLORY OF THE INVISIBLE KINGDOM.

CHAPS. 2 AND 3.

To him that overcometh."—(Seven times repeated.)

The indispensable condition of promised glory. Relation of this conflict to the rest of this book. 1. *Nature of this conflict.* The soul its sphere. Severe; self the great enemy. Entirely distinct from the conflict in the unrenewed heart. 2. *Its personal necessity.* Shown by the terms of these promises, and by the evils to be resisted in these churches. Not evaded by church connections, nor by change of circumstances. No truce. Not end till the last sinner is saved. 3. *Divine resources.* In Christ, our Head. Initiated by the Holy Spirit. Sustained by the Spirit. By the providence of God. All-sufficient encouragement. Relation of the visible church to this conflict, and its importance.

LECTURE X.

THE PROMISES " TO HIM THAT OVERCOMETH,"—(IN EACH CHURCH.)

CHAPS. 2 AND 3.

The prize, the glories of the triumphant kingdom. 1. Paradise restored. Life in Christ. 2. Death destroyed. The immortal body. 3 Priestly privileges. " Hidden manna." " White stone "—Urim and Thummim, direct and constant access to God, and knowledge of His will. 4. Kingly honours. Fellowship in Christ's dominion and triumph. These four exhaust the types of the old dispensation. 5. Perfect holiness and public adoption. 6. Union in one glorified family and city, and mutual participation in each other's bliss. 7. Fellowship with Christ in

His everlasting kingdom, when His mediatorial reign shall have ended. Present power of these promises. *Inf.* In what the triumph of the present visible church consists; not in the complete perfection of any present outward organizations, but in gathering and perfecting the elect.

PART III.

THE TRUE CONCEPTION OF THE KINGDOM.

Chap. 4.

LECTURE XI.

ITS DIVINE NATURE, AND SPIRITUAL PRIVILEGES.

Chap. 4: 1-6.

New division of the book. Change of method. The time and circumstances recalled. Nature of the vision, "in the Spirit." Teaching by symbols; its advantages. This the scene of all succeeding visions,

A symbolical picture of the essential elements of the spiritual kingdom. Seven of these: 1. The throne, and its formless occupant. God in His church, revealed and concealed in the glory of His own attributes. 2. The rainbow. Covenant mercy. 3. The twenty-four elders. The priestly and kingly dignity of the Redeemer. 4. The lightnings, thunderings and voices. Energies of His providence and Word. 5. The seven lamps of fire. Manifold enlightening energies of the Divine Spirit, the source of light in the kingdom. 6. The sea of glass. Exhaustless purifying influences. All a picture of present privileges conferred on each member of the kingdom. Their reality and glory.

LECTURE XII.

THE SPIRITUAL LIFE.

Chap. 4: 6-8.

Power of visible and material things over fallen man. Design of these symbols to counteract this by giving increased vividness to things unseen. *The four living creatures: the spiritual life of redeemed sinners, or the life of God in man.* This life the most stupendous and mysterious thing in creation; hence the strange and mysterious symbol. Proofs: 1. Must indicate something essential to the redeemed in chapter 5: 8, 9. 2. History of the symbol. Co-extensive with the history of redemption. In Ezekiel; in the tabernacle; at the gate of lost Paradise. 3. Its perfect adaptedness to represent this life, and nothing else. Beyond the range of nature; combined of the four most perfect forms of creature life on earth; this intensified by the profusion of eyes and wings. Image of the divine perfections in the creature. Sets forth the three leading properties of this life: (1) holiness, (2) spiritual knowledge, (3) and untiring activity. "In the throne:" secure and eternal. Now imperfectly manifested. Real, though mysterious.

LECTURE XIII.

THE GLORY, CLAIMS, AND PRIVILEGES OF THIS LIFE.

Chap. 4: 6-8.

This symbols forth: I. The glory of this life. (1.) In its being the moral image of God. (2.) In its origin, a new creation: the purchase of redeeming blood. (3.) In its results: perfect deliverance of soul and body from the curse, and of the earth itself. II Its claims and privileges. This symbol shows: (1.) The perfections we must cultivate; a fourfold view of holiness, spiritual power, submission, benevolence and communion with God. (2.) The spiritual perception and active energy to perceive and do the will of God, which this life supplies. Value of this and the accompanying symbols. Hence, (1.) The riches of God's Word; (2.) The vanity of the world; (3.) Comfort in affliction; and (4.) Nature's helplessness and refuge.

LECTURE XIV.

THE WORSHIP OF THE KINGDOM.

Chap. 4: 8-11.

Design of this whole chapter, to present the true spiritual kingdom in contrast with the imperfections of the visible church. Hence, not only its elements, but its activities are symbolized. THE WORSHIP OF THE KINGDOM. This has its origin in the symbol of life, its results in the prostration and praise of the elders. 1. All true worship is from a renewed heart. 2. *Adoration* of the Divine character, its first essential element. These living ones never rest in their praise; so Bible saints. Serious defect in devotional exercises. 3. Other essential element, *consecration.* Prostration and praise of the elders. Consists: (1.) In profound and cordial submission; (2.) Sense of obligation to Divine grace; (3.) Recognition of the will of God, as the creature's sole end and rule. This teaches, (1.) The nature and test of all acceptable worship, in outward forms, in the whole life. 2. External forms contemptible. 3. A cause of low piety, and its corrective.

PART IV.

ITS MEDIATOR KING, AND HIS REIGN.

Chap. 5 : 1—8 : 1.

LECTURE XV.

THE ADMINISTRATION OF THE KINGDOM ASSUMED BY THE SLAIN LAMB.

Chap. 5: 1-7.

Previous picture of the kingdom. Subject of this section; by whom and how it is administered. Leading topics of this chapter. 1. The book in the hands of Him that sits on the throne. Secret and all-comprehensive purposes of God. *Seven* sealed; covers the whole period of the mediatorial reign. 2. The proclamation of the mighty angel. No creature power or skill can conduct its affairs. Despondency from such expectations. Requires divine power. 3. The Lamb only able to do it. His seven horns, and seven eyes. Head over all to the church. "Weep not," on account of difficulties in your own salvation. Or, on account of afflictions. Or, on account of the perils of the church. Rejoice that the Lamb reigns; work for Him; opposition futile.

LECTURE XVI.

INVESTITURE AND PRAISES OF THE SLAIN LAMB.

Chap. 5: 8-14.

Grandeur of the scene. 1. New song of the redeemed. New in reference to song in chap. 4: 11. New in its object, subject and occasion.

Never ceasing. Will you join in it? Four things in it, and what follows. 2. Christ's right to administer the kingdom. His redemption. This no mere offer. Effectual grace. Providential agencies. Highest dignities conferred. 3. Hence, the assurance of triumph. In regard to the believer. In regard to the church. Reign of the saints. 4. The whole creation joins in the praise. No more curse. Implies not the salvation of devils, and all the wicked, but the opposite. A renovated earth the inheritance of the perfected church. Glimpses of this elsewhere in the Bible. 5. Overwhelming evidence of our Lord's divinity.

LECTURE XVII.

THE REIGN OF THE LAMB; ITS AGENCIES AND RESULTS.

Chap. 6: 1—8: 1.

The Lamb unsealing the book, Christ reigning. Relation of these seals to the trumpets and vials. *Seal* 1. Christ, in His gospel, conquering. All these agencies come at the call of the living creatures. *Seal* 2. War smiting the earth in its social joys. *Seal* 3. Want smiting the supports of its life, both of body and soul. *Seal* 4. Death, by all these instrumentalities, smiting the life itself. These four comprise all the agencies of the church, and Providence. Not confined to particular periods. *Seal* 5. The spiritual church bleeding, waiting, praying. Long period of conflict. *Seal* 6. Triumph, in three parts: (1.) Power of the world overthrown, revolutionized, and all enemies destroyed. (2.) Saints prepared during this delay by the Spirit's sealing. (3.) Their number and glory perfected. *Seal* 7. End of all conflict. The eternal Sabbath. *Note.* The half hour's silence.

LECTURE XVIII.

THE GREAT REVOLUTION.

Chap. 6: 12-17.

The overthrow radical and universal. Shows the world's essential ungodliness. Questions in regard to physical changes and to instrumentalities, here excluded. Does it teach a complete moral revolution? I Meaning of these symbols. Literal events impossible. Interpretation fixed in the old prophets. (1.) Is. 13. (2.) Is. 34: 4, &c. Striking parallel: (3.) Joel 2: 28-32. (4.) Hag. 2.

II. Meaning of this passage not satisfied by any past changes effected by Christianity. What it does require. Includes also past triumphs. The Christianized Paganism of modern civilization. Changes wrought not to be underrated, nor overrated. This moral earthquake required, (1st.) By the ungodliness of all governments, and of political principles. (2d.) By the whole habits of social and business life being divorced from God. (3d.) By the character of education, its spirit and aims. (4th.) By the extent of Sabbath desecration. (5th.) By the defection of the church from the primitive model. All that worldly men live for, doomed. To each that day of wrath may be near. Flee.

PART V.

ITS CONFLICTS AND TRIUMPHS.

Chap. 8 : 2.—Chap. 11 : 18.

LECTURE XIX.

THE PRAYERS OF THE SAINTS.
Chap. 8 : 2–6.

Design of this section. As the seven seals show Christ's agency, the seven trumpets show the working of the human agencies employed or resisting. Cover the same ground. 1. The seven angels and trumpets. All human and created instrumentalities called forth by influences sent out from the throne. Angels the appropriate symbols of these, therefore. 2. The incense and prayers. The angel: the divinely appointed agency by which these prayers are called forth. Incense: Christ's intercessions. All judgments in answer to prayer. No unanswered prayer. Answered not according to form, but ultimate design. Influence of prayer on an ungodly world. 3. Fire of the altar. Truth of Christ crucified in contact with the world. Like fire, in the heart, and in the nations. Hence these commotions. Scripture parallels. The power of truth and of prayer.

LECTURE XX.

THE EARTHLY GOOD SMITTEN : THE FIRST FOUR TRUMPETS.
Chap. 8 : 7–13.

These angel trumpeters; warning for all. Prepared from the beginning. Though successively called forth, these agencies then act simultaneously. 1. First four, a separate group. Smite the whole worldly system, the land, the sea, the fountains, and the lights. "*Earth*" and "*heaven,*" symbols, not of place, but character; of things earthly and heavenly: of the earthly and heavenly sphere. 2. Instrumentality and effect of each. (1.) The storm of war upon consolidated social order. (2.) Overthrow of government in anarchy and blood. (3.) A church becoming a political or earthly power, and poisoning the purest springs of human happiness. (4.) No new instrumentality introduced, but as the final effect of all these, the world's lights darkened. Three instrumentalities so different cannot symbolize events so perfectly similar as the various inroads of the northern barbarians. 3. Design of each, and their application to the whole history of the church in its relation to the world during the early and middle ages. The prediction of the angel in mid-heaven; these calamities may well awaken apprehension of more terrific woes. 4. Application to all succeeding ages, and to the present. Admonition to the church and the world.

LECTURE XXI.

THE SOUL SMITTEN: THE CURSE OF ERROR. FIFTH TRUMPET.
CHAP 9: 1-11.

The earthly good, though smitten, still trusted. Result. The fifth angel. *Scorpion locusts, hordes of soul-destroying errors.* 1. Their origin. A fallen star, a spiritual power degenerated into an earthly. Hence, having the keys of hell, instead of heaven. 2. Their forms; strange and unearthly. "Doctrines of devils." 3. Their king: Satan. 4. Their commission: peculiar, not against earthly good, but the souls of the unsealed. Cannot hurt God's children. Cannot kill or destroy the unsealed race, but only torment. Danger of unbelief. This torment unendurable. 5. The limit to this infliction. Five months, not all the year. No deception can last. Such errors, limited in their very nature, die in their own desolations. Observe, (1.) The sin of unbelief produces the curse of error. Observe, (2.) Special examples: apostacies and delusions of the middle ages; Mohammedan, Papal, and Greek. Spiritual despotism. Illustration of verse 6: death itself no escape. 2 Thess. 2: 3-12. Observe, (3.) The value of the Bible. Observe, (4.) Sealing of the Spirit the only security.

LECTURE XXII.

THE REACTION OF THE WORLD'S POWER AND WISDOM. SIXTH TRUMPET.
CHAP. 9 : 12-21.

First and second woes; cause and effect. Cause ever working. The principles are here described, before the organized systems they produced, which are described in latter part of the book. The sixth trumpet. 1. The second woe comes at the call of the Intercessor in answer to prayer. 2. Its agencies. The powers tormented by this spiritual despotism, and restrained by it. "In the Euphrates;" in the nations supporting the spiritual Babylon. They are summed up under a fourfold classification; love of power, of wealth, of sensual pleasure, and of knowledge. 3. How restrained. By the delusions that tormented them. Prepared for the moment appointed of God. Historical illustration. 4. Extent of influence. "Myriads of myriads;" yet limited to *two* of these. The world's power and its wisdom embrace all. So the two beasts of chapter thirteen. 5. Their true character. The cavalry of hell. Their twofold means of inflicting injury; violence and serpent cunning. Impossible to locate this on any particular event of history. Whole history of the church full of illustrations. 6. Their utter incompetency to produce repentance. The sins mentioned express the ungodliness and immoralities of all spiritual delusions.

Inf. 1. The divine authorship manifest. 2. The inveteracy of human depravity.

LECTURE XXIII.

THE GRACIOUS DIVINE AGENCY, AND THE HUMAN INSTRUMENTALITY WHICH IT PROVIDES.
CHAP. 10.

Necessity of a different agency in order to salvation. The next four leading symbols show what this is. 1. The mighty angel. The presence and power of Christ in His church. The open book, the Gospel. The seven thunders, whose utterances were unwritten : the mystery of His almighty power in grace and providence. No more delay. 2. *The human instrumentality.* The seer himself becomes a part of the symbolic scene. The church not only to see and adore, but to be the channel of the grace. The little book received and eaten ; the truth incorporated into the spiritual life. Expresses itself as a divine testimony. "Again." True nature of the church's testimony.

LECTURE XXIV.

THE WITNESSING CHURCH, AND THE RULE AND SUBJECTS OF HER TESTIMONY.

Chap. 11 : 1, 2.

How is the charge just given to be fulfilled ? I. The act of measuring. Truth must be ascertained. The divine rule. Human opinions worthless. The written word. II. Objects to be measured. (1.) The temple. God dwelling in and among men. Christ and His mystical body. True unity of the church. All human ordering excluded. (2.) The altar. Blood of atonement. (3.) The worshippers. A separate and consecrated priesthood. Adherence to the cross and crown of Jesus. We have here another picture of the true church. The whole matter of her testimony.

LECTURE XXV.

THE POWER OF THE WORLD IN AND OVER THE VISIBLE CHURCH.

Chap. 11 : 2.

Unmeasured things. 1. Externals of the church given over to the worldly minded. Such mere externals to be rejected. How fulfilled. 2. The period of this desecration limited. Precisely defined in the divine plan and purpose ; and hence encouragement. But why so specific ? Not that we may antedate events. Yet a very important use. Location of these periods in history impossible. Theory of a day for a year uncertain. Early purity of the church brief. Assumed dates of 606 and 755, etc., unsatisfactory. The beginning in each place known only to God. This indefiniteness does not lessen the value of these numbers. They symbolize the enemy's failure. Their previous typical and historic use. Their comparative value evident and precious. What is your position ?

LECTURE XXVI.

THE POWER OF A CHURCH, WITNESSING BY HER WORSHIP AND GOVERNMENT, DURING THESE CORRUPTIONS.

Chap. 11 : 3–10.

Necessity and difficulty of faithful witnessing. This whole passage the words of the angel; its design. 1. Who are these two witnesses ?

The two great functions of the church by which her testimony is borne: her *worship* and *discipline*. Nature and importance of these to this end. 2. Power of these witnesses. Like that of Moses and Elijah. Effect of a rejected Gospel. Slaying saints is not killing the witnesses. In persecution their voice the clearest. 3. *Killing* them. By corruption of worship and discipline. By the beast from the pit, the worldly power and wisdom. 4. Their dead bodies preserved. Lifeless forms; dead churches favourites with the world. Preserved in the streets of the great city, in the organizations of a corrupt and apostate church. These principles always working. Began early; at length in almost the whole church. Does it imply a universal silencing of these witnesses at once? Present alarming tendencies.

LECTURE XXVII.

THE VITALITY OF GOD'S WITNESSES, AND THE TRIUMPH OF A PURELY SPIRITUAL TESTIMONY.

CHAP. 11 : 11–13.

These witnesses indestructible. 1. Their safety is in delivering their testimony. Only when they cease to testify are they killed. 2. Their speedy reviving. The brief suspension of life enough to show their entire dependence on the Holy Spirit. He is the Author of their reviving. A revival of pure religion is a reviving of pure worship and discipline. 3. Elevation of these witnessing agencies to a purely spiritual and heavenly sphere. 4. Effects of this. Overthrow of the world's power in the church. "Seven thousand names of men:" all mere human authorities and opinions. The church cleansed and God glorified in it. Second woe ended. All the revelations of the sixth trumpet viewed in connection. All relates to the deliverance and purifying of the church. The restoration of Pentecostal times. Glorious prospects. No new agent intimated. The Spirit our hope. Present duty and encouragement.

LECTURE XXVIII.

THE TRIUMPH.

CHAP. 11 : 14–18.

Seventh trumpet calls upon a grand vision of victory. Comprehensiveness of these visions. 1. Celebrates the triumph as completed.

Includes all triumphs from the beginning. By no other agencies than those already revealed. Except the final acts of vengeance and of love, to end the conflict. 2. It *consummates redemption.* This the idea of the "*seventh.*" The last woe. Quickly follows the second in its very nature always. A long period of triumphant witnessing *may* intervene before the end comes. This language, however, describes not merely the commonly expected millenium. It is *Christ's eternal reign on the earth.* This in harmony with other Scriptures. Whole history of the kingdom points to this. This song of the elders requires it. Living creatures of chapter fourth and fifth, etc., no longer present, the life being now perfected and actually possessed. This song not one of expectation, but of thanksgiving: all enemies destroyed. The curtain falls. The new heavens and the new earth.

INTRODUCTION,

BY

CHARLES HODGE, D. D., LL. D.

It can hardly be questioned that a portion of our brethren, both in this country and in Great Britain, pay undue attention to the prophetic parts of Scripture. On this account they have been designated the "Prophetical School." While there are many exceptions, it is yet a characteristic of this class of writers, that they seem more concerned in future hopes than in present duty. They have no faith in the conversion of the world under the present "dispensation of the Spirit." They often speak in disparaging terms of the work of the Spirit, saying that the gospel has never yet converted a single town or village, and that it is therefore vain to expect that it will convert the world. The world, according to their theory, is to be converted through the terrors and judgments attending the second advent of Christ: not otherwise, and not before.

GENERAL NEGLECT OF THE PROPHECIES.

While all this is true, it is still more obviously true, that the great majority of Christians, and of students of the Bible, unduly neglect the prophecies. The historical books of the Old Testament are far less interesting than the evangelists of the New; so the doctrinal writings of the Old Testament have less to command the attention than the doctrinal instructions of the New. To the mass of Bible readers the doctrinal and practical portions of the Scriptures have more interest than the prophetical. Another cause of the comparative neglect of the latter is found in the fact that they contain much that is peculiar and hard to be understood. They require more study, more strict and well-considered rules of interpretation, with more self-command and self-subjection to the laws of exegesis, which nothing but necessity will induce the student to adopt. The difficulty attending prophetic interpretation is sufficiently attested by the number of failures exhibited in its history. The views that have been given of the visions of Ezekiel, of Zechariah, of Daniel, and of the Apocalypse, are scarcely less numerous than are the authors who have attempted their exposition. It is no wonder, therefore, that those who do not feel any special vocation to the work show so little alacrity to enter upon a field which is strewn with the wrecks of the labours of their predecessors.

Besides, the remark has often been made that the study of the prophecies either finds a man insane or makes him so. Although this remark is unjust, and is contradicted by numerous examples,—by none more conspicuous than that of the sainted Dr. Ramsey,—it nevertheless contains enough truth to render it a warning. It is true that the habit of mind induced by efforts to solve enigmas deemed of the utmost importance is more or less abnormal. One becomes disposed to accept what, in the judgment of ordinary minds, is all but impossible: to regard as certain, and to estimate as absolutely conclusive, what ordinary men consider doubtful or of very little weight. The members of the "Prophetical School" sometimes believe confidently that in which none but themselves have the slightest faith. Many, for example, believe that the expressions in which the Scriptures describe the destruction of the world, such as that the heavens and the earth shall be burnt up, shall pass away, and be melted with fervent heat, imply only the partial destruction of the wicked; that after this destruction—which is to change the earth less than the deluge did—men will continue to be born and die, to be convinced and converted, to all eternity. And even when they do not entertain opinions so contrary to the general faith of the Church, they hold, with the greatest confidence, views widely at variance with each other. Thus, some hold that Babylon of the Apocalypse is pagan Rome, others that it is Papal Rome, others that it is the Papacy in its worldly power.

While what has just been said does in some measure account for the general neglect of the study of prophecy, it does not by any means justify that neglect. "All Scripture is given by inspiration of God, and is profitable for doctrine, for reproof, for correction, for instruction in righteousness, that the man of God may be perfect, thoroughly furnished unto all good works." 2 Tim. 3: 16, 17. As the prophecies are a part of the Scripture, they are given by inspiration, and are useful for all the purposes above stated; and the man of God, whether he be layman or minister, cannot be properly furnished for his work, unless he be well versed in the knowledge of this department of revelation. This, however, as already remarked, is far from being the case, either as to the people or the ministry. Many even of our oldest ministers, if asked the meaning of some unfulfilled prophecy, must answer, not merely that he does know, which might be excusable, but that he has never examined the question, which would be, as a general thing, inexcusable. If asked to state the peculiar principles of prophetic interpretation, he will have to answer that he has never studied the subject. Questions so important as these may be presented: What will be the future of the Church militant? Is it to be a splendid earthly kingdom, with Christ at its head, or a spiritual kingdom, consisting of "righteousness, and peace, and joy in the Holy Ghost?" What will be the "new heavens and new earth," that shall be introduced when the heavens and earth which now are shall have passed away? These ever-recurring questions, which concern the very nature of our eternal future, cannot be answered with any intelligent confidence by multitudes even of our oldest ministerial brethren. The faith of most Christians upon this subject rests upon tradition. That is, they believe in relation to it what the mass of Christians for the last thousand years have believed, and for that reason. This, certainly, is wrong. A whole department of the revelation of God ought not to be thus neglected. The treasures of truth contained in the prophetic writings ought not to be thus undervalued; and we are offenders and losers if we close our eyes in the light which these writings throw upon the future of the Church.

WHO WERE THE PROPHETS?

When any one who has hitherto been guilty of this neglect of prophecy is providentially called to make them a subject of study, the first question which presents itself is, Who were the prophets? What constituted a man a member of that sacred class, and what were the functions of his office? We whose great blessedness it is to have been taught from infancy to believe all that the Bible teaches, are happily freed from the necessity of discussing these questions at the bar of reason. Every Christian admits the Bible to be the word of God in the sense that whatever it says God says; and therefore, the "thus saith the Lord" is for Christians the last and highest evidence of truth. The Bible clearly teaches that a prophet is a spokesman—one who speaks for another; so that what one says the other says. The man, therefore, who stands in the relation of prophet to God, is, so long as that relation subsists, the mouthpiece of God: the thoughts which he utters are the thoughts of God, and his words are the words of God. Hence it is that the sacred writers so uniformly renounce any self-derived authority for their messages, and claim for them the authority of God, and that they so often begin their discourses with the words, "Thus saith the Lord." This gives us the clearest and simplest idea of inspiration, and the clearest idea, also, of what it was to be a prophet. A prophet was a man inspired: a man under such an influence from the Spirit of God as rendered him an infallible messenger from God. Hence the Jews were accustomed to divide their sacred books into "the Law and the Prophets," a classification sanctioned also by the Apostles. Acts 26: 22; Rom. 3: 21. As the Law, or Pentateuch, was written by Moses, the greatest of the Old Testament prophets, it follows that all the sacred writers of the Old Testament were prophets, that is, inspired men—

men called to be the messengers of God. All men ordained to the ministry, whether under the old dispensation or the new, are in one sense messengers of God. We are therefore taught further, that none but inspired—that is, infallible—messengers are called prophets. This, under both dispensations, was the discriminating difference between ordinary teachers and prophets. This distinction is made specially clear in 1 Cor. 14, and in Eph. 4: 11. In the latter passage prophets and teachers are clearly distinguished. All pastors were teachers, but they were not all prophets. That is, it was inspiration—often including revelation, 1 Cor. 14: 30—which was the essential characteristic of a prophet. There was, however, a distinction among the prophets themselves. Some were permanently inspired, and were recognized as the official organs of God among His people. Such were the Apostles, and such was Moses. Others were only occasional recipients of that divine influence which made them prophets. Hence the Apostles spoke to them and of them as their official inferiors. 1 Cor. 14: 37. Hence, also, we hear of their receiving sudden revelations. 1 Cor. 14: 30. And hence, under the Old Testament, the prophets often speak of "the word of the Lord" coming to them; of "the hand of the Lord being upon them;" and other forms of expression are employed indicative of occasional accessions of divine influence. It seems, however, that there was a class of men who were recognized as the special organs of God in dealing with the people, and who were, so to speak, prophets by profession: men to whom persons of all conditions—kings and widows—resorted when they needed special instruction from God. Such a class did exist, and it seems, from 1 King 18: 4, to have been at times very numerous; for we are told that Obadiah took "an hundred prophets of the Lord, and hid them by fifties in a cave," on account of the persecution by Jezebel. However, Elijah was able to say, in the same chapter, verse 22, " I alone remain a prophet of the Lord." When, therefore, we read of "the schools of the prophets," we are not to understand schools consisting of prophets, but schools presided over by prophets, in which young men were trained for the prophetic office. For it is to be remembered that the prophets were teachers, and needed to be instructed in the religion and in the history of the people. It is not the ordinary mode of God's dealing with His people, to do by supernatural agency what can be effected by natural means. For that part of the prophet's work for which a man could be prepared by human training, such training was employed; and from this class of trained men, as a general rule, were taken the recipients of those supernatural gifts which made a man a prophet in the strict sense of the word. It is no less true that the word was sometimes popularly used, in a looser sense, to designate holy men, who enjoyed peculiarly intimate relations with God. Thus, in Psalm 105: 15, it is said, "Touch not Mine anointed, and do My prophets no harm. This language was used of the patriarchs, specially of Abraham, who had intimate fellowship with God, and to whom He revealed Himself as He did not to the world.

A prophet, then, was a teacher sent of God. He received his designation, not from the nature of his message, but from its source. It mattered not whether the message referred to past sins, or to present duties, or to future events. If it came immediately from God, if the messenger could say "Thus saith the Lord," if the word of the Lord was put into his lips, and he was commanded to deliver it to the people, then he was a prophet. Jeremiah describes his inauguration when he says, "The Lord put forth His hand, and touched my mouth. And the Lord said unto me, Behold, I have put My words in thy mouth,"—Jeremiah 1: 9, —and "Whatsoever I command thee, thou shalt speak," verse 7. And David said, "The Spirit of the Lord spake by me, and His word was in my tongue." 2 Samuel 23: 2. Hence, constantly in the New Testament the testimony of the Old is quoted, not as the testimony of men, but as that of God. The formula of quotation is usually "God said," or "The Holy Ghost said," or "The Holy Ghost by the mouth of the prophet said." The most didactic statement, however, of the nature of prophecy, or of what constituted the peculiar distinction of a prophet, is to be found in 1 Peter 1: 20, 21, "No prophecy of the Scripture is of any private interpretation. For the prophecy came not in old time [at any time] by the will of man; but holy men of God spake as they were moved by the Holy Ghost." No prophecy is a man's own interpretation of the will or purpose of God. It does not come from himself, from his own wisdom, experience, feelings, or foresight; but holy men of God spake as they were moved by the Holy Ghost. It is here denied that the prophets uttered their own thoughts, or used their own language. It is affirmed that their thoughts were the thoughts of God, and their words the words of God; so that, in the strictest sense of the terms, what the prophets said God said. It is to be remembered that the word prophet is used by the apostle in this connection in a sense which includes all the sacred writers.

Besides this comprehensive sense of the term, which makes it include every man who was the organ of God, or inspired, it is also used in Scripture in a narrower sense. It is to be borne in mind that Israel was saved "in hope:" they waited patiently for the good things to come. Their whole system was predictive, or typical: a shadow of the things that were to come. The plan of salvation was the same for them as for us; but it was revealed slowly, by a process of historical and doctrinal development. There was to be a redemption. That redemption was to be by blood. There was to be a Redeemer. That Redeemer was to unite in Himself all the offices of Prophet, Priest, and King, and in his Person the attributes of God and man. He was to subdue all nations. His kingdom, and with it true religion, were to extend to the ends of the earth. To Him every knee should bow, and every tongue should swear. The patriarchs obtained a good report through faith, but received not the promise, God having provided some better thing for us, that they without us should not be made perfect. It was not the purpose of God that the great work of redemption should be consummated in the days of the fathers, so as to exclude the millions who since their time have enjoyed its benefits, and the millions more yet to come. Everything under the old dispensation pointed to the future. Toward the expected Redeemer every eye was directed: His Person, His work, and the blessings of His advent, became the great object of all prophetic instruction. The sins of the people were reproved, judgments were denounced, restoration and favour were promised, all in a theocratic form, or with distinct reference to the great scheme of redemption which had been announced from the beginning,

Hence it unavoidably came to pass, that the general character of the prophets, as inspired teachers, became more and more merged into that of predicters. Foretelling the future had always been one of the great functions of their office; and hence the question, "Is there no more a prophet of the Lord in the land?" was the constant and anxious inquiry of both prince and people when their horizon was overcast. And throughout the New Testament, the predictions of the Old, as fulfilled in Jesus of Nazareth, are appealed to as proofs of His Messiahship. This distinction between the prophets, as inspired men and as predicters of the future, was early recognized by the Jews. This is the ground of the division which they made of their sacred books into three classes: the Law, the Prophets, and the Hagiographa; the Law being of course the Pentateuch; the Prophets those whose writings are characteristically predictive; and the third class all others, differing greatly among themselves, which did not fall under the other heads. This distinction seems to be clearly recognized in the New Testament, as in Luke 24 : 44. In the Church it has been universally received, so that, when the Prophets, or the prophetic writings, are spoken of, every one understands what books of Scripture are referred to. A prophet, therefore, in the comprehensive sense of the word, means an inspired man: one employed by God as His infallible organ of communication with men. If the word be taken in its stricter Scriptural sense, it designates those selected to reveal the purposes of God in relation to the more or less remote future of the Church and of the world.

NATURE OF THE PROPHETIC INFLUENCE.

The second question for the student of prophecy to answer concerns the peculiar influence which constituted a man a prophet: its nature, and its subjective effect upon its recipient. The Scriptures describe it when they speak of the power of God, or the hand of God, or the Spirit of God, coming upon him, or state that he spoke as he was moved by the Holy Ghost. Although it is impossible for us to understand or to explain how the Spirit of God operates upon the soul, so as to determine its character and acts, yet it is clearly revealed that He does thus operate, while much is revealed, both negatively and positively, of the effects thus produced.

The Bible everywhere teaches and assumes that there is a God; that this God is a spirit, a self-conscious, intelligent, voluntary agent; that He is everywhere present and active; governing all His creatures, and all their actions; acting with means, through them, or without them. It is the denial of one or the other of these Scriptural truths which lies at the foundation of all the philosophical and religious errors of our age. Hence the necessity of the people being thoroughly imbued with the philosophy of the Bible, which is the philosophy of God.

As God is everywhere present, and everywhere active, there are different classes of events which differ according to the relations which they bear to the divine efficiency. First, those which are called natural, which are due to forces inherent in the creature, whether physical or mental, in the production and control of which God exercises no other power than that which is constant and universal: a power which, so far as we know, adds nothing to the efficiency of the second causes themselves. Thus, in the ordinary changes of climate, the occurrence of heat and cold, of rain and snow, natural causes are efficient to the production of such effects, although constantly guided by the will and power of God. Thus, also, when a man thinks, speaks, or writes, he acts in accordance with his nature; the effects produced do not exceed the power with which, as a creature, he is endowed. All these are, in the proper sense of the words, natural events.

In a second class of events, however, there is a manifestation of intelligence and will, which are not attributes of matter. Even naturalists teach us that "life is not the product of organization, but organization the product of life." Much less is intelligence, will, consciousness, or conscience, the product of unintelligent matter. No combination of the molecules of matter can rationally account for either life or intelligence. They must be referred to the intelligence of God. But as the effects here alluded to are produced in the exercise of the *potentia ordinata* of God, we are not accustomed to speak of the organization and growth of plants and animals as supernatural events. They are natural, because produced in accordance with the uniformly acting laws of nature.

There is, however, a third class of effects, due to the power of God without the co-operation or intervention of any second causes whatever; that is, they are to be referred to the immediate efficiency of God. Such are creation, regeneration, revelation, inspiration, and miracles. Miracles are distinguished from the other events with which they are classed, in that they belong to the external or sensible world. There are such events, and it is proper that they should have a distinctive name. When our Lord said to the leper, "I will, be thou clean;" or to the blind man, "Receive thy sight;" or to Lazarus, "Come forth," there was no secondary cause brought into action; nothing intervened between the will of Christ and the effect; and as these were sensible events, occurring in the external world, they determine the definition of a miracle.

When the Spirit of God quickens, or brings to life, a soul spiritually dead, there is no intervention or co-operation of second causes. Such co-operation, in the case of infants at least, is seen to be inconceivable, or impossible. Regeneration is an act of God's almighty power, which precludes all co-operation. This is the proper sense of the term "supernatural;" and it is in this sense that the influence by which a man was made a prophet was supernatural. He did not become such by any natural process whatever. The Spirit of God came upon him. His thoughts were not the product of his own mind, nor were his words of his own selection. What he spoke God spoke. The first great point to be learned concerning these holy men of God is, that the influence under which they spoke was not natural, but supernatural. This latter word, however, is used by writers of the highest class in meanings so different that to determine the sense in which it should be understood is a matter of great difficulty and importance.

The true sense of the word "supernatural" is determined by that of the word "natural," and the meaning of "natural" by that of "nature." But, unfortunately, few words are used in such a variety of senses as the word "nature." Very often it means the external, sensible world. This is the meaning commonly attached to it when we speak of the laws, or the phenomena, or the forces of nature. All natural forces are universal, uniform, blind, and, as the moderns say, are correlated; they are mutually convertible, and relatively equivalent. So much heat will produce a given amount of motion; and so much motion will produce the precise amount of heat expended in its production. If this is the proper sense of the word "nature;" if everything that is natural is physical, then whatever is voluntary, intellectual, or moral, is supernatural. This is the sense in which the word is used by Coleridge, and by Dr. Bushnell in his work on "The Natural and Supernatural." So also Huxley, Tyndall, and other modern scientific men, when they deny that there is anything "spontaneous" in nature, mean by "nature" the external world. They intend to deny that there is any manifestation of intelligence or will in the phenomena of nature.

Much more commonly, and more in accordance with the signification of the word, nature is made to mean everything made or produced. Then everything is natural which is due to the efficiency of created agents, or of second causes; and that only is supernatural which is divine. According to the great body of theists, there is a constant concursus or cooperation between the First and all second causes; and according to some of them, of whom the Duke of Argyle is an example, this concursus is the only supernatural element in the ordering of the universe. In his "Reign of Law," he teaches that God never acts except in accordance with law, and by means of second causes. Even a miracle he defines to be an event brought about under the direction of God, through some law of nature unknown to us. By law, in this connection, must be meant a uniformly acting force. But how can that be a uniformly acting force which causes iron to float, the blind to see, or the dead to live? According to this use of the word, a miracle is no more supernatural than any other event since the creation; indeed, the Duke says that the creation itself was by law. Another consequence of this definition of the term is, that it makes all events equally supernatural, because the divine efficiency is operative in all.

There are two senses of the word "supernatural" which should be adhered to, because they are graven upon the mind of the Church. The first is that which characterises the efficiency of God when it acts without the intervention of any second cause, as in creation, in miracles, in revelation, inspiration, or regeneration. The second is based upon the clear distinction made in the Bible between the providential efficiency of God, acting constantly and everywhere, and the gracious operations of His Spirit, who distributes His gifts severally to each one as He wills. Hence the latter are distinguished from the former as supernatural. Thus, while increase of strength or knowledge is natural to man, faith, repentance, and all the graces of the Spirit, are supernatural.

We may seem to be wandering from our subject in devoting so much space to the discussion of the meaning of a word; but when we say that the prophets spoke under a supernatural influence, it is well to know what we mean: we mean that they were under such an influence as gave to their thoughts and words the authority of God.

THE SUBJECTIVE EFFECT OF THE PROPHETIC INFLUENCE.

On this point it is to be remarked, that the effect was different in different cases. The neglect of this obvious fact has led to much confusion and misrepresentation. Because certain phenomena attended the prophetic inspiration in one case, it has been inferred that they were characteristic of all cases. The Apostle, however, tells us, that God of old spoke to the people in " divers manners" by the prophets.

There are three general views as to the state into which this divine influence brought its subjects. The first is, that they were thrown into a state of furor. They were maniacs. Their senses ceased to make upon them their normal impression. Their control over their minds was lost. They were unconscious of what they said, and when restored to consciousness, were entirely ignorant of all that had passed. Such, according to the Montanists, was the state of the ancient prophets when under this supernatural influence. This condition they called " amentia." So Tertullian said that, when a man saw the glory of God, and spake directly to Him, he of necessity lost his senses.

Secondly, even Hengstenberg, in the first edition of his Christology, came very near this doctrine of the Montanists. He said that the Christian fathers were right in renouncing the Montanist theory of *amentia*, but wrong in repudiating that of *ecstasia*. What does ecstasy mean? Tertullian, in the passage above referred to, uses the words as synonymous: "Defendimus in causa novæ prophetiæ, gratiæ ecstasin, id est amentiam, convenire."[1] The word, however, is used for any violent disturbance, either of the mind, produced by strong emotion, whether of terror, astonishment, or joy, or of the imagination. It is, indeed, too comprehensive in its application to afford any definite notion of its import. In the New Testament it is three times rendered "trance." Acts 10: 10; 11: 5, 22. Elsewhere it is used for amazement or terror. Mark 5: 22; Luke 5: 26; Acts 3: 10; 16: 8. The usage of the word, therefore, in Scripture does not determine its meaning when used with reference to the prophets. Hengstenberg, as may be gathered from his whole dissertation, understands prophetic ecstasy to have been,—(1.) An abnormal, unnatural state. The mind, and the power of perception through the senses, were not in their ordinary state; (2.) That this abnormal condition was not only a matter of consciousness to the prophet himself, but produced effects visible to others. As in 1 Sam. 10: 6, it is said of Saul, "The Spirit of the Lord shall come upon thee, and thou shalt prophesy with them, and shalt be turned into another man." In verse 11, also, the people are repre-

---

[1] Henstenberg, Christologie, Band iii., Zweite Abtheilung, p. 158.

sented as saying, "What is this that has come upon the son of Kish? Is Saul also among the prophets?" In 1 Sam. 19, it is narrated that Saul sent messengers three times to apprehend David, and every time they approached the company of prophets that surrounded Samuel and David, they were seized with the influence, and began to prophesy. At last Saul himself determined to go; "And the Spirit of God was upon him also, and he went on and prophesied. . . And he stripped off his clothes also, and prophesied before Samuel in like manner, and lay down naked all that day and all that night. Wherefore they say, Is Saul also among the prophets?" Tholuck,[1] with whom Hengstenberg seems generally agreed on this subject, refers, in illustration of the prophetic state, to the "jerks," as they were called in this country. The "jerks" were violent, involuntary bodily agitations, which at times, both here and in North Germany, attended revivals of religion. It frequently happened that even those who came to mock were seized by the sympathetic influence, and became as violently affected as any of the others. Hengstenberg also refers, as evidence that the prophets were "beside themselves," or "out of their senses," to the fact that by worldly men they were thought to be insane. 2 Kings 9: 11. He quotes C. B. Michaelis in support of this view, who says, "Videbantur vulgo prophetæ non satis compotes mentis." Delizseh, to the same effect, says that, $\dot{\varepsilon}\kappa\sigma\tau\tilde{\eta}\nu\alpha\iota$, *to be out of one's senses*, is antithetical to $\sigma\omega\varphi\rho\text{o}\nu\dot{\varepsilon}\iota\nu$, *to be self-possessed*, or *to be sober minded*. Another characteristic of the prophetic influence or state, according to these writers, was that it was sudden and brief, or, as Tholuck calls it, momentary.

Reference is also made to the cases of Peter and Paul. Of Peter it is said, Acts 10: 10, "He fell into a trance, and saw heaven opened." The Greek word rendered *trance* in all these cases literally means *ecstasy*. Hence the condition in which these apostles were while in a trance is regarded as illustrative of the prophetic state in general. A trance, as defined by physiologists, is a state of catalepsy, where the

---

[1] Propheten und ihre Weissagungen, Hamburg, 1861.

subject is profoundly asleep as to the body, but awake as to the soul. The mental state, however, of a man in ecstasy is often described as that in which the understanding—or discursive faculty—is dormant, and the reason—the intuitive faculty—is active. The prophets, it is said, were seers; they saw by intuition, or immediate vision, all that they revealed. Even Principal Fairbairn, in his admirable work on Prophecy, says, "The ancient view of the prophetic state is beyond doubt substantially correct. It supposes the prophet, when borne away by the influence of God's Spirit, to have been transported out of his natural condition into a higher, a spiritually ecstatic state, in which, losing the sense and consciousness of external objects, he was rendered capable of holding direct intercourse with heaven, and, surrendering himself wholly to the divine impressions conveyed to his soul, he for the moment ceased from his ordinary agency, as one released from the common conditions of flesh and blood, and entered into the purely spiritual sphere, to see the vision of the Almighty."[1]

It has already been admitted that the subjective influence of the divine afflatus was no doubt different in different cases. It is no doubt true, that the power of the Spirit coming upon a man was at times attended by utter prostration, or violent agitation. But this does not prove that these were the uniform, or even the common attendants of prophetic inspiration. Because the "jerks," so called, accompanied certain revivals of religion, it does not follow that they are a characteristic of every true conversion, or even of every revival.

The common opinion of the Church in all ages upon this subject has been, that neither the body nor the mind of the prophets was thrown out of its normal state by the coming of the Spirit upon them. This is proved, (1.) From the nature of their discourses. These are not the ravings of half-distracted men; nor of men in whom "reflection," or

[1] "Prophecy, Viewed in its Relation to its Distinctive Nature, Special Function, and Proper Interpretation," by Patrick Fairbairn, D. D., Principal of the Free Church College, Glasgow. New York: Carlton & Porter, 1866, p. 119.

any other faculty of the mind, is in abeyance; nor of men who neither saw, nor heard, nor felt. They are the discourses of men in the full exercise of all their powers of mind and body. (2.) The whole conduct and mode of action of the prophets, as of Elijah, Elisha, Isaiah, and Jeremiah, are those of men in their normal state. They went about from place to place, conversed with all classes of men, admonishing, instructing, and warning them of coming events, in the manner of ordinary men. (3.) In such didactic passages as 1 Cor. 14, we are taught, (*a*) That the spirit of the prophets was subject to the prophets. It did not carry them away, destroying their self-control, and forcing them to speak as soon as they felt its influence. One could wait until another had finished his discourse. (*b*) That their discourses were those of men in their sober senses. They did not need to be interpreted. They were adapted to the learned and to the unlearned; suited to convince and to convert. (4.) It is to be remembered that the Apostles, in the scriptural and proper sense of the word, were prophets. They were inspired, and therefore infallible messengers of God to men. Whenever they wrote or spoke in that character, all that they communicated had the authority of God. But the prophets of the New Testament certainly, and probably most of those of the Old, were inspired from time to time, as God called them to deliver certain messages to the people.

So far from the prophetic influence generally producing bodily and mental disturbance, it is probable that, in many cases, the prophets were not conscious of the divine guidance. As men, when renewed by the power of the Holy Ghost; when brought to the exercise of faith, repentance, or love; or when the glory of Christ is so revealed to them that they are transformed into His image, are unconscious of the Spirit's operations, so, doubtless, the prophets, specially the writers of the Psalms, when they sat down to pour out the fulness of their own hearts before God, were often led to use expressions and representations which, in their full meaning, suited only the Messiah, of whom the writer was probably not thinking. Let any one read the 8th Psalm, with the exposition of it given by Paul in Hebrews 2, and he will be convinced that there is a hundredfold more in that psalm than David ever thought of.

While it is contended, agreeably to the general doctrine of the Church, that the prophetic state was ordinarily one of composure and self possession, freedom from agitation, either as to mind or body, allowing the prophets the free exercise of their own peculiarities of thought and style, it is freely conceded that there was something in them—*i. e.*, in those who were officially prophets—which distinguished them from ordinary men. There was a full assurance and invincible conviction that they were, in a supernatural sense, the messengers of God, so that their words were the words of God. It is as unreasonable to attempt to explain how this assurance was produced, as to undertake to explain how Christ healed the sick, stilled the waves of the sea, or raised the dead; or how the Spirit now quickens those dead in sin, and works in them to will and to do according to His good pleasure.

Tholuck further insists that the prophets were distinguished by spirituality or personal holiness. He considers it inconsistent with the nature of the prophetic office, that it should be held by any one not in intimate fellowship with God. This idea is generally connected with the doctrine that the gift of prophecy was a high state of spiritual illumination. We know, however, that at the last day many whom Christ will reject will be able to say, "Lord, have we not prophesied in Thy name? and in Thy name have cast out devils? and in Thy name have done many wonderful works?" The remarkable history of Balaam, as recorded in Numbers, chaps. 22–25, is a clear proof how intimately God may reveal Himself to the ungodly. The Scriptures teach that the extraordinary gift of the Spirit has no sanctifying effect; that He gave supernatural strength, wisdom, and skill, to artizans, without thereby making them holy men. We read also in John 11: 51, that Caiaphas, being high priest for that year, prophesied that Jesus should die for the people. It was one of the functions of the high priests, irrespective of their religious character, to act as prophets in cases of emergency. Although this is true, it is equally true that the prophets as a class were called "holy men of God."

MODE OF COMMUNICATION.

The Scriptures make mention specially of three modes of communicating to the minds of the prophets the messages which they were to deliver to the people. The first is that of direct address; the second that of dreams; the third that of visions.

It is utterly inscrutable to us how external things operate on our minds through the senses. We cannot understand how a word uttered by one man can awaken thought or feeling in the minds of others. Much less can we understand how disembodied spirits communicate their thoughts and feelings to other such spirits. The Spirit of God is a Person, and can have personal communication with other persons; can converse with them, communicating thoughts and exciting feeling. He can control all the operations of our minds, so that all our thoughts and feelings shall be due to His agency. The Jews held the doctrine, that it was the peculiar prerogative of Moses to have this immediate intercourse with God, whereas to all others He communicated Himself only through dreams and visions. The same view is very generally held by modern writers. Principal Fairbairn, though one of the very best of the recent authors on the Prophecies, says[1] that an ordinary prophet "was taken out of his natural state, and raised, merely for a moment, in his spiritual part, into communion with heaven. Such was God's ordinary mode of communicating with prophets, usually so called; but not His mode of communicating with Moses, otherwise he had, in this respect, enjoyed no peculiar distinction." "The employment of ordinary converse, and, as a consequence, the disuse of dark or enigmatical sentences: this is precisely such a distinction in behalf of Moses which the whole circumstances would lead us to expect." This opinion is founded principally upon Numbers 12: 6–8. It is there stated that Miriam and Aaron spoke against Moses, and that God summoned the three before Him, and said, "If there be a prophet among you, I the Lord will make

---

[1] "Prophecy," by Patrick Fairbairn, D. D., pp. 484, 485.

Myself known unto him in a vision, and will speak to him in a dream. My servant Moses is not so, who is faithful in all My house. With him I will speak mouth to mouth, and not in dark speeches, and the similitude of the Lord shall he behold." As to Moses seeing "the similitude of God," that is explained by Exodus 33: 19–23, where Moses prayed, "I beseech Thee, show me Thy glory;" and Exodus 24: 9, 10: "Then went up Moses and Aaron, Nadab and Abihu, and seventy of the elders of Israel; and they saw the God of Israel." In the same sense, Isaiah—6: 1—says, "I saw the Lord on a throne, high and lifted up." All this is, of course, consistent with the frequent and solemn admonitions given by Moses to the people, "Take good heed unto yourselves, for ye saw no manner of similitude on the day that the Lord spoke unto you in Horeb, out of the midst of the fire;" and with the testimony of St. John, "No man hath seen God at any time." John 1: 18. Nevertheless, even we, with our poor eyes, are said to see "the glory of God in the face of Jesus Christ." 2 Cor. 4: 6.

That the passage quoted above from Numbers does assign Moses a higher position than ordinary prophets is admitted; but that superiority consisted in more intimate access to God, and in the greater clearness of the revelations which he was to receive. That it did not consist in God's speaking unto Moses with words, and revealing Himself to ordinary prophets only in dreams and visions, is plain, (1.) From the very passage itself. It is said, "The Lord spake suddenly unto Moses, and unto Aaron, and unto Miriam, Come out, ye three, unto the tabernacle of the congregation. And He said, Hear now my words." Here was neither dream nor vision, but direct address: just as direct to Aaron and Miriam as to Moses. (2.) Much the larger part of the writings of the prophets are simple prose compositions, historical or didactic. Moses surely was a prophet; but was he in an ecstasy—out of himself—when he wrote the history of the deluge, of the dispersion of the nations, of Joseph, of the exodus, of the giving of the Law on Mount Sinai? The greater part of what proceeded from the prophets, in the restricted sense of the word, was not capable of being communicated by signs. Signs may reveal events, but how can they reveal abstract truths? Isaiah might have seen the Messiah, "the servant of the Lord," in the form of a poor man; the whole scene of the crucifixion might have been prefigured before him; but how was he to know that those sufferings were expiatory? that the Sufferer died for us, and that He made His soul an offering for sin? Paul not only says, but insists, and proves that his knowledge of the gospel was derived, not from man, but by direct revelation of Jesus Christ. Does any man believe that the contents of his epistles were made known to him in dreams and visions: all his knowledge of the law, of sin and grace, of the person and work of Christ, of the whole plan of salvation? Such an idea probably never entered any human mind. It is only by confining the word "prophet" to its most limited sense, and "prophetic inspiration" to the smallest portion of what the prophets reveal, that any such thing can be maintained. The simple Scriptural idea is, that "holy men of old spake as they were moved by the Holy Ghost." If they sat down to write history, the Holy Ghost guided them from the commission of error. If they undertook to instruct the people, the Spirit suggested to them what and how to speak, so that all they uttered came with the authority of God. So also, when the prophets warned, exhorted, or instructed the people, the Spirit filled their souls with the fire of a divine eloquence, so that they wrote and spoke with a force they never could of themselves have attained. As the infinite God is everywhere present, in His knowledge and power, always working, with or without second causes, producing all the infinite variety of effects in the world around us, so the Holy Spirit dwells in all the people of God, working in each and all according to the good pleasure of His will; of old making some apostles, some prophets, some healers of diseases, some speaking with new tongues, some interpreters of tongues, some evangelists, some pastors and teachers. It is obviously vain to try to explain how all these different effects were produced. All we have to do is to protest against whatever is contrary to the facts and teachings of the Bible. It is doubtless true that the Spirit sometimes spoke in a still small voice, which produced no disturbance in the prophet's mind. At other times He overpowered them, so that they became as dead men; at others He raised them so high that nothing was visible to them but things eternal and divine.

DREAMS.

No one has ever been able to explain the physiology of dreams. Familiar as we are with their ordinary phenomena, they remain as mysterious and as fearful as ever. There is nothing in our present state of existence so adapted to produce alarm and dread of the future as dreams. That every man should, on an average, be one third of his life out of his own control, capable of believing absurdities and impossibilities, and liable, under these hallucinations, to suffer all the horrors to which humanity is here exposed, is enough to make us feel on what a slender thread our happiness here depends. And nothing can be more appalling than the thought of the soul being launched into space in the state in which it is during sleep. It is a great mercy to know that, when out of our own control, we are still in the hands of God.

It is intelligible, from the powerful impression which dreams are capable of producing, that faith in them as premonitions of the future should have prevailed from the earliest times, and that "dream interpreters" should be a constituted profession. The Greeks were accustomed to say, "dreams came from Jove;" but long before the time of the Greeks, as we learn from the Bible—in the days of Abraham, Joseph, and Daniel—men had faith in dreams, and earnestly sought for trustworthy interpreters. This is the reason why reliance upon them, or consulting those who professed to explain them, is associated with necromancy,—spiritualism, as it is now called,—and denounced, even on the pain of death. Lev. 20: 6; Deut. 13: 1–5; 18: 11, 12.

Dreams are of three general kinds: first, where they are disconnected and preposterous; second, where they are connected, as in a natural series of events, there being nothing absurd or impossible about them; and third, where the higher faculties of the mind are clearly and consciously at work. Men have often solved in a dream mathematical problems, which baffled all their efforts at solution while they were awake. Intricate subjects, of which no clear or consistent view could be obtained, have often opened up in clearness and consistency during sleep. Notwithstanding the fantastic character of dreams in general, He in whose hands we are at all times can give them a clear significance, to be known at once by their character, or by the attending declarations of His will. Thus, in the case of Abimelech, without the intervention of any image, God warned him in a dream that Sarah was Abraham's wife. Gen. 20 : 3–6. Joseph's future pre-eminence over his brethren was foretold by the image of their sheaves doing obeisance to his sheaf, which he and his father understood without an interpreter. Gen. 37 : 7. But the dreams of the butler and baker in prison needed an interpretation, which Joseph only could give. So, also, the dreams of Pharoah were significant; but their true import was known only to God, and revealed through Joseph. Gen. 41 : 15, ff. In the remarkable vision of Jacob at Bethel, little comparatively was made known by what he saw, while the whole scheme of God's purpose regarding his descendants, and all the nations of the earth, was made known by the words which the Lord uttered in his ears. Gen. 28 : 12–15. Thus, in the case of Joseph, when "the angel of the Lord appeared unto him in a dream, saying, Arise, and take the young child and his mother, and flee into Egypt, and be thou there until I bring thee word; for Herod will seek the young child, to destroy him,"—Matt. 2 : 13—the revelation was by words. In the case of Nebuchadnezzar, the image seen in his dream was significant enough; but its true meaning could be given only by one enlightened by the Spirit of God. In dreams, therefore, it seems that God revealed His will sometimes by symbols presented to the mind, so simple as to need no interpretation, as in the dream of Joseph about the sheaves. Sometimes the scene presented to the mind of the sleeper was full of significance, but needed an inspired interpreter, as in the dreams of Pharoah and Nebuchadnezzar. More frequently God spoke to the prophet, or the recipient of His revelation, while asleep, as to Jacob at Bethel, and to Joseph when warned to take the young child into Egypt.

VISIONS.

A vision, in the sense in which the word is here used, is something seen. Peter, in Acts 11 : 5, says he saw a vision. What he saw was a great vessel, like a sheet, descending out of heaven, filled with all manner of living creatures. These things had no real corporeal existence; but figures of them were presented to his mind. The impression was as distinct and vivid as though it had been made through the senses. This is an illustration of the mode in which God communicated His will to the prophets of old. It has already been remarked, in opposition to a popular opinion of our day, that this was neither the only nor the common way; nevertheless, it was a way not unfrequently adopted.

1. As to these visions, or visual representations, some were very simple, intelligible at once, and without any explanation. Thus, when Jehoshaphat asked the prophet Micaiah, "Shall we go up against Ramoth-gilead to battle, or shall we forbear?" the prophet answered, "I saw all Israel scattered upon the hills, as sheep which have no shepherd." This was enough. The king understood it at once. 1 Kings 22 : 15–17.

2. At other times the visions were very complicated and obscure. At times, at least, the prophets did not understand them, but prayed to have them explained; which explanation, when given, went a very little way. Indeed, it is altogether probable that the prophets understood as little of the symbols presented to their view as those to whom they were afterwards announced. It was not the object of the visions to reveal the future more distinctly to them than to the rest of the people. The Apostle Peter represents the ancient prophets as inquiring and searching diligently into the meaning of their own predictions. It is an admitted fact, that the Old Testament prophecies regarding the first advent of Christ were universally, and more or less grossly, misunderstood by the Jews of His day. It is inconceivable that those prophecies should have been correctly understood by the ancient prophets. In that case they could not have failed to impress their true meaning on the people, and would

have produced a permanently healthy state of the public mind.

3. This suggests the remark, that the prophecies were not designed to gratify curiosity, to antedate history, but to produce a good moral and religious impression on the minds of the men of that and of coming generations. Their great subject was Christ and His kingdom. To our first parents, immediately after the fall, it was promised that a Redeemer should come. With ever-increasing clearness, His person and His work were set forth. This sustained the hope of the Church until His actual coming. The knowledge, faith, and hope of the people were preserved, and even as a nation they waited for the salvation of Israel.

4. It is also to be considered, that no one of these visions took in the whole of the future. One presented one feature; another a different one. Of those concerning the Redeemer, some represented Him as King; some as a Priest; some as a Prophet; some as a Man of sorrows, and acquainted with grief; some as a Victor; some as a Victim. It was not easy, perhaps not possible, to combine all these representations into a consistent whole, until they were explained by the mode of their accomplishment. Still, this was enough. Hereby the gospel was preached, by the Law and the Prophets, and a strength of faith produced, as we learn from the eleventh chapter of the Epistle to the Hebrews, which puts to shame the faith of us modern Christians.

5. The symbols presented to the minds of the prophets in their visions were almost all borrowed from their national history, and from objects with which they were familiar. The whole Old Testament was typical of the New. The bondage of the people of God in Egypt; the preservation of their first-born by slaying the paschal lamb; the passage through the Red Sea; the healing of the people by the brazen serpent; the manna from heaven; the water from the rock: which rock was Christ; the whole journey through the wilderness; the passage over Jordan, and entering the promised land, were all shadows of good things to come. From that day to this Canaan has remained a type for the rest which remains for the people of God. And as the

Church on earth and the Church in heaven are one, what is a type of the one is a type of the other. Hence, those who dwelt in Canaan are, in the language of the prophets, "those who are nigh,"—nigh to God: in His Church;—and those who dwelt out of Canaan " were afar off,"—*i. e.*, Gentiles,—Eph. 2: 13. Thus, to be cast off from the people was to be cast out of the Church, and to be restored to the dwelling-place of their fathers was to be restored to the Church. And when the conversion of the heathen is predicted, it is under the figure of their coming to the Holy Land, and participating in the sacred festivals there observed. In like manner, Jerusalem is a type, at once of the Church of God—Gal. 4: 25, 26—and of heaven, as often in the Apocalypse.

So also Zion, the seat of the theocracy, is the constant type of the kingdom of the Messiah, in all its phases, or stages of its development. In such passages as Isaiah 40: 9, " O Zion, that bringest good tidings, get thee up in the high mountain;" Psalm 2: 6, " I will set My King on My holy hill of Zion;" " Walk about Zion, and go round about her;" " He said of Zion, this and that man was born there;" "The redeemed shall come with singing unto Zion;" "Awake, awake, put on thy strength, O Zion;" "For Zion's sake I will not hold My peace, and for Jerusalem's sake I will not rest," Zion always means the Church. When, therefore, the prophet saw in vision Zion lying desolate, the prediction was that the theocracy, the kingdom of Christ, or the Church—all equivalent expressions—was to be desolated. If he saw Zion exalted, then the Church was to be prosperous. If he saw the nations flocking to Zion, the conversion of the Gentiles was predicted. This symbolical use of the word " Zion," has impressed itself indelibly on the minds of all Christians. It seems constantly in our prayers and hymns. When a man prays for the prosperity of Zion, every one understands him to pray for the prosperity of the Church. As the people of God under the Old Testament were called Israel, they are thus called now. " We,"—*i. e.* Christians—says Paul, "are the true Israel." And in the ninth chapter of the Romans, he proves that the promises were not made to the Israel after the flesh, but to the Israel after the Spirit: that is, to those who are the children of Abraham because they have the faith of Abraham. Hence, when the prophets predict the future glory of Israel, they, according to Paul, are to be understood as predicting the glory of the true Israel, *i. e.*, of the Church of God.

Illustrations of this kind might be continued indefinitely. The Messiah was to be a King. Hence, the theocratic kings were symbols of the Messiah in that character. He is called David, Ezek. 34: 23, 24; He is said to sit on the throne of David; the key of David was to be upon His shoulder; and the covenant or sure mercies promised to David, especially that his posterity should sit on his throne for ever, and that he should be the heir of the world—Rom. 4: 13—were fulfilled, so far as the perpetuity of his kingdom is concerned, by the resurrection of Christ from the dead,—Acts 13: 34,—and as far as the possession of the earth is concerned, by believers being the seed of Abraham, to whom the promise referred. Rom. 4: 13–18. This the apostle directly asserts, "If ye be Christ's, then are ye Abraham's seed, and heirs according to the promise." Gal. 3: 29. It is needless to refer to the frequency with which the high priest, his sacrifices and services, are used as symbols of the office and work of Christ. They were types of what He was to be and to do. As He was to be a King, but not such a king as the eyes of men had ever seen, so He was to be a Priest, but not after the order of Aaron; but a Priest without predecessor, and without successor, and without end of days; who by the one offering of Himself, hath for ever perfected them that are sanctified.

6. Another marked characteristic of the prophetic visions is, that they often represent things as contemporaneous which are widely separated in time. They have aptly been compared, in this respect, to the stars, which are apparently equally distant from our eyes, although separated from each other by measureless portions of space. Thus, the advent of the Redeemer is at times connected with the final triumph of His kingdom. In the third chapter of Malachi, the coming of Christ and His work of judgment are described as one operation "In the prophecy of Isaiah respecting Babylon,

the whole drama of her coming downfall and ruin is set forth in an unbroken delineation, which in one rapid sketch embraces the history of ages, and connects with the first stroke of vengeance inflicted by the Medes the last sad proofs of her utter prostration."[1] Illustrations of this peculiarity of the prophetic visions may be seen in all the leading Messianic psalms, in which the sketch of the Redeemer's career is given as a whole. In many other cases, one phase of the Messiah's work is given in completeness, and other phases are left out of view. Joel, for example, gives no other characteristic of the Messianic period than the general effusion of the Spirit. In one vision Christ is represented only as a suffering Man; in another only a conquering King. Again, the same vision may contain the most opposite characteristics. The person whom Isaiah described in the sixth chapter of his prophecies as Jehovah, before whom the seraphs veiled their faces, he saw as born of a virgin, and nevertheless recognized as the Wonderful, the Mighty God, the Prince of Peace.

In the verbal communications which are interjected into almost all the visions, intimations are sometimes given of the chronological succession of the events which they indicate. These indications, however, are so few and so indefinite as to render it impossible, prior to fulfilment, to write history out of prophecy.

7. This is not a subject to be exhausted in such a paper as this, or by its writer. One other important characteristic of the visions of the prophets, however, may be mentioned. They do not use symbols, so to speak, capriciously, so that the same symbol sometimes means one thing and sometimes another. As a general rule, the same symbol has the same meaning, not only in the writings of the same prophet, but throughout all the prophetic writings of the Bible. We have already seen that the land of Canaan is everywhere in prophecy the symbol of the rest of the people of God; the Hebrews, as the theocracy, is the symbol of the true Israel, or God's elect; Zion is the Church; the enemies of the Jews, Egypt; Moab, Edom, Babylon, represent the enemies of the

---

[1] Fairbairn, p. 179.

Church. A mountain commonly means a kingdom, a beast a dynasty, etc.

RULES OF PROPHETIC INTERPRETATION.

1. The first and most obvious rule for the interpretation of unfulfilled prophecies is, that they are to be explained in accordance with the way in which the fulfilled prophecies have already been accomplished. A wrong method of interpretation, as is universally admitted, led the Jews to wrong conclusions as to the first advent of the Messiah, and the nature of the kingdom which He was then to establish. It would seem to be an obvious dictate of wisdom to avoid their method in reference to the predictions yet to be fulfilled. The Jews erred on the side of literalism. They applied all that was predicted concerning Israel to the natural descendants of Abraham, through Isaac and Jacob. Paul teaches that those predictions and promises pertained to the spiritual seed of Abraham, whether Jew or Gentile. They expected that they as a nation were to be exalted over all other nations, and to be, as the Apostles expressed it, heirs of the world. They, therefore, anticipated a Messiah who should redeem them from their oppressors, conquer all their enemies, and by terrible judgments force them to acknowledge Jehovah as the only true God. They anticipated the time when Jerusalem would be the capital of the world, and when the temple and all its services would be reverenced and trusted in by all nations. Some of the most eminent of modern interpreters of prophecy go to the same extreme. Auberlen, for example, in his exposition of Daniel 7: 18–22, where it is said, "The saints of the Most High shall take the kingdom, and possess the kingdom for ever, even for ever and ever," says that, by "the saints of the Most High" must be understood the Jewish people.[1] Daniel, he says, could have understood the promise in no other sense. It matters nothing to us how Daniel understood the promise. He was inspired to announce, but not to explain it, which he has not done. We know with certainty, from the teachings of the New Testament, that it

---

[1] Auberlen, "David and the Apocalypse," p 219.

is those who are "Christ's who are the seed of Abraham, and heirs according to the promise."

2. A second obvious rule is, that the design of prophecy must be kept constantly in view, and nothing more be expected from it than it was intended to accomplish. That design, as we have seen, was not to anticipate history: to enable us to read the future as we do the records of the past. Its great object was to keep alive and active the faith and hopes of the people in the exceeding great and precious promises which had already been made. It did not instruct them clearly in what way those promises should be fulfilled. Much less was it intended to enable them to foresee the chronological order of events by which they were to be accomplished. "It was not given them to know the times or the seasons, which the Father hath put in His own power." Acts 1 : 7.

3. The symbols are not to be taken to mean all that they may be made to signify. There is an usage in regard to symbols as well as in regard to words; and, therefore, when any symbol has been found to have a settled meaning, that meaning is not to be departed from. This remark applies specially to the interpretation of unfulfilled prophecies. If in those which have been fulfilled a symbol has a certain sense, that sense is not to be ignored in the explanation of those which remain to be accomplished. An old commentator interprets the symbol of a flying eagle in one of the prophecies to mean the United States of America, because he fancied that there was a resemblance in the geographical configuration of our territory to an eagle in its flight. There would be no end to fanciful interpretations of this kind, if the rule that prophetic symbols have a fixed meaning be disregarded. It sometimes happens that a word must be taken out of its ordinary sense; but this does not invalidate the rule that the *usus loquendi* is a cardinal law of exegesis. The same is true with regard to prophetic symbols.

4. The doctrinal portions of the Scripture are to control the interpretation of the prophetical portions. The reasons for this rule are obvious. First, the whole Bible is the word of God. It must be consistent in all its parts; and secondly,

the didactic portions are far more clear than the prophetical. The doctrine of justification by faith is far more certainly taught in Scripture than what is meant by the wheels of Ezekiel, or the mystical Babylon of the Apocalypse. If, therefore, the Scriptures clearly teach that there should be no distinction between Jew and Gentile in the kingdom of Christ, any interpretation of prophecy must be erroneous which makes it teach that, after the conversion of the Jews, after the second coming of Christ, they are to be exalted over their brethren. A Jewish convert, a man of education, once said to the writer, while a guest in his house, that the Apostles had made a great mistake in amalgamating the Jews and Gentiles into one Christian church. "There ought," he said, "to be two such churches, the one Hebrew, and the other Gentile, in order that the former might retain their pre-eminence." In proof that the Jews were thus superior to the Gentiles, he referred to the language of Christ to the Syrophenician woman: "It is not meet to take the children's food and cast it unto dogs;" and then added, "The Gentiles are dogs, and should be content to feed on the crumbs which fall from a Jew's table." This did not sound very Christian, but it was the legitimate result of his principles of prophetic interpretation. Many interpreters teach that the temple in Jerusalem is to be rebuilt, sacrifices again offered, the old festivals to be observed, and the whole Mosaic ritual reintroduced. According to the common judgment of Christians, all these things have been done away with for ever, and God has provided for his Church something better than an eternity of Judaism. Whatever may be thought of these illustrations, there can be no diversity of judgment as to the validity of the rule that the clearly revealed doctrines of the New Testament are to control the interpretation of unfulfilled prophecies.

5. Another principle which should regulate the interpretation of the prophecies is, that the distinction between what is to be understood literally, and what spiritually, should be determined by fixed rules. It is admitted that some of the prophecies are to be understood literally, and some figuratively; and hence there are two schools of interpreters, the literalists

and the spiritualists. A man is not to allow himself to pass from one side to the other as it suits him, explaining a passage literally if it agrees with his doctrine, or figuratively if it contradicts it. This rule, though very simple, is frequently violated. If the interpreter departs from the literal meaning of a prophecy, he is bound to show good reasons for that departure; and on the other hand, if he insists on the prediction being taken literally, he must be able to prove that the laws of exegesis require such explanation. This is too wide a subject to be here entered upon. Hengstenberg, in the second part of the third volume of his "Christology," has laid down eight rules by which the figurative and literal sense of the prophetic predictions may be distinguished. Most of these are plain enough. If the literal interpretation involves an impossibility; if it makes the prophet contradict himself; if it be inconsistent with the mode of its accomplishment, as in the case of the appearance, in the person, of John the Baptist; if it contradicts the teachings of the New Testament, or the analogy of faith, it must, of course, be abandoned.

THE APOCALYPSE.

A few words in an introduction to a volume of lectures on the Apocalypse concerning the book itself must not be omitted. Such words, however, cannot have for their object anything more than to bring into view the nature of the work which the author of the lectures undertook to perform.

First, the portion of sacred Scripture which he proposed to illustrate is one of special interest and importance, in the first place, because so large a portion of its contents consists of the very words of Christ himself, addressed to His people for instruction, admonition, and encouragement. In the second place, because it treats almost exclusively of the person of Christ, and of the work which He is now carrying on in the world, in bringing His kingdom to its final consummation. Thirdly, because it unfolds the glorious future which awaits the Church. These are the things which the angels desire to look into. The Apocalypse itself, in one sense, is the book which no one in heaven or earth could open but the Lion of the tribe of Judah, the Root of David. None but He could prevail to open it, or could accomplish the purposes of God therein revealed. It has, therefore, always excited great interest in the Church; and perhaps more study has been devoted to it, and more has been written to illustrate it than any one book of the sacred canon.

A second characteristic of the Apocalypse is its exceeding difficulty. It is true that almost every enthusiastic interpreter maintains that it is all plain enough, provided the reader gets the right clew, and follows the path which the commentator points out. Nevertheless, to other persons the book remains as much an enigma as ever. The main source of this difficulty is, that so much of it consists in unfulfilled predictions. Such predictions were intended to be obscure. How could the first great promise of redemption, "The seed of the woman shall bruise the head of the serpent," be understood before Christ came, as we now understand it? How could the promise to Abraham, "In thy seed shall all the nations of the earth be blessed," which Paul says contains the whole Gospel, be understood before it was accomplished? How was any one to know that "thy seed" referred to one man, when almost everywhere else in the Bible it means the natural descendants of Abraham? How natural it was for the Jews to believe that it was their nation that was to bless the world, to be the means of extending the true religion, to conquer all nations, and bring them into subjection to themselves and their Messiah: that they might at least feed on the crumbs which fell from their own overladen table. The Messianic prophecies, the predictions concerning the person, work, and kingdom of Christ, were all but universally misunderstood until they were fulfilled. Then they became clear as day. It seems very unreasonable to expect that the New Testament prophecies relating to the future should be read with the certainty which belongs to history, when those of the Old Testament were so sadly and so generally misinterpreted.

Another source of difficulty in explaining the Apocalypse is to be found in the circumstance that so large a part of its predictions are presented under the veil of symbols. It is self-evident that simple prose is more intelligible than symbolical representations. This every man knows to be true from his own experience. Yet even the simple predictions of the Old Testament, in which the words employed admitted of only one interpretation, were, as a general thing, entirely misunderstood. It is, therefore, to expect more than can be accomplished when it is thought that the veil of obscurity and uncertainty which rests upon so large a part of the Apocalypse can ever be removed by man.

This does not impair the usefulness of this important part of the Word of God. The Old Testament prophecies were not useless because they were obscure. They kept alive the faith and hope of the Church from the fall of Adam until the coming of Christ. In like manner, although we may be unable to explain with certainty the details of the visions recorded in the Apocalypse, their general design and import are evident. They assure the Church that, although it will be assailed by many enemies, and have to pass through manifold trials and persecutions, its final triumph is sure: a consummation awaits it, the glory of which it has never entered into the heart of man to conceive. This is enough, until God sees fit to give us more. The venerated Dr. Archibald Alexander was accustomed to say, that although he understood but little of the Apocalypse, he perused it constantly, because a special blessing was promised to those who read it. It is a blessed thing that the objects of faith need not be understood.

A third remark concerning this book is that, setting aside the school of rationalistic interpreters, there are among those who believe it to be a revelation from God entirely different methods or theories concerning its purport and structure. According to one class it relates exclusively to the past; it is a delineation of the struggles through which the Church passed during the early ages of Christianity, until its final triumph under Constantine the Great. Another and very numerous class regard it as a prediction of historical events in chronological order; and they, therefore, endeavour to determine to what particular event each vision refers. Others regard the visions very much as the parables of our Lord:

those of the sower and the ten talents, for example, which have no regard to chronology, but give a view of God's purpose in regard to the Church from the beginning to the end. So the several great visions of the Apocalypse go over the same ground, and trace the destiny of the Church to the end. According to this view, the seals, the vials, and the trumpets refer to events which are synchronous, and not successive. This is true, as already remarked, with regard to the Old Testament prophecies. In Daniel the destiny of the Church, in its relation to the kingdoms of the world, is first set forth under the symbol of Nebuchadnezzar's image, and the stone cut out of the mountain, and then under that of different beasts, and one like unto the Son of man.

As there is this diversity of opinion as to the whole structure of the Apocalypse, there are endless differences of opinion as to the import of particular symbols. What is meant by Babylon? By the two witnesses? By the river Euphrates? The answers given to these, and many similar questions, are almost as numerous as the commentators. It is out of the question, therefore, in any exposition of this portion of Scripture, that certainty or unanimity is to be attained. Its great design, however, remains plain. It purports to show the people of God "the things which must shortly come to pass." This "shortly" may, however, include thousands of years; for we know that with the Lord one day is as a thousand years, and a thousand years as one day. Almost by common consent, although nearly two thousand years have passed since these revelations were given, the things predicted have not all come to pass. We have not even yet entered upon the millenium, which is therein so clearly foretold. Besides, although much in this part of the sacred volume is obscure, much is comparatively clear; and of every truth enough is revealed to give the Apocalypse power to sanctify and elevate the people of God.

THE REV. JAMES RAMSEY.

It is clear, from what has been said, that the task of an interpreter of prophecy, and especially of an expounder of the Apocalypse, is one of peculiar difficulty. It requires great humility and soundness of judgment, great familiarity with the Scriptures, and great spirituality of mind. These qualifications the late Dr. Ramsey possessed in an eminent degree. He entered the Theological Seminary, Princeton, New Jersey, in the year 1836. Thirty-six years have since passed away. The population of this village has been in that period almost entirely changed; only one of his old instructors remains alive; yet his memory is still cherished with affectionate reverence. He was revered even in his youth. There was about him such an elevation above the world, such constant evidence that he was a temple of the Holy Ghost, that he was sacred in the eyes of all who knew him. Although the impression which he made on his associates was principally due to the holiness by which he was distinguished, all who knew him also recognized in him the evidence of a clear and strong intellect, and of remarkable soundness of judgment. These characteristics of the man are clearly impressed upon this volume. In reading its pages, I recognize the spirit and the power which marked him as a student. The leading characteristic of these lectures is their spirituality. The author has expressed, if such a figure may be allowed, from the sacred text the pure water of life. He has compressed it as he would a sponge. His object is obviously to render the truths presented the means of growth in grace to his readers. To a greater degree, therefore, than any commentary within the writer's knowledge, this volume is adapted to spiritual edification. No believer can read it without finding himself a better Christian, nor can he fail to be made wiser. The clear strong sense which it everywhere exhibits will make him understand at least the inner truth of this portion of Scripture better than he ever did before. His sound judgment has preserved him from those fanciful interpretations of which the Apocalypse has been such a fruitful source. These lectures, therefore, we doubt not, will be a lasting memorial of the man, and a lasting blessing to the Church.

The writer of this introductory chapter feels it due to the friends of Dr. Ramsey to say, that the delay in its preparation is due to causes over which he had no control.

PART I.

INTRODUCTORY.

Lecture I. The Promised Blessing.
" II. The Gospel of the Kingdom.
" III. The Consolations of the Kingdom.

THE SPIRITUAL KINGDOM.

LECTURE I.

THE PROMISED BLESSING.

Rev. i: 3. "Blessed is he that readeth and they that hear the words of this prophecy, and keep the things which are written therein; for the time is at hand."

"ALL Scripture is given by inspiration of God, and is profitable for doctrine, for reproof, for correction, for instruction in righteousness, that the man of God may be perfect, thoroughly furnished unto all good works." If, however, we were to judge from the treatment which some portions of Scripture receive from many professed Christians, we should conclude that there is much which they consider very unprofitable. This is especially true of the Book of Revelation. By many this book is regarded as of little or no practical benefit, except perhaps the second and third chapters, and some other detached passages. However the learned may possibly find in it some food for faith and hope, or however beneficial it may be to the church in some future age, when its mysteries shall be unveiled, and the light of a complete accomplishment thrown upon its present obscurity, yet to the multitude of believers now, they think it must remain a sealed and a useless book.

I. It was not without reason, therefore, that the Holy Spirit, foreseeing this tendency to slight it, directed His servant John to introduce it in the very first words after its title, by this solemn declaration of a peculiar blessing upon every one who should attend to the things written therein. "Blessed is he that readeth, and they that hear the words of this prophecy, and keep those things which are written therein; for the time is at hand."

§. *Neglect of this book guarded against.*

These words, one would very naturally think, ought to have prevented that low estimate of the spiritual and practical value of this book which has so widely prevailed. Such a benediction is attached to no other book of Scripture. It is indeed true in regard to every part of God's word, that they are blessed who read and keep it; but such a special declaration as this prefixed to this book only, indicates a special importance attached to it, and a special kind or degree of blessing to be secured by its devout study, or at the very least a gracious warning against some special danger of neglect, and of spiritual injury arising therefrom. The language is very forcible, and the phrases take their shape from the practice of those times when books were all in manuscript and very scarce, when the knowledge of them was obtained principally by hearing them read, and when most obtained their knowledge of them only by hearing them read. "Blessed is *he* that readeth, and *they* that hear," i. e., every one who comes to the knowledge, even though but partial and imperfect,—as that of a mere hearer must usually be,—"of this prophecy;" 'and keeps,'—observes, 'those things,' and governs his faith, his fears, his hopes and his conduct by the revelations it contains.

Why, then, the question naturally arises, why has it been so much neglected? The answer to this is not difficult, and very properly leads to the consideration of its practical value to the church and the believer.

§. *Reasons of this neglect.* (1.) *Its mysteriousness.*

First, because of the mysteriousness of very much of it. In connection with this, there has prevailed the mistaken idea that there could not be any real advantage from what could not be understood; whereas that very mystery is often the chief source of the blessing, when it arises from the inherent grandeur and glory of the subject, and the natural imperfection and felt littleness of the creature. To humble man's proud heart, and put him in his proper place before the throne, no revelation is more important than that a divine plan pervades every part of the world's history, whose deep mysteries are as inscrutable as the wisdom that formed it is infinite, and capable of being expressed only in symbols of like mysterious import. To know assuredly that there is a mystery in everything which we cannot comprehend, as well as an unfathomable wisdom and power and love which we may forever trust, is no mean attainment.

A second reason of this neglect is to be found in the very common error in regard to prophecy in general, that since it cannot be perfectly understood until fulfilled, its chief value must be to confirm the faith of those who live after its fulfilment, by the evidence thus afforded to the divine origin of Christianity, and to the perfections of God. There could scarcely be a greater mistake. On the contrary, the chief value of prophecy, as well as its first, direct and most evident design, has been to cheer and sustain the faith and fainting hopes of God's people during the long ages of trial and sorrow that precede the glorious consummation it predicts; and its value as an evidence of inspiration, or of the divine Omniscience, which is the only value it can have after its fulfilment, so far from being its chief design, is entirely subordinate and incidental, though in the present state of our world very important. Indeed, this could never have been the design of this book, at least taken as a whole; for its re-

(2.) A mistake as to the design of prophecy.

velations of the future sweep onward over all the nations and ages of the earth, and find their complete fulfilment and perfect explanation, therefore, only when this whole state of things shall have forever passed away, and when in the experienced joys and woes of an eternal and unchanging state, all such proofs become forever antiquated and worthless.

A third reason that has prevented many from securing the blessing here promised is the very general error that the symbols so mysterious and unique with which the book abounds, must find their corresponding realities, their true fulfilment, each in some one specific event, instead of in vast series of events of a similar character repeating themselves throughout the history of the church, and all together tending to one grand definite result—the eternal triumph of the Cross, and the eternal ruin of all that oppose it. Now, the very nature of a symbol is such that it can represent its correspondent reality only by presenting as in a picture some one or more of its characteristic traits. If these characteristics are so perfectly distinguishing that there is but one event or object to which they can apply, then of course it must have this specific application. But if these traits are such as to characterize with equal clearness whole classes of objects or events, then must the symbol be applied to the whole, unless in some other way such application be definitely restrained. But in such a case the symbol is imperfect. In other words, symbols are representatives of character and of principles, and of events and objects just so far as they embody these. Now, as the symbols of this book are pictures of the church's sorrows and triumphs, and of the overthrow of the powers of the world, it arises from their very nature as symbols, and from the very nature of man and of God, which constantly secure the repetition of the same sins and judgments and deliv-

(3.) Too specific application of its symbols.

erances, that there will be an almost endless variety of applications of which they are capable, if regard be had to specific events. Accordingly, learned commentators, well read in the history of the church, have each found peculiar applications of these symbols, according as the mind of each has been peculiarly impressed, some by one, some by another event in that history, or by the peculiar and stirring events of his own times; and insisting upon this as the specific event designed in the symbol, and the scheme of interpretation required by this as the only true one, there has arisen a great variety of conflicting theories, and a great number of various applications of the same passages in this book to events separated by ages from each other. One effect of this has been to utterly unsettle the minds of less learned men, and to destroy all confidence in the possibility of ever arriving at any ascertained meaning of these predictions, at least by those who had not spent half a lifetime in accurate researches into history. Perhaps nothing so much as this has tended to increase the apparent obscurity, and to lessen the spiritual influence of this book, and the blessedness here promised.

It must however be here observed that what has often been found true in regard to other things of the kingdom of God, has happened here; that while these things have been hid from the wise and prudent, they have been revealed unto babes. God has made foolish the wisdom of men, and amply rewarded the faith and diligence of the humble and earnest believer. Where the pride of human learning has stumbled, and where the strength of human reason and the cravings of a vain curiosity have been baffled, and have turned from it as useless, because they could not understand it, the humble and simple-hearted believer has found the richest encouragements of faith and hope. While it is doubtless true that where there is

(4.) The idea that great learning was necessary.

this simplicity of faith and humble docility of mind, the more knowledge any one may possess of God's dealings with the church and the nations through past ages, the deeper and clearer will be his impressions of the great truths taught in this book, inasmuch as he has so many more striking illustrations of them, and sees them pervading and shaping the whole current of the world's history; yet it is also certain that there will not be a single truth of importance or source of consolation and spiritual strength found in it by him, that will not also be found by the most unlettered saint who is able to understand the words as he reads them, however mysterious the descriptions may appear. We shall never forget the impression of this fact received many years ago in circumstances of no little interest. The Sabbath had been spent in preaching in a settlement of Choctaw Indians on the upper waters of Red river, not far from Fort Washita, and we were passing the night at an Indian cabin. Quite a number of Christian Indians had assembled for a night meeting, and to get all the benefit they could from further intercourse with the missionary and his interpreter. The translation of the New Testament into their language had just been completed, and the first copies received and circulated. Much of it came to them with the freshness of a new revelation from heaven, but none more so than the book of Revelation. They turned to its closing chapters, and read, inquired and commented in their own way on the splendid imagery of those chapters, the city of the New Jerusalem descending from heaven, its massy walls, its pearly gates, its twelve foundations of precious stones inscribed with the names of the twelve apostles of the Lamb. To these untutored children of the forest, was all this an unintelligible jargon? Or, did they, in their simplicity, take it in its literal and material sense as describing an imaginary heaven differing from the hunting grounds which their fathers expected beyond the grave, only as a magnificent city differs from a prairie and forest well stocked with game? Far from it; their simple minds, though they had never heard anything about the laws of symbolic interpretation, and though many of the terms were strangely mysterious, seemed promptly to catch the grand leading ideas intended to be conveyed by the Spirit of God; and their natural and simple remarks, and the vivacity, energy and joyousness of their tones showed very clearly how truly their faith and hope were feeding upon these pictures of heavenly glory and purity and bliss, awaiting them in the presence and communion of their glorified Redeemer and His perfected church. We very much doubt if any learned commentator ever entered more truly into the spirit and real meaning of this splendid imagery than did they. This is but one of the many proofs that God's wisdom is above man's in the perfect adaptation of His Book, and of these most mysterious portions of it too, to the nature of the human mind and for the consolation of the spiritual heart,—of that mind and heart untaught by anything but His Holy Spirit. Over such indeed this teaching by striking symbols that fix in the mind a visible picture, has a power that no mere abstract statements ever can have.

Neither in the obscurity of this book therefore, nor in its prophetic nature and design, nor in the discordant views of commentators, nor in the want of human learning and culture, do we find anything at all inconsistent with the declaration, "Blessed is he that readeth, and they that hear the words of this prophecy."

II. This plain and simple declaration of its divine author must of itself be sufficient to satisfy every sincere believer in regard to the value of this book. But when we carefully and devoutly mark the things that are written therein, we cannot fail to see reasons for such a special

Its practical value.

blessing, and strong inducements to its prayerful study. We find them in its very title, in its general scope and design, in its special discoveries of truth, and in the very mystery that pervades its style.

Each of these, however, derives special force from the reason assigned in the text, which demands our first attention. "*For the time is at hand.*" This invests the things spoken of with an interest nothing else could give them. They are not matters in which only distant generations have any personal interest, but they concerned the duty and peace of even that generation to which the book was first given, and hence of every generation since. The alarming dangers it foretells were even then at hand, and so shortly to come to pass, that every one who heard these words would need its warnings and consolations, and would find in them such guidance and support as would fill him with blessing even in the darkest hour.

(1.) The nearness of the time.

It cannot be meant by these words, "the time is at hand," that the whole of the prophecies of this book were to be accomplished immediately; for by the consent of all it embraces the whole course of time, and reaches beyond the end of all things earthly. It can only mean that the conflicts and triumphs which were to end only when death and hell were to be cast into the lake of fire, were even then about commencing; and that very soon the whole of the principles of the long and fearful strife would be developed in events of stirring interest and importance to the church, and such as would require all the light and strength which these deep and far-reaching views of God's mighty and gracious purposes could give. These things must shortly come to pass; the mystery of iniquity was already at work; already had the malice of Satan been stimulated to stir up false brethren within, and excite violence without the church; and storms fierce and furious as hell could raise would soon be bursting over her,—storms that, even when calmed, would again and again repeat themselves. The time, therefore, was at hand when all these warnings of danger and glorious promises of triumph would be needed. And if needed then, they would be needed always. In every age, as the conflict waxed hotter and the final victory drew nearer, there would be the same or increasing need of the light which this revelation alone would be able to throw on the pathway and progress of the spiritual kingdom. Hence in all ages, blessed would every soul be who would hear and keep these words of warning and encouragement.

Again, the very title of the Book expresses its value.

(2.) By the title. *"The Revelation of Jesus Christ which God gave unto Him, to show unto His servants things that must shortly come to pass."*
The word "*Revelation*" or "*Apocalypse*," which last is only the Greek word in an English form, means "the uncovering," taking off the veil from what was before kept secret. Every one knows how the fact of a thing having been kept secret sharpens curiosity, its secrecy implying its special importance. With what intense earnestness men labor to extort from nature her secrets, spending their lives and making martyrs of themselves to discover her deep mysteries; and with what joy they announce such discoveries when made, and how eagerly a listening world welcomes them. The astronomer in his midnight vigils, and his life-long calculations,—the naturalist in his toilsome explorations among all the forms of being, from the snowy tops of Himmelayah to the deepest depth of ocean that plummet can be made to sound,— the traveller in unknown lands and savage tribes, the recluse student poring day and night over some question in philosophy or science in the solution of which he expects to unfold some mighty secret that will entrance the world,—these all are instances of this intense desire of

new revelations. How eagerly, too, men in all ages and conditions seek to pry into the unknown future; and what success attends every lying pretender to such knowledge, the whole history of the world attests. But here is a revelation infinitely more important and glorious than anything that the mightiest efforts of human genius ever extorted from the mysterious depths of nature. Here, too, a veil is lifted from futurity; and many of its real forms in distinct and awful grandeur pass before us, and gleams of its mysterious glory animate our longing hearts. Here God Himself has been pleased in a most wonderful degree to disclose to us the general character of His purposes and future dealings with our world and the church in all their changes through ages. The infinite importance of this revelation is intimated in the peculiar language here used:—"the revelation" "which God gave to Jesus Christ," to Him as the Head and Mediator of His church, and to whom alone access could be given to all these secret counsels of the Eternal mind, who came forth from the Father's bosom to reveal them, and who hence is called the Word of God. It is this revelation of things to come to pass here on earth in order to the full restoration in it and over it of the kingdom of God, the whole of these, so far as He was in His work of Mediator commissioned to unfold them for the benefit of His waiting people. Shall not a revelation thus solemnly announced, thus prepared for us in the secret counsels and mysterious intercourse of the persons of the Godhead, of the purposes of that Godhead toward our world and of His dealings with it, awaken our deepest interest? And can its study possibly fail to bring with it the blessing here promised?

John here further entitles it the testimony of Jesus Christ, made known by an angel commissioned for the purpose, and actually made to pass before his eyes in prophetic vision. Christ Himself here testifies;—an angel

THE PROMISED BLESSING.

is the instrument He employs. In this book there is less of the human element than in any other book of Scripture. Its revelations are not first passed through a human mind, and moulded by its habits of thinking and forms of speech to the degree that the apostolic epistles are. It is a simple report of the divine words or the divine symbols which he heard and saw. And perhaps more than any other book of the New Testament does this bear upon its very face the signature of its divine author. No man, with any tolerable knowledge of the powers of the human mind, and the productions of genius in different nations and ages, can deliberately and candidly read this book, in connection with the other Scriptures, and then admit the possibility of its mere human origin. In its very style, and its whole form, as well as in its matter, it is as far beyond all human productions as the living tree or man is beyond the imitations of the painter or sculptor. So manifestly emanating immediately from the bosom of the Godhead, and bearing the impress of divinity, blessed indeed must all those be who hear and keep it.

As already intimated, it was not intended to give beforehand a history of particular events, (3.) By its scope and but to present the principles that were design. to shape the world's history, so far as it concerned the progress of the divine kingdom, in their chief combinations and workings, and so to unfold the general course and grand characteristics of God's dealings with His church and the nations during all the long ages of conflict and darkness through which that church was to pass,—the various forms and combinations of evil that should oppose her, and the power by which she should overcome, and the glory that should eventually crown her triumph. And this, too, in order to cheer her heart and confirm her faith during the long night of her conflict, and while crushed and bleeding under the might and malice of her foes. As therefore she goes from age to age along her pathway of strife and tears and blood, with the world's powers all combined against her and externally triumphant, and holding her spiritual origin, glory, and destiny in contempt, she has only to look up to that window which John saw opened in heaven, and thence derive fresh courage and joy in her deepest tribulations. She thence learns not to think it strange concerning these fiery trials, but to see them as her destined path to an eternal triumph. She there sees these powers that the world deifies and adores,—political, literary, fanatical, infidel and heathen, all characterized as beasts of hideous and monstrous forms,—beasts, looking down to the earth on which they tread, and only there, lording it for a time over a suffering church and a prostrate world, until having exhausted all their skill and malice under the hellish inspiration of the great dragon, they are all together cast into the burning lake, and her own shout of triumph rings through all the earth, "Alleluia; the Lord God omnipotent reigneth." Surely, "blessed is he that readeth and they that hear" these words of divine cheer.

(4.) By its special revelations. For nearly all we know of Christ glorified, beyond the facts of His ascension and session at the Father's right hand, and investiture with universal dominion, and the promise of His second coming, we are indebted to this book. All the most stirring views of our blessed Lord in His glory, and in the exercise of His dominion—the mighty sweep of His Providence over the nations and the invisible world, and on behalf of each suffering saint, as well as our fullest and most impressive views of the future bliss and glory of the redeemed, and of our world delivered from the curse, and Paradise restored, are derived from this book, mysterious as it is. We are not merely told here what He will do, but we see Him doing it, and are made more sensibly to realize His living person and presence with us and in every event of life.

It is the very mystery which still enshrouds the symbols here used to reveal His works and His glory, the grandeur of His spiritual kingdom, and the horrid enormity and malignity of the world's opposition, that gives to us our truest and highest conception of them. How could we obtain even a true glimpse of the invisible world—and of those mighty spiritual forces that are battling so fiercely for the possession of the earth and of human hearts, and of the awful magnitude of the hidden dangers and hellish influences that encompass us, or of the matchless blessings and glories of the spiritual kingdom,—things beyond the power of earth's language to express, and the power of earth's objects to picture,—except by such unearthly mysteries of glory and of terror as these sublime visions present? He cannot but be blessed whose heart treasures up these wondrous things, written in this book, of our enthroned king and our heavenly home.

(5.) The mysteriousness of its symbols.

Thus it has always been. The blessing here pronounced has always been more or less enjoyed. This book has never been held by the church in vain. The whole experience of the church in every age testifies to its power. Whence those conceptions of the future world and heavenly glory—the vision of the city, and the river, and the slain Lamb, and the new song, and the harps of gold, and the day without a night, and Paradise restored, that have been wrought into all the thinking and speech of the church even in the darkest periods of her history? Whence were derived those views and that inspiration that produced those bursts of divine song—those bright and joyous anticipations of heavenly bliss, that have cheered the hearts of suffering saints in every

(6.) In all the church's experience.

age, in all their solemn assemblies, in the dens and caves of the earth, on the bed of death, and at the martyr's stake? Especially from this book. Whence did David Dickson catch the strains of that sweet song that has expressed and elevated the devotions of thousands of saints,—"Oh mother dear, Jerusalem," or as we have it in our books, "Jerusalem, my happy home?" And was it not from this same vision of John in Patmos, that Bernard of Cheny, in 1483, learned those heart-stirring strains that then cheered the church's gloom and brightened her hopes, and which ever since, translated into various tongues, have wafted to heaven her brightest anticipations and most earnest longings? With a few verses of this we may not inappropriately close this lecture, and may the Spirit of God enable us all in these times, when the true patriots of every land are in fear, looking after those things which are coming on the earth, to know the blessedness of the hope that looks up to that heavenly country and claims it as a home.

"For thee, O dear, dear country
  Mine eyes their vigils keep;
For very love, beholding
  Thy happy name, they weep:
The mention of thy glory
  Is unction to the breast,
And medicine in sickness,
  And love and life and rest.

"Beside thy living waters
  All plants are, great and small,—
The cedar of the forest,
  The hyssop of the wall.
Thy ageless walls are bonded
  With amethyst unpriced;
The saints build up its fabric,
  The corner-stone is Christ.

"There is the throne of David,
  And there, from toil released,
The shout of them that triumph,
  And the song of them that feast,

  And who, beneath their Leader,
   Have conquered in the fight,
  Forever and forever,
   Are clad in robes of white.

"Jerusalem, the glorious,
  The glory of the elect,
O dear and future vision
  That eager hearts expect!
Even now by faith I see thee;
  Even here thy walls discern;
To thee my thoughts are kindled,
  And strive and pant and yearn.

"Thy loveliness oppresses
  All human thought and heart;
And none, O Peace, O Zion,
  Can sing thee as thou art;
The Cross is all thy splendour,
  The Crucified thy praise:
His laud a benediction
  Thy ransomed people raise.

"O sweet and blessed country,
  Shall I ever see thy face?
O sweet and blessed country,
  Shall I ever win thy grace?
I have the hope within me
  To comfort and to bless;
And shall I see thy glory?
  O tell me, tell me, yes!

"Exult, O dust and ashes!
  The Lord shall be thy part:
His only, His forever,
  Thou shalt be, and thou art!
Exult, O dust and ashes!
  The Lord shall be thy part:
His only, His forever,
  Thou shalt be, and thou art."

LECTURE II.

THE GOSPEL OF THE KINGDOM.

Rev. i: 4–8. "John to the seven churches in Asia, Grace be unto you, and peace, from Him which is and which was, and which is to come, and from the seven spirits which are before His throne: and from Jesus Christ, who is the faithful Witness, and the first begotten of the dead, and the Prince of the kings of the earth. Unto Him that loved us and washed us from our sins in His own blood, and hath made us kings and priests unto God and His Father: to Him be glory and dominion forever and ever. Amen. Behold He cometh with clouds, and every eye shall see Him, and they also which pierced Him: and all kindreds of the earth shall wail because of Him. Even so, Amen. I am Alpha and Omega, the beginning and the ending, saith the Lord, which is, and which was, and which is to come, the Almighty."

JOHN, the favoured instrument by whom the wonderful revelations of this book were given to the church, needs no introduction to any reader of the New Testament. He himself delights in the title, *'the disciple whom Jesus loved.'* Of the twelve he was one of the select three admitted by our Lord to be special witnesses of His glory and of His secret sorrows. Of these three he seems to have been privileged to be nearest to his Master's person, and to enjoy the most confidential intercourse with Him. At the last supper we find him reclining next to Him so as to lean upon His bosom. His character is often greatly misunderstood. He was loving and lovely; but though gentle, affectionate and confiding, his was no mere passive and yielding nature, none of that soft and pliant tenderness so often attributed to him. On the contrary, he was dis-

The author.

tinguished above most of the others for the calm decision and fervid energy of his character, causing him and his brother James to receive from their Lord the surname of 'Boanerges,' or sons of thunder; thus reminding us that it is not to the most forward, bold and demonstrative, like Peter, but to the calm, thoughtful, and the retiring even, that we are to look for the highest specimens of real energy, courage and manly strength. In his peculiar mental character and habits as these appear both in his gospel and epistles, he seems to have been specially disposed and fitted to penetrate into the deeper spiritual mysteries of redeeming mercy, and to unfold the great principles of God's truth and dealings. There thus appears a beautiful harmony between the character of this apostle, and the privilege and duty to which he was here called of unfolding the grand elements of the vast scheme of God's Providence through future ages, to comfort and encourage His fainting and struggling church.

That church in every age is here represented by "the seven churches of Asia." These are supposed to have been under the more immediate care of this apostle in his last days. Now, too, all the other apostles are believed to have already joined their ascended Lord. His words here and in his gospel are the last apostolic utterances to the churches, and hence to whomsoever addressed would be received with equal reverence by all and of common interest to all. The "*Asia*" here spoken of, is only the western extremity of the peninsula now called "Asia Minor." The name, we are told,[1] originally belonged to a still smaller section, "the Asian meadows on the banks of the Cayster," as Homer has it. It was afterwards applied more definitely to the whole of what became, by the will of Attalus, king of Pergamos, a Roman province, and hence termed Proconsular Asia. These seven churches

[1] Conybeare and Howson, vol. i., p. 237.

were the churches of the chief cities of the province, and are afterwards named[2] in the order in which they would naturally be visited by a person starting from Ephesus the capital city. But just as the epistles of Paul to the Romans and Corinthians, and other churches, were intended for the instruction of all churches in all ages, since the relations between God and His church are always the same, and her duties, motives and consolations substantially the same,—so was this also a revelation equally for all: it was to these seven, only in order that through them it might come to all of us. On the one hand, then, we have here this beloved disciple receiving at the hands of our glorified Lord this revelation of His future purposes of grace and glory to His redeemed; and on the other, we have these seven churches receiving it directly at the hand of John, in trust for the church of every age and nation. So that "John to the seven churches of Asia," is equivalent to—'Jesus Christ to the churches of every people and age,' and therefore to us.

The one great subject of this revelation is the kingdom of Christ. It is this spiritual kingdom in its conflicts with and its triumphs over the power of Satan and the kingdoms of the world. And these verses which introduce and sum up the whole book, may appropriately be styled—*the gospel of the kingdom*. They announce its blessings and its triumphs, and these to be consummated by the coming of its divine King. In them we have, first, its message of mercy from a Triune God: "Grace be unto you and peace, from Him which is, and which was, and which is to come; and from the seven spirits which are before His throne; and from Jesus Christ, who is the faithful Witness, and the first begotten of the dead, and the Prince of the kings of the earth." We have, secondly, the church's glad and grateful response, in an ascription of praise to her redeeming

Its subject.

[2] Ch. i., 11.

God, in view of the magnitude of this mercy, and price at which it was procured: "Unto Him that loved us and washed us from our sins in His own blood, and hath made us kings and priests unto God and His Father; to Him be glory and dominion for ever and ever. Amen." Thirdly, we have a solemn warning to all the world in view of the coming of this redeeming God to accomplish the purposes announced: "Behold, He cometh with clouds; and every eye shall see Him and they also which pierced Him: and all kindreds of the earth shall wail because of Him. Even so. Amen." The whole is appropriately closed and enforced by the introduction of the divine author Himself, this coming Redeemer, in His own person declaring Himself as the origin and end of all,—the self-existent and unchangeable God, omnipotent to fulfil all the vast purposes of redeeming love to a wretched world: "I am Alpha and Omega, the beginning and the ending, saith the Lord, which is, and which was, and which is to come, the Almighty."

The highly spiritual and practical character and design of the whole book will clearly appear in considering the three leading topics of this passage; the message, "Grace and peace" from a Triune God; the church's response, "Unto Him that loved us, &c.;" and the world's warning and the church's hope, "Behold, He cometh."

I. First, then, we have the message of the gospel or glad news of the kingdom, as the burden of this whole book. That message is "grace and peace" from God the Father, the Son and the Holy Ghost. "Peace" sums up the blessings of this kingdom; "grace" describes their origin.

I. The gospel message.

All the blessings that come down from heaven to guilty and helpless man, laboring under the fearful burden of unforgiven sin and the dread of impending wrath and the misery of conflicting passions, unsatisfied desires, and earthly woes,

"Peace."

are forcibly and touchingly included in this one word, 'peace,' the peace that is from God and that reconciles to God. Without it you may gather to yourself all that earth calls good, all that for which men put forth their mightiest energies, and the eager strife for which fills the earth with "the waves of human agitation billowed high," and you have gained only dust and ashes. Without it, the more you have gained of the world's honours, pleasures and wealth, the greater the vexatious burden of vanity you have to bear, and the bitterer the cup of sorrow mingled for you at last. The want of it turns the best of earthly blessings into poison, and makes them only smooth your downward way to a deeper perdition. The possession of it, on the other hand, gives to all earthly good its only real value, and transmutes its sorrows, pains, and tears into healing medicines for the soul, and preparatives for eternal joy. It cannot do less; for it is called "the peace of God which passeth understanding,"—the peace which God gives, and by which God is reconciled. What more than this can a creature want? It brings him into loving communion with God, his maker; it secures sweet serenity and harmony in the soul itself; it satisfies every desire. Nature, in all her thousand processes, Providence, in all its minutest, vastest and most complicated movements, and even the unseen hosts of angels, all range themselves as the ministering servants of the soul at peace with God. "All things are yours."

"Grace" is its only source. Hence this message of the kingdom is "*grace* and peace." No true peace can come into any soul except through grace. Let not the frequency and flippancy with which this word is repeated make you insensible to the force and glory of its blessed meaning. It is the gratuitous, undeserved and sovereign favour of God, springing out of the depths of His own nature and with

"Grace."

all the gushing force of divinity, exhaustless as His own fulness, either by the creature's wants or the lapse of ages, and finding its true symbol in that river of the waters of life that John saw bursting out from beneath the throne of God and the Lamb.

Such is the glad news the gospel brings to you and to me, oh helpless sinner! Such the nature of the blessings which the whole resources of this spiritual kingdom of God are employed in bestowing. Mark well the two great truths taught by these words, "grace and peace," in regard to your native character and condition in the sight of God. The very words that come to you laden with heaven's richest mercies, to gladden and to save your soul, imply that God regards you as by nature at enmity with Him, and under the penalty of His holy law; and that deliverance from this state of sin and misery cannot be procured by any works or merits of yours or of any creature, but must be His perfectly gratuitous gift.

The infinite magnitude and preciousness of the blessings thus announced are most impressively taught by referring them to their origin in each of the persons of the blessed Trinity. It is, first, "grace and peace," "from Him which is, and which was, and which is to come." These words seem intended to represent as far as possible that incommunicable and mysterious name by which God revealed Himself to Moses, "I am that I am," or as it might be equally well translated and as it also means, "I will be what I will be." The words used in the original Greek here are very remarkable. They violate the most ordinary and fixed rules of grammar, as if to intimate that the very name of God must burst through all the ordinary laws of human language in order to find fitting terms—that indeed no human language can bear the burden of this name. And so it is of that grace and

From the Triune God.

peace which is but the expression of this name—of the divine character toward the believing sinner. They are as unchangeable and eternal as the Father's nature and eternal purpose of love, whence they sprang.

Again, it is "grace and peace," "from the seven spirits which are before His throne." Seven is the number of covenant perfection or completeness; "*before the throne*," indicates them as the ever ready messengers of its power and grace. This is but a striking symbolical expression after the manner of this book for the perfect and manifold variety and fulness of the operations of the Holy Spirit bestowed upon all the churches of Christ. In the covenant of redemption, and in the actual arrangements of the spiritual kingdom, the Holy Spirit takes the place and office of carrying forth by His perfect and fitting influences this grace and peace, that proceeds from the throne of divine sovereignty. It is, then, a grace and peace infinitely efficacious and all-sufficient as imparted to the soul by the Omnipotent Spirit.

Again, it is "grace and peace," "from Jesus Christ, who is the faithful Witness, and the first begotten of the dead, and Prince of the kings of the earth." It is grace and peace attested by the Son of God Himself, made sure by His resurrection from the dead as the first fruits of them that sleep in Him, and carried forward to its perfect consummation by His supreme and universal dominion.

Such is this grace and peace announced by the gospel, bestowed in this kingdom. It is boundless and exhaustless as the fulness of an unchanging God; mighty and efficacious as the manifold influences of the omnipotent Spirit; and firm and secure as the eternal throne of our risen and ascended Saviour. It is a "grace and peace" proclaimed in some form by all the works and ways of God to our sin-accursed world; proclaimed even by the very frame work of nature and its processes, standing as it does to be the theatre on which God shall display the working of redemption; proclaimed by all the vast sweep of His Providences, however clothed they may be in gloom and terror as they roll over us, for "all things work together for good to them that love God, who are called according to His purpose;" proclaimed too by every page of this blessed Book as it comes attested by Heaven's broad seal, and by no part more clearly than this closing revelation of the Kingdom; and most powerfully though silently proclaimed by the still small voice of the Spirit in your hearts, drawing you with loving strivings to flee from the wrath to come.

And futhermore. The offer of it in this proclamation of the Kingdom is limited by nothing but the sinner's willingness to accept it. "Whosoever will, let him take the water of life freely," are the express terms. Oh how unlike the ways of men! How unlike the pardons and amnesties of earthly powers, all full of limitations and exceptions, that make them savour far more of vengeance than of love and peace. Here no sinner is excepted; though your rebellion has been long and open and determined, involving the deepest and most damning guilt; though your soul may have every reason to tremble in the prospect of that dreadful wrath which its sins deserve; yet to you—aye, to the chief of sinners, the proclamation of heaven's grace and peace comes breathing nothing but love,—matchless, free, unbounded love. It comes to each of you,—what is your response? Who so mad, so bent on self-ruin as to treat with indifference this divinely attested message of grace and peace from God the Father, the Son and the Holy Ghost? "How shall we escape if we neglect so great salvation?"

Some of you have already received this grace with humble, penitent and believing hearts; you have felt this holy peace diffusing itself sweetly and powerfully through your sin-stricken and burdened souls. Surely you will most heartily unite in the joyful response of the church which follows: "Unto Him that loved us and washed us from our sins in His own blood, and hath made us kings and priests unto God and His Father: to Him be glory and dominion for ever and ever. Amen."

This is the second division of our text,—the believer's glad and grateful response to this gospel or glad news of the Kingdom. The language here seems to burst spontaneously from the heart of John as he contemplated that wondrous grace and peace he had just announced. It is too, and this should be specially noted, the actual expression of this divine peace as imparted to and dwelling in the soul; and shows its depth, its joyousness and its triumph. It is the utterance of an aged, persecuted, banished sufferer, on behalf of himself and the church upon which then the worldly power, with Domitian at its head, had placed its iron heel to crush out its very life. And yet here is not a tone or a trace of sadness; instead of groans and tears and dark forebodings every note rings with the very gladness and triumph of heaven itself.

II. The church's glad response.

Three things we may briefly notice in this response. 1st. The conscious dignity, power, and privileges even now enjoyed in this kingdom. "Hath made us kings and priests unto God," i. e., before God, in His estimation. Despised by man, poor, oppressed, or even driven to the stake, still in His eyes the believer is crowned with a royal dignity, and clothed with a priestly sanctity. To those whose notions of what is great and glorious are confined to material splendour and earthly power, these may seem strange words. All they imply is indeed not now enjoyed, and will not be until the whole mystery of redemption shall be finished; but they do imply that such a change has already taken place in the believer's

(1.) Conscious dignity and privileges.

relations and character as is the pledge and the foretaste of that future fulness of blessing. If to be a king is to possess dignity, dominion, power and riches, and to be a priest implies the still higher glory of holiness, friendship, and communion with God, then is there far more reality in the spiritual kingship and priesthood of the Christian, than ever belonged to any mere earthly monarch or Aaronic priest. And it is your privilege, believer, to feel this, and to feel it far more constantly and vividly than most of us do.

Distinctly then answer a few questions. Do you consciously welcome this message of grace and peace to your heart? Do you *trust* Jesus Christ, the Faithful Witness? Do you *choose* Him as your *Lord* and *Master?* I ask not now whether you feel the burden of a corrupt nature, and are ashamed and humbled on account of your daily sins. I know you do, you must, if you are a true believer. But do you accept God's grace in Christ as your only hope, and Christ's will as your only law? If you do—then what must be your real state and relations before God? Are you not united to Christ by an indissoluble union? Are you not adopted into the family of God? Are you not an heir of God through Christ? Is not your inheritance a share in the kingdom of glory, incorruptible and that fadeth not away? Are not nature and providence all working in subserviency to your interests? Are not angels your ministering servants? Is not the Spirit of God dwelling in you? Have you not continual access to the mercy seat? In a word, are not all the resources of the Godhead pledged to bring you off conqueror over earth and death and hell? Do not the explicit promises of the everlasting covenant render all this certain? In proportion, then, as you take God at His word, it is your privilege to say with this same John, "Behold, what manner of love the Father hath bestowed upon us, that we should be called the sons of

God. .... Now are we the sons of God, and it doth not yet appear what we shall be; but we know that when He shall appear, we shall be like Him: for we shall see Him as He is." What earthly crown or consecrating oil could even impart such hopes and dignities as these? Oh, dear brethren, do, I pray you, realize your real dignity and blessed privileges, and praise the bleeding Lamb that He *hath* made you "kings and priests unto God."

That you may do this more fully, consider the second thing taught in this response, the source and cost of these blessings—the love and blood of your redeeming God: "Unto Him that loved us and washed us from our sins in His own blood." Oh, my brethren in sin and in heavenly hope, what a theme is here for the praises of heaven and eternity! Earth's language is too utterly feeble, and man's loftiest conceptions too utterly mean. See how the inspired Paul labours to express the thought when he prays that we "may be able to comprehend with all saints, what is the breadth and length, and depth, and height: and to know the love of Christ which passeth knowledge."

<small>(2.) Cost of these blessings.</small>

This love of Christ is just as incomprehensible as the mysteries and glory of the Godhead itself. You see Him dwelling there in the bosom of the Father in bliss and glory unutterable, receiving the homage of a holy universe; and then flinging all this aside, He comes down through all the ranks of the higher intelligences, lower and still lower, till He reaches the depths of suffering in Gethsemane and on the Cross, and there pours out His blood that He may wash us from our sins. "From our sins,"—from their deep guilt, and so procuring our eternal forgiveness and God's favour; and from their power and pollution, and so procuring our restoration to the holy image of God. It may well be believed that those for whom all this was done, those whom the Son of God so loved and washed in His own blood, however low and vile and guilty before, would be thus advanced to whatever of dignity or privilege it was in the power of Omnipotence to bestow upon such creatures. Is any blessing too great for such love to give? Is any sin too black for such blood to wash away? Is there any degree of holiness or height of bliss beyond the worth of this blood to purchase? Oh, fellow-sinners and believers, is there a joy so great, a heavenly hallelujah so rapturous, as that of the redeemed sinner—as that in which you and I, ere many more years of sorrow shall have rolled away, shall unite? With some sense of this love upon our hearts, we cannot but join most gladly in

(3.) Ascription of glory and dominion to the Redeemer. The third idea of this joyful response, its ascription of glory and dominion to our redeeming Lord: "Unto Him be glory and dominion forever and ever. Amen." This is not a mere ascription of praise, a mere declaration that such glory and dominion belongs of right to Him; but that it is now and ever shall be our highest joy and effort to give Him this glory—to glorify Him in our bodies and our spirits,—living, suffering and dying, cordially submitting to His government, rejoicing in His dominion, and seeking to extend His blessed reign.

Here is the very essence and spirit of this response to the church. In view of His love and blood, and the kingly and priestly honours and privileges they have secured, she joyfully acknowledges that the glory of her salvation belongs exclusively to Him, both in its purchase, its application, and its final consummation; and expresses her desire and determination to yield herself up wholly to His dominion, both in providence and grace. Can He, beloved, require less? Can we dare to offer less? The objects of such love, the purchase of such blood, the recipients of such blessings, is there any work too hard, and any self-denial too great, any suffering too severe by which you may extend His dominion over this wretched world for which He died, and manifest your grateful love to Him? Is there any sacrifice of personal effort or property by which His kingdom may be advanced, which you can possibly make, that you can dare to withhold? And can there be any days so dark, any providences so mysterious, any calamities so crushing, that you can doubt the perfect wisdom and love of that dominion which He exercises over all things?

Consider, thirdly, the other leading idea of this passage: *the world's warning and the church's hope,*

III. The world's warning and the church's hope.

in other words, the *consummation* of the gospel of the kingdom. This comprehensive passage not only presents to us the message of this gospel, and its actual welcome and present power, but directs us forward to the period and the power which shall end the conflicts and perfect the glory of this kingdom. "Behold, He cometh with clouds, and every eye shall see Him, and they also which pierced Him: and all kindreds of the earth shall wail because of Him. Even so, Amen." These last words, *even so, Amen,* are not a response to the preceding announcement,—but are a double asseveration of its truth and importance; like the *verily, verily* of our Saviour, designed to attach to the declaration a special preëminence.

This declaration is indeed preëminent over all other prophecies; it is the sum and the end of

§. Consummation of salvation and damnation.

all threatenings and all promises. It at once fixes the mind upon that day and that event announced by the shining ones to the bereaved disciples on Olivet, as they were gazing on the clouds of heaven that had just received their risen Lord out of their sight. "This same Jesus, which is taken up from you into heaven, shall so come, in like manner as ye have seen Him go into heaven." However the waiting people of God may differ as to the time and circumstances of this second coming,—differences arising chiefly from the attempt to make the time and the manner more definite than the express terms of Scripture make them,—the glorious fact stands forth with a brightness that commands universal and joyful assent, that this second coming of our Lord in His glorified humanity is the end of the church's conflicts, and the consummation of her glory. It is the grand goal toward which all the multifarious movements of God's providence are hastening onward. Then the grace and peace here announced are to end in the fulness of glory; then the saints shall receive their complete investiture with the kingly and priestly honours here pledged by sweet and blessed foretastes; then shall they reign upon the earth, the last enemy being destroyed, and the militant kingdom end in the eternal and peaceful dominion of the redeemed in eternal union with Christ their living Head.

In answer to the question what shall take place at His second coming, let the express words of revelation be here a sufficient answer. "When the Son of man shall come in His glory, and all the holy angels with Him, then shall He sit upon the throne of His glory; and before Him shall be gathered all nations, and He shall separate them one from another, as a shepherd divideth his sheep from the goats. .... And these (the wicked) shall go away into everlasting punishment, but the righteous into life eternal."[1] "We which are alive and remain unto the coming of the Lord shall not prevent them which are asleep. For the Lord Himself shall de-

---

[1] Matt. xxv: 31-46. "Eternal life," and "everlasting punishment," as here inflicted, are something very different from national judgments; so that this is no mere judgment on the nations as such, but on the individuals of all the nations—of all the race. It is a judgment, the very grounds of which are the secret motives of the heart—*not* the mere external act,—love to Jesus, or rejection of Him, as He is represented in His people.

scend from heaven with a shout, with the voice of the archangel, and with the trump of God: and the dead in Christ shall rise first. Then we which are alive and remain, shall be caught up together with them in the clouds, to meet the Lord in the air: and so shall we be ever with the Lord." (¹) "It is a righteous thing with God to recompense tribulation to them that trouble you; and to you who are troubled, rest with us, when the Lord Jesus shall be revealed from heaven, with His mighty angels, in flaming fire taking vengeance on them that know not God, and that obey not the gospel of our Lord Jesus Christ, who shall be punished with everlasting destruction from the presence of the Lord, and from the glory of His power: when He shall come to be glorified in His saints, and to be admired in all them that believe." (²) Speaking of the sure fulfilment of "the promise of His coming," Peter says, "The heavens and the earth which are now, ... are kept in store, reserved unto fire against the day of judgment, and perdition of ungodly men. .... But the day of the Lord will come as a thief in the night, in the which the heavens shall pass away with a great noise and the elements shall melt with fervent heat, the earth also and the works that are therein shall be burnt up. .... Nevertheless we, according to His promise, look for new heavens and a new earth wherein dwelleth righteousness." (³) "And there shall be no more curse, but the throne of God and of the

(¹) 1 Thess. iv: 15–17.

(²) 2 Thess. i: 6–10. Compare with this predicted glorification of the "saints," and of "all them that believe," and "this flaming fire taking vengeance," the language of Peter, in proof that it is no partial judgments on *some* of the nations,—but universal and final, resulting in a complete change in all the conditions of earthly existence, requiring, in order to such judgment, the resurrection of the wicked, and to be followed by "a new heaven and a new earth,"—in which the consummated and perfected church shall eternally reign.

(³) 2 Pet. iii: 4–13.

Lamb shall be in it"—the glorified church, the new Jerusalem,—"and His servants shall serve Him."

Oh! if the eye of saint and sinner could be fixed more steadily and believingly on this coming day of wrath and terror to every impenitent soul, and of glory and perfected bliss to every child of God, how eagerly would this message of "grace and peace" be welcomed, and how joyously would this ascription of praise ring through all His suffering church even now! That "glory and dominion" procured by His love and blood, and the "grace and peace" that blessed dominion brings to those who submit to it, you may now despise. You may, by your practical treatment of these things, regard them as if they were unreal—unsubstantial imaginings, of less interest than the earthly good that perishes in the using, or that you perish in grasping. Oh, infatuated sinner! this delusion must very soon vanish. Now, you know Jesus Christ only by His gospel and these offers of peace,—as the bleeding Saviour and the Friend of sinners. He once was here and shed His blood for you, and it is the loving tender tones of His voice on the way to Calvary that you hear. Now He is on His throne. But He has gone there only to complete His kingdom here by His Word and Spirit and Providence. Jesus Christ must reign. He will reign. "To Him every knee shall bow, and every tongue confess that He is Lord, to the glory of God the Father." "He must reign till He have put all enemies under His feet." "Kiss the Son," then, "lest He be angry and ye perish from the way, when His wrath is kindled but a little;" and you be found, together with those who pierced Him, among the throng of those from "all kindreds of the earth" who "shall wail because of Him."

"Because of Him." That will be wailing indeed! Wailing because of the very one that came to save you, because of Him whose love is the eternal theme of heaven's highest hallelujahs. Christ rejected, an offered salvation neglected, a day of grace wasted, this is the thing that will give the lost sinner his keenest anguish, and wring from him at the last a bitterer wail than devils ever uttered.

Premonitions of this triumph and ruin He is even now giving us. As the final victory of a long and bloody war is only the result and design of all the thousand struggles and victories that may have preceded, and may be said to include them all,—so this final coming may be regarded as including all the progress of His kingdom towards it, as He by His Providence and grace is preparing and hastening on all things toward it. In all the developments of these He *is coming.* "Behold, He cometh with clouds." Similar language is elsewhere used in a way that seems necessarily to include the manifest glorious, visible progress of His kingdom of grace from that generation in which it was established, on toward that final consummation, as it is advanced from age to age by the mighty movements of His Providence. [1] These, as they sweep over the nations, remove obstacles, and, combining with the Word and Spirit, prepare the way, by successive victories of grace and judgments, for the final triumph of this grace and peace. He is thus coming now as in the clouds of heaven. The revolutions that shake the nations, that fill the world with desolation and blood, are but the footsteps of His Providence, levelling the mountains, and filling the valleys to make a highway for the onward progress of His kingdom. Terrible indeed to His enemies are all these unfoldings of His mighty plan; how terrible, we in this land know and feel in some degree at least. How He sweeps away

§. Coming now in the progress of His mediatorial reign.

[1] Comp. Dan. vii: 13, 14, with Matt. xvi: 28, and Mark ix: 1. Luke ix: 27, also with Matt. xxiv: 29, 30, 34. Mark xiii: 24, 26, 27, 30. Luke xxi: 25–27, 32.

all human hopes, and blasts the proudest expectations, and writes vanity and vexation of spirit on all man's schemes of happiness and glory, and makes the richest and loveliest of earth's heritages a scene of desolation and distress! To those who have no part or lot in the grace and peace of the gospel, oh! how bitter and crushing are many of the providences that now are sweeping over them so resistlessly, and bearing away all their earthly idols! And all the wailing that fills the land, and the households over which His judgments have swept, is "*because of Him,*"—to punish some for their rejection of Him, to chasten and purify and save others, and to show the world the malignity of sin. Be assured, my hearers, wrap it up as you may, talk as you will of political causes and human agencies, of man's folly, ambition, wrath and malice, the real cause is just "Christ rejected," the claims of His kingdom ignored. All of this is just the Prince of the kings of the earth vindicating His rejected claims, and showing a careless and ungodly world the worthlessness of its dependencies, while yet the grace and peace of His kingdom may be secured and is freely offered.

Let the world and the nations and every sinner take warning. "The Lord reigneth; let the people tremble." But let the church rejoice in hope, and let all this suffering and groaning creation rejoice with her. "For He cometh; for He cometh to judge the earth: He shall judge the world with righteousness and the people with His truth." He is coming to remove the obstacles that have so long prevented His triumphs; He is coming to sweep away all systems of error and delusion, to right all wrongs, to end all apostacies, to humble all the proud powers of this world, and to fill the earth with His glory.

§. Tremble and rejoice.

"For this tempestuous state of human things,
Is merely as the working of a sea

> Before a calm, that rocks itself to rest.
> For He whose car the winds are, and the clouds,
> The dust that waits upon His sultry march,
> When sin hath moved Him and His wrath is hot,
> Shall visit earth in mercy; shall descend
> Propitious in His chariot paved with love;
> And what His storms have blasted and defaced
> For man's revolt, shall with a smile repair."

And that we may rest in the full assurance of this, however dark the days that may be passing over us, however severe the conflicts through which the church may be called to go, however mighty the opposition of earth and hell, or however long the delay of His coming, He adds—"I am Alpha and Omega, the beginning and the ending, saith the Lord, which is, and which was, and which is to come, the Almighty."

LECTURE III.

THE CONSOLATIONS OF THE KINGDOM.

Rev. i: 17, 18. "And when I saw Him I fell at His feet as dead. And He laid His right hand upon me, saying unto me, Fear not; I am the first and the last; I am He that liveth, and was dead; and behold, I am alive for evermore. Amen; and have the keys of hell and of death."

THESE words convey the spirit and design of this whole book. They are a message of consolation direct from the lips of the glorified Redeemer. They were occasioned by the terror with which the vision of His glory, described in previous verses, had filled the heart of His beloved disciple. So overpowering was the sight that John had fallen at His feet as dead. With a tenderness equal to His godlike majesty, He lays His hand upon the fainting apostle, restores his strength, and revives his trembling heart with the assurance, "Fear not," reminding him of His divine nature, His dying love, and His universal dominion.

But not for John's sake alone were these words uttered, any more than for his sake alone was this grandest of all visions granted to him. The fact that he was twice directed to write all this, and all that should afterwards be revealed, in a book, and send it to the churches, shows that it was intended for other fearful hearts. Such were the circumstances of that time, as to make these consolations most needful and appropriate.

It was somewhere between the years 90 and 95 A. D. Domitian was on the Roman throne. "Being of a gloomy and suspicious temper, he encouraged a system of espionage; and as he seems to have imagined that the Christians fostered dangerous political designs, he treated them with the greater harshness. Flavius Clemens, a person of consular dignity, and his own cousin, was put to death for his attachment to the Christian cause; and his near relative, Flavia Domitilla, for the same reason, was banished with many others." Church history further informs us that the extent and virulence of the persecution was shown also by his causing to be dragged to Rome two grandsons of Jude, called the brother of our Lord, as dangerous rivals; though when he found their extreme poverty and obscurity—that they were joint proprietors of a small farm in Palestine, which they cultivated with their own hands, he let them go. (¹) In such times it could not be expected that one so distinguished and influential as John, the only surviving apostle of our Lord, could escape, even though old and feeble. Accordingly we find him an exile in the barren rocky isle of Patmos, and here addressing himself to the churches as their brother and companion in the tribulation and kingdom and patience of Jesus Christ; being "in the isle that is called Patmos, for the word of God, and for the testimony of Jesus Christ." The churches, oppressed and bleeding under the arm of imperial power stretched out to crush them, must have been filled with fears, not merely on account of personal danger, but for the cause of Christ so dear to their hearts. Welcome therefore beyond expression must this language have been, coming direct from the lips of their glorified King, and most cheering the view here given of His personal glory, and His providential care.

§. Circumstances of the church when written.

(¹) Killen's Ancient Church, pp. 169, 170.

But when has been the time in which the same assurance has not been more or less welcome to the church and the believer?

§. Still the same need.

Is it not still true that to be a partner in the kingdom of Christ, is to be a partaker in tribulation, and in trials and conflicts that demand patient endurance, and awaken earnest longing and waiting for His coming in delivering grace and power? Must we not, through much tribulation enter the kingdom of God? If we would reign with Christ, must we not suffer with Him? Can we wear the crown without bearing the cross? And as the church's perils and necessities and fears are still the same, so are her Lord's love and care. Neither time nor distance can change His heart or lessen His infinite resources. His churches now are just as dear to Him as ever. Not a single member of those seven churches was any more tenderly regarded by Him than each one now who, amidst trials and temptations, with many fears and tears, is seeking to follow His bleeding footsteps, and longing for His full salvation. To such, then, just as much as to John and these seven churches, are these words addressed: "Fear not; I am the first and the last, and the living One; and I became dead, and behold, I am alive forevermore, Amen; and have the keys of hell and of death." Such is their literal rendering.

In evolving the consolations of this passage, there are to be considered these four particulars — your fears are groundless; your Redeemer is divine; His atonement and intercession are perfect; and His dominion is universal.

I. "Fear not;" for your fears are groundless. You are affrighted at your own mercies. The

I. Fears of the believer groundless.

thing you fear is the very thing that brings to you salvation. It was so with John on this occasion. It was no real danger, but the personal glory of his own Saviour that filled him with alarm,—the very thing that of all others was his surest, indeed his only defence, and when fully understood, his highest joy. All he saw were but the symbols of His eternity and divine majesty,—"His head and His hairs were white like wool, as white as snow;" of His heart-searching Omniscience,—"His eyes as a flame of fire;" of His holy and resistless Providence,—"His feet like unto fine brass, as if they burned in a furnace, and His voice as the sound of many waters;" and all these as He in royal and priestly robes walked in the midst of the seven golden candlesticks, His churches,—upholding by His right hand his messengers and authority among them,—"the seven stars;" ministering His all piercing word,—" out of His mouth went a sharp two-edged sword;" and shining with the light and power of unapproachable holiness,—"His countenance as the sun shineth in His strength." That was indeed a vision of matchless and overpowering glory. But with all this awful and impressive grandeur, it was only a presentation in a single view, of all the grounds of confidence and joyful hope which flow from infinite power and wisdom and love. So that in these very things John had the brightest evidence of his own and the church's eternal security and triumph; and yet never, not even when he stood in the presence of the Cross, or afterwards of his persecutors, had he been so utterly overwhelmed as now. It was this excess of glory that, for the time, blinded his perception of the grace and love that gave it such glory. So it is still. Only we faint and tremble at the blessed reality of which John saw the mere symbols. As this beloved disciple, who had leaned with such confidence on his Lord's bosom at the last supper, fell at His feet as dead, overwhelmed by the display of His personal majesty and glory, so His people in every age have often been filled with terror at the display of these same attributes in His providential dealings with themselves and with the church. Our fears often, nay, generally arise from our misconception of the nature of those means and influences and processes of spiritual discipline and outward providences by which He is working out our salvation. Poor old Jacob almost despaired under the pressure of those providences in regard to Joseph that were the very means of saving his whole house. The Babylonish captivity, that desolated the land of Israel, was the very thing that purified and saved the church, and secured the fulfilment of God's most precious promises; and yet under its crushing burdens the captives hung their harps upon the willows, and wept bitter tears of sorrow and disappointed hope. And when the disciples saw their Lord nailed to the cross, and during the sad hours of that Jewish Sabbath when His body lay in Joseph's tomb, how completely did their hearts faint and their hopes fail! And that, as they soon learned, at the very event which laid forever secure the foundations of His kingdom and their own eternal salvation! Where, indeed, is the child of God who has not fainted in heart, and sunk in anxious fears, and wept bitterly over dispensations of God toward him, which he afterwards found out were only the instruments of good and the messengers of grace to his soul? Remember this, ye fearful saints! It is only your own misconceptions, your ignorance and imperfection that give to the events you dread the aspect of terror. Did you understand them, you would see cause to rejoice. The mystery which is now spread over them, however, is necessary. It is itself a part of the discipline of faith; a means of still more fully unfolding the tenderness and grace of your redeeming God. Away, then, with your fears. You are afraid of your own mercies.

> Ye fearful saints, fresh courage take,
> The clouds ye so much dread

Are big with mercy, and shall break
In blessings on your head.

Secondly, your Redeemer is God,—the author and the end of all things, in nature, in grace, and in Providence. "I am the first, and the last, and the living one." The original, perfect divinity of our blessed Lord is the very corner stone of our hope, the one deep exhaustless fountain whence every possible stream of consolation flows forth to a guilty world. In Him dwelleth all the fulness of the Godhead bodily. In Him are hid all the treasures of wisdom and knowledge,—of everything that we can need through eternity. If Jesus is yours, then all things are yours. For He is "the living One," who has life in Himself, and is the fountain of all life, natural, spiritual and eternal. He is therefore the first and the last in Creation. All things were made by Him and for Him. "For Him;" all therefore of nature's laws and processes must be such by their original constitution as shall work in perfect harmony with the good of His redeemed, and with perfect efficacy for His glory as their Redeemer. He is the first and the last in Providence. All its movements originate in His holy will, and are compelled to help forward His grand designs of redeeming mercy. Every event, great or small, from the sparrow's fall to that of an empire, receives from Him its commission, and brings back to Him its due revenue of glory. Those mighty convulsions which roll on, as the sea and the waves roaring, causing men's hearts to fail for fear, are His voice, like the sound of many waters, and the march of those feet of burning brass, consuming and treading down with resistless energy whatever opposes His kingdom. He is the first and the last in redemption. In His eternal purpose to meet, by the sacrifice of Himself, the claims of eternal justice, and so to redeem a chosen people from our ruined race, this plan of mercy had its

II. His Redeemer Divine

origin; and all the means by which that glorious plan has been carried forward since the fall, and applied to each individual believer, have had their origin in Him, and have derived from Him their efficacy. And the grand end of all is to secure and gather and perfect all the vast multitude of believers, and unite them in one glorious whole, and by an indissoluble union to Himself as His own body; so that the perfect and eternal salvation of each is inseparably connected with His own glory, and essential to the completion of His own mystical body. The church "is His body, the fulness of Him that filleth all in all." (¹) He is thus, believer, the Alpha and Omega of your salvation. He is the author and the finisher of your faith. He is, in every step, from first to last. He who has begun will finish. All is His own work. "Of Him, and through Him, and to Him, are all things: to whom be glory for ever." The one voice, therefore, of every one of nature's laws and processes; of every change and movement in the progress of this world's affairs; and of every fact, doctrine, threatening, and promise of His word and kingdom of grace to every believer, in all circumstances, is just this, "Fear not; I am the first and the last and the living one."

Again. "Fear not;" for His atonement is complete, and His intercession perpetual. "And I became dead, and behold I am alive forevermore." The Living One has died. Oh, believers, could we only enter more fully into the meaning and the glorious and necessary results of that death on the cross, we should never again fear the powers of either earth or hell. We should be ever singing even in tribulation, the new song, "Worthy the Lamb that was slain;" we would not find, so often as we do, our trembling spirits shrinking from the sweet strains of the apostle's glad response to the gracious mes-

III. His atonement and intercession all-sufficient.

(¹) Eph. i: 23.

sage of the kingdom, "Unto Him that loved us and washed us from our sins in His own blood, and hath made us kings and priests unto God." The merits,—the redeeming power of that death can be measured only by the infinite dignity of His person. It was because the fulness of the Godhead dwelt in Him, that that blood became a full satisfaction to the penalty of God's law, and secured for His redeemed a full and eternal atonement. "I died," says the Living One; "I who had power to lay down my life and take it again, I came down from my own throne, I bare your sins in my own body on the tree, I suffered there as your substitute,—then you cannot die. I died; then your sins are already atoned for, and forever gone, justice is perfectly satisfied, and unites with mercy in securing your salvation." God is reconciled, peace restored, all heavenly influences provided, and salvation made sure to every soul who trusts in this blood.

This is further confirmed by the assurance that He who died is alive for evermore. This is stated with a special emphasis—*Behold!* It is the crowning fact of salvation; it leaves no possible exigency through eternity unprovided for; it is eternal life. "Because I live, ye shall live also." The life of the body is bound up in the life of the head. "Your life is hid with Christ in God." He is alive to intercede for and to secure to every believer all He died for; Him the Father heareth always. His intercessions never cease. "Wherefore He is able to save them to the uttermost that come unto God by Him, seeing He ever liveth to make intercession for them." Then let His suffering, struggling people ever rejoice. While He lives, they live. While He prays for them, no good thing can be withheld. While He prays, every mistaken prayer of theirs will be corrected by His wisdom, and every unuttered sigh and groan will find its full expression before the throne of the heavenly grace.

Once more. "Fear not;" for His dominion is universal, extending over the invisible world. "I have the keys of hell and of death." Hell here is not the word used to express the place and state of eternal punishment; but the state of the dead—the unseen world with all its secrets of glory and woe, with all its mighty powers of good and of evil, everything beyond the grave. Death is His servant. Its sting is removed. It can no longer injure the soul united to Christ. Its very nature to them is changed, so as to become a means of final deliverance from the curse; or rather a process by which the body so polluted and cursed by sin shall be laid aside, to be in due time renovated and fashioned like unto Christ's glorious body. Death—the dissolution of the body—is the form in which Christ comes to sever the last link that binds His redeemed to the first Adam, and through which the curse was inherited. It had already been severed as to the soul, and so the claim of the curse even to the body had been annulled. Christ's holding the keys of the unseen world and of death, beautifully expresses His presence and agency in the whole process of dissolution and transition. Disease and violence, in whatever forms they may come, though in those most appalling to mere nature, are not the agents; they are the mere forms which *He* in His wisdom chooses, to effect the change, and in them He would have His presence recognized. Not a soul can pass from this world to the next, except just at the time and in the circumstances which He ordains. He presides over the whole process of your departure, believer, and that of those you love; His own loving hand must fling back the bolt that holds you a prisoner here; death, which is the form of the curse as it relates to the body, is thus, as the result of redemption from the curse, compelled to place the crown upon the believer's brow, compelled with His own hands, as it

IV. His dominion over death and the grave.

were, to sever the last tie which binds the curse upon the redeemed. That tie severed, the all-seeing eye of this Redeemer watches the sleeping dust, till His voice shall call it forth in a form of eternal youth and vigour.

Not only its entrance, all the powers of that unseen world are under His control. All those vast domains where mighty spirits transact the stupendous concerns of the spiritual world; the hosts of rebel angels, and of ministering spirits unto the heirs of salvation, are under His eye and hand; and neither angel nor devil wings his flight of mercy or of wrath but by His power and at His will.

Thus from the chamber of death and the gloom of the grave, and the mysterious powers of the unseen world; from all nature and providence, as well as from the cross of Calvary, and the blood of Jesus, and the majesty and glory of the Mediator's throne, there arises in universal harmony this one assurance to every believer, "Fear not." It is the voice of our Redeeming God in all His works and ways, to all His church and each of His fearful saints.

§. These topics pervade the book.

We said that these words express the spirit and design of this whole book. All who earnestly and devoutly study it, not to gratify curiosity, or to pry into the times and seasons which God hath put in His own power, but to find spiritual strength and consolation in the way of holiness, will find this eminently true. The four topics of consolation included in these precious words of our Lord, are indeed the same which, in an endless variety of form, are presented all through the Scriptures,—from the first promise, "The seed of the woman shall bruise the serpent's head," unto this last vision of that glorified Redeemer. But here they are brought out with a vividness, a concentration, a comprehensiveness, and a directness of application to all the possible phases of the church's experience and conflicts, that gives them peculiar power. This is because, first, Christ's personal glory and actual presence in the administration of all earthly things, is the one grand theme of it all; and secondly, it brings out clearly and fully the glorious consummation of His present mediatorial reign in the perfection and blessedness of the everlasting kingdom of His own redeemed. In each of the five parts into which this book naturally divides itself, the words of the passage before us find a fuller and more impressive unfolding—dispelling fear and confirming the faith of His people. In the messages to the seven churches showing the presence of Christ in His visible kingdom in its imperfect state; ([1]) in the glory of the spiritual kingdom and its administration by the slain Lamb; ([2]) in the progress of the conflict, and the triumph of a witnessing church; ([3]) in the character, progress and fate of the organized forms of evil, until even death and hell are cast into the burning lake; ([4]) and in the transcendent glories of the New Jerusalem, ([5]) in all these revelations our Mediator King seems to be laying His hand upon His fearful and often prostrate church, saying to her, "Fear not."

Be of good cheer, then, believer. Rejoice in the Lord always. Whether it be some deep mystery of God's truth—the undiscovered secrets of His holy and eternal plan, that troubles your heart; or the mystery of His spiritual discipline, the conflicts with corruption and temptation, that fills you with sore distress and anxious fears; or the mysteries of His providences, in the midst of which you stand powerless, as their numerous and conflicting influences meet and clash, and unite and roll on resistlessly, bearing before them men's wisest schemes and highest earthly hopes, imperilling the interests of the church, and desolating your home and your heart; what-

---

([1]) Ch. ii and iii.   ([2]) Ch. iv—viii; 1.   ([3]) Ch. viii; 2—xi; 18.
([4]) Ch. xi; 19—xx; 15.   ([5]) Ch. xxi; xxii.

ever it be that causes you to fear or faint,—look up and behold your glorified Redeemer as he appeared to John. Realize His continual, His personal presence, His unspeakable glory. Meditate upon it daily. Cultivate earnestly personal communion with Him. Think of Him as a living person walking always at your side, with His flaming eyes of love and holiness beaming upon you, searching your heart, and inspiring it with courage and peace. So shall you feel His right hand laid upon you, and these words of His cheering your spirit.

All these grounds of consolation are in Christ. For a guilty and suffering world there is no comfort, but in a divine Mediator. Nothing else and nothing less than this can meet the wants of a sinner. Human and angelic mediators, and all their united might, can never still the fears and remove the anxieties of a single soul. Have you, O sinner, a part in this only Mediator? You, too, must stand before Him. You, too, shall see His glory. His burning eye is even now upon you. He rules over you. He holds you in His hand of power. This is the day of His longsuffering. His great salvation is now offered to you. This is no mere theory, or figure of speech. These manifestations of His glory and grace, and offers of salvation, are facts as certain and real as the life you now possess, the guilt that now burdens your soul, and the death and judgment to which you are hastening. You who have hitherto neglected and rejected Him, are you prepared to stand before Him? Your day of grace is rapidly passing. You will soon have heard His last message, and enjoyed your last Sabbath, and felt the last strivings of His Spirit. "Behold, He cometh with clouds, and every eye shall see Him, and they also which pierced Him, and all kindreds of the earth shall

§. All in Christ. None elsewhere.

wail because of Him." "Behold, now is the accepted time; behold, now is the day of salvation."

> "Believe and take the promised rest,
> Obey, and be forever blest."

PART II.

THE MANIFESTATION OF THE KINGDOM.

Rev., Chap. 1: 19—Chap. 3.

Lecture IV. The Mission of the Visible Church.
" V. The Authority of the Visible Church.
" VI. Imperfections and Varieties of the Visible Church.
       (1.) Declining Love.
       (2.) Persecution.
" VII. Same Subject.
       (3.) Friendship of the World.
       (4.) Heresy.
" VIII. Same Subject.
       (5.) Spiritual Deadness.
       (6.) Spiritual Power.
       (7.) Lukewarmness.
" IX. The Individual Conflict.
" X. The Prize of Glory.

LECTURE IV.

THE VISIBLE CHURCH—ITS MISSION.

Chap. i: 12, 20. The golden candlesticks.

THE design of all this first part of this revelation to John, is to set forth the true outward manifestation and representative of this spiritual king-
§. Design of this part. dom. It does this in regard to its true mission, its spiritual authority, and its actual and various development.

Whoever can unite in that burst of praise with which the apostle welcomes this revelation of his Lord,—"Unto Him that loved us, and washed us from our sins in His own blood, and hath made us kings and priests unto God and His Father,"—possesses a dignity and distinction no earthly crown could ever give. He is a sharer in all the blessings of the spiritual kingdom of God. It is His high privilege, as it was John's, to have the King in His power and love lay His hand upon him, and dispel every doubt and fear by the precious assurance, "Fear not, I am the first, and the last. I am He that liveth, and was dead: and behold, I am alive for evermore, Amen; and have the keys of hell and of death."

But this distinction, precious and glorious as it is, is a hidden one. These members of heaven's
1. The true kingdom invisible. royal family are found in the hovels of poverty, oftener than in the halls of wealth and power. They have no immunity from earthly calamities; no visible badge of their high relationship.

(73)

Even they themselves are often in doubt about their right to its privileges. Such is, at times at least, the active power of remaining corruptions and the burden resting on their consciences, that they dare not unite in that song of praise. "Can we," they ask, "say that we are washed from our sins, while we feel the chains of sin still binding us, and a body of death still clinging to us?" They forget how Paul, in almost the same breath in which he makes the same sad confession, joyfully adds a thanksgiving for the deliverance and victory in prospect—"I thank God, through Jesus Christ our Lord."

But even when they themselves can hold fast the confidence and rejoicing of the hope, this distinction of theirs is invisible to others. "Behold," says John in his first epistle, (ch. iii: 1) as he gazes in rapture on the blessings of this heavenly adoption, "what manner of love the Father hath bestowed upon us, that we should be called the sons of God; therefore the world knoweth us not, because it knew Him not." No mortal eye, therefore, can trace the precise limits of this kingdom. No herald of it even, as he comes proclaiming the offer of its blessings, can point to it, saying, Lo, here! or Lo, there! "for the kingdom of God is within you." "The kingdom of God is righteousness, and peace, and joy in the Holy Ghost."

2. *The visible church its true and divinely constituted representative.*
It is the defects of its present development in the hearts of those who are its real subjects, that not only renders its extent undiscoverable, but its whole manifestation so imperfect. So very partially are its spiritual blessings now enjoyed, that but few beams of its power and glory appear. But however secret its workings, and obscure its limits, and partial the development of its power, the evidence of its actual presence and heavenly nature is irresistible. Such an evidence is found in the very

existence of what we call "the visible church of Christ."

The visible church is a body of persons representing Christ's interests in the world, by professing subjection to Him, and testifying to His character and claims. If Christ had no true subjects and witnesses here, the existence of such a body would be impossible. The visible church is a thing so entirely unique, so completely in contrast with all the organizations produced by mere human influences and agencies, that we are compelled to admit the presence of another and a divine cause, or deny the first principle of truth—that like causes produce like effects. No influence originating in a mere human heart, in mere earthly motives and principles, and from a nature so selfish, so corrupt, so sensual, so averse to whatever is purely spiritual and holy, could ever have wrought out such an effect as the church of Christ. Of such influences the true and the only effects are seen in the imperfections, pollutions and inconsistencies that stand out even in the eyes of the world itself, in such striking contrast with the principles of this church, and with their actual legitimate effects in the character and life of multitudes of her people. The real peculiarities that distinguish the true visible church from all earthly things, are such as no earthly cause can produce or has any tendency to produce. They are the results of the secret agencies of the invisible kingdom. His church, therefroth, stands forth here on earth by its complete singularity—in its high and unearthly claims, in its spiritual teachings, in its moral elevation, and in its power over human hearts and character, as the true representative, because the necessary visible outworking of the invisible spiritual kingdom of Christ.

It is manifest that it can only be a true representative of the spiritual kingdom, as it presents a true embodiment of its truths and principles, its spiritual character and privileges. Only as it does this can it share in the promises or protection of the King. Just so far as it fails in this must it forfeit all claim to the divine promises, and become itself the object of the Lord's displeasure, chastisement and desolating judgments.

<small>3. Importance of clearly distinguishing the true from a false church.</small>

It is therefore greatly important that this representative kingdom—the visible church, be clearly defined both as to its *design and character*. This is so, in order that whatever through human infirmity or corruption might mar its character, or make it a false representative, might be clearly distinguished from that which constitutes it the true pattern of the invisible and glorious reality, and ensures to it the protection of its divine King. That this distinction should be clearly drawn and understood, is necessary in order that on the one hand no true church be rejected because of its imperfections; and on the other hand that these imperfections receive not the sanction of divine approval, or even of church authority, as an inherent part of this representative kingdom. There are two opposite errors on this subject to which the world has always been tending, to prevent both of which this distinction is necessary.

The first of these is the serious error of confounding the true spiritual kingdom with the external church, so as to make a participation in spiritual blessings to depend upon an external organization,—or so as to regard a share in the privileges of the visible church as securing a right to the blessings of the spiritual kingdom,—or so as to mistake the nature and design of those defeats and sufferings to which the former is subjected, as if they gave ground for discouragement to the true children of the kingdom. The other is the opposite and perhaps equally dangerous error of undervaluing the visible church; regarding it because of its necessary imperfections in the present state, as a thing of comparatively little importance, and its organization and administration as matters of mere human authority and of comparative indifference—not materially affecting men's spiritual and eternal interests. To fully avoid each of these, we need to have the true church divinely defined.

The distinction between a true and false church is indeed very clearly taught all through the Scriptures. But it seemed specially desirable that now, when the last of the apostles was about to leave the world, and this church to go forth on her world-wide mission with these inspired records as her only guide, this distinction should be more definitely marked. This was indispensable to a right application of the promises and threatenings, the encouragements and warnings of this book, in which the visible kingdom of Christ as an organized body, and the various forms of organized evil are presented in close and deadly conflict. Only thus through the confusion and dust and smoke of the battle could the true church be recognized. And for practical purposes no mere abstract logical definition could suffice. It required one that would present such a picture or pictures of the church in its actual working, as whenever seen in actual life and history would at once be recognized, and render all except wilful mistakes impossible; not one that by its general or abstract terms would be capable of endlessly varied interpretations and applications.

This accordingly is most fully and clearly done by the interpretation of the leading symbols of the previous vision, and by the epistles to the seven churches which follow.

4. The true church defined by symbols and by examples.

Thus by a twofold method the true visible church is here defined. First, by the symbols of the candlesticks and the stars,—the golden candlesticks in the midst of which the glorified Saviour is walking, and the stars held in His right hand. Secondly, by an actual description of the condition of the seven separate churches thus symbolized, as they were at that time, each presenting a different phase both of character and outward state, but all together forming a complete view of the church as it is during its militant condition, so that every church in all ages might find in one or more of them its own likeness both as to excellencies and defects, and so receive appropriate encouragement and warning. Thus by a comparison both natural and easy, we may readily detect the degree in which any visible organization conforms to the true model or comes short of it. We may thus too be enabled to trace the progress of the spiritual kingdom; the living church, through all the ever varying phases, declensions, apostacies, and revivals of all ages, until at last she comes forth in her bridal beauty and perfection to meet her descending Lord.

I. THE TRUE CHURCH SYMBOLIZED.

It will not be unprofitable to dwell at some length upon the instruction contained in the symbols here set before us by our Lord Himself as a picture of His true church. All the magnificent symbols of that vision recorded in the previous verses, whose glory had so overwhelmed the apostle, were designed to set forth clearly and vividly just two things,—Christ Himself, and His visible church, and these in their relation to each other. The only two symbols that directly describe the church are the seven golden candlesticks and the seven stars; and these are the only two that the Lord here explains. He calls them a mystery; something which contained a deeply hidden significance which needed to be pointed out. And He speaks of them as the mystery which was the subject of all He commanded John to write, of all he had seen, of all then passing, and all that was yet to be revealed. "Write the things which thou hast seen, and the things which are, and the things which shall be hereafter; the mystery of the seven stars which thou sawest in my right hand, and the seven golden candlesticks." As much as to say, that the whole subject of his writing in reference to the past, the present or future revelations, was this mystery of the stars and candlesticks. Thus clearly does our Lord declare that the subject of the whole book is the church as symbolized by these candlesticks and stars. The first of these sets forth at a glance the nature and design of the church, and the second her spiritual authority, as appointed and upheld by Him.

"The seven candlesticks which thou sawest are the seven churches." These were the first objects that met the apostle's gaze, as he turned round, startled by the trumpet tones of his Redeemer's voice; and it was in relation to these that all the other symbols were intended to be viewed, all those which set forth the glory of her risen and reigning Lord, walking in her midst. It beautifully and forcibly expresses the true mission of the visible church. A candlestick, or lampstand as this was, like those in the tabernacle and temple, is for the purpose of holding up light in the darkness. The church is God's appointed light-bearer in this dark world. She is not the originator of the light she gives; she gives light only by preserving, holding forth, and disseminating the light entrusted to her. That light is gospel truth and influences. Her great, and indeed her only business, is to hold fast this truth and hold it forth, until its light penetrates into the darkest corners of the earth. She is not only utterly destitute of all elements of light in herself, and of all power to make it; but she cannot in any way improve the light entrusted to her. All she can do is to steadily support it, in its right and true position, so that it may be in a condition to burn and to shine into the darkness around. She can neither make truth, nor improve truth; but she has a vast work to do in receiving fully and holding forth clearly what has been committed to her care in the lively oracles of God. Whenever she

1. The candlesticks; the church's mission.

attempts anything more than this, when she seeks to improve or modify the light itself, when she would become a political power, or a teacher of philosophy, she is no longer the golden candlestick of God's appointment; she is unfaithful to her simple, spiritual mission, and her light becomes darkness, or a lurid glare that burns only to deceive.

In fulfilling this mission, she is not a mere passive and involuntary instrument. What the candlestick does as passive, unconscious matter, the church, composed of living souls, can do only by the active employment of all her energies—her intelligence, her gifts and her graces. To hold forth the light of God's salvation is to be the sole end of her being and its activities. To use her powers and gifts for any other purpose is a mal-appropriation of the most important and solemn trust ever confided to human beings. To use them for any selfish or worldly end, is as if the priest in the tabernacle had taken the golden candlestick and melted it down into money for his private use. This, in fact, is just what covetousness does; it turns this consecrated gold into filthy lucre. Ambition, in like manner, uses this golden candlestick as a pedestal for the display of its own glory, and slothfulness for its own self-indulgence. It is nothing but this unfaithfulness that has so sadly disfigured this beautiful spiritual creation of God, the visible church, and withered her power. Every covetous man in the church, instead of using his property to uphold the light, really melts down his share in this golden candlestick into coin for his own use; at once robbing God and abjuring his own part in God's service and salvation.

Her true nature therefore is that of a witness, a witness for God. Her great work is to bear a testimony. That testimony is perfectly definite and fixed. She has no power to add to it or take from it. She has no right to deliver it

The church a witness bearer.

in any other way than as a divine testimony, a charge committed to her, and resting solely on the divine veracity. She is to declare it, not on her own authority, or on the authority of mere logical reasonings, or demonstrations of philosophy, claiming the world's assent on such grounds. The penetrating brightness and power of her light depends solely on the degree in which she is seen to base every utterance on this exclusive ground, "Thus saith the Lord." This it was that gave to the apostles' testimony such power; it was the simplicity and purity of their witness bearing, and that of the primitive church, that caused the light of the gospel to spread so rapidly and to penetrate the darkest dens of Satan's power. And what the church now needs is just the reviving of this spirit of witness-bearing, in opposition to the rationalistic spirit, in all her people and her pulpits, in all her courts and enterprises. We need to hear the voice of God ringing in our ears continually, "Ye are my witnesses, saith the Lord." It is not by the force of our logic, however perfect, nor by the extent and variety of our learning, however useful, nor by the polished beauty, the glowing rhetoric or fervid eloquence of the preacher's utterances, that the truth of God finds an entrance into the dark recesses of the human heart; but by the simple utterance of faith in the name of the Lord. We need to catch anew the simplicity of the apostolic commission as it fell on the ears of the primitive church, "Go ye into all the world, and *preach the gospel*,"—herald the glad tidings—"to every creature," "teaching them to observe all things whatsoever I have commanded." "Preach the gospel," "teach my commands,"—this is her great business. "Announce it as glad tidings from heaven, not as a conclusion reached or established by man's reasonings; and teach as duty all that I have commanded, and nothing else." Though we may all believe all this, we yet need to catch anew in far mightier power the spirit of the great apostle to the Gentiles, as he expressed it to the proud and wisdom-loving Greeks of the Corinthian church. "I, brethren, when I came to you, came not with excellency of speech or of wisdom, declaring unto you the testimony of God. For I determined not to know anything among you, save Jesus Christ, and Him crucified. And I was with you in weakness and in fear and in much trembling. And my speech and my preaching was not with enticing words of man's wisdom, but in demonstration of the Spirit and of power, that your faith should not stand in the wisdom of man, but in the power of God."

What has just been said might seem to make this witness-bearing the exclusive function of her §. By her worship. public ministry. But this is very far from being so. It is the work of the whole church. This truth is to be the expression of her whole life. It is to mould the character of every member, and to direct all their activities in all the relations of life. It receives its first articulate expression in all her ordinances of worship. In her prayers and her praises and her holy sacraments, this truth is held forth in its most impressive form. In these every feature of her whole relation to God, every distinctive truth of the gospel of Christ, and indeed all the claims of His holy law are practically presented. The verbal declarations of her pulpits and books are to be tested by these, and in these their true nature and design appears.

But this is not all. The truth must be lived. It must control all the habits, business and cares of life; and it is especially by so doing that it makes the church the light of the world. The testimony of a holy life tells with special power on a world of sin. This presents the truth in its living force and heavenly beauty. It is a testimony that cannot be gainsaid or resisted. Darkness flies before it. Without this effect the verbal testimony would soon become worthless, and the ordinances would be powerless and unmeaning. Without it indeed both would be speedily corrupted. Without it they would prove themselves destitute of the very seal to which they lay claim, the seal of a divine, transforming power accompanying the truth.

This is the testimony to which the apostle refers when he says to the Philippians,—"That ye may be blameless and harmless, the sons of God without rebuke, in the midst of a crooked and perverse nation, among whom ye shine as lights in the world; holding forth the word of life." This is what Christ means when He says, "Let your light so shine before men, that they may see your good works, and glorify your Father which is in heaven."

This service of preaching and other *ordinances* of worship, and of a holy life exemplifying the truth, is the scriptural idea of "worship." "Pure religion—[Greek, worship] and undefiled before God and the Father is this, to visit the fatherless and widows in their affliction, and to keep himself unspotted from the world." It is thus the church worships, and in her worship witnesses for God, and pours her light on the world's gloom.

To the end that the church may be a true witness for God, He has constituted her with a government and power of discipline so as to exclude from her membership all that are living in open inconsistency with the truth and claims of Jesus; and from her ministry, all who teach contrary to the truth as it is comprehended in Christ crucified. To the same end also is her deaconship, or that function which takes charge of temporalities; that thus she may bear witness to the unity of her people in love, by the abundance of one being made to supply the wants of another; and that the means may be supplied by which the light of her whole testimony may be made to shine over all the earth. Her whole government, therefore, is

§. By her government.

designed to train and discipline her to be a witness-bearer. And just in proportion as her ministers, office-bearers and people keep constantly in view this work of witness-bearing for God as the very design of the church's existence does she answer to this symbol of the golden candlestick, and is truly God's light-bearer in a dark world.

A second thing taught here by this symbol as presented to John in this vision is the source of the grace by which she is enabled to fulfil this mission,—Christ the author and the supporter of her light. If the church is but a candlestick, or lampstand, a mere light-bearer, then must her light soon go out unless constantly supplied from some other source. In the vision of Zechariah this was represented by two living olive trees which through golden pipes poured the oil into the golden lamps, and which are there explained as "the two anointed ones which are before the Lord of the whole earth," that is, the two Messianic offices of priest and king. Now that the Messiah Himself has appeared the types disappear, and instead of the olive-trees, we have the Redeemer Himself clothed in the habiliments of the High Priest, and with divine and kingly majesty, walking in the midst of these candlesticks, and by His grace and discipline feeding and trimming these lights which He Himself has kindled and placed upon them. It is His presence that makes them shine; the withdrawal of His supplies or care would leave them in utter darkness and utterly worthless. What more worthless than a candlestick in the dark, without a light? So nothing is more worthless than a church without Christ—a church in which Christ's presence is not manifested by the effulgence of truth and holiness cherished by His indwelling Spirit. Witness the effete organizations that still retain the name of churches in the lands once visited by the

2. The church's dependence on the presence and grace of Christ.

apostles, and irradiated by gospel light,—the Nestorian, the Abyssinian, the Greek and the Roman churches. All our forms and ordinances, all our organizations and assemblies, and our new plans for eliciting light and power, are just as worthless for this purpose without the presence of Christ working in us and by us, as would even a *golden* candlestick be without any light on it. No working, or changing, or tinkering of the candlestick, can make it give light. We must have the presence and grace of the great Light-giver. When the light burns dimly, when the darkness seems to thicken, and the fogs and dampness that are ever exhaling from the pit resist her feeble and struggling rays, there is but one resource. To that we cannot resort too quickly, if we would keep our light from entire extinction. It is in despair of any other help, to cry to our Great High Priest and King with unwearying importunity, for those divine influences which will kindle anew the flame of zeal and love, and enable her, from every enlightened soul, and from every official station, to give forth a clear and convincing testimony.

It is further implied by this relation of these symbols to the glorious Being in their midst, that our encouragement to expect this is fully equal to our dependence. The same symbol that shows our need, shows Him as ever present to supply that need. It presents Him as actually fulfilling the promise with which He accompanied the great commission given when He withdrew His bodily presence, "Lo, I am with you alway, even unto the end of the world." It was that promise made visible. It shows that it is in and by His church that He manifests His priestly character and sanctifying power. There He is seen in His priestly robes, girded with His covenant faithfulness, and detecting with His eyes of flame every deception and secret impurity, and noticing every breathing of desire toward Him, however faint, and every unuttered prayer and groan; there He displays His divine majesty and the stately steppings of His grace, and unfolds the design of the mighty movements of His Providence as with feet of burnished brass He treads down the nations; and there too the voice of His power is heard, bowing the sinner's heart, filling it now with terror and anguish, and anon with a joy that passeth knowledge. There too He declares His threatenings, and manifests the avenging and corrective, as well as the saving efficacy of His word, which is as a two-edged sword; by "the breath of His lips slaying the wicked" and purifying His people. Elsewhere this church is called the house of God, of our Redeeming God. In it He dwells, in it He works, from it His power goes forth, and by it He shews forth His glory. Hence these seven candlesticks—His churches, and not the nations at large, nor even heaven itself, are presented to John in vision as the sphere of a glorified Redeemer's movements. Among these He is ever walking—for these He is ever working; "Head over all things *to* the church."

In this symbol John would also see the identity of the church in all ages. It would at once remind him of the golden candlestick in the tabernacle and in Zechariah's vision. There indeed it was a single candlestick or lampstand with seven branches and seven lamps; here it is seven of these lampstands,—the same term is used as that which describes the one in the tabernacle. They are separate from each other, as seems evident from the Lord walking in their midst, answering thus to the seven distinct churches which they are afterwards said to represent.

3. The church's identity in all ages.

This symbol would therefore at once identify in the apostle's mind, the church of Christ with the church of the old dispensation, both under Moses and as restored under Zerubbabel after the Babylonish captivity. It would vividly set forth the truth that these churches scattered among the cities of the Gentiles as the seven churches of Asia were, had succeeded to the honours and privileges once accorded exclusively to the Jewish people. Though they had been cut off, and their temple perished, yet the true temple and priest and candlestick remained. That very thing for which Israel of old had been called and separated, these churches of Christ were constituted to accomplish, and that far more effectually. Indeed the accomplishment of that design was reserved for this dispensation. Abraham was called, and his descendants set apart as a separate people—the church, the *" called out"* from among the nations,—in order that in him all the nations of the earth might be blessed. To carry this promised and prepared blessing to the nations, to diffuse the blessed light of the salvation of God over all the earth, is the peculiar work of the church of this age and dispensation. The one had now become seven: the minor had become of full age; the church had put on her true spiritual form, perfectly adapted to all nations. The light no longer emanated from a single centre, but from centres as numerous as the bodies of believers gathered from among the nations. The gospel placed these candlesticks among all nations, and in all the cities of the nations. The churches thus gathered inherit the privileges and the offices of ancient Israel, only in fuller measure and with mightier power. They succeed to her very titles; they are the true Israel; they only are real Jews in the covenant sense. The true Jerusalem, the city of the living God, the Mount Zion in which her Messiah reigns, is that New Testament church to which the apostle in the epistle to the Hebrews represents all believers as having now come. The olive tree of Paul is the same; and the branches, though they differ in substance, have the same life and produce the same fruits of holiness. Even their covenant relation to Abraham, so far as it secured any real spiritual blessings, is the same. "If ye be Christ's, then are ye Abraham's seed, and heirs according to the promise."

But while the apostle would thus behold the identity of the old church with the new in office and privilege, he would also see that the old visible unity had disappeared. It was no longer a unity of visible organization as in Israel of Old; but a unity resulting from their relation to the same living Head dwelling equally in them all, and upholding in each a distinct spiritual authority. Here are seven churches with their seven stars or angels, each one a church with its divinely upheld authority. One single shaft, with its seven branches, was no longer the proper symbol of the visible church, but a seven-fold multiplication of these light-bearers, each bearing the same relation to the One glorious Being in their midst,—a multiplication as numerous as the separate churches or bodies of congregations, as numerous as the wants of the nations should demand.* All these are indeed united, but not by any visible bond of organization; only by their relation to their Divine Lord, and in the unity of that spiritual truth by which they shine. It is a "unity of the Spirit," says Paul to the Ephesians, and he thus describes the bonds that bind it into one spiritual body. "There is one body, and one Spirit, even as ye are called in one hope of your calling; one Lord, one faith, one baptism,

4. Her unity not visible, but spiritual.

---

* Why, then, it may perhaps be said, did not the multiplication of this same symbol in Solomon's temple, where there were ten candlesticks, imply that even then there was no *visible* unity? Simply because it could not. The visible unity of the Jewish church was then an existent fact; and the multiplication of the symbol, as also of the tables and lavers, of which there were ten each, could only be regarded as a repetition of the same symbol, to impress the true character of the church. But when viewed as types of the church under the Messiah, it might seem to *prefigure* the *indefinite multiplication* of the visible churches of Christ, and hence, as a matter of necessity, that then their unity could be only spiritual, a unity of relation to their divine Head, and a unity of function.

one God and Father of all, who is above all, and through all, and in you all." And the goal of perfection to which her Redeemer's ascension gifts are represented as bringing her, here and under this dispensation, is, we are told in this same connection, "the unity of the faith." "Till we all come in, [literally, unto,—εις] the unity of the faith, and of the knowledge of the Son of God, unto a perfect man, unto the measure of the stature of the fulness of Christ."

The preciousness of the visible church is also clearly symbolized. Like the candlestick in the tabernacle, these are "*golden.*" While this may represent the required purity of the church, it certainly does represent its actual preciousness. This preciousness is manifest from the peculiar relation in which it stands to Christ, as the representative of His mystical body, and as His appointed instrumentality in gathering and perfecting that body. It becomes thus the theatre on which and by which He displays the glory of His grace and wisdom and power.

5. The unspeakable value of the visible church.

The visible church is not a mere voluntary society, in which membership and government are matters solely of human choice. It is a positive institution of God. It is indeed a necessary outgrowth of the invisible kingdom, a necessary result of the election of grace and the effectual call of the Spirit through the word. But while it is the manifest outgrowth of the spiritual life, the Redeemer—the author of this life—did not leave to the imperfectly sanctified hearts of His people to form it according their own wisdom, or impulses. Its design and functions are too intimately associated with His own glory and the accomplishment of His mediatorial work to be left entirely to the inventions of human wisdom, or the management of human skill. Its constitution, its functions, and the offices necessary to their right administration have, in all ages, been of divine appointment. The precision with which He condescended to establish all its minutest regulations under the old Dispensation, requiring everything to be framed and ordered according to the pattern showed to Moses in the Mount, every reader of the Bible must have been struck with. This was so, not only in what was directly and expressly typical, but as to all the regulations necessary to secure their proper observance. Thus, under that typical dispensation, it was shown how all the more spiritual ordering and worship and outward administration of this more spiritual dispensation must be by His authority and His alone. The visible church, therefore, as well as the invisible body which it represents, is a society ordained by God, constituted by Him, and receiving from Him at least its general form, its officers, its ordinances and its laws. It is a heavenly thing,—it is the *kingdom of heaven.*

Most appropriately, therefore, it has a "golden" symbol. Infinitely superior to all other visible organizations here, as being directly formed and ordered and arranged by divine wisdom, she demands the supreme affection and attachment and reverence of all. Appointed not only to represent the body of Christ—the elect, redeemed, regenerated children of God who are begotten to a heavenly inheritance, and who are to reign upon the earth; but also to be the chosen instrumentality by which this redeemed body is to be gathered and trained and perfected for its eternal and glorious inheritance, until Christ shall come again to be glorified in His saints, it becomes invested with an importance and preciousness second only to that invisible and spiritual reality.. Its officers and ordinances are Christ's great ascension gifts to His spiritual kingdom, His invisible church. "When He ascended up on high, He led captivity captive, and gave gifts unto men. ...... And He gave some, apostles; and some, prophets; and some, pastors and teachers; for the perfecting of the saints, for the work of the ministry, for the edifying of the body of Christ; till we all come in the unity of the faith, and of the knowledge of the Son of God, unto a perfect man, unto the measure of the stature of the fulness of Christ."

Imperfect, therefore, as the visible church is, and always has been; marred, as was the church of Sardis and of Laodicea, by the corruptions that still dwell in the hearts of her members, and by false professors, she is still, in the eyes of our Redeemer, infinitely more precious than all the kingdoms of the world and the glory of them. Even the churches of Sardis and Laodicea have a *golden* candlestick as their symbol, as well as the pure and uncensured churches of Smyrna and Philadelphia. Compared with the pomp and might of earthly powers, men very generally regard the church as a feeble and insignificant thing, a power of but little account in the world; but the time approaches when she shall come "forth as the morning, fair as the moon, clear as the sun, and terrible as an army with banners." While the proudest and mightiest dynasties of earth are crumbling into ruins, she shall go forward, building upon those ruins the kingdom of her Lord and Saviour, until He come and sweep away all opposition, and destroy all the enmity, and crush the old serpent forever, and she gives place to His true invisible spiritual kingdom, which shall reign with Him on the earth forevermore.

§. The central object of the book.

Hence this visible church, as God's light-bearer in a dark world, becomes the great central object of this whole book. The grand struggle is to make and preserve her purity:—that so she may truly represent the spiritual kingdom. Hence though sometimes corrupted, and often persecuted, and otherwise rebuked, yet in the sweep of God's Providence, all agencies and powers are made to bow before her. It is the visions of her toils and trials, of the struggles of her light with the darkness, and of its triumph over it, that are here made to roll before us in strange and awful magnificence.

Beware, then, that you do not under-estimate this "golden" instrumentality and representative of God's kingdom. Ever remember that the government, the ordinances, the offices, the discipline, and the spiritual enterprises of this church are divinely appointed; they are heavenly means of a heavenly power for heavenly ends. To neglect or turn away from the privileges of this church is to reject God and His Son. If you have any love to the King Himself, and to His invisible spiritual kingdom, you cannot but love and cherish this visible kingdom which He has ordained to represent it and to be the channel of its blessings to a perishing world. If you love the light, you will love the golden candlestick which supports it, and without which it would soon go out, or at least give forth its light but feebly and in a narrow sphere It is the world's only hope. No light can shine upon the world's deep darkness, so as even to alleviate its sin, its misery, or its ignorance, but that of which it is the bearer, and with which it is furnished by the grace of a glorified Saviour. Whether, therefore, you regard His honour or the salvation of man, you will regard no sacrifices too costly, and no labours too severe by which the interests of this church can be advanced. Your heart's most earnest feeling will be that of the captive Jews by the rivers of Babylon—"If I forget thee, O Jerusalem, let my right hand forget her cunning: if I do not remember thee, let my tongue cleave to the roof of my mouth: if I prefer not Jerusalem above my chief joy."

> If e'er to bless thy sons
>   My voice or hands deny,
> These hands let useful skill forsake,
>   This voice in silence die.
>
> If e'er my heart forget
>   Her welfare or her woe,

> Let every joy this heart forsake,
>   And every grief o'erflow.
>
> For her my tears shall fall;
>   For her my prayers ascend;
> To her my cares and toils be given,
>   Till cares and toils shall end.
>
> Beyond my highest joy
>   I prize her heavenly ways;
> Her sweet communion, solemn vows,
>   Her hymns of love and praise.

That any one should regard such strong attachment to the visible church and external ordinances as in any kind of antagonism to spiritual realities, and out of pretence of supreme regard to the latter should lightly esteem the former, is as if one should despise the candlestick out of professed regard for the light it bears; or as if he should dash away the cup in which the cooling draught is presented to his burning lips, out of professed regard for its precious contents. If any are so foolish as to cling to the candlestick without any light, surely we need not reject the candlestick as it bears on it heaven's own pure light. Because others will have the empty cup without and instead of the waters of life it was designed to convey, we need not commit the egregious folly of trying to secure these waters of life by refusing the cup.

Professing members of the church of God! Are you fulfilling the end of your calling? Are you shining in the beauty of truth and holiness? Do you prize the truth, and hold it fast, and hold it forth in the darkness, so as to give light to those around you? And are you doing all you can to make the church to which you belong a bright and shining light?

You are called to be a witness for God. You are a witness of some kind. You are giving forth a daily testimony. What is that testimony? Is it the truth, purity, beauty and love of the gospel and cross of Christ? Is it such a testimony both of the lips and life as leads the world to see the excellency of the gospel, and to confess its power?

Or, are you, by your inconsistency, and self-indulgence and worldliness; by your unbelief, or lukewarmness or despondency, bearing false witness for God? You are His witnesses. You are upon your solemn oath. That oath has been taken over the memorials of a Saviour's blood. If such is your testimony, then are you guilty of a species of perjury before God, by conduct that falsifies His truth, brings dishonour upon His gospel, yea, upon His very blood, hardens sinners in their unbelief, and confirms them in their way to perdition; and persistence in this course must bring down upon you the dreadful plagues that are written in this book. If the very possibility of incurring such guilt makes us tremble, as well it may, for it is daily incurred by multitudes, let it stimulate each one to pray, with daily earnestness, the prayer of the Psalmist—"Create in me a clean heart, O God; and renew a right spirit within me. Cast me not away from Thy presence; and take not Thy Holy Spirit from me. Restore unto me the joy of Thy salvation; and uphold me with Thy free spirit. Then will I teach transgressors Thy ways; and sinners shall be converted unto Thee."

LECTURE V.

THE VISIBLE CHURCH; ITS AUTHORITY.

Chap. i: 20.

"The stars are the angels of the seven churches."

THE first mark of a true church of Christ is found in the fulfilment of her mission as a spiritual light in a dark world. The second is the authority by which she acts. This is our present subject.

The golden candlesticks are beautiful and expressive symbols of her spiritual mission. But they necessarily leave out of view the other equally important feature of the true church, the authority by which she is governed. This is indeed the distinctive feature that presents her before the world as the visible representative of the invisible spiritual kingdom. To set forth this is the design of the only other symbol in this vision of which Christ gives any explanation—the stars in His right hand. This completes the view of what is essential to the visible church. She is not only a light-bearer, but a kingdom, having the authority of her King exercised by visible representatives acting under His commission. "The stars are the angels of the seven churches." These angel stars, as we shall see, most perfectly symbolize the spiritual authority constituted by Christ Himself in every one of His churches.

§. Stars symbols of authority.

Used as a symbol, stars represent the function of ruling, and rulers. This rests upon a manifest analogy. The stars belong to a sphere above us, they give light, and their light and movements are not controlled by earthly things, but earthly things have always been regarded as controlled by them. They thus aptly represent that lawful authority which is from above, and sheds upon the path of duty its only light, and without which all teaching and acts of government would be without any value or force. With this usage every Scripture reader is familiar. ([1]) The seven stars in the right hand of Christ, therefore, present the simple idea of the spiritual authority of Christ as exercised in each of these churches. Its explanation, '*angels*' or *messengers*, necessarily implies the fact that that authority is vested in and exercised by human instruments sent by Him. The symbol itself sets forth all authority in the church as Christ's; the single word by which it is explained, describes that authority as found only in those who are His messengers, saying and doing just what He bids them, and nothing more. This seems so evident that we might at once proceed to unfold the importance of this mark of the true church, and to apply the principles of truth and duty which it involves. The variety of views, however, which have been taken of these "*angels*," and the importance of the general subject makes it proper first to present at length the grounds of the view just stated.

I. Meaning of these Star-Angels.

That a spiritual authority in each church is designated by these words, nearly all seem to be agreed. But a great deal of unnecessary controversy has arisen as to what particular kind of officers are here intended by the term "angel." Such a controversy is necessarily interminable, because of the plain fact that

§ 1. Angel not a designation of any specific office.

([1]) Compare Num. xxiv: 17. Matt. ii: 2. Rev. ii: 28; xxii: 16. Job xxxviii: 7. Is. xiii: 10. Ez. xxxii: 7, 8. Joel iii: 15. Amos v: 26. Dan. viii: 10. Ps. cxxxvi: 9.

neither the word itself nor anything else in the context designates any particular office. It is a general term designating the ruling function of the church in whomsoever deposited, just as the candlestick denotes the church in its light-bearing function. The supposed obscurity of the language has arisen from the attempt to make that specific which Christ here designedly made general, and which general sense is essential to the force and fulness of the meaning. The silence of Scripture is just as expressive as its revelations. If it uses language of wide and general signification instead of specific terms, if it is silent in regard to any specific limitation of their meaning, it is because no such specific ideas were intended.

Now the word *angel* is not and never was the title of any particular officer in the church. It was used indeed, we are told by later Jewish writers, as the title of the reader of prayers in the Jewish synagogues, the leader of their worship. But in the whole Bible there is no trace of even this application of the word, nor of any such officer, as this is represented to have been. At the same time there are other terms constantly used in the New Testament to express every kind of officer appointed by Christ in His church. These terms were perfectly familiar. Their meaning was definite. If now it was the design of our Lord here to express a particular officer, it is incredible that He would have refused to use the proper term which He Himself had taught His inspired apostles to use, and have used instead a term which had no such official application, was not a name of office at all, but which was in familiar use as a functional designation perfectly equivalent to our word *messenger*, and just so used frequently in the New Testament, as its equivalent was in the Old.[2] The use of such a word to designate the meaning of an important symbol, is proof positive that

[2] Mark i: 2. Luke vii: 24. ix: 52. 2 Cor. xii: 7. Jas. ii: 25. Mal. iii: 1.

we have no right to substitute for it any such specific terms; and that to do so, is to narrow down, if not completely to lose the great and broad idea here taught.

What is that idea? What does the word angel here mean, and why is it used? It must mean either messenger in this broad general sense, or *angel* as used in English. It has no other meaning. In the last sense it is clearly inadmissable here. The epistles which follow, intended for the instruction, warning and encouragement of each of the seven churches, and addressed to the angel of each, were most certainly not addressed to unseen spiritual beings.

2. Designates the nature of all church authority.

We are therefore necessarily thrown back upon the generic sense of messenger. As used in the addresses of these epistles, it must represent some relation held, or some function exercised by men, by which they were constituted a proper medium of communication to those churches from their divine Lord and His apostle. What else can this be but that spiritual authority which He has committed to His church, and lodged in officers of His own appointment, and by which He rules in and over her? The true nature of this authority is precisely and clearly designated by this word "messenger," by which all mere human authority is at once excluded, and all authority in His church declared to be dependent on a divine commission from her King, and to consist in nothing else than the execution of a divine message. The specific use of the term to express heavenly beings as messengers of God, would suggest and render specially appropriate this word to denote messengers acting by *divine* authority. The symbolic use of it in this book— denoting invariably a spiritual influence or power, or an assemblage of such powers, would render this term, used in its generic sense, suggestive of the same kind of messenger. The whole range of language, therefore, could not apparently have furnished a word so fully expressive of the positive character of all official authority in the visible church, and at the same time so exclusive of all human assumptions of power by which the exercise of this authority has been so sadly marred, as this simple word, '*messenger*,' used in explanation of the symbol of the stars in Christ's right hand, and therefore meaning a messenger from Him. It expresses, in one word, the great truth that there is no rightful authority in Christ's visible kingdom except what He has commissioned and sent; and that every one vested with that authority is bound to keep, both in word and in action, within the precise limits of His commission.

This explanation of the word "angel" preserves the true force and significance of the symbol which it expounds. A star is something very different from a candlestick or the light which it sustains. Though both give light, they do it very differently; the candlestick is a mere light-bearer, and the light it bears must be kindled and sustained by a power without itself; a star is a heavenly body whose very nature is light, and represents therefore a heavenly source of light and power, and not a mere light-bearer. The thing indicated by it differs from what these candlesticks and their lights indicate just as a star differs from a candlestick, otherwise there is no definite meaning whatever in symbols. The candlesticks and their lights represent the church as holding forth by her organization, ordinances and holy example, the word of life in a dark world. The stars, on the other hand, represent, not the light the church gives or the influence she exerts, but that which her Lord gives to her; that authority which He has vested in messengers raised up and sustained by His right hand, as walking in her midst He cherishes and brightens the flame of her holy example and teaching.

3. This shown by the stars, their nature and position.

The position of these stars, in the right hand of the Redeemer, is just as important a part of the symbol as the stars themselves. The meaning of it is evident. The right hand is the seat and the symbol of power. These stars being in His right hand as He walks among His churches, represent them not merely as upheld by that power, but as the instruments by which He exerts it. They appear, not as rising from or supported by the candlesticks, not as originating from or dependent on the churches, and so varying with all its changes of declension and revival, but as deriving all their light and influence from Christ alone,—as immediate and permanent emanations of His power. They must then represent His own divine authority as exercised in and for His church by instruments of His own appointment. His authority in and over His people never varies with the changes in His churches: whether the light of each burns brilliantly and purely like that of Smyrna and of Philadelphia, or is almost extinct like that of Sardis and Laodicea, its star in His right hand changes not, His authority is the same, unchanging as Himself.

It is indeed very true that those in whom this authority is vested may and do change, and often cease entirely to be faithful to their high trust; but then, too, they are no longer messengers of Christ, and have no longer any share in what these stars represent. So far only as they preserve the character of messengers, and truly represent the authority of Christ, are they stars, and their light certain and unchanging. The authority of Christ cannot be wrenched from His right hand by the unfaithfulness of those through whom it is exercised. Such only wrench themselves from the protection and care secured by being His messengers. This they cease to be whenever they do not truly represent His authority. It thus still more clearly appears how fully this word "angel" or *messenger* in its widest sense, interprets this symbol of the star. It is only as the various offices in the church of Christ are exercised by men who act purely as His ambassadors, not in their own, but in His name, not from expediency or mere human reasonings, but as executors of His laws, as only the bearers of His message, that they fulfil their true function. Then the authority thus exercised is not theirs, but His; the light is not that of human wisdom, but of express divine authority; the requirements and laws enforced and the decisions pronounced are the fixed unchanging light of a divine and unchangeable power:— it is a star, and not a lamp, a star in Christ's right hand.

It should not pass unobserved that this symbol of the stars is in the vision itself, presented not immediately after the mention, in verse 12, of the seven golden candlesticks, the first great object that caught the eye of the seer,—but not until verse 16, at the close of a full description of the person of the glorified Redeemer as He walked in their midst, and as the first of the three closing characteristics which marked the display of all His power and grace toward them. In other words, *these stars are a part of the description of Christ Himself as He dwells in the midst of His churches.* "And He had in His right hand seven stars: and out of His mouth went a sharp two-edged sword: and His countenance was as the sun shineth in his strength." The very fact that these stars are thus presented, not as a part of the church, though, by the explanation, belonging to it, but as a part of the manifestations of Christ Himself, is decisive evidence of their design, as symbols not of persons, or particular offices, but of His delegated authority wherever deposited. In this grouping of these symbols, there is great beauty and force. The two-edged sword of His all-penetrating word, and the sunlight of His countenance, representing His life-giving approval, are thus presented immediately after, and in immediate connection with

marginal note: 4. The relation of these stars to the other symbols in the vision.

these seven stars in His right hand: so that in immediate connection with His appointed authority in each church we have the all-piercing truth, and the grace that enforces it. His laws and claims as King are enforced by the word of His threatenings, slaying the wicked, and the light of His countenance, irradiating the souls of His people and the mansions of glory.

"The seven stars are the messengers of the seven churches." Every church has its own messenger from its Lord: one church is not over another, but Christ's authority directly in each. From this language some have inferred that these were messengers of these churches, in the sense of being sent by them to John while an exile in Patmos, to express their affection and to receive his directions. This would be very plausible if this word were used independently, instead of being the exposition of the stars in Christ's right hand. Such messengers, representing no power of Christ, no permanent function or blessing granted to His churches, but a mere temporary expedient to meet a special emergency, cannot possibly satisfy the meaning of this striking symbol, which, as we have just seen, is one of the chief manifestations of the Redeemer's glory as He appears in the midst of His churches, along with the two-edged sword of His mouth, and the sun-light of His countenance. The same fatal objections lie against the view that these *messengers* are so called, as indicating their office of leading in the worship and conveying to God the desires of the people. But in the sense we have seen to be alone consistent with the symbol, that of messengers of Christ clothed with His authority, they are also messengers of the churches; just as Paul is "the apostle," i. e. the *messenger* "of the Gentiles," as well as of Jesus Christ;—while he is *from* Christ, he is *to* them, so that they had a special property in him. So to each church the Lord

5. To each church its own star and messenger.

has given a representative of His own authority. To no one has He given authority over others, much less over all. There are as many of these messengers as there are churches. Each receives directly from Christ spiritual authority to administer the affairs of His kingdom within its own limits. This is not inconsistent with a joint authority arising from the union and agreement of those to whom, in the different churches, it has been entrusted.

Each church too has but *one* angel or messenger. Yet we read in Acts xiv: 23, that a plurality of rulers were ordained in every church; "*when they had ordained them elders in every church*," where the churches must have been only single congregations. Some of these seven churches of Asia, certainly at least Ephesus, must have embraced many congregations; and it is certain that it had many elders or bishops whom Paul summoned to meet him, on all of whom the whole care of the church was to devolve after Paul's departure, and to all of whom he expressly commits it.[3] Still even in these, this spiritual authority is represented as a unit, implying that a number of individual congregations were united in one body under one government; that though the rulers might be many, the authority must be one, and would be, if really Christ's. The union and agreement of these rulers in different congregations, in teaching and enforcing the same truths and duties, on the sole authority of Christ as the only lawgiver, becomes the strongest possible evidence, that the authority by which they act is one, and is Christ's, and gives to their decisions the highest possible force. The assembly of the apostles and elders at Jerusalem to decide a question referred to them by the church of Antioch is the divinely provided example of this.

This oneness, therefore, of the symbol of Christ's au-

[3] Acts xx: 28-31.

thority, and of the term used to explain it, can decide nothing as to whether this authority is vested in one person or in many: in either case it must be a unit in order truly to represent the authority of Christ. This could be properly set forth only by a single star and messenger. Indeed the divine, '*messenger*' character of this function appears the more manifest, and the evidence of it is clearer, where there is a plurality of persons entrusted with it, than when vested in an individual. Even if any one thinks on other grounds that each of these churches were subject to a prelatical bishop, yet the relations, duty and privileges implied in these stars and messengers, cannot be restricted to him, unless he be the sole repository of authority, and all subordinate authorities be excluded from any share in the privileges, responsibilities and encouragements which these symbols express. But this is contradicted by the whole tenor of these epistles, which are evidently designed for the whole of each church, and addressed to its spiritual authority as representing it, including all those whose agency was the proper and necessary means by which these messages of the King were to be conveyed to the people, and obedience to His charges secured and enforced.

Such appears to be the meaning and design of this beautiful symbol. How important and decisive a mark of a true church it is, and must ever be, is evident. Surely that society can have no claim to be a part of the visible kingdom of Christ, which does not acknowledge Him as its Head, by submission to His sole authority. And it can neither have nor give any evidence of participation in His kingdom, of its being a true church, except as its constituted authorities speak and act as deputies of the King, teaching and enforcing nothing but what He commands, and all that He commands.

§. A decisive test of a true church.

Taken in connection with the symbol of the golden

candlesticks, the two together make up a complete and decisive test of a true church furnished by the Head of the church Himself. The one marks it completely in its relation to the world; the other marks it as completely in its relation to its divine Head. These two, though inseparable, are perfectly distinct. They are as distinct as her work, and the authority by which she works. And just as inseparable. Her light-bearing mission to the world can never be fulfilled, except as she is governed by the sole authority of her King. That mission is discharged, as we have seen, by her witness-bearing. But this is worthless except as she speaks and acts by Christ's authority. This is just her giving to the world what she has received from her Lord without adulteration. Hence in speaking of this in the previous lecture, some things were necessarily said implying this authority. Yet the two things are just as distinct as these two symbols,—as her work and her commission.

If, therefore, a church fulfills this mission, no matter what subordinate measures or instrumentalities it may employ in diffusing the light of truth and holiness, no matter how it may conduct its missionary operations, or administer its sacraments, or arrange its acts of formal worship; provided, secondly, that it always bows to the King's authority, and its rulers and teachers act and speak only as He directs, constantly regarding themselves as His messengers, and without any right to teach or enforce anything He does not teach, no matter whether that authority is exercised by a pastor alone, or a church session, a prelate or a presbytery, or in any other possible way,—it is a true church of Christ: it has the candlestick and the star in Christ's right hand, and it stands equally with these seven churches of Asia as a part of His visible kingdom. We do not mean to say that these are matters of no, or even of little, importance. On the other hand, the efficiency of a church in fulfilling her great mission will depend very greatly on her conformity in all particulars to the principles and pattern in the word. But mistakes and imperfections here cannot vitiate a church's claim to be a true church of Christ.

Let us now more fully unfold and more definitely apply some of the chief points of instruction and encouragement involved, comparing them with other teachings of Scripture.

II. APPLICATION OF THESE PRINCIPLES.

All authority in the visible church emanates from Christ only. He is King. The church is His kingdom. The *visible* church is a kingdom established by Him to represent His invisible or real church, His true spiritual kingdom. It is, in its true nature, neither an aristocracy, a democracy, nor a republic. It is just what it always was, a theocracy, not indeed in the form in which Israel of old was—a civil government with a Divine Head; but a government still directly dependent upon and administered by a Divine Head. The attempts that have been made to run a parallel between the government of the church and republican civil government are calculated to mislead; just as also the attempt to compare it with an earthly monarchy. In the manner of the selection and appointment of officers in His church, much may be suggested doubtless that may guide in the arrangements of human governments, and especially in guarding against the abuse of power. But in all such parallels, there is great danger of having the true nature, source, and limitations of church-power obscured, and the obligations to obedience sadly lowered, or placed on erroneous grounds. In the church all power is from above, and not from the people; all they have to do is carefully to seek out and designate those whom the King has commissioned by His gifts and the internal call of His Spirit. He makes the

1. All authority in the church from Christ

laws; He appoints the offices; He calls the officers; He prescribes their qualifications; He furnishes the qualifications; and the spiritual perception necessary to enable the church to recognize these qualifications, is also His gift. All things here are from Him, and from Him not as the God of Providence merely, but as the church's redeeming God, dwelling in all His redeemed people, for whose sake He has constituted this visible kingdom, and whose influence and character must be predominant in it, if it be any true representation of His real spiritual kingdom. It is just in proportion as the church fully recognizes and feels His *real, personal,* though invisible presence in her midst, and this entire dependence on Him as her living Head, imparting His Spirit to her true members, that the affairs of her government can be rightly administered, and its high and holy ends attained.

All this seems to be implied in this symbolic view of Christ's authority in His church. Compare with it the language of Paul in Eph. iv: 8–12. Having in the previous verses enjoined them to keep the unity of the Spirit in the bonds of peace, and then defined that unity in the words, "There is one body and one Spirit, even as ye are called in one hope of your calling; one Lord, one faith, one baptism," he shows how it is preserved and perfected by that spiritual authority, the origin and various forms of which he declares to be from Christ, as His ascension gifts. "When He ascended up on high, He led captivity captive, and gave gifts unto men. ...... And He gave some, apostles; and some, prophets; and some, evangelists; and some, pastors and teachers; for the perfecting of the saints, for the work of the ministry, for the edifying of the body of Christ, till we all come in the unity of the faith and of the knowledge of the Son of God, unto a perfect man, unto the measure of the stature of the fulness of Christ." It is this gift of authoritative teaching and ruling, sent down from His throne to each of His churches, and conferred on men called and qualified by Himself, which constitutes the grand instrumentality by which He trains and perfects them. Thus He puts forth the right hand of His power, and secures full effect to His word and Spirit in building up His true spiritual kingdom. In each church this spiritual authority of the King is the sole star of its hope and guidance and security; and, as exercised by living messengers of His own providing and sending, the great agency by which He is gathering and training His church, until it be complete, and grace be perfected in glory, and the visible and real spiritual kingdom become identical.

Since Christ bestows such gifts, since He sends His messengers to every church, a weighty responsibility rests upon it in regard to their reception. This is the aspect in which her election and ordination of men to office is here presented. It is her reception, her acknowledgment of her Lord's commissioned messengers. When by His Providence and Spirit the gifts and graces are bestowed necessary to make up the qualifications which His word requires, these are the credentials of His own call and commission. To ascertain the possession of these in each particular case is one of the church's most responsible duties. Serious mistakes here must be fatal to her purity and prosperity. But when, as seems to have been the case in some instances at least, in apostolic times, ([4]) the call of the people unites with the decision of those already in authority, and when by both this voice is uttered as the result of a faithful and prayerful application of the tests of Christ's appointment, it is truly the voice of the Spirit speaking in His people, and gives the strongest security against error. But if this last be wanting, if the selection and ordination of men to official

2. The responsibility of the church in receiving these messengers.

([4]) See Acts vi: 2 6. xiv: 23. 1 Tim iv: 14. v: 22.

station in the church be without this earnest seeking for and reliance on the guidance of the Spirit, and faithful application of scriptural tests, and a sense of the great responsibility incurred, and if mere human wisdom and earthly motives control her action, the result cannot but be disastrous. Here is the great entrance of all apostacies and defections. Those are received as His messengers whom He never sent, and those rejected whom He has sent, and so His authority is set aside, the channels of His gifts and graces obstructed, and communication with Him being cut off, disease and spiritual death is the result. If the divine guidance furnished by His word and Spirit be neglected in this matter, nothing can preserve the church from despising the spiritual gifts of her Lord, and from the influence of pretenders and false teachers, and a desolating spiritual despotism. The whole history of the church is full of the proof of this. Her whole track through ages past is blackened with the fearful ruins thus produced. Again and again has the symbol been verified,—the falling star becoming wormwood and poisoning all the fountains of life.

To the credentials of the apostles and other inspired men Christ set His own immediate seal by the miraculous gifts conferred upon them. Having thus given a fully attested and sufficient record of doctrine and precept and promise and warning, to guide His church till He come again, and having also pledged to her prayers His indwelling Spirit, He has left resting upon her the whole responsibility of applying this revealed word to ascertain and authenticate those who are His commissioned messengers. Hence in the first of these epistles which follow —that to Ephesus—a high commendation is bestowed on that church by her Lord, "because," says He, "thou hast tried them which say they are apostles, (i. e. sent) and are not, and hast found them liars." And a severe censure is pronounced, and heavy judgments threatened upon the church of Thyatira, because she by her authorities had suffered that woman Jezebel, calling herself a prophetess, to teach and to seduce the people. Hence too such injunctions as these. "Lay hands suddenly on no man." "The things that thou hast heard of me among many witnesses, the same commit thou to faithful men, who shall be able to teach others also." "Beloved, believe not every spirit, but try the spirits whether they are of God."

The churches of Christ cannot be too constantly and earnestly reminded that no more important and responsible duty ever devolves upon them, than the selection and setting apart of those who are to teach and administer the affairs of His house. It touches the very centre of the church's life and purity and power. To put her seal on those whom God has not sent, or refuse it to those whom He has sent, are both alike fatal to her spiritual interests, and highly insulting to her Lord. It becomes church members and officers and judicatories therefore, whenever called upon to choose or set apart men to office, to bear in mind the solemn nature of the act, and its far-reaching consequences, affecting the very fountains of life and salvation to a perishing world. Let them remember how very nearly it touches the honour of the King, and how deeply it affects the prosperity of His kingdom. In authenticating as the King's messenger—as either a teacher or mere ruler in the church, one whom God has not sent, a wound is inflicted on the body, deep and injurious in proportion to the abilities and attainments of the individual. Let no brilliancy of talent or extent of acquirement, no worldly power and wealth, have any influence here, except as they are under the control of strong gracious principles, especially of deep humility, and a complete submission of intellect and heart to the simple word of Christ. We repeat it, that the sad divisions that have marred the peace of the church, as also all her apostacies, and the feebleness of her testimony, are traceable to this as the first overt step.

The leaders of the host have been unfaithful, in a greater or less degree, to their high trust, and so error in doctrine and laxity in discipline have snapped the bonds of union, and broken her marshalled ranks, and rendered her, instead of that conquering army who follow the Lamb, described as the "called and chosen and faithful," an easy prey to an ever watchful and hostile world. If the church is to dispel the darkness of the world, if she is to be acknowledged as a true representative of the visible kingdom, she must recognize and follow as her leaders only the stars in Christ's right hand,—only those who shine with a heavenly light, and manifest in themselves the power of His right hand,—only those who as *teachers* come not with excellency of speech or of wisdom, but in demonstration of the Spirit and of power, and who as *rulers* exercise the meekness of heavenly wisdom, and cheerfully bow their own necks to the yoke of Christ.

All authority committed to the visible church is entirely spiritual, and for edification, not destruction. It is a kingdom of truth. Jesus Himself distinctly renounced the aid of civil power and force in stating to Pilate His high claims to be a king, "My kingdom is not of this world: if My kingdom were of this world, then would My servants fight, that I should not be delivered to the Jews: but now is My kingdom not from hence. Pilate therefore said unto Him, Art thou a king then? Jesus answered, Thou sayest that I am a king. To this end was I born, and for this cause came I into the world, that I should bear witness unto the truth. Every one that is of the truth heareth My voice." Force or political power, then, either in the propagation or defence of this kingdom, is utterly inadmissible. No civil pains or penalties, honours or dishonours, can convince of truth

<small>3. Church authority purely spiritual, and for edification.</small>

or convict of error. This church authority or power is the heavenly, spiritual influence of these stars. It is not a sword to punish, or a rod to chastise, or a voice of terror to alarm, except by spiritual warnings addressed to the understanding; but a star to enlighten and attract. It is vested in a messenger armed only with the word,— the word of instruction, of warning, of comfort, and of spiritual power to admit or exclude from the privileges of this kingdom. All the censures inflicted even to the extreme of excommunication are not properly punitive, but disciplinary, adapted and designed, so far as the offender is concerned, to bring him to repentance. Even the deliverance of the incestuous person at Corinth unto Satan, was "that the spirit might be saved in the day of the Lord Jesus."[5] And no greater outrage has ever been committed by man on the rights of God, and no more flagrant abuse of power, or more horrid conversion of light and mercy into darkness and hellish hate and cruelty, than the infliction, by church authority, of temporal pains and penalties, the assumption by frail mortals of the right to take vengeance in the name of God. "Vengeance is mine, I will recompense, saith the Lord." It finds its true representation in this book, in the star fallen from heaven, and receiving the keys of the bottomless pit, and letting forth the darkening smoke and locusts of hell upon a suffering and wasted church: or as fully developed, in the whore riding the scarlet coloured beast, and drunk with the blood of the saints.

These stars in Christ's right hand, while they shine in the lustre of heavenly love, proclaim indeed an almighty power to punish, if that love be slighted. These messengers, even when announcing the terrors of the Lord, and excluding from the privileges of His kingdom, are however always to speak with tears and tones like His who

[5] 1 Cor. v: 5.

wept over guilty and doomed Jerusalem. How terrible, then, this perversion of power! The time has not yet come when the danger of this perversion, horrible as it is, of this holiest trust, has ceased. Nor will this danger completely pass away while this sacred trust is committed to imperfectly sanctified men, and while tares are mingled with the wheat. A misguided and fanatic zeal is still ready to hurl its thunderbolts of vengeance, or to invoke the aid of the secular power, in the very name of love and mercy. The language of Paul, with all his inspiration and miracles, still needs to be inscribed on the commission of every church officer and judicatory,—"Our authority which the Lord hath given us for edification, and not for destruction." (6) Even when intimating the sternest exercise of this authority, he says again,—"Not for that we have dominion over your faith, but are helpers of your joy." (7)

To all who are vested with any authority in the kingdom of Christ, this representation of their functions as that of stars and messengers of Christ, suggests most solemn admonition and precious encouragement.

4. Admonition and encouragement to church rulers.

Both the symbol and its explanation—messenger—fixes attention on the *function*—the official duty rather than the *person*, so that no person, however high his official position, is either a star or angel, except as he identifies himself with the high and holy duties these imply. It is not the personal influence or gifts of any one that gives him any share in the honour or the privileges of one of these messengers, or makes him a channel of Christ's light and power for the edification of the church: it is simply the faithful exercise of that spiritual authority entrusted to him, and which he can be enabled to do by divine grace alone. In such official position, therefore, there is no ground for pride or boasting.

(6) 2 Cor. x: 8.   (7) 2 Cor. i: 24.

At the same time, such are reminded very impressively of the solemn responsibility resting upon them as messengers of the King of Zion, representatives of His kingly office before the church and the world; that they are entrusted with a work in which His highest honour, and the most precious interests of His blood-bought church and a perishing world are all deeply involved. How weighty such a trust! How fearful such responsibility! It made an apostle tremble; its weight would crush the mightiest angel unsupported. It will fill the heart of every one who rightly regards it with holy and trembling solicitude, and cause him to look up and cling to that glorious right hand as his only support, and to walk softly and circumspectly, giving anxious heed to all his steps and words. He will shrink with dread from uttering, in the name of the Lord, one syllable more or less than he has been taught. As a ruler, he will equally refrain from making the slightest change in the law of Christ's house—from adding to or taking away anything in the terms entitling to its privileges. As he dreads the withering rebuke of his Lord, as he values the approval of that countenance that shineth as the sun, and the sweet and powerful upholding of that mighty arm, will he implicitly follow the very letter of his instructions.

In doing this, and generally just in proportion as he does this, will he meet with opposition and have to endure suffering. The servant is not above his Lord. The messenger can expect nothing better from a wicked world than the King Himself, whose message he bears, received, if he speaks all the truth and faithfully applies all the discipline which Christ has commanded. For one of these, in the fulfilment of his embassy to a world in rebellion, to be expecting a life of worldly ease and comfort, a snug settlement where, cheered with merited honours and congenial gratifications of taste and intellect, and freed from anxious cares, he can quietly and successfully fulfil his high trust,—is one of the wildest dreams that ever entered a Christian's brain. With such an experience, he would no longer be in the footsteps of Jesus or of Paul, or of any other of the host of worthies who have carried the standard of the King. Such earthly good, such exemption from suffering in his relation to an ungodly world, need be *expected* only at the expense of recreancy to his trust and treason to his King. But if in some exceptional cases where the messenger is surrounded by the children of the kingdom, there should be comparative freedom from persecution and want, it is certain that the great enemy who assaulted Christ Himself with his fierce temptations will sorely perplex and harass and torment these, His feeble messengers. They are the especial objects of Satan's hate. How unspeakably precious the comfort, therefore, and how powerful the stimulus to faithfulness which this symbol affords! In speaking and enforcing Christ's truth and laws, every teacher and ruler is in Christ's right hand, sustained and protected by His Almighty power. The very condition of their holding this high and secure position is that they act as His faithful messengers. Whenever they assume to speak in their own name, or to seek their own honour or ease, they in just that degree cease to fulfil their star-like function, and forfeit His protection. But, on the other hand, just so far as they are stars, shining with the pure light of truth and holiness, and as messengers doing what He bids them, just so far they feel the grasp of His hand of love and might, and just so far, even in their greatest feebleness, can they defy the powers of earth and hell. The conscious feeling of identification with Christ in administering the government of this immoveable kingdom—a feeling possible only in the degree that all selfishness and ambition is swallowed up in a regard to His glory,—will make them, like Paul and Silas, fill the midnight dungeon with the songs of praise. They can say with Paul, "Most gladly therefore will I glory in infirmities, that the power of Christ may rest upon me. Therefore I take pleasure in infirmities, in reproaches, in necessities, in persecutions for Christ's sake; for when I am weak then am I strong." ([8])

Being thus held up in Christ's right hand did not keep the angel and the church of Smyrna from being cast into prison and the prospect of a violent death; nor Antipas in Pergamos from a martyr's cruel fate; but it was still more strikingly shown in holding them up in these persecutions, and enabling them to brave and triumph over death itself.

Christ's own mission from the Father as the angel of the covenant is the pattern in its execution of theirs from Him. "As thou hast sent me into the world, even so have I also sent them into the world." Hence He says, "If the world hate you, ye know that it hated Me before it hated you. If ye were of the world, the world would love his own; but because ye are not of the world, but I have chosen you out of the world, therefore the world hateth you. Remember the word that I said unto you, The servant is not greater than his Lord. If they have persecuted Me, they will also persecute you; if they have kept My saying, they will keep yours also. .... These things have I spoken unto you, that IN ME ye might have *peace*. IN THE WORLD ye shall have *tribulation:* but be of good cheer; I have overcome the world." ([9]) Addressed as these words were originally to the apostles, they have a special force in regard to rulers and teachers of the church in every age.

5. *The esteem and obedience due them.*
The esteem and obedience due to the authority of the visible church is here taught. Regarded as stars in His right hand, and messengers from His throne, each word and act

([8]) 2 Cor. xii: 9, 10. ([9]) John xvii: 18. xv: 18–20. xvi: 33.

in His name and according to His word is as if He Himself did it. When the plain and rough-clad ambassador of Rome uttered, in the name of the senate and Roman people, their stern demands to the proud and hesitating *Egyptian King*, and drew in the sand with his staff that scarce visible circle requiring instant compliance, the haughty monarch heard in those few words, and saw in that sandy circle, all the resistless power of the mistress of the world. "He," says Christ, "that heareth you heareth Me, and he that despiseth you despiseth Me; and he that despiseth Me despiseth Him that sent Me." "He that receiveth whomsoever I send, receiveth Me, and he that receiveth Me receiveth Him that sent Me." "He, therefore," says Paul, "that despiseth, despiseth not man, but God." [10] No higher insult can be offered to a king than to treat with contempt his authorized representative; no juster and surer cause of vengeance, according to his power. He may as well abdicate his throne at once, as suffer his authority to be thus trampled on, by not avenging those whom he has, even in the slightest degree, clothed with it.

Let the church, then, ever regard her rulers as the stars in Christ's right hand. But then let her so regard them only so far as they appear in His hand and act by His authority. In themselves they are the same helpless and ignorant sinners that others are, and all their opinions and acts outside of the testimony and laws of Christ's house, are of no more account or force than those of other men. But within that sphere every member of the church is bound to regard them as the representatives of Christ's power for his own edification and salvation. But whenever they presume to carry the influence which this gives them into outside spheres, and to confirm or advance opinions on other subjects, it is a gross and wicked perversion.

[10] Luke x: 16. John xiii: 20. 1 Thess. iv: 8.

The terrible abuse of church power in past ages, and still in corrupt churches, "lording it over God's heritage," has become one of the most desolating curses upon the nations; and the infidel scoffer loves to point to priestly ambition and tyranny, and to "the arrogance of the clergy," as if to fix the origin of this worst form of human oppression on the church, instead of on the world as it has entered into and corrupted the true church. This has led to a directly contrary extreme—the almost entire prostration of real spiritual authority in the church. It would be well for all to ponder well the deep import and practical bearing of such passages as these, addressed both to rulers and ruled. "Them that sin rebuke before all, that others also may fear." "Reprove, rebuke, exhort with all longsuffering and doctrine." "These things speak, and exhort, and rebuke with all authority. Let no man despise thee." "Let the elders that rule well be counted worthy of double honour, especially they who labour in the word and doctrine." "And we beseech you, brethren, to know them that labour among you, and are over you in the Lord, and admonish you; and to esteem them very highly in love for their work's sake." "Remember them that have the rule over you, who have spoken unto you the word of God; whose faith follow, considering the end of their conversation." "Obey them that have the rule over you, and submit yourselves: for they watch for your souls as they that must give account." ([11])

The admonitions, warnings, and censures of the church then, as uttered by its authorities in truth and love, are no mere idle words. Let every wanderer from the fold, every backslider in heart, remember that they come with all the authority and love of the King Himself. Let the baptized youth of the church remember that that autho-

([11]) 1 Tim. v: 20. 2 Tim. iv: 2. Titus ii: 15. 1 Tim. v: 17. 1 Thess. v: 12. Heb. xiii: 7, 17.

rity of the kingdom over them arising from their birth of Christian parents, is no mere nominal thing. It may inflict no sensible pains, it may deprive of no valued enjoyments by its penalties; and its precious privileges and powerful protection may be unseen and unfelt; it may seem to be as powerless, and as little to be heeded as the blessing or the curse of some wandering soothsayer, but it is fraught with results of infinite magnitude. It is the expression of the righteous and merciful claims of your redeeming God. It is the word of the Lord which endureth forever. To slight, despise, or rebel against it, is to inflict upon the soul a deep and painful wound which only that rejected mercy can heal, and which, even if healed, will bring bitter tears and heart-agonies. "He that despiseth, despiseth not man, but God."

LECTURE VI.

VARIETIES AND IMPERFECTIONS OF THE VISIBLE KINGDOM. THE SEVEN CHURCHES. EPHESUS AND SMYRNA.

CHAPS. II. AND III.

I. GENERAL CHARACTER OF ALL THESE EPISTLES.

"HE that hath an ear let him hear what the Spirit saith unto the churches." This claim on universal attention is annexed to each of the epistles to the seven churches. It is a declaration by our Lord Himself, that these messages of His, though addressed each to a particular church, were intended for all; and that every individual who hears them has a deep personal concern in them. Let us take heed to the divine injunction, and devoutly attend to what the Spirit saith.

The body of each of these epistles is filled with details relating to the actual and peculiar condition and character of the church addressed. That which gives to them their peculiarly universal application is the fact that they present an epitome of all the phases of the visible church in her militant and suffering estate. Hence the very number of the churches addressed is the established symbol of completeness in things pertaining to the covenanted kingdom, and not a mere accidental or arbitrary thing. It is almost certain that these were not all

§. A seven-fold picture of the church as it is.

the churches, as they certainly were not all the cities of even that province. These seven appear to have been chosen from the rest, and all the developments of grace and of error in them to have been so ordered, that they might present in this seven-fold form such a complete view of the varieties and imperfections of the visible church, that every true church in all ages and nations, recognizing its own likeness, might feel itself addressed through them; so too that every church which had no claim whatever to be a true representative of the spiritual kingdom, might be clearly distinguished from the true even in its greatest imperfection.

These epistles, therefore, by giving us a complete set of examples of the true church with its actual imperfections, furnish us with a practical definition of it of universal and easy application. The candlesticks and the stars set forth the heavenly mission and spiritual authority of the church; these epistles set forth the actual imperfections in the execution of her mission and the exercise of her authority as these were committed to imperfect men. At the same time, the danger of regarding any of these imperfections and corruptions as a part of her true character, or as necessary to her development, is effectually prevented by the perfectly clear discrimination of these in the commendations and censures of our Lord. The severity with which he rebukes these evils, furnishes also the most effectual warning possible against them.

§. A definition of the church, by examples.

Regarding these two chapters as presenting a complete picture of the visible church as she then was, we cannot fail to perceive their intimate and essential connection with the rest of the book. They set clearly before us, what it is very important should be borne in mind, in order rightly to estimate the progress of the church, and to account

§. Relation to the rest of the book.

for her defections and reverses. They present her as she actually was at the close of the apostolic period, when fully furnished for her mighty work and started on her long career of conflict. They show her precise condition when the apostolic gifts and miraculous powers which had furnished and authenticated her testimony were withdrawn, and with the naked word of that testimony, and the sole guidance of the Holy Spirit, she entered on that course of trial and suffering so graphically and grandly described in its principles, progress and results, in this wonderful book. Here are the beginnings of all the evils that afterwards grew to such mighty proportions, and brought down such fearful judgments; and here too are all the simple agencies and forces that were to crown with eternal triumph this spiritual kingdom. So far, therefore, from these epistles being distinct from and nearly unconnected with the succeeding portions of this book, as they are too often treated, they form an integral part of it, and indispensable to a right understanding of its mysteries, and to the full spiritual comfort and guidance it was intended to convey.

The practical bearing of much in these epistles on the daily life of the believer is manifest, and is a frequent theme in the pulpit. To illustrate and apply them with this view would be entirely uncalled for, and is not our present design. We desire here to present these seven varieties of the church at the close of the apostolic age in one summary view, as representing the leading phases of the varied imperfect mixed condition of the visible church during its militant career, and embodying the final charges and promises of her King as adapted to these states. We shall thus obtain the clearest conception of the design and meaning of this interesting portion of Scripture, as a whole, and in doing this, most of its practical lessons will be necessarily suggested, and their force perhaps even more fully felt.

The merest glance at these epistles shows a great variety in the condition of these churches. Only two of them are without censure, Smyrna and Philadelphia; three receive both commendation and censure, Ephesus, Pergamos and Thyatira; the other two receive only the severest rebukes,—in one of them, Sardis, a few names being singled out for special praise,—the other, Laodicea, being without even such a remnant. Before considering the epistles to each of these separately, three things are to be observed in regard to all of them.

I. General Characteristics.

The style of these epistles, their forms of thought and expression, is very different from all the other writings of John, or those of any other apostle. They remind us strongly of the words and manner of our Lord when in the flesh, as these are reported by the four evangelists. They are His very words uttered by His own lips. In the apostolic epistles, we have the truth as moulded first into the form of a human conception or argument, and expressed in connection with the holy emotions it produces. In this form, and to show what shape the truth assumes, as it comes in contact with a human heart, it has a special adaptation to our wants. Nor is it at all inferior in its divine authority, since both the conception and expression are under the infallible guidance of the Spirit. "All Scripture is given by inspiration of God." But valuable as that form of His teaching is, it is not the form which in His wisdom He here adopts. He does not here employ John to speak for Him. These are not John's words. He is merely the amanuensis. They come directly from our glorified Lord. Though ascended up on high, He is still so really with His church that He can

1. Their style.

speak to it His own words. He is not absent, though invisible. These epistles make us sensible of His presence as otherwise we could not be. As we read and ponder their pregnant words and truths, we seem to feel a peculiar sense of awe, as listening to a voice directly from the throne,—from within the vail. We bless Him for the impressive view thus given of His constant care and speaking nearness,—in addressing us, even after He had ascended to the right hand of the Father, crowned with glory and honour, in like words and tones to those He used when in the flesh.

These last words of Jesus, these final messages of His love, we may well expect to be words of power, rich in instruction, warning and comfort, and we shall find them such. They are a constant repetition of the blessed assurance—"My presence shall go with you, and I will give you rest."

Each one of these epistles is introduced by our Lord's announcing Himself in a distinct character, and one specially adapted to the character and state of the church addressed.

2. Christ's titles.

These distinctive characteristics are nearly all drawn from the description of His personal glory as presented in the vision just before recorded, and from the midst of which he utters these several messages. From the abounding fulness of His glories, from the manifold aspects of His holiness, wisdom, power and love, He selects that one most suited to the need of each. We are thus reminded that there is no form which the ever-varying state of His churches here can assume, which will not find in the revelation which He has given of Himself some aspect of His divine fulness exactly fitted to it. Thus also are we taught that the safety and comfort of the church must depend upon her views of Christ. The earnest and continued contemplation of His glory and His grace is the only thing that can meet every emergency, and supply every want. Without this, all His messages will be only in word, not with power.

Each of these epistles is introduced by the words, "I know thy works." In every condition of the church and the believer, this is the first great fact to be impressed upon the heart, after the glory of Christ Himself. By the term "works" here, we must understand every manifestation of character. Their true nature depends upon the motive,—the secret principle of the soul which prompts them. But who can understand his own heart? Who can unravel the complicated net-work of feeling and emotion, of hopes and fears and desires and aims that enter into every action—how much or how little of self and the world may be mingling with love to Jesus and a regard for His glory? Who but He whose prerogative it is to search the heart? With infallible certainty His eyes of flame penetrate the secrets of the soul, and with infinite ease detect and separate the mingled forces of thought and feeling that control every action. We may be deceived, we are very likely to be; He cannot be. Other men may be deceived, or deceive us. The authorities of the church can never tell the heart; their judgment, therefore, can never decide our real relations to the kingdom of Christ. This is His own prerogative. Let none dare to invade it. "Who art thou that judgest another?" Without this omniscience, He could not be a perfect Saviour. By this He knows the extent of the horrid disease; and how far, if at all, the remedy is working; and these epistles teach us that He will, by His word and Spirit, unveil to His trusting people precisely what they need to know of themselves and their works.

3. Their common introduction.

But this is not all the force of these words. Who but He can estimate correctly the ever-varying forces of temptation with which His people have daily to contend, arising from secret causes, from peculiar temperaments and constitution, from disease, from earthly relations and pursuits, and from the cunning wiles and fiery darts of Satan, so as to weigh aright the works and struggles of His people? The child of God is often sadly and cruelly misjudged on this account by his dearest friends. These friends, we say not enemies, too often assume to judge of what it is utterly impossible for them to know, unless they could perfectly perceive the whole of these circumstances. Who, too, but He can enter that other dark chamber of the heart, where are treasured up all its sorrows, and whence many of them never once emerge to any fellow-creature's ear—secret woes that no words may utter, and no ear may hear, and which not even the nearest friend ever dreams of? Yet how greatly these control and modify all our works, every one knows. All these, in their minutest shades and deepest depths, Jesus takes into compassionate consideration when He says, "I know thy works."

Precious words! with which thus to introduce every message, whether of warning, of comfort or of approval. Let the church have them ever ringing in her ears. Let her disregard the opinions of man, his praises or his censures, his threats or his promises they are utterly worthless as guides in duty, or sources of comfort. But let her never forget that there is one all-searching eye upon her always, in all her backslidings, and sorrows, and conflicts, and fears, and labours,—in her feeblest efforts to promote His glory, and in the darkest days of Satan's power; the eye of one whose approval can turn sorrow into joy, toil into pleasure, and suffering into triumph. "I, even I, am He that comforteth you: who art thou, that thou shouldest be afraid of a man that shall die, or of the son of man, which shall be made as grass; and forgettest the Lord thy Maker?"

II. THE SEVENFOLD VARIETY.

1. EPHESUS. DECLINING LOVE.

A Church Strong, Orthodox in Doctrine, Order and Morals, but having left its first love.

Chap. ii: 1–6.

In external things this was the most favoured of the seven. Ephesus was the chief city of the province, its great seaport, and the natural outlet of all these other cities to the sea. It was indeed at that time the most important city of Asia Minor, and is said to have had a population of not less than six hundred thousand. A temple of "the great goddess Diana," regarded, on account of its size and magnificence, as one of the seven wonders of the world, gave to it a peculiar celebrity; and in reference to this, the strange designation, "Temple Sweeper," was regarded by the city as its most distinctive and honourable title. It was the chief seat and fountain of magic arts, so that the very name of these in ancient writers was "*Ephesian letters.*" It thus had become a place of resort for all nations. Its wealth and influence, therefore, were very great.

Its church had been founded by the apostle Paul, and had enjoyed his personal labours for three whole years. In it Timothy also had laboured under his direction. To its assembled elders, whom he had summoned to meet him at Miletus, he had given that final solemn charge, recorded in the twentieth chapter of Acts,—a charge which still stirs to its depths the heart of God's ministering servants. In its formation, early training, and discipline, therefore, nothing could be wanting that even inspiration and apostolic presence and authority could give. It very early gathered into it many of the chief men of Asia, and must have had a numerous membership and embraced many congregations. Another apostle, John himself, had, according to the uniform tradition of the church, been now living there for many years.

This church is commended for two things. (1.) First, its labour and patience in exposing the claims of pretended apostles, and in securing a pure ministry and government. "I know thy works, and thy labour, and thy patience, and how thou canst not bear them which are evil; and hast tried them which say they are apostles, and are not, and hast found them liars." So marked was their zeal for His honour and authority in this, that He repeats in the next verse His commendation with additional emphasis; "And hast borne, and hast patience, and for My name's sake hast laboured, and hast not fainted."

§. Commendations.

(2.) A second ground of commendation is appended to the censure which is next introduced, as if to temper its severity. This is its hatred to the deeds of the Nicolaitanes. "But this thou hast, that thou hatest the deeds of the Nicolaitanes, which I also hate." The very name of these Nicolaitanes has become synonymous with antinomian and licentious indulgences. Enough only is known of them to make it certain that they indulged in and defended licentious practices, lowering the obligation of the moral law. Everything else about them has been designedly suffered to perish, that there might never be any ambiguity in the meaning intended,—never any doubt as to the kind of conduct our Lord meant under this distinct name to hold up to the abhorrence of His church in all ages. With special distinctness and force He thus warns her against the fatal poison of suffering unholy practices within her pale under any pretext.

These commendations settle at least two leading objects of the church's care and labour. She must never tolerate false teachers, or immoral practices. She must never weary in her labour to drive such entirely out of her pale.

Twice this labour and patience without fainting is mentioned in connection with the testing of these pretended teachers. Notice this. There is no part of the discipline and government of the church that makes such large demands upon her labour and patience, none in reference to which she is more apt to fail, than in openly and firmly resisting the insidious teachers of error, those who claim to be apostles and are not.

Observe also how resistance to false teachers and to immoral practices go together. Loose doctrines and loose morals are intimately connected. A spurious charity for teachers of error is not seldom equally indulgent to laxity of morals. A low estimate of truth is inseparable from a low estimate of practical holiness. The conscience that is not tender enough to be wounded with false doctrine, is not tender enough to be hurt much with unholy practices. Christ's authority as King will be but little revered, if His authority as teacher be lightly regarded.

§. Censures.

But notwithstanding all this external prosperity and internal soundness, there was ground for heavy censure. There was a secret and fatal disease fixing itself on the very seat of life. "Thou hast left thy first love," is the weighty charge. How serious this is, is evident from the admonition and warning that follow. "Remember, therefore, from whence thou art fallen, and repent, and do the first works; or else I will come unto thee quickly, and will remove thy candlestick out of his place, except thou repent."

A church, therefore, may be large and prosperous, zealous for truth and order and purity, labouring patiently and successfully for the name of Christ, and yet there may be, unseen by human eyes, and unsuspected even by herself, a secret defect that silently but surely threatens her very existence. No external zeal can compensate for declining love. Love is the very principle of life; and yet it is alarmingly true, that its vigour may so decline, even beneath the most flaming zeal and patient labours, as to imperil life itself.

This censure is administered in close connection with the praise of their zeal in exposing these false apostles, and before the second ground of praise is mentioned, implying some real connection between this zeal against false teachers, and their declining love. There is such a connection, and it should never be forgotten. When any are called to contend earnestly for the faith, when patience is tried by daring and persistent error, and when at length the pretensions of false teachers are exposed, the process is apt to chafe and embitter the spirit, and success to foster spiritual pride; thus holy love to Jesus and His people insensibly loses that first fervour with which it gushes forth in faith's first view of the cross and the extinguished curse.

§. Lessons to all churches.

Ephesus, then, may teach the churches of every age, that if they would enjoy the approbation of their Lord, they must labour faithfully and patiently to uphold His sole authority, by contending for a pure ministry and a holy practice,—by refusing to follow any but the stars in His right hand: while, at the same time, her long extinguished light and removed candlestick will be a standing warning that all this will not avail to save them from ruin if their love is suffered secretly to wane. The evil, therefore, which imperilled her existence, was not an evil in the working of her organization, was not any imperfect or wrong official action, but an evil which had its origin, its seat and its power in the affections of the individual believer. It was therefore only as these warnings and admonitions of our Lord were applied to the individual hearts of the members of the church of Ephesus that they could be of any avail to save it. By such a personal application only can they be of any benefit to us.

Let no one, then, even cursorily read these things without such an application. You are ortho-
§. And to individuals. dox, you are zealous for outward purity and order, but may your Lord say of you—"Thou hast left thy first love?" Once your soul melted in penitence and grateful love as you thought of His sufferings and your sins; once you wrestled with intense fervency, in your closet and in the house of God, for greater holiness for yourself, and for the salvation of your unconverted friends and others; once you felt the claims of redeeming love drawing your heart out in cordial consecration to His service and self-denying labours for His kingdom; is it no longer thus? Has the sweet thrill of tenderness, the yearning of desire, the springing energy of love passed away, leaving a painful consciousness of departed joys in your devotions and your services? Then the horrid leprosy, which the sprinkled blood seemed to have cleansed, is again bursting forth in its dark, polluting spots over your soul, and your life also. When the sick man, who has been nigh unto death, and so far restored as to feel the power of the disease broken, and the process of recovery established, again feels the old symptoms returning day after day with increasing power, his appetite for wholesome food failing, and his strength decreasing, he will be, if in his senses, at once alarmed, and will not lose a moment in hastening to resort to the remedy that before relieved him, if within his reach. Your case, declining Christian, calls for far greater solicitude.

"Remember from whence thou hast fallen." Recall the past experiences of His grace. Re-
§. Admonitions. member the divine mercies, your lost joys, and broken vows, and departed

usefulness. "Thou hast fallen," yes, fallen from grace, there is such a thing, and the condition is a dreadful one. David complaining of his broken bones, and Peter weeping his bitter tears, would tell you so. And though you have not yet, by any overt act, displayed your decay of love to that, or even a worse result, it must bring you, unless speedily restored. There is but one way of restoration. "Repent and do the first works." Look to the cross, the blood, the righteousness, the Spirit, as at the first; take hold of the invitation and offer of the gospel as a lost and helpless sinner, and believe the love that God has to you. Waste no time in examining and analyzing past experiences, but at once "do the first works;" repent and believe in the Lord Jesus Christ. You must again feel the strong grasp of His loving hand, you must again repose on the blood of the everlasting covenant, you must again feel the sweet influences of that Spirit of love melting, warming and reviving your heart, or all is lost; your light will go out entirely. Repent, repent; or the light of the church which you have thus, by your decay of love, obscured, will cease to shine upon you, and the very ordinances which once cheered your soul with hope and joy, be utterly withdrawn or worthless: the candlestick will be removed by your Lord coming quickly in judgment.

Such are the admonitions which this message to the orthodox church of Ephesus is ever uttering to every church and every heart where love is secretly declining. How very widely this phase of character prevails in the visible kingdom, the sad confessions and the spiritual feebleness of the whole Christian world testifies.

Besides these admonitions, this message presents the true remedy and preventive of such declension. It is found in the character in which the Lord Jesus announces Himself to this church, and the promise at its close to him

§. Remedy and preventive.

that overcometh. Behold Him ever personally present with you, and in all the worship and government of His church. See Him always walking in the midst of the golden candlesticks, not merely as a witness, but to supply their oil, and trim their lights; and holding the stars in His right hand, enforcing the authority of His messages with divine power. What can more effectually preserve love in its first freshness, together with earnest and untiring zeal, against every innovation of His sole authority, than a constant realization of His loving, personal presence? And to those struggling against the emissaries of dangerous error,—error that subverts Christ's sole authority over the soul, and so poisons the very bread of life, and who, in the struggle, are in danger of enfeebling their love, which is the very principle of that life, what can be more cheering and invigorating than to see at the end of this conflict, the Paradise of God, and to hear the promise to eat freely of the fruit of the tree of life which is in the midst of it,—the promise of an immortality of truth and of love?

In striking contrast with this powerful but spiritually declining church is the second,

2. SMYRNA. PERSECUTION.

A Church Poor and Persecuted, but fully approved.

Chap. ii: 8–10.

Of all these seven churches, no one stands higher in the estimation of her Lord than this. Yet in outward estate she is the worst of them all. Poverty and persecution are her present lot, and prisons and death are awaiting her. Her record here is not one of active labours and triumphs for Christ, but of poverty and tribulation for His sake; and no record shines more brightly, or secures a higher reward. Over against her poverty is the assurance of her Lord,

§. Its state.

"but thou art rich,"—a precious pledge of heavenly treasures; and over against the rage of her persecuting foes is the voice of His love and power, saying, "Fear none of those things which thou shalt suffer. ...... Be thou faithful unto death, and I will give thee a crown of life."

This church and city is not elsewhere mentioned in the New Testament. But one of the most interesting scraps of early church history relates to it, and furnishes a striking illustration of this epistle. A little more than seventy years after this, in a fierce persecution led on and stimulated by the Jews, Polycarp, its chief bishop and a disciple in his youth of the apostle John, suffered martyrdom here in extreme old age. The narrative has been often repeated, but we cannot refrain from giving here at least the answers of the aged martyr when summoned before the proconsul, and addressed in the customary language— "Swear, curse Christ, and I will set you free." "Eighty and six years have I served Him, and I have received only good at His hands. Can I then curse Him, my King and my Saviour?" "I will cast you to the wild beasts, if you do not change your mind," said the proconsul. "Bring the wild beasts hither," said Polycarp, "for change my mind from the better to the worse I will not." "Do you despise the wild beasts? I will subdue your spirit by the flames." "The flames which you menace endure but for a time, and are soon extinguished," calmly rejoined the martyr; "but there is a fire reserved for the wicked, whereof you know not; the fire of a judgment to come, and of punishment everlasting." These flames soon did their work. By his death, the rage of the populace, to which already many victims had been sacrificed, was so far satiated that the proconsul suspended the persecution, and this poor suffering church had a respite. Not only here and in history, but on the very spot where it suffered, the testimony of this faithful

§. Polycarp.

church still lives. While the great city and temple of Ephesus have utterly perished, and every vestige of its large, wealthy, but declining church has been obliterated, the faithfulness of this martyr church is still celebrated, and the spot of this early martyrdom shown in this city of Smyrna, now greater and more celebrated even than in the times of the martyr; and there again the true witnesses for Jesus are revived and uttering their testimony.

§. Consolations. During those years of bitter trial, when not only her apostolic leader, but many of her members were carried to prisons and to death, how precious beyond conception must these words of Jesus have been! "Be thou faithful unto death, and I will give thee a crown of life." As they were read in her assemblies and her families, and recollected by her sufferers, they calmed many a troubled heart, and prepared many a feeble saint for the crown of martyrdom.

Still further comfort and encouragement were administered to this church by the character in which Christ here presents Himself to them, and in the promise to him that overcometh. His titles here set forth to this suffering church—His divine power and His human sympathy. He is "the First and the Last," the Author and End of all things, universal and absolute Sovereign; and yet He "became dead, and is alive." While, therefore, in their pathway of blood, they are only walking in His footsteps; and walking there, they not only see Him holding out to them the crown of life, but hear His assurance that though they die a martyr's death, "they shall not be hurt of the second death."

How precious this experience of the church of Smyrna, and this message and these promises to her, have been to thousands since, the blood-stained annals of the church in all ages attest. With this church of Smyrna before their eyes, none can ever think it strange concerning the fiery trials through which they are passing. And with such promises and assurances, they may, on the other hand, rejoice. inasmuch as they are counted worthy to be partakers of His sufferings.

But let no suffering church or believer overlook the important fact, that while this church receives not one word of censure, but only confirmation and comfort, this comfort does not consist in any promise of deliverance from their suffering estate while here, but only of grace to bear it. On the contrary, the promise implies that these persecutions shall continue, and shall be suffered to run their complete natural course, indicated here, after the manner of this book, by ten days, expressing a complete but indefinite period. This does indeed imply a real limit beyond which even Satan could not go, but then that very limit may be reached only by a cruel death. Be it so, however; it is only ten days of suffering,—then what? Not a mere temporal deliverance from the persecutor's rage, but "eternal life." The tender love of our Lord is not shown here so much by removing external evils, as by sustaining His people under them, and by making them occasions of larger spiritual attainments, and means of working out a brighter reward.

§. Suffering not removed, but grace to endure.

The great lesson, then, here taught in regard to the church, is that outward wealth or power, or safety or success, is no mark of a true church. All these may be wanting, and yet there be great spiritual riches, and the approving smiles of her King. We here see that in this sevenfold picture of the church, one of the two churches on which His perfect approval is bestowed is the one most bitterly persecuted and impoverished. Singular holiness and faithfulness is sure to beget the hatred of the world. This very hatred is then made the instrument of still higher spiritual attainments, and so the occasion of a richer blessing. "All that will live godly in Christ Jesus

§. Outward good no mark of a true church.

shall suffer persecution." This is not yet an obsolete truth, as some seem to think it at least in a state of advanced civilization such as we live in. The offence of the cross has not ceased. The world has not become Christian; it is the world still, though polished and learned, instead of savage and barbarous. But the church has become worldly, and that to a fearful extent, so as often to seek to justify her worldliness. Whenever she completely renounces the world, and utters a clear, consistent and faithful testimony in her life as well as her doctrines, against sin in all its polished as well as disguising forms, this inherent enmity of the world will be just as fully manifested. It may be in a different way. It generally at least must be more indirect. If the world does not persecute the church, it is either because it has corrupted her so far that her testimony does not seriously interfere with its more refined indulgences, or because it regards her as too powerless to be worthy of her notice.

It is not, then, to the church with the richest endowments, and the highest worldly honours and influence, that we are to look for the greatest spiritual power, or for the purest representation of the spiritual kingdom. As we trace the path of that kingdom through the ages, we are not to look for it in the chief seats of power and wealth, but in the caves and dens, in prisons and on scaffolds, in poverty and obscurity; and even when in power, as bitterly hated and misrepresented; but everywhere shining with the light of divine truth and holiness.

But it is not merely the world as such, in its professed neglect of the gospel and opposition to its claims, that hates the true and faithful church. Its most bitter enemies and fiercest persecutors, as here foreshadowed, have been false and apostate churches, who retained the name, the forms, and a certain outward succession, and therefore claimed to be the only chosen people of

§. Apostate churches, the bitterest persecutors.

God, like these persecutors of Smyrna, who said they were Jews and were not, but were the synagogue of Satan. The Jews, by rejecting Christ, cut themselves off from all covenant relations and privileges, and no longer were Jews in the sense of the covenant made with Abraham; and by still claiming it, became guilty of blasphemy, and more guilty and further off from God than other nations, the very synagogue of Satan. A like condemnation rests upon all who claim such an exclusive relation to God on mere external grounds instead of spiritual conformity, and also the guilt of a terrible pre-eminence in persecuting violence.

Here, again, the message can only attain its end by a personal application. The charge is,—

§. Faithfulness. "Be thou faithful." This word may mean believing, exercising a firm faith in Christ; and this is, of course, the only source of all unswerving adherence to Him, and faithfulness in the use of all He has entrusted to us, which last we regard as the idea here. Be trustworthy; one whom Christ can trust; can trust with His commands, His honour, and His messages of mercy to other lost sinners. Be one who will not use what Jesus has entrusted to you for your own private indulgence, or squander it in ease or neglect, but faithfully employ it for the sacred purpose for which it was given. And what have you that has not been given by Jesus to be used in advancing His kingdom within and around you? Can you name one thing that is not a sacred trust for this object? Bodily health, talents, knowledge, influence; home and all its comforts, children, friendships; property, religious privileges, Bibles, good books—all are sacred trusts. They cost His blood. Have we perverted them from their holy design?

"*Unto death.*" This is the measure of this faithfulness. It does not mean 'until death,' merely, but though death, a violent death, be the result. Though the use of our time, our talents, our property and influence for His glory, may bring us to death; though conformity to His will and example should involve not only self-denial, toil and suffering, as it assuredly will, but the loss of life itself, faithfulness demands it. No crown without it. Professed follower of Jesus, can He trust you? trust you to do your duty, your whole duty, whatever it may cost you? Only by His Almighty grace can any helpless sinner do this. May we all "obtain mercy of the Lord, to be faithful."

LECTURE VII.

THE SAME SUBJECT CONTINUED.

Chap. ii: 12–29.

PERGAMOS AND THYATIRA. THE FRIENDSHIP OF THE WORLD. HERESY.

THESE two churches are, in some respects, very much alike. In each there is a very remarkable mingling of good and evil, the good, very good, and the bad, very bad. In both there are the same foul results, but produced by very different means.

3. Pergamos. The World's Friendship.

A Church Faithful under the World's Violence, but yielding to its friendship.

Verses 12–17.

The distinctive evil which this church presents is the friendship of the world. Though it had been faithful under persecution, it was sadly corrupted by worldly alliances. It had borne the brunt of a fierce and bloody persecution, in which the faithful servant of Christ here named, but of whom nothing else is now known, suffered martyrdom. It had endured all this without yielding anything of the truth or the honour of Christ. For this, therefore, it receives His hearty commendation, but now incurs His censure, by yielding to the friendship of the world. It was tolerating unholy alliances with the world, which had already corrupted many of its members, and rendered necessary the threatening of disciplinary judgments. "Thou hast there them that hold the doctrine of Balaam, who taught Balak to cast a stumbling-block before the children of Israel, to eat things sacrificed unto idols, and to commit fornication. So hast thou also them which hold the doctrine of the Nicolaitanes, which thing I hate." This doctrine of Balaam and of the Nicolaitanes were not two separate and distinct defections. The word '*also*' in verse fifteenth, is to be taken with *thou*, not with *Nicolaitanes;* so that the meaning is not 'Nicolaitanes in addition to Balaamites,' but ' thou also, as well as Israel,' in like manner with Israel, hast in these Nicolaitanes those who hold the same corrupting principles that Balaam taught. This additional designation and description of the Nicolaitane doctrine is no mere variation; but brings out with impressive distinctness the characteristic features of this violation of church purity. Balaam, though warned of God, and highly favoured with the visions of the Almighty, "loved the wages of unrighteousness," and in perverse resistance to the light given him, counselled such alliances between Moab and Israel, as involved many of the latter in the most shameful excesses of idolatrous worship, and incurred the fierce wrath and judgments of God. Unholy alliances and admixtures, counselled by covetousness and other worldly motives, and which lead the separated Israel of God to unite with the enemies of the spiritual kingdom, and conform to their worldly idolatry and pleasures, are without any doubt the peculiar evil here presented in such odious and fatal characters. The effect of such alliances where open idolatry prevails, is necessarily to produce conformity to idolatrous practices, and the sensual indulgences connected with them. Hence in the early church conformity to the world, when acted out fully, took this form literally—"to eat things sacrificed to idols, and to

§. Balaamites and Nicolaitanes.

commit fornication." And even where these results, as literal acts, no longer follow, the constant usage of the Bible in describing all forsaking of the pure worship of God and violation of consecration vows, as a spiritual whoredom and fornication, makes them appropriately describe the true nature of all worldly conformity.

Sin changes its forms, but not its principles. There are no temples of Diana, and Venus, or of Boodh and Vishnu among us, enticing back to their licentious indulgences those who were once devoted worshippers there. But the temples of Mammon, of Pleasure, of Ambition, rear their alluring fronts and open their wide portals along every walk of life. Many professed worshippers of Jesus openly enter these temples with the thronging crowds, and while they profess to reject their worship, evidently eat with zest of their dainties, and drink from the cup of their intoxicating joys until they become spiritually debauched, and live in open violation of their solemn vows of consecration to Christ. There are many churches, too, which, though they might hold fast the truth against the violence of persecution, yet, like Pergamos, they are unable to resist this more subtile and powerful attack from the friendship of the world, and who have and acknowledge as fellow-disciples those who plead for these worldly alliances, and for habits, pleasures and pursuits which are most truly described as sitting down in the temples of these modern gods of the world, and eating the things sacrificed to them, until the soul is all polluted with the guilt of broken vows and a spiritual adultery.

§. Worldly conformity, the same in principle.

Pergamos thus presents us with another very distinct phase of the visible and imperfect church. Those worldly alliances which formed the dark blot upon its otherwise noble character, have always been a most prolific source of

§. Satan's power in it.

corruption. It was so with the antediluvian church, when the sons of God went in unto the daughters of men. It was so with Israel during every period of its history, in the immediate family of Jacob, in Egyptian bondage, in the plains of Moab, and especially in the days of her greatest prosperity—the splendid reign of Solomon, and so outward until the very last warnings of the prophetic oracle by Malachi, and afterwards, until her light had almost expired under the corruptions thus introduced. The virulence and power of this evil is here intimated, first, by the designation given to the place where it prevailed, as the place where "Satan's throne" was, "where Satan dwelleth." Nothing more fully proves his presence and power. In places like Pergamos, which had once been the capital for a century and a half of a wealthy kingdom, and which still was renowned for its magnificence, riches, and the treasures of learning stored in its vast library, Satan very generally reigns with special power, and that too by means of this doctrine of Balaam. Under the elegancies and refinements and embellishments of an advanced social state, he conceals the real enmity of the world, and allures the church to its embrace. By these alliances between the church and the world, he did in Pergamos what he could not do in Smyrna by his synagogue and his fires.

But the enormity of this evil is still more fully exposed by the whole language of Christ to this church. The very title He assumes in addressing them, as "He which hath the sharp sword with two edges," implies their need of sharp and penetrating judgments. His rebuke may well startle every one who cultivates the friendship of the world. "Repent: or else I will come unto thee quickly, and fight against them with the sword of My mouth." No compromise is permitted for a moment with this evil. It is not treated as something partly evil and partly good,

§. Incurs the severest rebukes.

requiring nice discriminations to be made, but as utterly and manifestly contrary to the whole nature and spirit of His kingdom. Nor is this true merely of the peculiar forms of this evil in Pergamos; the same divine authority is equally explicit in regard to the ungodliness of it in every form, no matter how concealed and refined. "The friendship of the world is enmity with God," is the strong and sweeping language of the Spirit, without any explanations, limitations or distinctions. In regard to it in every form, the charge is an uncompromising call to repentance. To the church, Christ says—'Repent; put away this evil from among you in the faithful exercise of that authority which I have entrusted to you, and by the earnest use of the means of grace I have appointed. Purge out this Balaamite doctrine that would conceal or blot out the eternal distinction between My church and the world.' If not, "I will come unto thee quickly, and will fight against them with the sword of My mouth." If the church neglects its duty, He will take this matter of its discipline into His own hands, and by His purifying judgments cleanse it.

Observe, however, how tenderly and carefully He discriminates between His church, defective and censurable as she was in the discharge of her duty, and those unworthy members who, by their worldliness, placed stumbling-blocks in the way of their brethren. "I will come unto thee quickly," but, "I will fight against *them*," not against thee. These visitations of His judgment have a two-fold aspect, (like the cloud that separated between the Egyptian and Israelitish hosts at the Red Sea); though they inflict deep and sore wounds upon His true people, they tend to their purification and salvation; but against those who seek the friendship of the world and the indulgence of the flesh, against all Balaamites and Nicolaitanes, He comes to make a war of extermination.

§. These judgments discriminating.

Every member, therefore, of His church who is courting the favour of the world, lowering the standard of separation from it, seeking to justify habits and practices which the most prayerful and earnest Christians condemn, and so putting stumbling-blocks in the way of the feeble, should tremble at these words. They remind us of those other words of His: "Whoso shall offend one of these little ones which believe in Me, it were better for him that a millstone were hanged about his neck, and that he were drowned in the depths of the sea. Woe unto the world because of offences; for it must needs be that offences come: but woe unto him by whom the offence cometh."

There is added for the encouragement of His people, who in such a state of the church contend against these wiles of Satan, and reject the delusive friendships and the proffered dainties of the world, the appropriate and rich promise that they shall eat of the hidden manna of communion with God in glory, and shall possess the precious pledge of His eternal friendship.

§. Prevalence of this conformity. Indefinite ideas of it.

Never, perhaps, in the whole history of the church did this Balaamite doctrine exert so wide an influence as now. Never did it have such facilities for covertly and insidiously creeping into the church and enticing the followers of Christ into the most ruinous worldly conformity. Trite as the subject is, much as has been said and written about it, it is one which never has been and never can be clearly understood by any but an earnestly spiritual mind. The great difficulty attending every effort to enforce upon the church the teachings of the Bible in regard to conformity with the world, is that every man, woman and child has a different idea of what it means. One regards it as engaging in those pleasures that are distinctly worldly, as the theatre, the ball-room, the gay party, and having no taste for or temptation to these, considers himself as above all censure; another—the high-minded merchant—regards it as conformity to the dishonest trading and trickery of business life, and so votes himself innocent; another regards it as applying to the extravagancies of fashionable life, which he regards as a foolish waste of money, and congratulates himself upon his virtuous self-denial; while still another regards it as specially directed against covetousness, and the desire of the honours and applause of the world, and so, with entire assurance, votes himself free from any sinful conformity. But this sin lies far deeper than any of these outward acts and habits; it takes every variety of form, and often assumes the garb and the name of some of the loveliest human virtues; and it dwells equally in the palace of royalty, the mansion of wealth, and the most abject hovel of poverty.

But whatever ambiguity the devil and the human heart may have contrived to throw around the meaning of the term "the world," as used in this phrase, "conformity to the world," there is no such ambiguity of meaning as used in the Bible. There its sense is definite and clear. It is everything from which God is excluded, no matter how lovely in itself, how humane, how apparently philanthropic, how noble and generous, how learned or intellectual: if God be excluded so that His glory is not the real and avowed end, it is "*the world.*" It is always the very opposite of the true church; it is indeed everything which has not in some way the stamp of the spiritual kingdom upon it, and is not employed in promoting its great designs.

§. Bible meaning clearly defined.

The language of the apostle John is decisive: "For all that is in the world, the lust of the flesh, and the lust of the eyes, and the pride of life, is not of the Father, but is of the world." If it is not of the Father, it is of the world. Conformity to the world, then, is compliance with the desires of the flesh and of the eye, and with the pride of life, instead of having every desire both as to its object and degree controlled by the Spirit of God and the love of Christ.

There are two things which tend to confound the distinction between the church and the world, and so to give currency and power to this Balaamite doctrine. (1.) First, the variable and defective standard of separation from the world. Multitudes have a standard on this subject which they certainly never got from the word of God, and which compels them to explain away almost entirely its strong and sweeping statements. It declares the separation must be entire; it admits of no friendship, no compromise. Wherever we come in contact with any earthly thing, which we must continually do, we must so touch and handle and use it, as to stamp on it a heavenly character, and turn it into a spiritual influence, and make it subserve spiritual ends, so as, in a word, to separate it with ourselves from "the world." Such a totality of separation is a thing possible only to a spiritual mind, and conceivable only by such. Hence this idea of conformity to the world will vary with the spirituality of each individual. If you know but little of communion with God and the joy of sins forgiven, you will see nothing but what is attractive, and perhaps even praiseworthy in many things from which the soul, habitually thrilled with the touch of the spirit of adoption, would shrink instinctively as incapable of giving either pleasure or profit, nay, as utterly godless. You may even find a savour of piety in that which, to the truly spiritually minded, will present only the corruption and loathsomeness of death. Just as those Balaamites, of Pergamos, justified their conformity by their doctrine

§ Causes. 1. Variable and defective standard of holiness.

and teachings. Many a pure lust of the flesh and of the eye, and much of the pride of life, is thus defended and justified.

(2.) Another thing which helps to confound this distinction, and give plausibility to many Balaamite counsels, and which is naturally suggested by comparing the sins to which it led in Pergamos, and those by which it manifests itself among us, is the change wrought by the church upon the world itself. Those old idolatrous civilizations have passed away before the gospel, and society has put on, in a very great degree, the outside dress of Christianity. Under this so-called Christian civilization, with its refinement and science and art, the danger of the church is greater than ever from this evil of worldly conformity. We have arrived at that state in which the effects produced by the church upon the world are in danger of enfeebling the church and arresting its further progress. Our present civilization, with all its humanizing and elevating influences on the mind of man, and on society, in all wherein it differs from the old civilizations of Greece and Rome, is the effect of the prevalence of Christianity, and a signal proof of its power. But, considered in itself, it is just as godless as they were. It takes the wild swine, and washes and pens and trains and teaches him to do wonders, but it does not change his swinish nature, as he is continually proving, by turning, even under all these influences, to the vilest abominations, like the sow that was washed to her wallowing in the mire. It polishes society, it cultivates the intellect, it changes the forms of human activity and the sources of enjoyment, it multiplies the comforts and the embellishments of life, but it does not bring the heart any nearer to God, it does not wean the affections from earthly good, it does not make it any easier to bear the

§. 2. Change wrought on the world itself.

cross or walk in the blood-stained path of the Man of sorrows.

Its effect indeed is just the opposite. It only intensifies and confirms the earthliness of the heart, by multiplying indefinitely the sources of earthly happiness, and expanding and invigorating the powers of the human mind. With the love of God controlling them, these are inestimable blessings; but they will never produce that love, and without it their direct effect is only to deify the world and man. This it has done, and is always doing, in the Pantheistic theories of the philosopher, and the practical atheism of the multitude. It takes up the very language of Christianity and adopts its forms, but neither feels its power nor aims at its spiritual ends. It may substitute the sublime study of the stars, or the hollow and artistic pomp of the modern stage, for the brutish stupidity and the war-dance of the savage, but a Laplace and a Garrick may be as far from God as the untutored Indian.

§. Intensifies earthliness.

Instead of separation from the world being the result, the bonds that bind the cultivated but unsanctified man to the world are rendered stronger and more plausible just in proportion as they are more refined and intellectual. Everybody knows that the love of God, of holiness, of the cross of Christ, of spiritual and eternal things, is just as fully ignored by all this externally Christianized civilization, as it ever was or could be by the old Roman or Greek idolatries.

But this has made the danger of the church far greater. In those days the distance between the church and the world was so great, that the external habits and actions of every man professing Christianity made it visible, as it still does, in heathen lands. Now the world has put on the outside of Chris-

§. Church's danger.

tianity to such an extent, without receiving its spirit, that no mere externals of the social or moral habits can at all distinguish between the child of God and of the devil, between the church and the world. The testimony, therefore, which is now required in the life of every true Christian to prove his separation from the world, is one that must show clearly the real ungodliness that lurks under all the moralities and polish and elegancies of modern civilization.

This outward conformity of the world itself to the church, and the high spirituality required in the church to meet it, render this doctrine of Baalam exceedingly popular.

§. *Its opposition to Christ's claims.*

Conformity to the world pervades the whole structure and habits of most modern Christian society, and spreads its polluting influence over many of our church plans and enterprises. The stress laid upon architectural display, and musical attractions, and oratorical power, and social and political influence, in building up and extending the spiritual kingdom, is a proof of this that meets us everywhere. But in nothing is its influence so disastrous, and so insinuating and unsuspected, as in the very principles that govern most professing Christians in their lawful labours and pursuits. The Christian is called to live in a new sphere, and for new purposes; he is called out of the world, where the end of men's activity is to answer the question, "What shall we eat? What shall we drink? Wherewithal shall we be clothed?"—and his Lord's charge to him is, "Seek not these things, for your Heavenly Father knoweth that ye have need of them; but seek first the kingdom of God, and all these things shall be added unto you." Being in this kingdom, he is required to labour for it with all his energies, and the King expressly engages that He Himself will provide for all his personal earthly necessities, or rather, that a sufficient supply of these will be made sure to him by spending his efforts for the advancement of the kingdom. He not only authorizes us to trust in Himself, He requires us to do so. Here is the real point of the distinction between the children of the kingdom and of the world in reference to the affairs of this life; the former look for their worldly support in serving the kingdom, and in advancing its interests; the latter look for it only to their own worldly energies and accumulations. But in actual life, where is there any apparent difference between the great multitude of men and women in the church and out of it? To a very great degree it is true, that in the real motives that call out and stimulate the activities of professed Christians in their daily business, there is no difference between them and the moral man of the world. In the pursuit of our various callings, what palpable evidence is given by each of us of any positive trust in our King—of such a trust as excludes distressing doubts and secures real peace? of our holding to Him such a peculiar and precious relation as we do, indeed of our holding any peculiar and intimate relation to Him and His daily Providence different from what other men do? It is in this feebleness of trust, and the consequent anxieties and feverish concern, and overwrought energies, absorbing almost all the time and thoughts, that this conformity to the world is most manifest, most powerful, and most disastrous in its effects on the church, and on our personal holiness and happiness. Hence it extends into everything we do, into every relation of life, and every service of our Lord, robbing us of our peace and joy and hope, and causing us to walk, if we walk at all, with crippled limbs and stumbling steps along the narrow way. Here, too, is the reason why our Lord so often and so sorely rebukes His church, why He is fighting against multitudes in it with the sword of His mouth, blasting their schemes, disappointing their hopes, and drying up their springs of earthly joy.

Oh, brethren in the kingdom and patience of Jesus Christ, when our Lord comes we shall get new light on this great subject. It will be a terrible surprise to many souls to find how completely they were conformed to the world, when they flattered themselves they were separated from it. Let us give earnest heed to those warnings of the word and Spirit, which cannot be too often repeated. "Come out from the world, and be ye separate, saith the Lord, and touch not the unclean thing." "I beseech you, therefore, brethren, by the mercies of God, that ye present your bodies a living sacrifice, holy and acceptable to God, which is your reasonable service; and be not conformed to this world."

4. THYATIRA. HERESY.

A Church Increasing in Works, but tolerating a foul heresy.

Verses 18–29.

This church presents a phase the very opposite to that of Ephesus. It is commended for its works of *charity*, as well as of faith, and because it had advanced in these instead of declining. "I know thy works, and charity, and service, and faith, and thy patience, and thy works—the last to be more than the first." But while abounding in charitable labours, it had not been zealous for the truth and authority of Christ; it had extended its charity even to dangerous error and false teachers. "Notwithstanding, I have a few things against thee, because thou sufferest that woman (or thy woman) Jezebel, which calleth herself a prophetess, to teach and to seduce My servants to commit fornication, and to eat things sacrificed unto idols." The church authority had suffered one who called herself a prophetess, claiming to be sent of God, and pretending to special wisdom and piety, to teach her foul heresies, and so seduce the people into carnal lusts and idolatrous practices.

Toleration of heresy is the characteristic defect of this church. What the particular doctrine was that this pretended prophetess taught, is not mentioned, as the guilt did not consist in the kind of error, but in the utterly unauthorized teaching, in the single fact that this teaching was without Christ's authority. The sin of the church was in not doing what Ephesus is so highly commended for, trying them which said they were apostles and were not, and proving them liars. And the whole epistle shows how great the evil is of tolerating in the church any teaching which has not the manifest stamp of Christ's authority upon it, no matter what may be its apparent wisdom or speciousness or harmlessness.

§. Effects of heresy.

The effects upon the character of those who listened to this deceiver, are the first things that strike us as showing the magnitude of this evil. They are the same as those charged upon the church of Pergamos,—fornication, and the eating of things sacrificed unto idols. They are here mentioned in an opposite order, as if to indicate the different order of their development, as well as their different origin. There the seducers were Balaamites; here it was a Jezebel. There the cause was covetousness and the friendship of the world; here it was heretical teaching, by one pretending to divine authority, and rendered attractive by the blandishments of worldly power and wisdom. But the results upon the life are the same, though reached by a somewhat different process. Sensuality and idolatry in some form or other are the invariable results of error. Whether apostacy begins in a secret covetousness or in doctrinal error, it ends in the same horrid depths of moral pollution.

§. Why called Jezebel.

The name Jezebel, applied to this pretended prophetess, indicates still further the true character of such teaching. It is equally unimportant and impossible to determine positively whether this was a real woman, or the personification thus of the heretical agency corrupting the church; the result is the same, and the very indefiniteness only makes the application more general and comprehensive. This name is used by our Lord, evidently to identify her character and relations to the true church, with those of that troubler of ancient Israel, the queen of Ahab. That Jezebel had been brought by marriage into Israel from the proud and idolatrous royal house of Tyre, at that time the foremost representative of the world's power. She had brought with her all the haughtiness and cruelty of her family which are notorious in heathen story, together with all her idolatrous attachments; and with all the blandishments of that licentious worship, and all the power of her throne, she strove to root out all pure worship of Jehovah. By giving her name to this corrupting and powerful teacher in Thyatira, Christ declares that what Jezebel was openly and avowedly, she was in reality, notwithstanding all her artifices. And the inference is necessary, that all such teachers as employ their influence and worldly wisdom in teaching in Christ's name what He has not taught, and so corrupting the church's purity and leading her members into a heinous spiritual adultery, are true Jezebels, with whatever attractions they may clothe themselves and their teachings; just as they who lay the stumblingblocks of worldly conformity are true Balaams. This one name applied to such, does more to describe their true character, to unveil their Satanic nature and abominable and ruinous influence, than whole chapters of description would have done.

A characteristic feature of all such false teaching and teachers, and by which it is rendered specially dangerous, is referred to in verse 24; its pretended "depths," its profound insight into the divine mysteries, and ability to

§. "Depths of Satan."

unravel them,—here styled by Christ, according to their real nature, "depths of Satan." "Depths," as they speak or pretend. Ever since the times of these Jezebelites of Thyatira, and the still earlier times of those false teachers of Corinth, who withstood Paul with their professions of superior wisdom, the defenders and propagators of error have laid claim to deeper insight and profounder views. They are ever boasting of a progressive theology, a system more rational and in harmony with nature, of certain profundities of reason, which are only depths of Satanic deception, cunning bribes to the proud and blind intellect of man. They have thus always put themselves in strong contrast with the true 'messengers' of Christ, whose office is to deliver to the world a simple testimony, nothing more, nothing less.

Thus far this message to Thyatira unfolds the nature of this evil. Its magnitude and heinousness appears still further from the judgments with which it is threatened. The destruction of this Jezebel was to be so complete and so signally appropriate as to impress all the churches with the Lord's abhorrence of such perversion of His truth and authority, and the certainty with which His all searching eye would detect and His power punish it. " Behold, I will cast her into a bed, and them that commit adultery with her into great tribulation, except they repent of their deeds. And I will kill all her children with death; and all the churches shall know that I am He which searcheth the reins and the hearts; and I will give to every one of you according to your works." How far this language is figurative it may be impossible to say positively; nor is it important, since whether literal or figurative the lesson to the churches is the same. It seems, however, evident that by " her children " are meant her disciples, those who had received their religious opinions and character from her ; and then it would

§. Judgments.

follow that those who committed adultery with her, were such as united with her in teaching these seductive heresies. They are united with her therefore in the punishment. What aggravated her guilt and doom was that He "gave her space to repent of her fornication and she repented not." The long suffering of God toward such deceivers only hardens and encourages them. She is, therefore, made to eat of the fruit of her own doings. Her sin becomes her punishment. She is to find the bed of her pleasures the bed of helplessness and wasting disease, her beauty and fascinations all gone, herself an object of pity and contempt. All such false teaching brings its authors to shame and disgrace. Of her children He says: "I will kill all her children with death." This language is very peculiar as well as strong. It seems to intimate that this loss of life threatened, was nothing that could be caused by such instrumentalities as affect the body only,—it was one inflicted by the curse of the law itself. They were to be given over to the full power of death, to become His special victims, pierced through with His eternal sting. In the matters of salvation, to follow any teachings but those of Jesus is to kill the soul itself. Surely the toleration of such teaching in the church itself must be a grievous sin, and one that imperils its very existence.

Our Lord then applies to this case the great principle which governs all His infliction of judgments upon His church. "According to your works." There is a sad tendency to forget the important and precise place which 'works' hold in the kingdom of grace. No works can bring a soul into the kingdom; no works, even by one who is in it, can entitle to any, even the very least of its blessings; grace, free and sovereign, only can do this. It does not however follow that in His treatment of those who are the objects of this grace, He does not regulate His

§. According to your works.

dealings, the manifestations of His displeasure and approval, perfectly "according to their works." In nothing is this always more distinctly manifest than in the consequences of our treatment of His truth. Perversion of this, or indifference to it is invariably followed by a terrible and an exactly proportioned retribution. Truth always takes a fearful vengeance on those who slight her. From such she hides her face, and turns away, and even when they see her they cannot recognize her. When they call she will not answer, when they seek her they cannot find her; "For that they hated knowledge, and did not choose the fear of the Lord: they would none of My counsel: they despised all My reproof. Therefore shall they eat of the fruit of their own way, and be filled with their own devices.... He that sinneth against Me wrongeth his own soul: all they that hate Me, love death."

Does not Thyatira thus set forth a type of church character, which, sad to say, has been widely and fearfully realized? Have not intense activity, earnest zeal in works of charity, in ministering to the wants and woes of suffering man, and faith and patience in enduring all the toils and self-denials which this has demanded, been found often in a church side by side with great charity to soul-destroying error and its teachers? Let the churches remember that there is no such system of compensations in the spiritual kingdom, as will allow zeal in one thing to make up for neglect of another. Works of charity cannot compensate for indifference to truth.

§. This phase of the church often realized.

This evil that polluted the church of Thyatira grew afterwards to gigantic proportions. And the manner in which it is here presented as originating with a woman, a Jezebel, a false prophetess, and made alluring by the blandishments of sense, makes it a clear foreshadowing of the

§. Gigantic growth in Rome.

foulest and most destructive heresy and apostacy that has ever polluted the visible church,—that harlot church and mother of abominations afterwards so fully depicted in this book. This Jezebel has her full grown form in that daring effrontery and yet apparent feminine tenderness, and these most cunning blandishments of a spiritual harlotry, with which a so-called church has impiously presumed in the name of Christ to inculcate doctrines leading to the foulest lusts and the rankest idolatry. The Jezebel nature of this mystery of iniquity which was then beginning to work such disastrous effects in Thyatira, was only fully developed when a few ages after the worldly power seized upon the visible church, and with a face of meekness, a heart of unscrupulous ambition, and an arm of terror, lorded it over God's heritage. To call this power a church, a true church of Christ, is as much an abuse of language and truth, as to have so-called the Jezebelites of Thyatira who were corrupting and ruining the church. The doom of the one too foreshadows the doom of the other, which is described in strikingly analagous language in the latter part of this book.[1]

Terrible however as this evil was, it had not yet gained the ascendancy in this church, so as to destroy its church character. There were those whom Jesus could thus address: "But unto you I say [and] unto the rest in Thyatira, as many as have not this doctrine, and which have not known the depths of Satan, as they speak." In such a state of the church, when error holds authority and occupies high places, and puts on its most attractive forms and cunning sophistries, it is no easy matter to hold fast to the simple truth and worship of Jesus; and to do so is all the burden He calls His true disciples to bear. He regards this as full proof of loyalty and love. When this is united, as it was in the faithful at Thyatira, with

§. Promise to the faithful.

[1] See chap. 17: 16, and chap. 18.

abounding works of love and faith, it marks a fulness and symmetry of Christian character upon which Jesus looks with special satisfaction, saying, "I will put upon you none other burden: but what ye have already, hold fast till I come." No burden which Christ lays upon us, can crush us by its weight, or even cause us to walk painfully and heavily. This especially is so pure and heavenly, so spiritual and elevating like the pure air itself, that it sustains the bearer. The danger is not that we sink under the burden, but that we let it go, through neglect, by grasping at earthly good, or at some glittering bauble of Satan.

The forces and wiles of error are innumerable. It assumes the very forms and usurps the very names of the most precious truths. Inspiration, divinity, atonement, consecration, Christ, the Holy Ghost, and every other term of the kingdom, are perfectly familiar to its vocabulary. Its false prophets in these days swarm everywhere; and fulfill to the letter the description of our Lord, that "they shall show great signs and wonders, insomuch that (if it were possible) they shall deceive the very elect." No human wisdom can enable us to hold fast divine and saving truth. It never can be held by the head; the heart alone can keep it. And *it* can keep it only as it works it into and assimilates it with the whole spiritual being. Nothing but the indwelling Spirit of God, the Spirit of life, can give even to the heart this power. Only that Divine Spirit that searcheth all things, yea the deep things of God, can keep the soul from sinking in these depths of Satan, depths of boastful wisdom, of sophistical reasoning, and Satanic cunning. But that can make even the foolish wise. "Ye have an unction from the Holy One, and ye know all things. . . . These things have I written unto you concerning them that seduce you. But the anointing which ye have re-

§. Dangers, warnings, and means of safety.

ceived of Him abideth in you, and ye need not that any man teach you: but as the same anointing teacheth you of all things, and is truth, and is no lie, and even as it hath taught you, ye shall abide in Him." ([2]) In these matters of religious truth and duty, we "need not that *any man* teach" us; it is not science, or learning, or logic that we want. Valuable as these are, they can never even tell us what God is, or what He requires, or what He will bestow; much less can they make us like Him. God Himself must be our teacher; first, in His inspired word showing us what is truth, and then by the enlightening Spirit renewing the heart and purifying the spiritual vision. Away with all human teachings, properly so-called; all man can do is to tell his fellow-man what God has already taught, to be a witness, to deliver a testimony.

In the midst, then, of all the devices of error, that under pretence of unfolding the deep and hidden things of God, are only bringing down the mysteries of His nature and government to the low level of man's thinking, let the true believer only remember the charge of his Lord to this church, and these words of His servant John just quoted, and let him hold fast to the truth revealed in the written word, and just as it is revealed, setting aside all human additions, and testify to it in the face of human pride and power, and he has nothing to fear. This is a burden we must bear, and to which we must hold fast,— to which the church and believer must cling till Christ comes. Not till then will error cease its assaults, and foul apostacy its desolations, and Satan no longer transform himself into an angel of light. Till then the light will not be perfect, till then spirits from the pit will talk like angels from heaven. Then, and not before, shall all darkness flee away, and all delusions vanish, and all the

[2] 1 John ii: 20–27.

mysteries which now baffle our reason, and try our faith, be cleared up in the undimmed light of an eternal day. Nay, not *all* mysteries. While God is infinite, and man is finite, there must ever stretch before the creature's vision a glorious and illimitable field of mystery, into the bright regions of which He shall be eternally progressing, and in the light of God discovering new wonders of wisdom, power and love.

Then, too, in those final victories of the Mediatorial reign, when He shall come, shall be fulfilled the glowing promise which appropriately closes this message to a church struggling against the wily force of error, backed by the power and wisdom of the world in its darkness. It is a promise that, through fellowship with Christ in His final triumph, the believer shall tread the powers of earth beneath his feet; and that the darkness of the long night shall for him be dispelled by Christ as the morning star ushering in the brightness of unmingled and eternal truth. "We wait for His appearing."

LECTURE VIII.

THE SAME SUBJECT CONTINUED: SARDIS, PHILADELPHIA, AND LAODICEA.

5. SARDIS, OR SPIRITUAL DEADNESS.

A Church honoured, but dead.

CHAP. III: 1-3.

FOR many ages this city had been celebrated for its wealth and magnificence. It was one of the most beautifully situated cities in all Asia. In allusion to its wealth, the river Pactolus, on which it was situated, is spoken of by the poets as flowing over its golden sands. It was the capital, six hundred years before, of the kingdom of Lydia, the name of whose last king, Crœsus, has become proverbial for unbounded wealth. In the time of John, it still retained much of ancient splendour. It is now a wretched village, inhabited only by a few shepherds and herdsmen, whose flocks and herds feed upon the rich pastures of the fertile plain that stretches away for miles before it.

There, in the midst of its wealth and profligacy, a church had been established, when or by whom, we know not. It had become distinguished among its sister churches, and seems to have been congratulating itself as being quite as prosperous, if not more so than most other churches of the province. There were no divisions within, and no fierce conflicts without. Thus satisfied with the good opinion of their brethren, and soothing any se-

§. A mere reputation for life.

cret upbraidings of conscience with the delightful unction that their reputation was high among the churches, that they were honoured on account of their outward prosperity as a truly live church,—how it must have shocked their self-complacency, when, as they were assembled together to receive this new message from the aged apostle in Patmos, to whom, they were told, Jesus had just appeared and had Himself delivered it, to hear, in the words of their ascended Lord Himself, "I know thy works, that thou hast a name that thou livest, and art dead." "I knew these works of thine, which have procured for thee this reputation for spiritual life; others see only the exterior, others therefore may praise you, and hold you up as a model church, and stimulate your pride to still further labours of self-righteousness; but I who search the heart, I know they are dead works; they are not the earnest spontaneous outgoings of a heart all alive with grateful love to Me. It is only a reputation for life that thou hast, 'but thou art dead.'" Such is the brief, terrible and startling charge against this church of Sardis.

Yet, in all that man could see, this may have been a model church. The Lord does not charge her with any special sin. Her liberality and charity, her adherence to sound doctrine and morals, her observance of ordinances were all such that the mere superficial observer could see nothing to censure, but very much to praise. The visitor from poor and persecuted Smyrna, and from weak and tried and labouring Philadelphia, which was only a day's ride distant, would go home and speak to their suffering brethren of what great things Sardis was doing, how liberally it supported its pastor, how it cared for its poor, what a fine church they had, and how little they were molested by the heathen around them, and indeed how even the heathen seemed to respect them, were quite friendly with them, and seemed often to enjoy their society. If a close observer and spiritually minded, the fear might have arisen that this apparent friendliness of the world might possibly come from some softening of the church's testimony against its ungodliness, and foul idolatries. Such a one, too, if admitted to their social meetings and family circles, would have felt that there was a great and palpable defect in the loving warmth and energy of their devotions, an appearance of formality and constraint in conversing on spiritual subjects entirely different from the earnestness and interest manifested in the business and political topics of that day, such as might well awaken wonder and fear lest all might not be just what it seemed to be.

Certain it is that Christ in this message says not one word about defects censured so severely in other churches; about divisions or heresies; about eating meat in idol temples or fornication; about Balaamites or Nicolaitanes, or a Jezebel, or even about any failure in discipline. Neither was it oppressed with poverty or crushed with persecution, as Smyrna was, so as to need consolation. Its whole state is described in these comprehensive and expressive words, "a name that thou livest, and art dead,"—honoured, yet dead.

This is a most sad and perilous condition for any church to be found in; and yet it is a very frequent state of churches outwardly prosperous. It is a kind of galvanized corpse. The motions of life are there, but life itself is gone. Men may be made, a church may be made, to go through the motions of piety for a while, by the force of other motives than the love of Jesus. It would be a hideous sight to see the dead body of a dear friend under some such galvanic influence, going through all the motions of the living organism, and stretching forth its icy arms to clasp you in their close embrace; but a far more hideous and abhorrent sight is it, in the eyes of a holy God, to see the motions and actions proper to the spiritual life simulated by a dead soul, under the force of a secret self-righteousness—reaching forth toward Him, not the living desires of a soul longing for His love, but the dead forms of heartless prayer, and a formal mercenary service, as destitute of true love as the corpse of life. But horrible as it is, it is very certain that many a church, and many a soul, since Sardis perished, has been just in this Sardian state, having a reputation for life, going through its outward motions, but spiritually dead.

Two other expressions of our Lord in this message elucidate this condition. First—"I have not found thy works perfect before God."

§. Works imperfect and defiled.

"Perfect" here cannot mean sinless perfection, the want of which could not be evidence of spiritual death. It means, "filled up," "completed;" their works were wanting in some essential element to make them what they professed to be. Observe, it was not the want of works for which they are censured, but for a defect in the character of their works. What that defect was, we have seen. They were works of dead, not of living souls; at least of souls in which spiritual deadness concealed any hidden life that might exist. Every work of such a church and of such a soul, every act of charity, and every form of worship, is defective in that which is its very essence. However full and complete before men, they are not "filled up" "*before God:*" in His sight they are hollow, mere shells without the precious kernel. Let every church standing high in the estimation of others, and prosperous in her external circumstances, remember that while men are praising, Christ may be frowning, and His judgments impending, as a thief in the night. Human eyes may detect no flaw, where the eye of Jesus sees only death.

The other expression referred to is, "defiled garments." This of course could not mean those daily defilements which are removed by constant resort to the blood of atonement, by one living near to the cross, and walking by faith in Christ. They are such as are contracted, not so much by sudden falls in the mire through the fierce assaults of temptation, as by wilfully and habitually walking and living amidst the dust and smoke and murky atmosphere of the world, and lying down on the tinselled but filthy bed of its pleasures. All this may be while yet the forms of godliness are gone through with, and to man's imperfect vision, no special dark spot be visible.

But bad as things were in Sardis, it was still a true church. Though the *deadness* was real and pervasive and paralyzing, it was not yet complete *death*. Some things remained, though even these were ready to die. These things cannot mean persons, referring to the few that were undefiled, though it includes their influence. There were still some gracious things, some latent sparks of life, some uneasiness of conscience, some sense of guilt, some feeling of shame, and some real desires after holiness, as well as an outward adherence to God's worship and word.

§. Things remaining.

To them, therefore, the charge is, "Be watchful, and strengthen the things which remain, that are ready to die." *Awake.* Such a church is asleep, and all its fancied prosperity is but the dreams of the spiritual sleeper. Such a soul never once seriously suspects its real condition, or if at any time a fear arises, it is quickly repelled by the thought of its unstained Christian reputation.

§. The charge and warning.

This insensibility is the most alarming feature of this condition. It is like the physical torpor that seizes upon the almost frozen traveller, and impels to sleep. Nothing but the most desperate effort can recover it. Indeed, left to itself, the poor soul will be just like such a traveller, it will sink down into the sleep of death. It usually requires, not only the reiterated warnings of God's word to be sounded in the ears, but generally some startling, crushing, humbling providences, to strike the stupid soul, and arouse it from its dreams of carnal security and worldly ease. Sickness, worldly losses, bitter disappointments, sore bereavements, or what is still worse, being left to fall into some open sin, are, one or more of them, the means used to awaken such, if there be any salvation for them. Nothing but speedy repentance under the awakening calls of His word, can prevent these and still worse judgments. Hence Christ says, "Remember therefore how thou hast received and heard, and hold fast and repent. If, therefore, thou shalt not watch, I will come on thee as a thief, and thou shalt not know what hour I will come upon thee."

If any language could, these words of our Divine Lord would startle, not only into wakefulness, but terror, every sleeping church, and every sleeper in it. "I will come as a thief." I will give no previous warning. As His coming at the second advent, so will be His coming to inflict judgment on every sleeping church and professor. "When they shall say, Peace and safety, then sudden destruction cometh upon them." When they are dreaming that all is well, the crash of judgment shall, like thunder, make them spring from their spiritual sleep, to feel the fragments of their earthly hopes and joys all shattered and tumbling in ruins around them; or they are suddenly waked up by finding that already some strong and fierce temptation has seized them in their sleep, and ere they were aware, dragged them down, like poor David and Peter, into the power of some terrible, lurking sin, and left them all wounded, bruised and bleeding. "Thou shalt not know what hour I will come upon thee." Literally, "*what kind of hour:*" whether in health or sickness, in prosperity or adversity, in joy or sorrow; in loss of friends, of reputation, of health, or of goods. All may seem like the fatal morning in Sodom, when the redden-

§. The sleeper's danger.

ing dawn, and the sun rising in his brightness, gave promise of a day bright as any that had ever shone upon her, just as Lot was hurrying from her gates, and the fiery storm of vengeance was about to burst forth. Fancy not that all is safe, because you can see no signs of danger,—because you neither see nor feel the preparations for coming judgment. You will never see the coming infliction till it falls.

Is there a reader of these pages who is sleeping amidst all the mighty and pressing interests of the kingdom of Christ and the world to come? Especially, a professed member of this kingdom, sunk down in spiritual sloth? Could the veil be lifted that conceals the preparations that are going on at this moment for your chastisement or signal punishment, your face would gather blackness, and your soul sink in dismay. But you cannot see them. Yet there they are, behind that impenetrable veil where God hides His coming providences, just as certainly as if we saw them. "If thou shalt not watch, I will come on thee as a thief."

But we have omitted thus far an important clause.

§. Remember past mercies.

Wrath may arouse the sleeper, but only love can melt the heart. It is the goodness of God that leads to repentance. This threatening of judgment, accordingly, is preceded by a tender appeal to the mercies of God. "Remember, therefore, how thou hast received and heard, and hold fast and repent." This "*how*," of course, has reference both to the matter and magnitude, as well as to the manner of the blessings bestowed. Let such a church review the past history of His dealings with her, and if there be a spark of love it will be enkindled. The hardest heart must melt in view of the magnitude and tenderness of redeeming grace, and long-suffering patience. Remember how largely, how tenderly, how undeservedly thou hast received! What abounding mercies, privileges, instructions, promises, warnings, ordinances, influences of the Spirit, and free offers of all the fulness of faith, and hope, and joy! Remember the everlasting covenant, the precious blood that sealed it, and that cleanseth from all sin, the baptism that pledges its blessings, the boundless love so often commemorated at His table, the tenderness of His human sympathy, the constancy of His all prevalent intercessions, and His divine power; and *hold fast*, and repent.

Even in such worldly and backslidden churches, however, there is often a remnant who are faithful; who, in the midst of general defection, keep themselves unspotted from the world, as there was at Sardis. "Thou hast a few names, even in Sardis, which have not defiled their garments." These are each known by name to Him, and marked with special favour, and assured of a far higher honour than that which comes from man; "they shall walk before Me in white, for they are worthy." This is a worthiness not of merit, but of fitness, and wrought by grace, and, therefore, excluding all boasting. Such a remnant, in such a church, is sure to be unpopular, regarded as enthusiasts or extremists, as narrow-minded, austere and impracticable. For all this, and much more, they find in this promise an all-sufficient compensation. Let every believer beware how he suffers his opinions and practices to be moulded by the mass of professing Christians around him. The state of the church is too often such that nearness to Christ, and a share in His promises, are only in proportion to your singularity, not only from the world, but in the church itself.

§. The faithful few.

Mark how appropriately Christ presents Himself to this church, and to others like it. "He that hath the seven spirits of God,"— *i. e.*, the Holy Spirit, in His perfect, all-sufficient and manifold operations; "and the seven stars,"

§. Encouragement.

whose authority pervades His churches, and gives efficacy to their teaching and discipline. If then they were dead, pervaded with the spirit of the world, instead of the spirit of holiness, it was not because of any deficiency in the agency, which was divine, or the instrumentality, which was of His appointment, and sustained by His power. When, therefore, He calls upon us to watch, to remember, to hold fast and repent, He thus reminds us that He holds an infinite sufficiency of grace to quicken our dead souls, and that, in the means of His appointment, the ministry and ordinances of His church, there is a divine adaptedness to secure that grace.

In the closing promise to him that overcometh, the same beautiful adaptation to the circumstances of the believer in such a church is evident. He shall be clothed in garments of purity and glory; His name shall never be erased from the book of life, as the names of these Sardian backsliders deserved to be from the record of the church on earth; and though despised and misunderstood, even by professed brethren here, he shall stand confessed of Christ before His father and the holy angels. This is honour indeed infinitely beyond all earthly reputation. This is life eternal.

6. Philadelphia, or Spiritual Power. A Church Feeble, yet Conquering.

Chap. iii: 7-11.

We have here another church which passes, without censure, under the searching eye of Jesus.

§. Uncensured. It is a most encouraging truth, that of these seven churches, two are uncensured; that even amidst all the imperfections of the present life, there are two to whom He sees necessary to utter only words of approval and encouragement. For that they are without censure, was not because these churches were composed of sinless saints; it was not that they were not sadly burdened with imperfections, and their character sadly defaced by shortcomings; it was not because, in the individual believers that composed them, He saw no sins that grieved His holy and loving heart. But what He saw and approved was that their sins were laid on Him; they were daily taking refuge in His blood, and turning away from their own best works, were looking for acceptance only in His righteousness. Being thus in habitual communion with Him in His death and merits, they were so also in His life, and hence were earnestly engaged in the daily struggle of the spiritual warfare, and grieving over the sins that grieved Him.

This is implied in the reason here assigned by our Lord for His approval. " For thou hast kept My word, and hast not denied My name."

§ Commendations.

..... "Because thou hast kept the word of My patience." The word of Jesus is, first of all, His word of justifying grace, that precious gospel of the kingdom that testifies to the efficacy of His blood and righteousness, for our perfect pardon and acceptance— " Christ, the end of the law for righteousness to every one that believeth." To keep that word, is so to wrap it up in the strongest and tenderest emotions of the heart, and especially in the living tissues of a simple and earnest faith growing all around it, that it becomes a part of our very being; and " we hold fast the confidence and the rejoicing of the hope firm unto the end." Then, too, will His word of authority be no burden, but precious as the shining light to the tempest-tossed mariner; " His commandments are not grievous." Then will His word of promise also be so received into a trusting heart as to minister the mighty grace of the Holy Spirit, strengthening for every duty and trial. That promise, " I will keep thee," will be held fast even when trials are sore and protracted, and long expected deliverances or spiritual consolations are delayed; and through the long night the soul will wait for His appearing and salvation; "the word of His patience"—ministering His patience—will be kept, and, being kept, it will keep the keeper. "Because thou hast kept the word of My patience, I also will keep thee."

Christ adds to this ground of commendation, "and hast not denied My name." It is such a keeping of the word of Jesus, and nothing else, that will keep a church, or a believer, from denying His name like Peter. His name as Teacher, in opposition to the pride of human reason and worldly wisdom,—His name as Priest, atoning and interceding,—His name as King, her almighty ruler and defender, will be infinitely precious. "Yea, doubtless, I count all things but loss, for the excellency of the knowledge of Christ Jesus my Lord." No soul ever yet denied Christ in any degree, who did not first neglect His word.

§ Yet feeble. Yet this was but a feeble church. In immediate connection with these commendations, it is first said as a reason of the usefulness promised her, "For thou hast little strength," not "*a* little strength," as in our version. "*I* will enlarge thee, for thou art few and feeble," is the idea. In every sense in which men estimate strength, in wealth, in worldly influence, and in numbers, this church therefore appears to have been weak. But it is just such that Jesus delights to honour. This very feebleness, united with such faithfulness, made it a specially appropriate instrument of His power. The treasure is placed in earthen vessels, that the excellency of the power may be of God. As the Lord said to Paul, "My grace is sufficient for thee: for My strength is made perfect in weakness," so He says to every feeble and faithful church and believer. And, with the apostle, such may respond, "Most gladly, therefore, will I rather glory in my infirmities, that the power of Christ may rest upon me." The want of earthly resources, of numbers and wealth, and worldly influence, and high social position, need never be any cause of solicitude or discouragement to the church. It should rather have the opposite effect. She should remember Gideon's three hundred. She should remember the rams' horns of Jericho. "Not by might, nor by power, but by My Spirit, saith the Lord of Hosts." She should cast away all dependence on external power, on the arm of civil government, and on the influence of wealth, or learning, or eloquence, when she has them; and, when she has them not, all longing for them as needful to her success; but looking up to the unseen throne of her risen Saviour, and waiting for Pentecostal effusions of the Holy Spirit, let her keep the word of His patience, in her weakness, saying with Paul, "Therefore I take pleasure in infirmities, in reproaches, in necessities, in persecutions, in distresses for Christ's sake; for when I am weak, then am I strong."

Now it is to this feeble, but faithful and waiting church, that our Lord gives the only special promise in all these epistles, of success in extending the triumphs of His kingdom. "I have set before thee an open door, and no man can shut it.(¹) . . . . . Behold, I will make them of the synagogue of Satan, which say they are Jews, and are not, but do lie; behold, I will make them to come and worship before thy feet, and to know that I have loved thee." This is an open door of usefulness, and these are victories of love. No higher honour can His church have on earth than this. When the King in His power opens the way to usefulness, not all the powers of earth or hell can close it. The nations may rage, as they have often done—may clothe themselves in all their pomp, and marshal their power, as at the Diet of Worms, with

§ An open door.

(¹) Comp. 1 Cor. 16:9. 2 Cor. 2:12. Col. 4:1:3.

a feeble monk summoned before them,—they imagine a vain thing. Infidelity may summon her strength, and multiply her sophisms, and pervert the lessons of Providence, and the facts of history, and the teachings of the stars and the rocks, as she has done, and is still doing: He that sitteth in the heavens shall laugh, and even men shall have them in derision. An apostate church may invoke the whole power of the world, may multiply her prisons, and kindle her fires, she can neither imprison nor burn the truth; she cannot shut the door that Jesus has opened to the feeble messenger of truth who goes forth only in His name, and in the secret might of His Spirit. So far from this, the most violent of the opposers, the members even of an apostate church—"the synagogue of Satan"—shall, like those apostate Jews of Philadelphia, come and bow down before the simple majesty and divine force of gospel truth, as seen in the earnest and faithful Church of Christ. It was so most strikingly at the Reformation, when, in the power of earthly weakness, and a simple, divine testimony, the true church arose and entered the open door her Lord had set before her, and thousands joyfully felt and acknowledged her power, and came to share in that love with which He had crowned her. So it ever has been, and shall be.

It was the word of God, which this church had kept, that enabled her to enter this open door, and armed her invincibly against all opposing powers. That word "cannot be bound;" neither can the church which makes it its treasure and its strength, of which it is the life.

> His very word of grace is strong
> As that which built the skies;
> The voice that rolls the stars along,
> Speaks all the promises.

It is the voice of Him who here declares Himself to this feeble church as "He that is holy, He that is true,"—He in whom are truly realized all the attributes of Jehovah, summed up in that one word "holy:" as "He that hath the key of David,"—the whole power of David's throne, as the Head of the kingdom of God—who has it now, and in His person has transferred it to the right hand of the Majesty on high, and is now administering it; as "He, therefore, that openeth and no man shutteth, and shutteth and no man openeth."[1] How this announcement of His present reign, and His irresistible power, to the saints in Philadelphia, must have sent a thrill of spiritual energy through all their souls, and infused a courage into the most feeble, to do and to dare great things for Jesus. And shall it not still animate to livelier faith and zeal His struggling church, until He come to crown all her triumphs?

This is not all. Beside the open door of usefulness, and the conversion of her enemies, still another blessing is promised to this church. It is security from the storm of fierce trial that was impending. "Because thou hast kept the word of My patience, I will keep thee from the hour of temptation, which shall come upon all the world to try them that dwell upon the earth." To be kept from, "out of" the hour of temptation or trial, cannot mean not to suffer temptation and trial, but to be saved from its power, to be kept through it, and brought safely out of it. A most precious assurance this to the church and the believer in a world whose very nature it is to tempt and to try, when the believer may be always apprehending the advent of that hour here predicted. For this is not to be taken as the prediction of a specific time of trial that was to come and pass away once for all, but as the announcement of the fact that none in any age, or

§ Security.

---

[1] Comp. Is. 22: 22. "And the key of the house of David will I lay upon his shoulder; so he shall open, and none shall shut; and he shall shut, and none shall open." And Is. 9: 6, 7. Jer. 23: 5. Luke 1: 32. Acts 2: 36.

place, or circumstances, can escape this hour. It must come upon all generations, as well as all nations and churches. No sphere of duty or usefulness, no degree of Christian attainment is secure, no place in the church so high or so low as to escape it. It shall come upon all the world, to try all them that dwell upon the earth. Only in heaven, and in the new world, wherein dwelleth righteousness, can we hope to escape its assaults. But all they who faithfully hold fast the word of Christ, shall be kept by His power, and brought safely out of it. In whatsoever form it may come, assaulting the soul through the body, the estate, the reputation, or the friends of our bosom, or directly striking the spirit itself with the fiery darts of Satan, still the promise, "I will keep thee;" keep thee *out of* it, from the lips of the King Himself, is enough. "God is faithful, who will not suffer you to be tempted above that ye are able; but will, with the temptation, also make a way to escape, that ye may be able to bear it."

These promises are all crowned with the assurance, "Behold, I come quickly." This to the struggling church and waiting believer is the sum of all promises. He comes in the prompt and mighty supports of His Spirit, in the deliverances of His Providence, in the reception of the disembodied spirit to Himself; but these are but the foretastes of the triumph at His second visible appearing. This is the assurance that soon the struggle will be ended, the battle fought, the victory won; that soon not only shall temptation cease to harrass, and indwelling sin to pollute, and hell to assault, and the purified spirit soar away to be with the spirits of just men made perfect; but that death itself, the last enemy, shall be destroyed, and the body itself raised and fashioned like unto Christ's glorious body, and the whole perfected church be admitted to the full glories of the resurrection state and the

§. Christ's coming, and her crown.

eternal kingdom. "Quickly," says Jesus. "Quickly!" let the church reply; and gathering from the bright and cheering hope fresh courage and energy, still keep the word of His patience, and enter with zeal each open door, and so be ready to welcome His appearing, both in its foretastes and its great consummation.

"Hold fast that which thou hast, that no man take thy crown." Let her hold fast by the grace of the indwelling Spirit, the word that has hitherto been her strength and comfort; let her hold fast to the self-denying service and toil to which her Lord has called her, that no enemy, by seducing her from her allegiance, into a life of selfish ease and worldliness, deprive her of her crown. That crown belongs only to conquerors. "If any man draw back," shrink from the toils and trials of this service, "My soul shall have no pleasure in him." But to the conqueror is here given the glowing promise, enough to stimulate to any labour and suffering, of a permanent and eternal dwelling place in the temple of God, amidst His revealed glory, and of bearing His image, and of admission to all the blessed privileges of citizenship in the new Jerusalem, and participation in the new name of Christ, the as yet unrevealed glories of His perfected kingdom.

§ His word and his work.

Surely no church of Christ, however feeble, can ever contemplate this example of a church in its weakness achieving these spiritual conquests for Christ, and inheriting such promises, and anticipating such glory, and yet be faint-hearted or fearful; or, in its weakness, turn to earthly helpers. Especially it will not, when it considers the contrasted example of the next and last and worst of all the seven.

7. LAODICEA, OR LUKEWARMNESS.

A Church strong, self-sufficient, but lukewarm and loathsome.

Chap. iii., 14-20.

This presents us with a phase of church character in every respect the opposite of the last.
§ The worst of all. Abounding in wealth, and every other external advantage, this church felt no need of any thing. The words plainly indicate great temporal prosperity, as well as spiritual pride. Filled with plenty, surrounded by splendour, supported by worldly power, and rejoicing in its ease and self-indulgence, it imagined itself equally rich in spiritual goods and the divine favour: it dreamed not of its utter loathsomeness, and how very near it was to utter rejection. Its real character is in terrible contrast with its pride and self-sufficiency. " I know thy works, that thou art neither cold nor hot. I would thou wert cold or hot. So, then, because thou art lukewarm, and neither cold nor hot, I will spew thee out of My mouth. Because thou sayest, I am rich, and increased with goods, and have need of nothing; and knowest not that thou art wretched, and miserable, and poor, and blind, and naked."

There is not one relieving trait, not one single feature upon which even the gentle and loving eye of Jesus can bestow a single commendation. Yet it has not apostatized from the truth; it is not guilty of foul heresy; it has followed no Jezebel; it is charged with no Nicolaitan doctrine or deeds; the whole is summed up in the expressive word, "lukewarm," "neither cold nor hot." For a church, or a follower of Jesus Christ, while recognizing His divine claims, His infinite love, His precious blood, His almighty Spirit, His sweet and holy service, and His promised glory, to treat it all with indifference, to be unmoved, or slightly moved by it, to manifest no warm affection, no earnest devotion, no self-denying and self-sacrificing zeal, is specially insulting to Him, and indicates a degree of insensibility almost past hope. It would be past belief, if it were not so common. For dreadful as this condition is, the very fact that no church of all the seven is so often referred to, and more familiar in the thinking and preaching of the churches generally, shows the universal consciousness that this Laodicean state has ever prevailed very extensively.

The worst feature of such a condition is, that it so effectually conceals itself. "Thou knowest not." To such self-sufficiency and spiritual pride, its vilest rags seem like royal robes; its filth appears to be gold and diamonds; its mercenary and proud services, a holiness that merits reward. It seems to itself on the very threshold of heaven when ready to fall into the lowest hell. Such a church, with all its self-complacency and confidence, has less of the marks of a true church than any other that Christ acknowledges. It is on the very point of utter rejection, and that with abhorrence: "I will spew thee out of My mouth." As thus translated, these words seem to express the fixed and unchanging purpose or decision to reject it. This is too strong. The precise meaning is, "I am about"[1] to do this; implying still a brief interval allowed for repentance, before it is thus with loathing and violence rejected.

§ Self-ignorance.

Hence, with a compassion, tenderness, and patience truly divine, He adds these counsels of salvation, these offers of His abounding grace; tried gold for their poverty, white raiment for their nakedness, and eye salve for their blindness. He reminds them, that as many as He loves He rebukes and He chastens; be zealous, therefore, and repent; a warning in which it is hard to say which most

§ Long suffering.

[1] μέλλω.

prevails, the tenderness or the holy displeasure. He then presents Himself to this very church, so careless, so proud, and so loathsome, in an attitude of infinite condescension and tenderness; enough, one would think, to move the most indifferent, and to melt the hardest heart. "Behold, I stand at the door and knock: if any man hear My voice, and open the door, I will come in to him, and will sup with him, and he with Me." In uttering these words, He would have His church regard Him in the character here announced,—"the Amen, the Faithful and true Witness,"—the only real, and perfect, and unerring revealer of the divine will and mercy; and "the beginning of the creation of God," the origin and author of the whole creation of God, who, therefore, has all power and wisdom to make good all He promises. It is He who thus combines with the tenderest sympathies of our human nature the all-sufficiency of God, who is standing at the door of His churches, and patiently knocking and waiting for admission, in order that every soul that opens to Him may enter into fellowship with Him, in all the fulness of His joys.

He, therefore, enforces all with the final promise, than which nothing can rise higher, of sharing with Him in His throne, not merely the blessings of His mediatorial reign, but in the spiritual power and glory of His consummated and everlasting kingdom.

III. CONCLUDING INFERENCES FROM THIS SEVEN-FOLD VIEW.

On the whole of this view of the varieties and imperfections of the visible church, or militant kingdom of Christ, we offer the following remarks:

1. *The completeness of this seven-fold picture.*—These examples so gather up and classify, and reduce to a few general principles, all the proofs of faithfulness,

and the forms of imperfection, and even all external states and temptations, that every church may recognize its own features, and receive its own message. Every enemy is distinctly pointed out; every snare and ambuscade of these foes exposed. The poison that works in secret, and the violence and blasphemy that defies the very heavens; the declining affection, the faint-heartedness, the worldly desires and fleshly lusts, indifference to true doctrine, regard for human honour, discouragements arising from weakness and opposition; pride, self-righteousness and indifference, these, and others like them, are here presented in their true character and tendency. Here is orthodoxy waxing cold, and the martyr spirit waxing worldly, and charitable zeal becoming heretical, and spiritual death concealed under a showy formality, and spiritual loathsomeness under a proud self-righteousness. Here is heathen idolatry and Jewish bigotry; defiant heresy and profound rationalism; Sadducean self-indulgence, and Pharisaic formalism.

Here, too, we have found warnings suited to every danger, counsels for every emergency, and rich consolations and promises for every sorrow and trial. The work of faith, and labour of love, and patience of hope; the union of holiness of life with purity of doctrine, and the power of a simple and faithful testimony, are all here crowned with the praise and blessing of Jesus. But loveliest and brightest among these seven candlesticks, flinging their radiance down all along the path of the church, through the ages of her conflict, shine those of Smyrna and Philadelphia. These are the types of a pure and faithful church; the one treading a bloody path to prisons and death; the other in her feebleness carrying forward the banner of the Son of David to fresh conquests of love and grace. But nothing short of the gathered and condensed experience of the militant church, in all ages, can show how perfect and complete this sevenfold picture of it is. The more these epistles are studied, the more wonderful will they appear, and the more worthy to have been dictated, just as they are, by the lips of a glorified Saviour, as with omniscient eye He gazed upon all the exigencies of His suffering church, and worthy to be His last direct messages, to guide and comfort her till His second coming.

It deserves special observation that in all these seven epistles our Lord never so much as alludes once to any outward forms. In this comprehensive view of the churches, in which everything deserving censure is censured, and every thing worthy of praise is praised, mere forms of worship, ritualistic observances, are not even noticed. Nothing could show more conclusively how utterly contrary to the whole nature of the gospel, and of the spiritual church, is the tendency to attach to such things any importance, much more to make them essential terms of Christian communion.

So far as these churches give any indication of their attention to such things, by the character given of them, we should conclude that the two most severely censured, were the two most noted of all for their punctilious observance of outward forms. All of these churches were so careful and punctilious in adhering to such things, that there was nothing to be censured,—or they were not. If they were, it did not keep them pure, it did them no good, and they receive no commendation for it. If they were not, the fact that Christ does not notice it, proves it to be a matter of no importance to their spiritual state, or their standing in His sight.

2. These messages have a *special application to the authorities of every Church*. Addressed immediately to the messenger of Christ to each church, they not only lay upon Him the responsibility of faithfully representing the message, but of seeing to its faithful execution. His is the responsibility of administering the law as well as

promulgating it. In the preservation of truth and purity, in upholding pure worship and discipline, the church must act through her rulers and teachers.

In these two things, her worship and discipline, the whole testimony of the church is concentrated. In her prayers, her praises and her preaching, and her daily consecration, Christ must be the supreme object of trust and love; and in her discipline, His authority alone must be regarded. If His cross be obscured, or His crown dishonoured, her power is gone, her glory departed. The vigour or the decline of love, of faith, of courage, of separation from the world, of pure doctrine, of earnest zeal and humility, always, and necessarily, become apparent and powerful for good or for evil, in precisely these two ways—worship and discipline. The messages to Pergamos and Thyatira especially show how a corrupted worship, tolerated by a lax discipline, had incurred the displeasure of the Lord. The most earnest watchfulness on the part of those entrusted with the worship and discipline of the church is essential to her well-being. If open inconsistencies are tolerated, if those who are openly disloyal to Christ are acknowledged as His by those who represent His authority in the church, her testimony is obscured or falsified, the honour of Christ is tarnished, the souls of the erring and backsliding endangered, and hearts of God's people made sad. The same neglect of discipline, which was so severely censured in the churches of Pergamos and Thyatira, repeated in other churches and ages, has opened the door to those errors and apostacies that have desolated so large a portion of the church. Let all, then, who have authority in the church be faithful to their high duty, and neglect no means of preventing corruption in her worship and discipline. It is a greatly mistaken tenderness to tolerate as nominal members those who virtually disown the authority of Christ. We must be careful, however, that in administering firmly the discipline of Christ's house, love wax not cold, and that all the tenderness of Christ, as shown in these epistles, mingle with and temper every act. Let space be given for repentance, as Christ gave even to the backsliders of Thyatira; let patience have her perfect work here as every where else; but let not Christ's honour, and the soul's salvation, and the church's safety be imperilled by neglecting to inflict those spiritual penalties which He has appointed for edification and not for destruction.

3. *The full display it presents of His perfect divinity.*— Prominent in all this picture of the church shines the glory of Christ Himself. He assumes the titles, and claims the attributes, and exercises the prerogatives of God, even when He walks as a man in the midst of the seven golden candlesticks. No creature, angelic or superangelic, could appropriate such terms. If these do not prove a divine person, a true and perfect God, no language can. To the believer, therefore, who has fled for refuge to Him, these views of His divine glory, in immediate connection with His offices as Saviour, and His nature as man, are infinitely precious. Upon this cardinal truth no shade of doubt can ever gather, without unsettling every true ground of trust and hope. To deny this doctrine is to exclude from all share in these messages, it is to deny Him. To acknowledge as a church of Christ any society that denies it, is treason to Him, and cruelty to souls, even to the souls of those denying it.

4. Not less forcibly do these epistles present *Christ as now in person reigning over His church and the world, and actually present with His people.* We are elsewhere told that He has ascended to the right hand of the Majesty on high, that the heavens have received Him until the time of the restitution of all things, when He will come visibly again to earth. But we are also taught abun-

dantly that that absence is merely a bodily absence, not a personal absence; not an absence inconsistent with His personal and real, though spiritual, presence. Strangely have the words personal and real, applied to the presence and reign of Christ, often been used as if opposed to the actual, present spiritual reign; as if, being spiritual, it were not personal and real; as if the spiritual was not more truly real and all-controlling, even over the outward and visible world of nature and Providence, than that which is visible and material. The spiritual is opposed only to the material and visible; not to the personal and real: it would be much nearer correct to say that the material and visible were opposed to the personal and real. This abuse of language has not been without injurious effect upon the conceptions of the faith of His church. In looking for His visible appearing in that glorified human body that ascended from Olivet, and confounding that with His personal presence and reign, they have too often, practically at least, lost sight of the blessed and cheering truth of His present real presence, and personal reign. Having become a man; having borne to the throne of His Father the body and soul He assumed as our Mediator, He still, as a divine person, holding that glorified nature in indissoluble union with Him, is, according to His promise, personally and always present.

And here, in these visions and messages, we see Him actually revealing Himself as personally present in and with His churches now; in every state and condition looking down upon them from His throne, witnessing all their works, Himself extending the succours of His grace, and inflicting the strokes of His rod, and in actual, living, personal communion with every soul that trusts in Him.

This present dispensation is His *personal reign*, and *His personal presence*, in a glorious and perfect sense, which it could never be if He were on earth, subject to the conditions of flesh and blood. We are taught, indeed, to look for a visible presence, and a visible reign, and, as we think, *with* His people here on earth; but it will be, and can be only when all the conditions of our existence are changed, and the whole earth itself so changed as to be adapted to them: a condition in which all things will be in harmony with the resurrection state, and of the visibilities of which, if we may so speak, we can form now no adequate conception. But His presence now is just as real, and as personal, for His person is divine, and only divine, as it will be then, though not visible and bodily. Let us realize this more, and rejoice in it. It is no mere shadowy thing. It is no mere figure of speech or of thought. It is as much a reality as the presence of the spirit of your dearest friend, when his body is in your sight. You see not his spirit, but you know it is there. His body is only the evidence of his spirit's presence. The body of Jesus is not before your eyes; but you have His repeated assurances that it is where its presence is the fullest possible evidence of His universal personal presence and reign. While His bodily presence was with His disciples, they could not comprehend and realize His divine presence; it was not until He had ascended, and the truth of His actual enthronement clearly revealed, that they reached those higher conceptions of His perpetual personal presence, that afterwards filled them with such joy and power. To His parting promise, then, let us seek to give a fuller meaning and realization, that in it we may have the assurance of something *more* than a bodily presence—a divine presence united with a human heart. "Lo, I am with you always, even unto the end of the world."

5. Finally, we would direct attention to the practical value of this whole picture of the visible kingdom, *as a test of the true church.* " What are the essential marks of

a true church ?"—and, "What degree of error in doctrine and duty, in worship and discipline, is necessary to exclude any body or society from the church of Christ ?" are questions that have been often and warmly discussed. It might have appeared to some that any serious departure from truth and duty, any open neglect of the administration of Christ's laws would cancel the claim to a part in the kingdom, or, at least, would justify one in separating from such. So, indeed, it has been. There are those who refuse communion with other churches, on account of what they regard as a grievous error in psalmody, or on account of a difference in the form of administering a sacrament; and those who even deny the name of church to those who are not organized according to what they regard as the apostolical form. Now, what was the character of those churches which Christ here acknowledged as His? All of them, except two, very imperfect; two of them tolerating most grievous doctrinal and practical errors; and two of them so greatly backslidden, that one had only a few unspotted members, and the other none whom Christ excepted from His severe rebuke. Yet in none of these churches were the defections such as to justify separation from them in order still to adhere to Christ. Not even the few in Sardis, who had preserved their garments undefiled, were called upon to come out from the rest—to renounce that worldly church. There were still two things common to them all; they acknowledged their mission to be that of spiritual light-bearers, and they professed subjection to Christ as their Lord; they received His messenger; they were candlesticks, and they had stars in His right hand. They had not become political powers, and assumed civil authority, as the church of Rome did; they had not rejected His messengers accredited by His Spirit, and substituted for His authority another—a mere earthly head, no longer subject to, and to be judged by, the written word, and confined to the limit of its instructions. They had not inaugurated a worship which set aside, as that of Rome does, the all-sufficiency of Christ's atoning blood, and justifying righteousness, and all-prevalent intercession; nor a system of discipline that changed the whole nature of the church from a spiritual to a mere external and compulsory power, and completely ignored Christ's sole headship and revealed will. Where these two things remain, its spiritual mission acknowledged, and Christ's sole authority confessed, the imperfections in the discharge of these functions, and in obeying and administering that authority, do not deprive it of its claim. Even Laodicea, as well as Philadelphia, still holds its place among the seven churches; and the duty of each faithful believer in her, is to bear a faithful testimony, not by withdrawal from her, but while Christ is knocking at the door of the church,—by himself opening the door to admit Christ to holy fellowship with himself. So, at length, the whole church shall feel His gracious presence and reviving power.

LECTURE IX.

THE INDIVIDUAL CONFLICT AND VICTORY, WHICH IS THE END OF THE VISIBLE, AND THE NECESSARY MEANS OF ATTAINING THE GLORY OF THE INVISIBLE, KINGDOM.

REV. II. AND III. CHAPTERS.

"TO HIM THAT OVERCOMETH."

EACH of these epistles concludes with a glowing promise of the glories of the church triumphant. These are all addressed, not to the churches as such, but "to him that overcometh,"—to the individual conqueror. The possession of these glories is suspended, therefore, upon an individual conflict. The suspension of every one of these promises upon this single condition, thus seven times repeated, shows that the very design of the visible church is to call men to this spiritual conflict, and to sustain them in it, as the only means of attaining the glories of the everlasting kingdom.

It is this personal conflict, too, that gives shape and character to the great conflicts of the church, as portrayed in the symbolic revelations of this book, and as already in part recorded in the history of the church. It, therefore, brings the whole of these great and stirring scenes of seals and trumpets, and vials and beastly powers, as well as of the New Jerusalem, in its descending glories, into immediate and personal contact with the spiritual life of each soul. It is the exigencies* of this spiritual and individual warfare that demand or give occasion to all the strange and vast movements of the mighty plan of God here on earth.

This subject, therefore, though often treated of, and in

pressing necessity (urgency)

many various forms, is always one of deep interest to every believer, and every earnest inquirer after the salvation of God. And its relations to the whole subject of this Book of Revelation, as just stated, render it proper and important to consider, attentively, its *nature*, and *personal necessity*, and *divine resources*, in connection with these other truths of the spiritual kingdom.

This conflict is the same so often spoken of and described in Scripture, by such language as the following: "Fight the good fight of faith." "The flesh lusteth against the Spirit, and the Spirit against the flesh; and these are contrary the one to the other; so that ye cannot do the things that ye would." "For we wrestle not against flesh and blood, but against principalities, against powers, against the rulers of the darkness of this world, against spiritual wickedness in high places." "This is the victory that overcometh the world, even our faith." The world, with all its power, its wisdom and its pleasures, the flesh with all its lusts, and the devil with all his invisible hosts, are the enemies to be fought and conquered. Against these, on the other side, is the new nature, created and sustained by the indwelling Spirit of God. It is a conflict in which the powers of heaven and of hell are engaged; and in which the prize is the eternal salvation or ruin of the immortal soul in which it is carried on.

§. 1. Its nature.

§. Its sphere, the soul itself.

The sphere of the conflict is the soul itself. This is the field where alone sin can be met, and Satan vanquished. Sin is a thing of the soul. It is not a substance, but a quality. It is a quality of spirit only; not of matter. It is not, however, a proper and original quality of it, such as those which are necessary to form its true nature; it is that which destroys its perfection, which spoils it. It is such a quality as rottenness is of the tree; as putridity is of flesh. Nor is it the effect of circumstances, or of our connection with a material body. Neither does it belong to organizations, and systems, and societies, except as it inheres in and pollutes the souls of those who constitute or control them. However widely it may extend its fearful consequences, penetrating and perverting all human activities, and sweeping its horrid blight over all the earthly interests of man, and bringing his body even down to the rottenness of the grave, it still has its seat, its very existence, in the soul, and no where else. And not in the soul merely as a resident or guest; as something separate and distinct from it, or as a temporary emotion of joy or sorrow; but as a quality of its very nature, a quality that has entered and changed that nature, just as the poison of an inherited scrofula pervades the whole body. It has thus completely reversed the blessed relation of the soul to its Creator, and cut it off from His loving embrace, and made it a rebel to His law, and a just subject of its awful penalty. All apparent resistance to sin, then, which does not disturb its place in the affections, the very centre and spring of the soul's activities, leaves it in its full power. Destroy it there, and the curse is repealed, Satan dethroned, God and man again in full and loving communion, and all warfare ended.

This renders the conflict most difficult and fierce, and most painful to flesh and blood, and utterly impossible to mere nature. For it follows, from the very nature of sin, that self is the great enemy in this conflict. The "flesh" is but another name for this corrupt self,—the natural heart, which regards the interests of this world,—of the flesh, as of more practical importance than those of the Spirit. This makes the world an enemy, and gives to Satan his power. The very essence of this conflict, therefore, is self-denial. Not the mere denial of worldly lusts and pleasures, and criminal indulgences; abstinence from these is a part rather of the Christian's pleasures

§. Severe. Self the great enemy.

than his self-denials. It is *self*, not the world and Satan merely, that are to be denied; self as opposed to God, to Jesus and His kingdom, in its manifold forms of self-righteousness, self-wisdom, self-dependence, and self-indulgence. It is not a single habit to be overcome; even that often involves a long-continued and severe struggle, and tests all the soul's energy. It is no amount or degree of superinduced habits, but all native tendencies and moral activities of the depraved heart that are to be resisted and totally changed.

There is, indeed, in the natural heart a conflict; but it is totally different from that here required. It is only the conflict between a higher and a lower, a more or a less intelligent selfishness, or between this and some natural affection. In it the love of reputation may be opposed to some present gratification of appetite or passion; the love of knowledge to the love of pleasure or of money; the fear of punishment or the lashings of a guilty conscience to the force of vicious propensities—one earthly desire to another, or conscience to the whole. Though it is a matter of much consequence to the earthly life, on which side victory shall rest in these conflicts, yet, so far as the soul's salvation is concerned, it matters not which triumphs, if no higher principle is engaged. Such battles are fought entirely outside the precincts of the spiritual kingdom, and without regard to its interests. Such victories have their reward, but it is earthly and only earthly, and perishes with the earthly life, and only leaves the victor in it to a deeper descent to the same perdition with the vanquished. This, not because he is worse in this matter, but because by his very position he rejected greater light and abused greater privileges. His is a Capernaum, a Chorazin and a Bethsaida fate, compared with that of Sodom and Gomorrah; the fate of a Pharisee compared with that of a publican or harlot.

§. Differs entirely from the natural conflict.

Now, it is the necessity of this conflict, in its personal, individual character, that in these epistles to the seven churches is so earnestly pressed.

§. 2. Personal necessity.

It appears, first, from the very terms of the promise. All these promises are made, not to the churches as such, but to individuals. "*To him* that overcometh," is the single condition seven times repeated, on which all the glories promised shall be bestowed. The candlestick of Ephesus may be removed; judgment may come upon Sardis as a thief in the night; a lukewarm Loadicea may be rejected with loathing; but this shall not prevent the acceptance and crowning of the single one that overcometh, of the few that have kept their garments clean, or the solitary soul that opens the door to a waiting and pleading Saviour. The churches are thus reminded that it is not in virtue of any outward connection with them, not by any sacramental grace or church power, or apostolic order that an entrance into the joys of the spiritual and everlasting kingdom is secured. Every member of every church is also reminded that it matters not how perfect the church organization may be; how free from every taint of error, or open unfaithfulness in service or discipline; how brightly its roll of martyrs may shine, or how earnest and successful it may be, like Philadelphia, in entering the doors of usefulness opened before it: all this will not secure to the individual members a place in the glorified kingdom. It is, in every case, only "to him that overcometh," to the individual conqueror in a personal conflict, that the reward is promised.

§. From the promise itself.

The necessity of such a conflict is further shown by the nature of the evils in each of these churches. The special evil to be overcome in Ephesus was the chilling of first love, by controversial zeal; in Smyrna it is the fear of

§. From the evils here presented.

personal suffering incurred by faithfulness to Christ; in Pergamos it is the world's friendship, enticing the heart to conformity with its idolatry and lusts; in Thyatira it is the high pretensions and cunning devices of error, deceiving the soul into the same indulgencies; in Sardis it is a regard for the praise of men, benumbing the soul's life, and defiling the outward walk; in Philadelphia it is the discouragements arising from conscious weakness, and the greatness of its work and trials; in Laodicea it is the lukewarmness of spiritual pride. In every case the personal and spiritual nature of the conflict required is manifest. It is no where one that can be waged merely by organizations and drill; ministers cannot fight it for their people, nor can a whole church of faithful officers and members, by their earnestness, and zeal, and courage, carry along with them a single soul, that has not itself fought its way into the kingdom. The conflict with such enemies as these cannot be carried on by delegating it to others; no priest, or minister, or church, can throw itself in between the soul and its enemy: each soul must grapple directly with the foe within it, and conquer or die.

Self-evident as this fact is, members of the visible church cannot be too often or earnestly reminded of it. In churches where there is any considerable zeal and activity in prosecuting the various enterprises necessary to the support and extension of the gospel, there is a constant tendency to merge individuality in organized effort, and to substitute the labours, and activities, and benevolence thus developed, for this personal conflict. It is no difficult thing for a deceitful heart, in the midst of the busy activities of a zealous church, to take a full share in these labours; and, borne along simply by the ranks all around it, as in an army, fancy itself a real sharer in the conflict, and in the victory which ensued. But in this spiritual conflict, no soldier can be thus carried to victory by the pressure

§. Not evaded in the church.

of earnest and determined men around him. Each must fight his own way, even as though there were no other on the field.

Neither can any child of the kingdom evade or lessen the severity of this personal conflict, by any change of circumstances. The attempt to do this by seclusion from the world, and perpetual exercises of devotion, only fearfully aggravates it. The records of monastic piety show the darkest pictures any where found of this conflict, and the greatest triumphs of Satanic power. What greater folly can there be than the attempt to conquer depraved self by a life that makes self the centre of all the thoughts and actions; and by a renunciation of all the duties and ties of social and domestic life? But even in the highest walks of Christian life and effort, the same conflict must be engaged in. In the study of the minister, it may rage just as violently as in the marts of commerce; in the loneliness of a desert life, as in the midst of the city's busiest throngs.

§. Nor by change of circumstances.

It admits of no truce. In the sweet retirement of the family, and in the perplexing cares and irritations of business, in every field of intellectual effort, in every walk of charity and work of usefulness, in the most sacred ordinances of the house of God, and in the solemn secrecy of the closet, the enemy is present, and the conflict pressing. No advancement in civilization, no refinement of social life, no extent of intellectual culture, no political reforms, not even the liberty which poets have sung, and for which patriots have bled, can ever even mitigate the real intensity of this spiritual warfare, or render the victory easier. No earthly culture can refine man into true holiness. These only change the form of the conflict; and often, when its form seems least violent, it is the most deadly, because most insidious. The struggle with religious self

§. No truce.

often wrings the soul with a keener agony than with vicious self. It is far easier to resist the devil when he comes as a fiend, than when he comes as a friend.

Again. The necessity of this personal conflict can never cease until the application of redemption ceases, until the final consummation. It is laid in the very nature of fallen man and of a holy God, and in the whole method of God in the application of redemption. It matters not how great the glory and power with which you conceive the visible church on earth to become invested at some future time, provided that it be not a glory inconsistent with men still dwelling in the flesh, and inheriting depraved natures: there will be still the necessity for it. These promises admit no other condition than this conflict and victory. They offer these glories of the eternal kingdom only "to him that overcometh." And so long as men are to be saved by the gospel, the word of the gospel can never be antiquated. That word is clear and decisive. "Through much tribulation we must enter the kingdom of God." "If any man will come after Me, let him deny himself, and take up his cross daily, and follow Me." "If so be that we suffer with Him, that we may also be glorified together." Never, until the work of redemption is completed, can such exhortations as the following cease to be appropriate, and necessary: "Watch and pray, that ye enter not into temptation." "What I say unto you, I say unto all, Watch." "Watch ye, stand fast in the faith, quit you like men, be strong." "Fight the good fight of faith." "Put on the whole armour of God, that ye may be able to stand against the wiles of the devil." "We, according to His promise, look for a new heavens, and a new earth, wherein dwelleth righteousness. Wherefore, beloved, seeing ye look for such things, be diligent that ye may be found of Him in peace, without spot, and blameless." "If ye do these things,"—that is, the things

§. Continues until redemption is complete.

included in the previous struggle enjoined,—" ye shall never fall: for *so* an entrance shall be ministered unto you abundantly into the everlasting kingdom of our Lord and Saviour Jesus Christ."

No triumphs of the gospel, however multiplied, shall ever convert the narrow way into a broad and easy one. Though all persecution should cease, and old Pope and Pagan should be not only confined to the mouth of their dens, gnashing their teeth, in their decrepitude, upon the passing pilgrims, but utterly destroyed, and nothing left to tell the world of them but their bones, still the lust of the flesh, and the lust of the eyes, and the pride of life, shall never cease to beset with new forms of temptation every traveller to the heavenly city, so long as the corruption of nature shall continue in any child of the kingdom. For so long as descendants of Adam shall be born on earth, they shall be born in sin. This of itself involves the necessity of a conflict on the part of all who arrive at years of responsibility. And this conflict implies, in addition to the inherited depravity, the continuance of the curse, the agency of Satan, and a world still suffering and groaning for a promised deliverance. Its necessity, therefore, can only cease when the last saint shall have put forth the last struggle, when the whole body of God's elect shall be complete, and the King shall come the second time without sin unto salvation, to destroy the last enemy, to crown with final victory His mediatorial reign, and end it, and to crown with its perfected glory His own everlasting kingdom, His triumphant church. That kingdom will then be found to be exclusively a kingdom of conquerors. The bright glimpses of its glory that flash upon our waiting eyes, from these promises to the seven churches, are seen only at the end of an unearthly, and mysterious, and severe conflict. The path to it is the same trodden by prophets, and apostles, and martyrs, and all the hosts of suffering saints; for it is the blood-stained path of their suffering, glorious Leader. Darkness and storms are seen gathering over it; it passes through flood, and through fire, and through hosts of earthly lusts, and Satanic spirits; but at every point it is clearly marked by the footsteps of the Lamb. Clear and distinct, above the warring of the floods, or the threats of the foe, are heard at every step His cheering words, "*Follow Me.*" And yonder, in His glory, we hear Him uttering these final words of promise,—enough to thrill with a hope and joy unutterable the heart of each struggling one, "To him that overcometh will I grant to sit with Me on My throne, *even as I also overcame*, and am set down with My Father on His throne."

§. 3. Divine resources. In Christ our head.

This last promise suggests to us what the Scriptures elsewhere so fully teach, that the ground of our hope and source of our victory in this conflict, are entirely in the conflict and victory of our divine Head. "*Even as I also overcame.*" "In the world ye shall have tribulation; but be of good cheer, I have overcome the world." "This is the victory that overcometh the world, even our faith. Who is he that overcometh the world, but he that believeth that Jesus is the Son of God." It is only because Christ has overcome, that such a conflict is possible; and His victory renders that of the believer sure. It was achieved for His people. By that victory He quenched the curse; He wrought out an everlasting righteousness; He destroyed death and him that hath the power of it: he has ascended His mediatorial throne, and is thence dispensing the infinite resources of the Almighty Spirit to all believers.

§. Initiated by the Spirit.

Though a personal and individual conflict, it can never be carried on by personal and individual strength. Nothing but the mighty, the omnipotent resources of the mediatorial kingdom can ever enable a feeble saint to win the victory over sin, the world and the devil. Nothing else can ever enable one who is, as all are, "born in iniquity," "without strength," "alienated from the life of God," "dead in trespasses and sins," to rise up and come forth from his helpless bondage to sin and Satan. An arm of divine love and might must reach away over into the regions of the kingdom of darkness and death, and not, indeed, by force, which is impossible, but by a power such as the Maker of Spirits alone can exert on the spirits He has made—a power in sweet and perfect harmony with the soul's nature—a power that sets the will, before enslaved by the soul's depravity, free from the horrid bondage that urged it on a course contrary to the soul's original nature and deepest convictions,—by such a power must translate it from the kingdom of darkness into the kingdom of God's dear Son. "No man can say that Jesus is the Lord but by the Holy Ghost." "Except a man be born again, born of the Spirit, he cannot see, he cannot enter the kingdom of God." "Jesus, being by the right hand of God exalted, and having received of the Father the promise of the Holy Ghost," has shed it forth on a helpless world.

§. Sustained by His Spirit and providence.

The conflict thus initiated is always represented as carried on by the same spirit, as the Spirit of Christ, the agent of His mediatorial power and grace. It is not flesh against the flesh; but "the flesh lusteth against the Spirit, and the Spirit against the flesh." "If ye, through the Spirit, do mortify the deeds of the body, ye shall live." All the fruits of holiness are "fruits of the Spirit." We pray "*in* the Spirit," we "walk in the Spirit," yea, we "live in the Spirit." "Fear not," then, ye struggling saints. "Be strong in the Lord, and in the power of His might." Behold Him on the mediatorial throne, with all the resources of the kingdom of God at His command, and employing them all for your salvation! He has surrounded you with the influences of this kingdom—the word of divine love, the attractions of the cross, the powers of the world to come, and these applied, not by human agency merely, but by the loving power and wisdom of the Divine Spirit. From that throne, too, He gathers up all the complicated agencies of His providence, and unites them into perfect harmony with His Spirit's work on the heart, making all things work together for your good.

It is only by these powers of the invisible, spiritual kingdom, that any soul can obtain the victory, and inherit its promised glories. While it unfolds these glories to our admiring view, and opens wide its heavenly portals to each spiritual conqueror, it also reaches down, in this way, its divine and gracious influence and protection to every sincere, struggling soul, in the midst of its enemies. It is thus that the kingdom perfects itself. It calls out each soul to engage in this conflict, it supports and directs all through it, it animates the faith, and hope, and love, that carries the feeble saint on from victory to victory, till the last enemy lies crushed beneath its feet.

While these words, therefore, "To him that overcometh," reveal a conflict of transcendent difficulty in order to salvation, every believer should remember that all the resources of the spiritual kingdom are on his side, and all its interests are concerned in his victory. What more than this can the most fearful and severely tried desire? What more do you want, or can you have, than the blood and the Spirit of Christ? Does not the voice of that precious blood silence every voice of condemnation? Is any working of corruption or temptation of Satan too strong for the power of that Spirit? Of those who fought with the great dragon, it is said in chap. 12: 11, "They overcame him by the blood of the Lamb, and by the word of their testimony; and they loved not their lives unto the death." So, too, we must overcome. "The word of their testimony" is but the work of the Spirit. Trusting in these

§. Encouragement.

two—the blood of the Lamb, and the power of the Spirit—Paul saw the triumph from afar, and even in the very heat of the conflict, uttered, on behalf of each suffering saint, these cheering words. In them it is the privilege of every believer to unite. So let us do. "Who is he that condemneth? It is Christ that died, yea rather, that is risen again, who is even at the right hand of God, who also maketh intercession for us. Who shall separate us from the love of Christ? Shall tribulation, or distress, or persecution, or famine, or nakedness, or peril, or sword? As it is written, For thy sake we are killed all the day long; we are accounted as sheep for the slaughter. Nay, in all these things we are more than conquerors through Him that loved us. For I am persuaded that neither death, nor life, nor angels, nor principalities, nor powers, nor things present, nor things to come, nor height, nor depth, nor any other creature, shall be able to separate us from the love of God which is in Christ Jesus our Lord."

While, however, it is as individual victors in a personal conflict that each member of the true church of Christ secures the promised glory, this does not render the ordinances of the visible church any the less needful. Hence, in concluding this view of the conflict, we call attention to a remark already made—that this personal conflict and victory is the one great end and design of the visible church. The very position in which the statement of this necessity of a personal conflict is found, appended to these messages to the churches, as the condition of every promise, shows that it was only in proportion as the church secured such victories that it accomplished its purpose. For this, all her organizations have been constituted, all her ordinances given. To this, all her energies are to be directed; for it, all her enterprises formed and prosecuted. The whole array of ecclesiastical government, of

§. Relation of the visible church to it.

officers, forms, worship, sacraments and discipline, is of no worth to any soul except as it is instrumental in enlisting it in a successful conflict with sin, the world, and Satan. Only as any church secures this result, does it preserve its purity, or show its true nature. Failing in this, it ceases to be a true church, and becomes a synagogue of Satan, and one of the most destructive of all his hellish agencies.

On the other hand, the ordinances of the visible church are perfectly adapted, by the wisdom and love of her divine Head, for this very end. To wilfully neglect them, to treat them as unnecessary, is, as we have already seen, to throw aside the cup in which the waters of life are offered. It is, therefore, to reject that life itself. To every true believer, the worship and discipline of the church is most precious, is felt, indeed, to be indispensable. "My soul longeth, yea, even fainteth, for the courts of the Lord." "Blessed are they that dwell in Thy house." "Those that be planted in the house of the Lord, shall flourish in the courts of our God." "He that believeth and is baptized shall be saved." "And let us consider one another to provoke unto love and to good works; not forsaking the assembling of ourselves together, as the manner of some is; but exhorting one another, and so much the more as ye see the day approaching." "Obey them that have the rule over you, and submit yourselves, for they watch for your souls as they that must give account, that they may do it with joy and not with grief."

The visible church is, therefore, the divinely appointed instrument in gathering and perfecting the invisible church, by securing this personal conflict and victory. The whole subject shows us how, as, one by one, each individual victor passes away to receive his crown, the imperfect and struggling visible kingdom is preparing the increasing throng of the invisible kingdom; and how, at length, when the last battle shall be fought, and the last enemy destroyed, and the last saint crowned, the visible shall be merged in the invisible kingdom, and the latter, as the triumphant church, stand forth as the consummated work and glory of redemption.

LECTURE X.

THE PROMISES "TO HIM THAT OVERCOMETH."

Rev. ii. and iii. Chapters.

THE body of these epistles to the seven churches gives us a picture of the visible church in the various phases of its militant state. The promises at the close of each show us what the church will be when the conflicts are ended, and the victory over sin and death complete. The picture of the church militant and of the church triumphant are thus brought close together. The glories of the latter are thus made to cheer the heart, and to invigorate the strength of the feeble saint during all the long conflicts of the former.

The possession of these glories is made to depend upon victory in a personal and individual conflict. This conflict is spiritual—its seat is in the soul—a corrupt nature, depraved self, is the great enemy to be overcome; and this is fortified by the world and the devil. Each soul must engage in it for itself—must fight its own way into the kingdom. But it can overcome only by divine strength. Divine resources are provided and offered in the blood and spirit of Christ, in all the powers of the spiritual kingdom of God, and in His providence, making all things work together for good to them that love Him.

In these promises the glorious and eternal prize of this victory is held out. By uniting all these in one view, we get a seven-sided, a complete and perfect view, so far as in our imperfect state we are capable of conceiving it, of the glories of the perfected kingdom. This we can only do by looking distinctly at each, and catching its meaning, as that is often bound up in figures drawn from the old dispensation, but which the Bible itself furnishes us with abundant means for understanding.

1. *First,* the promise to the church of Ephesus. "To him that overcometh will I give to eat of the tree of life which is in the midst of the Paradise of God." This promise carries us back to the bliss that Adam lost. It represents the promised glory as Paradise restored. Of that Paradise, the distinguishing privilege was eating of the tree of life. That the sin of Adam lost. The grace of Christ restores it. "I am come that they might have life, and that they might have it more abundantly." That life bestowed in the new birth is perfected in glory, and so becomes eternal. "He that believeth on Me hath everlasting life." But it is still a creature life; it is not self-sustaining. It is eternal, because it is eternally nourished from the infinite source of all life. Appropriate means are furnished in the provisions of the everlasting covenant for this, and these are here represented as the fruits of the tree of life. This tree appears again in the last chapter of this book, and is there described as bearing *twelve manner of fruits*—fruits suited to all classes and wants of God's redeemed; and yielding those fruits "every month," that is, always fresh and ready. It grows along the banks of the river of life, which flows from beneath the throne of God and the Lamb; it is the product of sovereign grace and atoning blood. The fulness of the living God, and the merits of the atoning Lamb, are the exhaustless source of these fruits of immortality. "Your life is hid with Christ in God. When Christ, who is our life, shall appear, then shall ye also appear with Him in glory." The Paradise, of which this is the central glory, is more, far more, than what Adam lost. No forbidden tree of knowledge grows

§. 1. Paradise restored.

there; no tempter can ever enter there; nothing can hurt or destroy; every influence and agency shall sweetly combine in filling with substantial joys the hearts of the redeemed. Probation is ended. It is the full life of God in the soul. "Because I live ye shall live also."

2. The *second promise* carries us back to the curse that Adam brought. It represents this blessedness of the kingdom as an entire and eternal deliverance from the curse of death. "He that overcometh shall not be hurt of the second death. Even death itself is conquered by him, and he shall for ever wear the trophy. "Be thou faithful unto death, and I will give thee a crown of life." The continued dissolution of the body, in the case of the children of the kingdom, rendered this specific promise needful. "It is appointed unto all men once to die." That death, though a consequence of sin, is to the spiritual conqueror no part of the curse. Its nature is changed. It is the first step towards the deliverance of the body from the curse, by its severing its connection with the first Adam, and preparing the conditions for its glorious reconstruction, when Christ shall come the second time. It is but the more lengthy form of that change which shall take place in the bodies of the living saints at the final consummation of the kingdom. It is but the transfer of the redeemed spirit from all those conditions of temptation and sorrow, to which in the flesh it must be exposed, to a home and rest " with Jesus," there to await, instead of here, the full perfection of its bliss. Even in the case of the impenitent, the death of the body is not the curse of the law, but only a mere incident of it.

§. 2. Death destroyed.

"It is not all of death to die."

"There is a death whose pang
Outlasts the fleeting breath;
Oh! what eternal horrors hang
Around the second death."

This second death is, in the latter part of this book, described as "the lake of fire" into which was cast whatsoever was found not written in the book of life. It is the eternal ruin of both soul and body, to be consummated at the last judgment, when they that have done evil shall come forth to the resurrection of damnation. It is this coming wrath that gives now to the sinner's bodily dissolution all its terrors and its sting. But, for the redeemed, this second death is destroyed. Over the spiritual conqueror, the feeblest saint that in the might of the Spirit maintains the conflict with temptations without and corruptions within, it has no power. When he approaches the end of the conflict, death itself, whether it comes amidst all the endearments of a christian home, or in the tortures of a cruel martyrdom, is compelled to be no longer the messenger of a curse, but the servant of a king, bearing the crown of life, and placing it on the conqueror's brow, and confessing that he is for ever vanquished.

"Be faithful unto death"—"be faithful," though it require you to die a bloody death, "and I will give thee a crown of life." Even in dying he is not hurt; he is not touched even by the second death. And at the last, amidst the crash of dissolving nature, and the fires that purify an accursed world, and consume all the works and monuments of a sinful race, he shall stand in his glorified and immortal body calm and secure beneath the spreading wings of eternal love. There is no more curse.

3. The *third promise* carries us back to the priestly privileges of the ancient church for its type, and represents this blessedness as consisting in the most intimate fellowship and communion with Christ as our great High Priest, in the highest privileges and the most sacred places of the spiritual kingdom. It selects as its type the highest honours and most sacred nearness and fellowship of the High Priest under the old covenant, when the tabernacle

§. 3. Priestly privileges.

was set up in its full glory, and God dwelt by a visible symbol among His people. But it goes far beyond the type. It describes a height of privilege to which, even in the shadows of that typical system, no Jewish priest was ever admitted. Israel ate of the manna that fell around the camp. "The hidden manna" was that memorial portion of it which was laid up in the ark of the covenant in the most holy place. Of this, not even the High Priest could eat; it was there to be sacredly preserved from all human touch and sight as a memorial and a type. It is of this that the spiritual victor shall actually partake, that is, of the joys of holy communion with God, of which it was the symbol. Of this hidden manna, Paul speaks when he says, "Eye hath not seen, nor ear heard, neither have entered into the heart of man the things which God hath prepared for them that love Him." They are in the ark of the covenant, covered by the mercy seat; they are laid up in Christ Jesus, and secured by His perfect propitiation—the same that satisfies the law, and covers over all its demands. Christ Himself, in all the fulness of His great salvation, in all the complete displays of His love and glory in His perfected kingdom, is this hidden manna. "As the living Father hath sent Me, and I live by the Father; so he that eateth Me shall live by Me. This is that bread that came down from heaven, not as your fathers did eat manna, and are dead; he that eateth of this bread shall live for ever." Now, indeed, we are permitted to eat of it as it falls round about the camp in our wilderness estate; but then we shall eat of that hidden manna that can be found only beneath the mercy seat, and under the spreading wings of the cherubim of glory. The spiritual victor shall be admitted into the holy of holies, where Christ unveils His glory; to him all the secrets of covenant love shall be uncovered, and he shall for ever feed on all the ark in the holy place not made with hands contains.

The other part of this promise has received various explanations, most of which are drawn from some rare heathen customs. We prefer the explanation adopted by Trench, and which is drawn like all the other figures in all these promises from the rich treasures of the old covenant, and God's own previous teachings, and from that very part of it, and the very time from which the figure of the hidden manna was derived. This "white stone," and "the name written" on it, "which no man knoweth, saving he that receiveth it," is thus made to refer to that mysterious Urim and Thummim, that unknown but most precious thing deposited in the curiously wrought breastplate of the Jewish High Priest, and on which was supposed to be inscribed the sacred name of Jehovah, but which none but the High Priest ever saw, and by which God, on special occasions, made known His will to the High Priest consulting it.

It thus beautifully indicates the possession of the certain and easy means of perpetual and direct communication with God, and of obtaining immediate and perfect knowledge of the divine will. No more darkness, no more ignorance, no more imperfect knowledge, no more doubt or perplexity. We shall not "see through a glass darkly; but then face to face." "We shall then know even as also we are known." It is such a present, perpetual revelation of the new name—the new and completed glory of Jesus our Eternal King and Covenant Head, as shall be perfectly adapted to every peculiar, personal, and secret want of man's nature for ever. It is all that could be typified by the constant possession and free consultation of the mysterious Urim and Thummim, Lights and Perfections; free and constant access to the divine mind by the complete indwelling of the Holy Ghost, filling the heart with divine light and love. "Ye have an unction from the Holy One, and know all things." This is but a foretaste and pledge of it. Its fulness is thus represented in the picture of the new Jerusalem, afterwards given in this book: "And there shall be no night there, and they need no candle, neither light of the sun, for the Lord God giveth them light."

4. The *fourth promise* unfolds the kingly privileges under the type of David's reign. It adds to these priestly privileges full fellowship with Christ in His mediatorial triumphs over the nations. Its language and imagery are taken from the culminating period of the glory of the old dispensation, the establishment of the kingdom in the person and family of David, and is in great part a quotation from the second Psalm, which describes the triumph of Messiah's reign. "He that overcometh and keepeth My works unto the end, to him will I give power over the nations; and he shall rule them with a rod of iron; as the vessels of a potter shall they be broken to shivers; even as I received of My Father." This power over the nations is a share in that power promised to the Son as King and Head of His church. In these triumphs of the King, even the humblest subject of the kingdom shall partake. They are all achieved for the sake of His redeemed. The opposition of the nations to His spiritual kingdom, the sufferings inflicted upon His people, their prayers and cries for deliverance, and their rejected testimony through long ages shall, in the hour of final victory, all be seen to have given force and direction to the strokes of that iron sceptre that shall break to shivers the proud potsherds of the earth, and sweep from it the whole of the present social and civil system, to prepare the way for the descending city of our God. So intimate is the union of His people with Him, that as members of His body, as sharers of His life, and constituting the very kingdom for which He died, their interests and salvation direct and control the act of judgment by which the powers of a world so long ruled by Satan shall be for ever crushed.

§. 4. Kingly privileges.

"Know ye not," says the apostle, "that the saints shall judge the world." "Like sheep, they," the wicked, "are laid in the grave—are driven to the grave; death shall be their shepherd; death shall feed on them; and the upright shall have dominion over them in the morning." "The kingdom, and dominion, and the greatness of the kingdom under the whole heaven shall be given to the people of the saints of the Most High, whose kingdom is an everlasting kingdom, and all dominions shall serve and obey Him." Even now, during the great conflict between the church and the world, it is fatal to the mightiest of earthly powers to set itself in opposition to the feeblest saint. In the tie that binds that saint to Jesus, and the faith-winged prayer that takes hold on His throne, there is a secret power that drives back and dashes to pieces the mightiest earthly forces that assail him. This is but the prelude to that victory by which the dominion of the world, lost to man in the fall, shall be restored to man redeemed, in which every saint must share. "And the armies which were in heaven followed Him upon white horses, clothed in fine linen, white and clean. And out of His mouth goeth a sharp sword, that with it He should smite the nations; and He shall rule them with a rod of iron."

The other part of this promise, "and I will give him the morning star," may seem at first sight to have no connection with these kingly triumphs. A closer inspection, however, will show it to be most intimate. There, as everywhere, the star is the symbol of authority; the morning star is the leader of the heavenly host, the King of Kings and Lord of Lords. Christ afterwards announces Himself to be this morning star, and that as the root and offspring of David. He thus appropriates to Himself the language of prophecy, in which the Spirit predicted the glorious rise and triumphs of the kingdom of God under David, as the type of the triumphs of David's greater Son; extorting the words from the lips of the unwilling Balaam, the world's own prophet: "There shall come a star out of Jacob, and a sceptre shall rise out of Israel, and shall smite the corners of Moab, and destroy all the children of Sheth. And Edom shall be a possession, and Seir, also, shall be a possession for His enemies, and Israel shall do valiantly. Out of Jacob shall come He that shall have dominion, and shall destroy him that remaineth of the city." This promise, then, represents Him as rising in the glory of His triumphant kingdom upon the long and dreary night of the world's darkness and conflicts, and ushering in the light of an eternal day. It is the consummation of the triumphs over the nations, the breaking upon the world of the glory of Christ's peaceful and perfected kingdom. "I will give thee the morning star," assures each spiritual conqueror that he shall share in the alleluias of that day of triumph; that, although his own individual warfare may have ended long before, and his body may have long mingled with its kindred dust, yet even he shall have his full share in that great triumph, that even the dawning of that day of glory shall be greeted by his joyful eyes.

"For if we believe that Jesus died and rose again, even so them that sleep in Jesus shall God bring with Him. * * For the Lord Himself shall descend from heaven with a shout, with the voice of the archangel, and with the trump of God, and the dead in Christ shall rise first; then we which are alive and remain shall be caught up together with them in the clouds, to meet the Lord in the air; and so shall we be ever with the Lord."

These four promises exhaust the riches of that typical dispensation, whose very design was to foreshadow the glory of the spiritual kingdom; and they also gather up every conception of the blessedness and glory of the perfected spiritual kingdom, so far as it is a perfect restoration from all the evils of the fall, and deliverance from all the trials of conflict. Paradise is restored; the curse of death abolished; every barrier to free and constant access to God removed, and every opposing earthly power that had grown up during the ages crushed out. The remaining three promises give us the more positive side of this blessedness and glory, and in forms and language drawn from the brighter and fuller revelations of the present dispensation of the kingdom.

5. The *fifth promise* brings us, accordingly, to the great central idea of the blessedness and glory of the spiritual kingdom. It assures the victor of perfect personal holiness, entire conformity to the divine image, and of a public recognition of his divine relationship. "He that overcometh, the same shall be clothed in white raiment; and I will not blot out his name out of the book of life, but I will confess his name before My Father and before His angels." This white raiment, we are afterwards told, is "the righteousness of the saints." This is two-fold: the righteousness wrought out by Christ, and imputed to them, by which they are justified; and the personal conformity to the divine law wrought in them by the Spirit, and wrought by them under its power. The first is already theirs, and it is because they are thus pardoned and accepted, that they are enabled to engage in this conflict. It is the second that is here meant. Growth in this is the very design of the spiritual conflict. This is the perfection of glory. Holiness is the glory of God. It is the sum of all His moral perfections. This beauty and glory of the divine image shall invest all these conquerors. Every power and emotion of the soul, and every faculty of the glorified body shall be under the perfect and sweet control of the will of God, and shall reflect His image. As such, Christ shall present Him before God, a spotless and eternal trophy of His redeeming love and power; the Father shall acknowledge him as His child, and angels

§. 5. Holiness and divine adoption.

shall welcome him to their joys, and learn from him the love of redemption.

6. The *sixth promise* represents the spiritual conqueror as having a permanent abode in the house of His Father, and as being bound together with all the multitude of others like him into one glorious and perfect society, in which each shall reflect upon every other the glory of God and the Lamb, each becoming a fresh revelation of the name, the glory, and the grace of God, and of the new name of the triumphant Redeemer. "Him that overcometh will I make a pillar in the temple of My God, and he shall go no more out; and I will write upon him the name of My God, and the name of the city of My God, which is New Jerusalem, which cometh down out of heaven from my God; and I will write upon him My new name." "A pillar" is evidently a figure, not of support, but of fixed and unchanging abode—"he shall go no more out." The name of God inscribed, represents God's right in him, and his right in God, and himself as a revelation of the divine glory. The name of the city inscribed, represents this as not a solitary bliss, but as the fullest possible development of the social element, as a participation in all the rights and privileges of a heavenly city, the New Jerusalem, whose glories are afterwards described. It represents the conqueror as one of a mighty throng, bound to each other by ties of eternal love and personal union to Christ, and having the bliss of each enhanced by a perfect and holy sympathy with every other. The "new name" of Jesus is a new manifestation of His distinctive glory; and seems most naturally to refer to that final manifestation of His glory consequent upon the completion of His mediatorial work, when He shall have subdued all things unto God, and shall, in His glorified body, dwell with all His glorified saints in that heavenly city, of which the Lord God almighty and the Lamb are the

§. 6. Divine citizenship.

light. This new name, inscribed on each, represents each as shining forth before all his glorified companions as a distinct manifestation, an eternal monument of the matchless love and power fully displayed at last in His perfected kingdom, when His mediatorial work is accomplished. Each one of these spiritual conquerors shall, as the result of the present personal conflict, possess not a mere individual bliss, but shall share in all the joys of a common salvation; shall drink not only of his own cup, but of the overflowing cups of bliss of all the myriads around him; shall have his own peculiar blessedness multiplied infinitely by mutually giving and receiving those rapturous pleasures that fill each soul, and in exercising together those untiring activities that shall find, in the service of the King, high, and holy, and ennobling employment; and shall be bound together with all the family of God into one organic whole, one everlasting kingdom, one heavenly city, one body of Christ, one—in living and eternal union with God and the Lamb.

7. The *seventh promise* crowns this glory. It leaves no conceivable element of blessedness wanting. "To him that overcometh will I grant to sit with Me on My throne, even as I also overcame, and am set down with My Father in His throne." This is far more than the "power over the nations," promised in the epistle to Thyatira. That is a share in the act of power and judgment which shall end the conflict, and crown the mediatorial triumphs, and make the universe to ring with the shouts of alleluia; this is to share with Him in the peaceful and eternal glories of the perfected kingdom which are to follow this triumph. "Even as I also overcame." He had a personal conflict here in the flesh on our behalf; He overcame the world, sin, death, and hell, and has been crowned with glory and honour on the right hand of the Majesty on high, as Mediatorial King, and there He must reign till He

§. 7. Royal inheritance.

have put all enemies under His feet. When He shall have done this, there is nothing more left for a mediator to do—the mediatorial reign ceases. But the fruits of that reign are eternal; these are the body of His redeemed and glorified people who are in living and eternal union with Him. As their living Head, He must ever reign in them, over them, and among them. This is His own peculiar throne, and His everlasting kingdom, as distinguished from His mediatorial reign. They shall ever reign with Him over a world redeemed, regenerated, and purified by the final conflagration from every vestige of the curse. In that new heavens and new earth wherein dwelleth righteousness, in that one great city of the living God descended from heaven, every redeemed soul shall share in a far more glorious dominion than that originally conferred on Adam, and lost by the fall.

This is beautifully and expressively represented as sitting with Jesus on *His throne*. The redeemed "shall reign for ever and ever," but not on a throne inherited in their own right, but in His who redeemed them; a throne founded in sovereign grace and redeeming blood. "*On My throne:*" "the throne which belongs to Me as the reward, the final and eternal result of My whole mediatorial work. It is Mine, but Mine for My redeemed to occupy, and rule over a world restored to holiness and harmony." There is something here which we are slow to conceive. To rule and reign, as exercised here on earth, so fully implies power to restrain and prevent, if not to punish, evil, that we find it difficult to conceive of a rule where there is no evil to be restrained or guarded against, and no enforcement of laws by the sanction of penalties. Yet such is the rule promised. It is a dominion where one desire, one aim, one will, pervades every soul, and that will the will of the King Himself. Then it is, and only then can it be, that every soul is king, every one *reigns* with Christ, for He lives perfectly in each. Then shall appear the completeness of the union of Christ and His redeemed: one life, one body, one throne. "Because I live, ye shall live also." "If we suffer with Him, we shall also reign with Him." Then shall this promise be fulfilled when He shall say, "Come, ye blessed of My Father, inherit the kingdom prepared for you from the foundation of the world." Then shall be realized the joyful hope of the crowned elders in the new song, when the Lamb took the seven-sealed book from the hands of Him that sat upon the throne. "We shall reign on the earth." "They shall reign for ever and ever."

Such are the visions of glory spread out by these precious promises to the longing eyes and hearts of all engaged in this spiritual conflict. Their brightness dazzles our feeble vision. It is unutterable. A whole new creation seems to sweep before us in unimagined beauty, purity, and grandeur, pouring its treasures at the feet of the spiritual conqueror; but all this is the mere sign or token of that more mysterious bliss included in these promises, in which we see all the fulness of God pouring its unsearchable riches into his whole being. Blessed be our God for these revelations of it! Weary, and sick, and wounded, and surrounded by darkness and storms, as we often are here, how cheering the glimpses of this coming glory, which ever and anon flash upon us, and assure our trembling hearts of the reality and glory of the invisible kingdom, and the heavenly prize. While thus we look, not at the things that are seen and temporal, but at the things that are not seen and eternal, we gather new strength for the conflict; and even the heaviest burdens, and the most crushing sorrows, appear but light afflictions, working out a far more exceeding and eternal weight of glory.

We must offer one concluding inference. This whole subject corrects all those unwarranted expectations of a perfect visible church which some indulge, and teaches us in what consists the certain final triumph of the visible church, so often promised. Most certainly not in this, that the outward organization or collection of organizations, can ever itself become, by any process of purification and union, the triumphant church—can ever be converted into it. However greatly it may be improved and purified, so as more effectually to accomplish its divine purpose, it can never cease to be imperfect, because composed of imperfect men. Tares must mingle with the wheat until the end. A pure, perfected church can never exist here, while men continue to live in the flesh; that is, until after the resurrection, when the present constitution of the order of nature shall have passed away. When, therefore, the Scriptures teach us the security and triumph of the visible church, they do not mean that these imperfect things that constitute it shall themselves grow into a kingdom of perfection, a glorious organization or system, in which all these promises shall be realized, any more than that these present bodies shall gradually grow into immortal ones. But they teach the precious truth, that this visible church, imperfect as it is, shall withstand the gates of hell, shall never be crushed out by all the fierce assaults of men and devils, but shall triumphantly accomplish the purpose for which it was constituted; that it shall stand secure amidst all the convulsions and upheavings of human society and nations, as the representative of God's chosen and invisible church, and as the channel through which the powers and blessings of the invisible kingdom flow forth upon a guilty world, until, through its instrumentality, every one of the truly called and chosen, (the κλητοι και εκλεκτοι,) the whole real church (εκκλησια) of God shall be rescued from the powers of evil surrounding them and in them, so constituting the triumphant and everlasting kingdom. Then it ceases, because not only the design of it is accomplished, but because the very conditions of its existence cease; and the redeemed, complete in number and in character, and freed from all admixture of evil, under the perfected system that shall succeed in the New Jerusalem, enter upon their princely inheritance. That inheritance is not the mere perfection of the school that trained them for it, but something far higher and nobler.

When a whole people have been formed into an army to resist aggression, or to conquer for themselves a home, and when the end is gained, and all enemies are conquered and destroyed, it can no more act as an army; its existence as such ceases, and its individual soldiers are merged into the triumphant nation, for the fulfilment of those higher functions, and the enjoyment of those nobler activities and pleasures, which were the object of the previous conflict. So with the militant church. When the number of the redeemed is complete, and the conflict in each soul ended, then the whole design, both of the visible church, and of the present course of nature in our fallen world, ends, and all these pass away together, and give place to that entirely new and infinitely glorious order of things represented by the New Jerusalem, in heavenly and mysterious splendours, descending out of heaven from God, where, by gradual accretions, she had been preparing for her final inheritance and glory.

PART III.

THE TRUE CONCEPTION OF THE SPIRITUAL KINGDOM.

Rev., Chap. 4.

Lecture XI. The Divine Nature and Spiritual Privileges of the Kingdom.
" XII. Its Spiritual Life.
" XIII. The Glory, Claims and Privileges of this Life.
" XIV. The Worship of the Kingdom.

LECTURE XI.

THE DIVINE NATURE AND SPIRITUAL PRIVILEGES OF THE KINGDOM.

REV., CHAP. IV: 1–6.

WE here enter upon a new division of this book. The revelation is, however, continuous, though the manner changes. Instead of words addressed to the ear, unearthly sights and sounds burst upon the soul. That we may not in this change lose the connection, let us recall the time and circumstances.

It was the morning of a Lord's day, about sixty years after our blessed Lord had ascended to His heavenly throne. His beloved disciple, and only remaining apostle, was a persecuted exile among the rocks of Patmos. As he gazed from its desolate heights across the Ægean sea to the shores of Asia, he could almost see the region of the seven churches, which he had recently left in deep distress. His loving heart yearned over them. In his banishment he could render them no help. The persecutor's heel was treading some of them in the dust. The blood of noble martyrs had already flowed there. Satan's seat was there, and his rage and malice was bursting forth with new power. External violence was by no means its worst form. This was no proper reason for discouragement—no occasion even for disappointment. Jesus had fully prepared them to expect this, and all the apostles

§. Time and circumstances.

had taught the churches that this was the condition inseparable from faithfulness to the interests of His kingdom. A far greater evil than this saddened his heart. Internal corruption threatened the very life of some of these churches. Even in Ephesus, love had waxed cold; in Pergamos and Thyatira, doctrines and practices as destructive as were those of Balaam or Jezebel to Israel of old, were spreading their poison; in Sardis the church had a name only for life, while dead; and in Laodicea spiritual pride and self-sufficiency had eaten out all zeal, and Christ and the world were placed on a level. Where was this to end? How could the church triumph, and the world be saved, if the church itself lost her purity, and became apostate like Israel of old? Never had she appeared to need so much the presence of her Lord and His apostles. And yet John himself, the last link connecting visibly the church and her glorified Lord, must very soon depart. Amidst such things, even the old apostle needed consolation—how much more the faithful believers of that time, and still more of after, and still darker, ages, when this full-grown apostacy had wound its deadly coils around the suffering, prostrate church! To meet this need, the following revelations were perfectly adapted; and they were given on that same Sabbath day, immediately after those messages to the churches which exposed their danger, and intended as her Lord's last gift, to pour their blessed light over her dark and bloody path through the coming ages.

The awe-struck apostle had not yet recovered fully from the shock produced by that overpowering vision of his Lord's majesty and glory, in the midst of the seven golden candlesticks; and the last words of those messages had scarcely died upon his ear, when the scene changes. That glorious vision suddenly fades away,—the heavens above him seem to open, as if to disclose the mysteries of

§. In the Spirit.

the invisible world, and he hears that same trumpet-toned voice of authority and power now addressing him from above, saying, "Come up hither, and I will shew thee things which must be hereafter." "And immediately," says he, "I was in the Spirit;"—it was not a bodily, but a spiritual ascent. His whole consciousness was severed from all connection with this world and its sensible objects, and elevated into a higher state, where it was entirely controlled by the Spirit, alive only to sights and sounds presented by the Holy Spirit. These sights and sounds were not real, material existences; it was not the real, actual heaven, the locality where the glorified Redeemer dwells with the spirits of His redeemed, which the apostle saw now in vision; but, as the imagination pictures before itself creations of its own as vividly as though beheld by the outward eye, so the Spirit of God now made these pictures of spiritual and future things to pass before the mental vision of the apostle.

In the epistles to the seven churches, John had only to write down the words of his Lord; in all the rest of this book, he has still only to record the scenes, and objects, and actors, as they are made to pass before him, and their acts and words. All that John does here is to tell what he saw and heard. None of these symbols are of his creation. All are just as much divine as the words of the seven epistles. Being presented thus by the Spirit to the soul's inner vision, they were so represented that every feature, act, and word in each scene, essential to give the full idea of the spiritual reality symbolized, would be reported, and that perfectly, and nothing else. There is nothing here, then, without a meaning, without its corresponding spiritual reality. In this whole book, therefore, there is less, far less of the human element, than in any other book of Scripture. In it there is scarcely any room to the writer for human thinking, and none for human illustration.

This method of teaching by symbols seems to many rather like hiding, than revealing, truth. Why these obscure images? Why not, instead of these, tell the things they mean in plain language, which all could at once understand? Whether we could give reasons for this or not, it would be enough to know, that since God has done it, it must be best adapted to the end designed. But we are able to see its wisdom in part, at least. We might ask in return, Why should nations have flags and seals, and place upon their flags and seals some symbol, rather than state in words plainly its meaning? Could any language ever present, as it were in a single point, the great mass of ideas, and truths, and interests, thus often presented at a single glance? Could it do it as impressively? Could it by any possibility so gather up all these as to fix them in the memory, and make them ready to pour through the soul their whole force, as a symbol can? And then as regards the symbols of this book, what if it should be found that almost every thing in it had been already stated in the plain language of Scripture, and spread out often in many forms of precept, promise, warning, parable and argument; and that, after all, most that we find here is the gathering up into distinct forms, and striking symbols and pictures, all these precious truths of the kingdom, by which the faith, and hope, and joy of God's people have been sustained; and that these truths are so gathered up and presented as to show them to be the great moving and controlling principles in all the future history of the kingdom—in all its trials, conflicts, and in its final consummation; and so, too, that under these impressive and concentrated forms, they might be more easily remembered, and more deeply and constantly influence the heart and life amidst the darkness of the ages to come, and counteract the influences of sense, and the obtrusive power of earthly things? As we examine each symbol,

§. *Teaching by symbols.*

all this will become more manifest, and that no other method could with such power accomplish the end designed; that the wisdom of God is just as fully displayed in the perfect adaptation of His revelations to human infirmities in this apparently obscurer method, as in the plainest declarations of other Scriptures. Strictly speaking, they are obscure only as men try to find out from them what they were never designed to teach; as when they seek to extort from them the hidden mysteries of the world of spirits, or a historical delineation of future events, with their times and seasons, so as to enable us distinctly to trace the succession of particular events, as by a prospective history. But when they are consulted to obtain spiritual comfort and guidance, to strengthen faith, and animate hope, and quicken zeal, their response is clear, and as stirring as that trumpet-toned voice that called to John, saying, "Come up hither."

§. Scene of the whole book.

The vision first presented after this call, and recorded in this chapter, forms the scene of all the succeeding visions. It is the high position from which the seer is made to view all earthly things, and especially all the movements of the spiritual kingdom. It is also the stage, as it were, on which, and the great objects amidst which, or in relation to which, all the rest appear and move. It must then be of the greatest importance to understand what this opening vision is designed to represent. This will be a key to the whole of these revelations.

§. General meaning.

What then is it? Of the answer to this there can be little or no doubt. IT IS A SYMBOLICAL PICTURE OF THE SPIRITUAL KINGDOM OF GOD IN ITS ESSENTIAL ELEMENTS. To this kingdom every thing here relates; the whole book is but a prospective view of its conflicts, trials, and triumphs; and therefore, of course, *in it* must be laid the scene on which all the mysterious beings and actions of the book move. It is a picture of the spiritual realities which are all around us, but whose invisible glory we here in the flesh find it so difficult to conceive of, and of which nothing in all the word of God presents such a view as this.

May the Spirit that gave it open our eyes to see its truths, and make our hearts to feel their heavenly power! The whole scene is made up of seven distinct objects.

1. *The throne and its formless occupant.* Of Him who sits on that throne no description is given; §. 1. God in its midst. He was above all description. It is only said He was in appearance like unto a jasper and a sardine stone; no form appears so as to be described; that seems to be concealed beneath the blaze of its own glories, which alone are visible. Those glories are compared to the jasper and sardine. The great variety of the most brilliant colours combined in the jasper, is an appropriate symbol of the variety of infinite and lovely excellencies that blend together in the character of God; and the blood red of the sardine or cornelian is an equally appropriate symbol of that justice that pervades, and is inseparably united with, all His other attributes. He is known only by the glorious displays of these attributes. In the very glory of the attributes that reveal Him, He remains concealed; yet, by these glories He is revealed as the Eternal, Invisible, and Incomprehensible One. How impressive the view thus presented of Him, who "dwelleth in the light which no man can approach unto, whom no man hath seen, nor can see;" and whose ways are as incomprehensible as His nature. "How unsearchable are His judgments, and His ways past finding out!"

2. Secondly, "There was a rainbow round about the throne." This we recognize at once as §. 2. The covenant. the appointed symbol, ever since the flood, of God's covenanted mercy toward a fallen world. "I do set My bow in the cloud, and it

shall be for a token of a covenant between Me and the earth." The same symbol encircles the sapphire throne of Ezekiel's vision, the throne of "the appearance of the glory of the Lord." As it appeared to John, it had a peculiarity which he describes as "in sight like unto an emerald." Bright and dazzling as a precious stone, in all its brightness the green predominated, the well understood emblem of *peace*, and gave its shade to all the other colours. The language of the covenant of redemption, is the song of the angels at the birth of its surety, "Glory to God in the highest, and on earth peace, good will toward men." It is God, in all the majesty of His power, and the splendours of His Godhead, who reigns in the midst of His church, with not a single attribute dimmed; but yet a God who has graciously bound Himself by a covenant of love, to exercise all the fulness of His attributes in working out the matchless mercy of that covenant, the perfect salvation of redeemed sinners. "Know, therefore, that the Lord thy God, He is God, the faithful God, that keepeth covenant and mercy with them that love Him, and keep His commandments, unto a thousand generations." "For this is as the waters of Noah unto Me; for I have sworn that the waters of Noah should no more go over the earth; so have I sworn that I would not be wroth with thee, nor rebuke thee. For the mountains shall depart, and the hills be removed; but My kindness shall not depart from thee, neither shall the covenant of My peace be removed, saith the Lord, that hath mercy on thee." While, therefore, the awful splendours of His holiness and justice fill every heart in His kingdom with awe, this precious symbol invites them near, assuring them that mercy has triumphed over wrath; so that "we have boldness and access with confidence," and may "come boldly unto the throne of grace, that we may obtain mercy, and find grace to help in time of need."

3. The third object accordingly represents those who compose this kingdom. Round about the throne are four and twenty subordinate thrones, and on them four and twenty elders with white robes and golden crowns. The word in the original translated "seats" in verse fourth, is the same as that translated "throne" in the second and third verses, and would, if so translated, better represent the original. Who these elders are, who thus surround the central throne, we learn from this same apostle's words in the first chapter: "Unto Him that loved us and washed us from our sins in His blood, and hath made us kings and priests unto God, even His Father." Also from the fifth chapter, where they sing the new song to the praise of the slain Lamb: "For thou wast slain, and hast redeemed us to God by Thy blood, out of every kindred, and tongue, and people, and nation; and hast made us unto our God kings and priests: and we shall reign on the earth." This was no new view of the character and dignity of God's covenant people. Even to Israel of old, at the foot of Sinai, God had said, "If ye will obey My voice indeed, and keep My covenant, * * * * ye shall be unto Me a kingdom of priests."[1] Paul speaks of those justified by faith as "reigning in life by Jesus Christ," and sitting with Him in heavenly places;"[2] of all believers as "having an altar," and as "offering the sacrifice of praise continually;"[3] and Peter, addressing them, says expressly, "Ye are a royal priesthood." These elders, then, most certainly represent the true and chosen people of God in their real covenant character, relations, and rights. They do not merely represent the glorified church, but all the royal priesthood of God's people viewed exclusively in their covenant standing, and their position in the spiritual kingdom. Hence, their number is twenty-

§. 3. Dignity of the redeemed.

---

[1] Ex. 19: 5, 6.   [2] Rom. 5: 17.   Eph. 2: 6.   [3] Heb. 13: 10, 15.

four,—two, the proper witnessing number, for each of the twelve tribes of God's covenant people. They are thus the beautiful and expressive representative, with their priestly robes, and their golden crowns, of the fulness, consecration, and dignity of God's chosen, the membership of the spiritual kingdom. They are your representatives, believer. Those thrones, and crowns, and priestly robes are yours. That position round and near to the throne of a covenant God is yours. Such is the place you occupy in the spiritual kingdom of God. Its purity, honour, power, and nearness to God are indeed, as yet, yours actually but in part; but if you are His at all in the covenant of His love, they shall be yours in actual possession, in all the glorious fulness of blessing and privilege which they imply,—yours for ever. Like the few in Sardis, see that you defile not your garments; like those in Philadelphia, "Hold fast that which thou hast, that no man take thy crown." To this you are encouraged by the next thing here mentioned.

4. "Out of the throne proceeded lightnings, and thunderings and voices." These can only represent the bright and powerful displays of the divine energy in fulfilling the promises of the covenant, by destroying all the opposition of earth, and hell, the flesh, and the devil. These voices, as well as the lightnings and thunderings, are "*out of the throne;*" they are not there the tumultuous voices of men, but the *manifold words of God*. We have here the mingled energies of His providence and His word—His word, with its many voices of precept, and warning, and promise, and comfort. The awful voices of wrath to all that oppose the interests of this kingdom mingle with the sweetest assurances of His love to all who submit to it. Amidst the lightnings and thunderings of His most awful judgments mingle such voices as these—"I, even I, am He that comforteth you; who art thou, that thou shouldest

§. 4. The Word, and Providence.

be afraid of a man that shall die, and of the son of man, that shall be as grass, and forgettest the Lord thy Maker? * * * I have covered thee in the shadow of My hand, that I may plant the heavens, and lay the foundations of the earth, and say unto Zion, Thou art My people."

But the combined energies of His providence and His word, proceeding out of the throne, are not all which He has in this spiritual kingdom provided for His redeemed. Mentioned in immediate connection with these, is—

§. 5. Divine light.

5. The fifth object: "seven lamps of fire burning before the throne, which are the seven spirits of God." What are these but the manifold and all-sufficient energies of the Divine Spirit, pouring forth their searching light and power through all the kingdom, dispelling all darkness, exposing all delusion and hypocrisy, and giving to all the thunders of His providence, and all the voices of His word, a spiritual efficacy? In this kingdom there is no other light than this. The Holy Ghost, by His enlightening power, fills it with the truth, and peace, and joy of God's salvation. All else on earth is darkness. And whatever thunderings, and lightnings, and voices of wrath may proceed from the throne, and make the earth to tremble, this blessed light of the Spirit of God shines with unremitting and steady brilliancy over all the spiritual church. None of the enthroned and crowned elders, or of those whom they represent, can ever be left in darkness. This Spirit "the world cannot receive, because it seeth Him not, neither knoweth Him; but ye know Him; for He dwelleth with you, and shall be in you." "If we live in the Spirit, let us walk in the Spirit."

§. 6. Purifying influences.

6. The next thing mentioned, and placed in close proximity to these lamps of fire, for it also was immediately "before the throne," was "a sea of glass like unto crystal." There is throughout a general correspondence between

these symbols and the typical symbols of the Old Testament tabernacle and temple; and, indeed, between the whole symbolism of this book, and the types, and figures, and facts of that whole dispensation. But to make this to be a level, glassy expanse, like the surface of a sea, or expanse of water, is in utter disregard of this analogy; in disregard, too, of the use of the sea as a symbol throughout this book, and a figure throughout the Bible, of the tumultuous nations; and not in accordance with the language here used, which does not say it was something like a sea, but a sea made of glass. It was evidently a magnificent reservoir of purifying influences, like that used in the temple of old. That was expressly called a sea; it was of molten brass; it contained about 24,000 gallons, or 400 hogsheads; and was, on account of its magnitude and splendour, one of the noblest and most striking objects which then met the eye of the worshipper, even where all around was so magnificent. It was devoted entirely to typical purposes, being used only in the daily purifications of the priests, to fit them for their approaches to God; other small and movable lavers being used for other and inferior purposes. This picture of the spiritual kingdom would have been evidently imperfect without this symbol of the abundant purifying influences provided in it to wash away all the pollutions of the redeemed, and to fit these spiritual priests for His worship and service. But this symbol, presented to the eye of the apostle, was one of vastly superior magnitude and glory to that molten sea of the old typical worship. It was one, indeed, that it was utterly beyond the power of man, or the capacity of the material, to form, and that could exist only in the spiritual perception, or the imagination. Instead of brass, its material was of pure glass, like unto crystal; thus indicating the transparent clearness with which the purifying influences of divine grace are now revealed in this spiritual kingdom. In the Old

Testament church these influences, though the very same in their real spiritual nature, were but dimly revealed. They were, indeed, known and received only by means of types and shadows, which, like the brazen sea, while they contained them, concealed them. Now, the accomplished facts and clearly revealed truths of the gospel, and the simple ordinances of a spiritual worship, are, as it were, a transparent sea of crystal, in which are not only provided and preserved the waters of life and purity, but by which their spiritual nature and abundance are clearly displayed to all His waiting people.

Large, too, as that was, it was nothing to the vastness of this. In the fifteenth chapter, all the multitude of those who had been kept clean from the defilements of worshipping the beast and his image, are represented as standing on its mighty sides. There, moreover, its contents are, as it were, mingled with fire; both the great purifying agents in nature being thus united in the symbol, as they are elsewhere united in the Scriptures to express the purifying power of the Spirit, in the baptism of water, and the baptism of fire. It is not only by the gentler power of the word, but by the severer efficacy of fiery trials, that the saints are made and kept pure. This is no reservoir that could ever have been filled with human hands; it contains the immeasurable fulness of the grace of God. All can have access to it; all the millions of the redeemed, and all the ages of eternity, cannot exhaust it.

This symbol thus presents, in a visible form, the truths expressed in all those passages of Scripture which teach the necessity of holiness, and of divine cleansing, to secure it, and the abundance of such influences provided in the kingdom of God. "Be ye holy, for I am holy." "Without holiness no man shall see the Lord." "Not by works of righteousness which we have done, but according to His mercy He hath saved us by the washing of regeneration and renewing of the Holy Ghost, which He shed on us abundantly through Jesus Christ our Saviour." "Christ loved the church, and gave Himself for it, that He might sanctify and cleanse it with the washing of water by His word, that He might present it to Himself a glorious church, not having spot, or wrinkle, or any such thing; but that it should be holy and without blemish." "Having, therefore, these promises, dearly beloved, let us cleanse ourselves from all filthiness of the flesh and spirit, perfecting holiness in the fear of God."[1]

"O thou afflicted, tossed with the tempest, and not comforted," see here the exhaustless fulness of sanctifying grace! I know you feel weary often with the agony of the spiritual conflict. The struggle with corruption within, and temptation without, leaves you sad and faint. You sigh for holiness, and peace as its fruit. You long from this body of sin to be free. Remember this sea of glass, these matchless and all-sufficient purifying influences of the kingdom of God, now so clearly, so transparently revealed. The Word has been made flesh; His glory revealed: a fulness of grace and truth. "And of His fulness have all we received, even grace for grace." In the constant, prayerful use of His word, and all the ordinances of His church, you are dwelling on its brink. Oh, bathe in it your polluted soul. It will make the foulest clean. No plague, no palsy, no leprosy of sin, can resist its efficacy. Wash, wash daily, and live, and rejoice.

The only remaining object in this scene is one of exceeding interest: the four living creatures which stand nearest the throne, and lead in the worship of the spiritual kingdom. These will form the subject of succeeding lectures. In the objects already considered, however, we have some of the main features of this kingdom; enough to feed our faith and animate our love, and to encourage

---

[1] 1 Pet. 1: 15.   Heb. 12: 14.   Tit. 3: 5, 6.   Eph. 5: 25–27. 2 Cor. 7: 1.

the heavy laden sinner to enter in and be saved. Here is the throne of Jehovah, spanned with the rainbow of the covenant, revealing Him as displaying the glory of His attributes in working out its gracious purposes; here are redeemed sinners in their pure and priestly robes, and with their crowns of glory, on their thrones of spiritual dominion and dignity; mighty thunderings, and lightnings, and voices of God's providences and word are issuing from the throne to secure its safety and triumph; the all-searching, divine light of the Spirit of God pervades and illumines it; and with this, in inconceivable fulness, are the strangely mingled waters and fires of spiritual purification.

Now, this is not a picture of the heaven to come, let it be remembered. That is very differently represented in the New Jerusalem. No purifying sea will then be needed to wash away pollutions; that will have accomplished its work. This is a picture of what now is, a picture of the present spiritual position, and relations, and privileges of the children of God. It represents the invisible church in its true nature, viewed as entirely distinct and apart from the world, with which, in actual life and to human eyes, it is so intimately mingled. The Holy Spirit has here clothed the precious truths and doctrines elsewhere taught with a visible form, so that, by these sensible images of glory, our hearts might be more deeply impressed with the surpassing excellency of things unseen and spiritual. It would be well for us if this symbolical picture of our state and privileges could be ever before our minds. It would help us in the midst of earthly vanities to perceive the higher glory of that spiritual world to which we belong. We shall realize this vision just in proportion as we enjoy spiritual influences—as we daily live and walk in the Spirit. With this power filling the church and our hearts, we shall know what it is to sit on

§. *Present privileges.*

the thrones of the crowned elders; what it is to gaze upon and approach the awful throne of our covenant and redeeming God; and to stand unmoved amidst the thunders of His judgments, to walk in the light of His Spirit, and the beauty of holiness. We shall know better than any commentator can teach us, the meaning of Paul's language of adoring gratitude: "Blessed be the God and Father of our Lord Jesus Christ, who hath blessed us with all spiritual blessings in heavenly places in Christ;" "who hath raised us up together, and made us sit together in heavenly places in Christ Jesus." Let us, then, more earnestly labour and pray for richer effusions of the Spirit on the church, that our spiritual experience may correspond more fully to our higher position and relations. "When the Lord shall build up Zion, then shall He appear in His glory."

Thus, too, does God teach those who are living only for this world, the reality and glory of His kingdom. These spiritual and unseen things have a glory and a permanence, a reality that no earthly and material things can possess, and which no earthly objects can even represent fully. How fearfully and fatally mistaken those are who are living only for the present world, and slighting the unseen and the eternal, a few days or years will terribly convince them. "The things which are seen are temporal; but the things which are not seen are eternal."

LECTURE XII.

THE SPIRITUAL LIFE.

REV., CHAP. IV: 6-8.

"And in the midst of the throne, and round about the throne, were four beasts full of eyes before and behind. And the first beast was like a lion, and the second beast like a calf, and the third beast had a face as a man, and the fourth beast was like a flying eagle. And the four beasts had each of them six wings about him; and they were full of eyes within."

WE are not brutes; we have souls that shall never die. We are indeed allied to the brute creation, and to this visible world, by our bodies; but by our souls we are still more closely allied to the unseen and spiritual world, and to God Himself. Of that invisible world, our souls form a part; in it lie all our highest interests. We are in just as close and constant contact with it as with this visible world. And yet such is the infirmity of our fallen nature, that the concerns of this perishing world, to which the body belongs, hides from our view that greater world to which our souls belong. Surrounded with visible things, and pressed by bodily wants, or the cares and evils of social life demanding constant attention, and obtruding themselves upon us even when from very weariness we seek to escape them, we find ourselves continually dragged down to earth, and all our thinking chained fast to its little and temporary interests. These two interests were designed to be perfectly harmonious, and if kept in their true relations, would have been so. But now the inferior excludes the superior; the care of the soul gives way to the care of the body; the creature shuts the Creator out of the heart; and the eternal realities of the spiritual world lose all their power. "Man that is in honour,"—by the possession of a rational and immortal nature,—" and understandeth not, is like the beasts that perish."

This debasing and fatal infirmity, even when we are most deeply sensible of its guilt and ruinous results, we find it most difficult to resist, so as to rise to the habitual spiritual mindedness which is life and peace. To do this is the triumph of that faith which is the substance of things hoped for, the evidence of things not seen. But such a faith implies a far clearer and more vivid conception of things spiritual than we generally possess; such a vivid perception of their glory and present importance as sense gives us of the material things around us.

§. Design of these symbols.

Now it is to secure this very impression, with something like this sensible vividness, that much of God's revelation is peculiarly adapted. The Spirit of God here wonderfully helps our infirmities; and one reason, at least, why these infirmities so continue to enfeeble us, is because we so much neglect some of His teachings. The whole sacrificial and ceremonial institutions of the Old Testament are such helps; so, also, are the sacraments of the New Testament. The same end was designed to be promoted by these symbolical pictures of these spiritual realities in this book. Here the Spirit helps us, by clothing these unseen verities in material forms, describing them by sensible images, such as, being retained in the imagination, must effectually, by their surpassing glory, weaken the force of all visible and sensible things over the heart. Let us, then, ponder well these strange sights presented to the apostle in Patmos, that so feeling the powers of the world to come, we may, in this particular at least, realize the blessing promised to those who study this book.

While these remarks apply to all the symbolical teachings of the Spirit, they have a peculiar force and appropriateness in connection with this picture of the spiritual kingdom, and especially with this most remarkable of all the symbols in it, those four living creatures.

No more strange, mysterious, and unearthly object was ever presented, even to the spiritual vision of the inspired prophets, than that described in these verses.

§. Meaning of these living creatures.

The reason is obvious. No more strange, mysterious, and unearthly thing is to be found in the whole range of created being, than that which it is intended to represent. It is nothing less than a visible picture of what the boldest human imagination would have pronounced impossible to be represented by a visible image: It is a symbol of THE LIFE OF GOD IN THE SOUL OF MAN, OF THE SPIRITUAL LIFE OF REDEEMED SINNERS. Or, to express the same idea in a somewhat more concrete form, as it presents itself in those who possess this life—it is *human nature as redeemed and regenerated, united to Christ, and made partaker of the divine nature.* It presents that life in its true nature, and, of course, in its full perfection. This nature can only be very imperfectly understood, as it is seen in imperfectly sanctified souls. This life, as wrought in the believer's soul by the Spirit, in uniting him to Christ, and sustained there by that Spirit, is the same in its nature now, as when at last it reigns supreme in the soul; but the soul itself in its actings now cannot show this nature fully while sin still pollutes it. We can only know what it is now, by considering it apart from the sinful imperfections which still influence the heart; and considered thus by itself, it is the same blessed and glorious thing in the struggling, and in the triumphant saint. In this symbol, then, we have a picture of that life in Christ which the believer now enjoys in part; and which will at length pervade his whole nature, when it shall have destroyed sin in the soul, and finally by the power of the Spirit dwelling in him, shall have quickened his mortal body by a glorious resurrection. It is, therefore, appropriately presented as the last of these symbols, which together set forth the nature and blessings of this spiritual kingdom, the crowning result of them all. A present and reigning God, His eternal covenant, royal and priestly privileges, divine protection, divine light, and purifying power, are the great ideas set forth in the previous symbols. These, however, essential and precious as they are, would give a very imperfect idea of this spiritual kingdom, without this spiritual life, the very design and result of all its other blessings, and the very essence of its existence.

That this is the glorious and hidden thing set forth to our view in this symbol of the four living creatures, is not a matter of fanciful conjecture, nor does it rest on the perception of accidental or arbitrary analogies; but on a careful examination of the history of this symbol throughout the Scriptures, and on the natural, and necessary, and Scriptural interpretation of their properties and forms.

That it cannot represent angelic intelligences is made certain by what is said of them in chap.

§. Share in redemption. 5 : 8, 9. They are there united with the four and twenty elders in worshipping the Lamb; and join with them in those words of the new song, "Thou hast redeemed us to God by Thy blood, out of every kindred, and tongue, and people, and nation." They must, therefore, represent the redeemed, or something essential to them; and yet they must mean something entirely different and distinct from the four and twenty elders, though in perfect harmony and union with them. Since the elders represent the personal dignity and priestly privileges of every individual believer, if this symbol represents their spiritual life—that life which they have only in God, which is hid with Christ in God—then these conditions are fully satisfied; both symbols are necessary to represent the redeemed in their complete character and standing in the kingdom, and each represents a perfectly distinct idea.

I. The whole Scripture history of this symbol is consistent with this view, and demands it.

§. I. History. That history is co-extensive with the history of redemption as revealed to man. These living creatures were, in everything essential, in everything distinctive, indeed, no new thing to the apostle. He would at once recognize in them the same mysterious forms that Ezekiel saw supporting the display of the divine glory revealed to him by the river of Chebar. They differed, indeed, from those in some particulars; but these were only in the manner in which these animal forms were combined, and the number of their wings: these animal forms are the same, and there is the same unnatural and unearthly profusion of eyes and wings. They are so nearly alike, that it is impossible they should be symbols of different truths. But those which Ezekiel saw, he expressly declares were the cherubim, and all through the tenth chapter he so calls them. "And I knew that they were the cherubim."[1] This identifies them in character with those figures that were attached to the mercy seat that covered the ark, and between which the glory of the God of Israel dwelt; which were also wrought all over the inside of the tabernacle and temple. They are thus identified also with the undescribed objects or beings placed at the gate of the garden of Eden, to keep the way of the tree of life, when our first parents were excluded from it.

From the very moment, therefore, that man was turned out of Paradise, and his only hope was the promise of a redemption that should restore him thither, was this symbol presented to his view. And all through the ages and changes of the old dispensation, until Christ

§. Co-extensive with the history of redemption.

[1] Ezek. 10: 20.

came and wrought out this redemption in our nature, and carried that nature in triumph and glory to His throne, as an eternal bond of union and fountain of life to His people, this same symbol is always kept before the eye of His waiting church, as if it were the very embodiment of its highest hopes. Now, here, at the very close of revelation, when the types of the Old Testament, and their antitypes in the New, are gathered up into one glorious view of the unseen realities of the spiritual kingdom of God, this same mysterious form stands out more fully developed, and more distinct in all its parts, than ever, and placed, as we shall see, in immediate connection with the whole history of the future conflicts of the church, until grace is lost in glory, and conflict crowned with eternal triumph. It must, then, have been intended to represent some great essential truth in regard to the kingdom of God, something that entered into its very nature, involved its very existence, embodied the highest hopes of man in every age, and to which God designed that the eyes of His church should always be directed. What could this be but human nature redeemed and regenerated—the life of God in man!

In every place in which this symbol is mentioned, this meaning is perfectly appropriate, and in some the only one it can well bear. The following are all the cases and connections in which it is found in Scripture, viz:

1. It was placed at the gate of Paradise after the fall, together with a flaming sword, to keep the way of the tree of life.

2. It was united at each end into one piece with the mercy seat upon the ark.

3. It covered the interior of the tabernacle and temple; and additional figures of it were placed in the Most Holy place of Solomon's temple.

4. It is spoken of in several places as the dwelling and chariot of God. 2 Sam. 6: 2. 2 Kings 19: 15. Ps.

18 : 10 ; 80 : 1 ; 99 : 1. [Dwelling between = Heb. Inhabiting.]

5. It supported the chariot throne of the glory of the Lord in the vision of Ezekiel.

And in this book of Revelation:

6. It appears in the midst of the throne and round about the throne.

7. It never ceases to praise, day and night.

8. It leads the service of the twenty-four elders. Vs. 9, 10.

9. It joins in the song of the redeemed, being there named first, as if leading it. Chap. 5 : 8, 14.

10. It calls for the agencies used by the Lamb for subduing the world. Chap. 6 : 1, 3, 5, 7.

11. It gives the seven last plagues to the seven angels.

Besides these uses of this symbol, there is only one other place where the word "cherub" occurs. That is in Ezek. 28 : 14, where it is evidently used as being an object of surpassing glory, as a figure to illustrate the extravagant pride of the king of Tyre, and can have no influence, therefore, in determining its symbolic meaning.

Now look at all these uses. What was it preserved and secured to fallen man a place in the Paradise of God, but redemption unto a new life; and how else can he regain possession of it but by this new nature, this spiritual life? What else than a regenerated life keeps the way of the tree of life?

The mercy seat upon the ark represented Christ as our satisfaction to the law; what could the cherubim of gold, united with it into one piece, represent, but redeemed and regenerated humanity in union with Christ; in other words, that new spiritual life that is the necessary result to the redeemed of the satisfaction of Christ?

As covering the whole inside of the tabernacle and temple, as indeed being wrought into the whole of the precious inner curtains, which really constituted the tabernacle proper, the other curtains being only coverings, it seemed to constitute His whole dwelling place: what, then, could it represent there but the multiplication of that spiritual life in the boundless multitudes of regenerated natures, which constitute His whole redeemed church, His spiritual temple, and the body of Christ?

As a symbolic support for the manifestation of Jehovah's glory, in inseparable connection with which that glory always appeared and moved, as in Ezekiel's vision, it had its most beautiful and striking significance in this spiritual life with which, in His church, God's glory is only thus connected and displayed.

And the position which they hold here, and throughout this book, is one that brings them into similar, if not the very same connection, with the throne. "*In the throne, and the circle of the throne*" is the literal translation of the words of the passage before us.* It most naturally expresses the closest possible connection with it without being on it. Is there any creature so near and intimately connected with the manifestation in the church of God's glory, as the "new creature," the spiritual life of the redeemed, the life they enjoy in virtue of their union with Him who has borne their nature to the throne, and which, therefore, comes to them directly from its fountain in the throne?

It is characteristic of this spiritual life, that its very nature is praise, and that it, and nothing else, prompts and leads the worship of the members of the spiritual church, the royal priesthood of saints.

---

* The Greek here will not properly bear the meaning which some commentators give these words, "Between the throne and the circle [*i. e.*, of the elders] around the throne." This would require the word $\varkappa \upsilon \varkappa \lambda \omega$ to be in the gen., as $\pi o \tau a \mu o \upsilon$ in Rev. 22 : 2. May not the words naturally imply that as the throne was lifted up, they were within the circumference of it and under it, and so corresponding exactly to their position in Ezekiel?

K

It is finally this spiritual life which demands for its full perfection in all the body of His redeemed, all those great providential agencies which the Lamb employs as He breaks the seals of God's hidden purposes, and unfolds the plan of His providence; it is this, too, which gives forth to the angels of the seven last plagues, those vials of the wrath of God, for the final destruction of all incorrigible wickedness—vials which have been filled by their hatred and violence toward this spiritual life of God's redeemed.

Having thus examined every relation and connection in which this symbol is used, and finding this view of its meaning fully sustained in every case, and believing that none of the other meanings which have been assigned to it are so sustained, whether that of angels, of the whole renovated and redeemed creation, which is but a necessary result of it, or of the ministry of the church, we feel authorized, with others who have virtually presented the same meaning, to regard this as fixed and settled, as much so as any symbol can be. It is a visible presentation of the great idea of THE SPIRITUAL LIFE, which shall at length pervade every redeemed soul in the kingdom of God.

II. Secondly, it will give still further confirmation to this view, and help us toward the rich practical lessons it contains, to consider the perfect appropriateness of this symbol to set forth the divine properties and excellence of this spiritual life.

§. II. Adaptedness.

This life is something entirely beyond the range of nature. It has its seat deep in the soul renewed by God's Spirit. It does not make the heart throb any more vigorously; it gives no more nourishment to the blood, or tension to the nerves, or vigour to the brain. It displays not its transcendent excellence by feats of intellect, or flights of fancy, or triumphs of genius. Hence, men whose vision takes in only the present world ignore it, and regard the claimant of it as a visionary enthusiast or impostor.

The very symbol shows that it is something that human imagination could not have conceived, much less human or natural power have created. It is something higher, nobler, and more enduring than anything man ever dreamed of in the wildest flights of his fancy and ambition. Nothing among all created living things can adequately represent it.

Hence the Spirit takes the forms of the four most perfect living creatures on earth which together would combine all creature excellence. They are the four leading representatives of the four chief classes into which, for common purposes, men divide the highest and noblest of the animal creation. For this same reason, too, each of these forms has been taken, in the common language of men, and also in Scripture, to figuratively represent some of the highest moral properties. The lion is the highest type of courage and power: "the righteous is as bold as a lion;" the ox, of patience and submission; the human face, of benevolence and intelligence; and the eagle, of soaring devotion and elevation above the world: "they shall mount up on wings as eagles." Together, then, these four become an apt symbol of all perfections of created being: of a life that combines all the highest excellencies of which created life is capable.

But still further to intensify the idea of this life, and to show how immeasurably it transcends all manifestations of earthly life, each of these living ones is full of eyes, before, and behind, and within; and covered with wings, having six each; indicating the most perfect perception of God's will, and sleepless vigilance, and untiring energy in doing it. We have, then, in this symbol, the very image of the divine perfections, so far as a creature can possess them: the life of God in the soul. Could any language, or any other conceivable forms, represent with such vividness and force as this does, the infinite excellence of this spiritual life?

By this symbol three leading properties of this spiritual life are distinctly and prominently set forth, by which it is perfectly described: holiness, divine knowledge, and unwearying activity.

§. Holiness.

This is its very nature. No one living form could even imperfectly shadow this forth. Four are here required to do it; four different natures, each setting forth one of its cardinal constituent elements, and, together, including every moral excellence. Here is lion-like courage in doing the will of God in the face of all difficulties and enemies; perfect meekness and humility, submission to the divine will; love to man as a brother; and eagle-like devotion to God, and communion with Him. What more can there be? To the perfect idea of holiness not one of these can be wanting; with these united, nothing can be wanting. It is by these that the various aspects of the new nature, the spiritual life, are manifested. Your temper and life must present these four distinct faces and forms of moral excellence, or you have no life in you, at least no evidence of it.

§. Divine knowledge, or spiritual insight.

This new life has a power of spiritual perception, a capacity to know divine things, entirely beyond mere nature or intellect, however enlarged. It is but the same thing expressed in such language as this: "The secret of the Lord is with them that fear Him, and He will shew them His covenant." "Evil men understand not judgment; but they that seek the Lord understand all things." "Now we have received not the spirit which is of the world, but the spirit which is of God, that we might know the things that are freely given to us of God." "The natural man receiveth not the things of the Spirit of God, for they are foolishness unto him; neither can he know them, for they are spiritually discerned. But he that is spiritual discerneth all things, yet he himself is discerned of no man." "Ye have an unction from the Holy One, and know all things. The anointing which ye have received of Him abideth in you, and ye need not that any man teach you; but as the same anointing teacheth you of all things, and is truth, and is no lie, and even as it hath taught you, ye shall abide in Him."[1]

Just in proportion as your soul is full of this spiritual life is it covered with eyes, to perceive the beauty of truth, and its adaptation to your wants, and in the same proportion is it secured from all error. From this there is but one sure preservative, a vigorous spiritual life, securing sleepless vigilance, and a quick perception of the divine will. No intellectual acumen, no logical acuteness, can secure the soul from destructive error.

This is another of these leading properties of the life of the Spirit. It belongs to the very §. Untiring activity. nature of this spiritual life, that it should never weary in exercising the functions of praise and obedience. We, alas, even the very best of God's children here, are apt to be soon wearied when the service is hard, for we as yet very imperfectly feel the power of this new life; the numbness of our natural estate of death still clings to us; but when it shall pervade the soul, filling every emotion and desire, then shall we serve as the angels do in heaven. Just in proportion as your soul is now under the power of this new life, is it full of wings, ever ready to fly promptly to do His will, never tiring in His sweet and blessed service.

This spiritual perception and untiring activity, is inseparably and equally connected with every form and manifestation of holy character. It directs and controls as completely the perfect development of holy courage

[1] Ps. 25: 14. Prov. 28: 5. 1 Cor. 2: 12, 14, 15. 1 John 2: 20, 27.

and humility, as of love and communion with God. In this respect, the four living creatures were alike. All partial developments of Christian character arise from retaining and cherishing in the heart some desire or temper which obstructs the growth of this life in that direction.

The crowning excellency of this life is, that it is *eternal*. These living creatures are in immediate connection with the throne. This life is beyond the reach of all earthly and Satanic foes. They are with the Lamb, who is also in the throne, and in their midst, (chap. 5, 6.)

"Your life is hid with Christ in God; and when Christ, who is our life, shall appear, then shall ye also appear with Him in glory."[1]

Until then, however, our experience of this life in its power and joy must be very imperfect, and marked by many vicissitudes. It has only entered your soul. It does not reign there alone; the power of that spiritual death from which it has plucked you, is still most fearfully felt. Now its presence is manifest by the spiritual conflict. If you are conscious of the struggle, if you have eyes to see the preciousness of Jesus, and winged desires to seek and do His will, you have begun to feel its transforming power, and shall at length enjoy its unutterable bliss and glory. The eyes, now so feeble, shall gaze into the depths of knowledge and glory; no more on fainting limbs and trembling steps will you serve Him as a weary pilgrim, but on wings of unmingled love and joy be borne upward and onward for ever, through the enlarging fields of glory and of service.

§. Why so mysterious.

Finally, we see why these symbols are so mysterious, so perfectly unique, without any counterpart in nature, and as material existences not only impossible, but inconceivable. It shows that the life they represent is deeply

---

[1] Col. 3: 3, 4.

mysterious, inconceivably glorious, and full of all perfections compatible with our nature; infinitely beyond any thing of which we can form any conception. The very mysteriousness of these images, and the utter impossibility of conceiving even of them as actual existences, is the very thing that makes them represent more completely the truth expressed by the apostle Paul, "Eye hath not seen, nor ear heard, neither have entered into the heart of man, the things which God hath prepared for them that love Him; but God hath revealed them to us by His Spirit."

There is such a life. It may be ours. It must be ours, or we can have no part in His spiritual kingdom. It must be ours, or we must die the second death. We cannot work it up in our own hearts. God the Spirit alone can bestow it. It is "born not of blood, nor of the will of the flesh, nor of the will of man, but of God." "Except a man be born * * * of the Spirit, he cannot enter into the kingdom of God."

LECTURE XIII.

THE SPIRITUAL LIFE: ITS GLORY, CLAIMS, AND PRIVILEGES.

REV., CHAP. IV: 6-8.

THESE living creatures, so unlike all earthly existences, are representatives of a life unlike and above all earthly life. It is not, however, the life of angels, or of some other highly exalted beings in some distant regions of God's great universe, but the new life of every new born soul, of every converted sinner. This life, existing as it does here in the flesh, in a soul still beset with native corruptions, and in constant and deadly conflict with them, exhibits but very imperfectly its glorious nature and mighty powers. Even to those of us who feel the deep throbbings of this blessed life, and its daily struggles with indwelling sin, its excellence but dimly appears. To know this we must contemplate it, not as obscured and obstructed by our corruptions, but apart, in its own high nature and powers, as the work of the Spirit of God. The germinating shoot that has just burst forth from its shell, and is yet struggling with the clods upon it, can give to the mere observer a very faint idea of the powers and capacities of the life that is working in it. Only as he considers its nature, and principles, and gradual development, and perfected results, can he know the life of the acorn or the oak. To aid us in forming distinct, vivid, and impressive conceptions of the spiritual life, this strange symbol, as we have already seen, was given, that in gazing on it " we might know the things that are freely given to us of God." Its general meaning has been shown in the last lecture. But its unique and complicated character, and the vast importance and comprehensiveness of the truth it represents, fully justify a further exposition, in order to unfold its practical value to the believer. This we shall do in this lecture, under these two leading heads, the glory of this life, and its claims and privileges.

I. This symbol sets vividly before us the *true glory of this hidden life*, and so the infinite excellence of true religion. As a hidden thing, it is despised, its very existence doubted, and its glory always obscured by the obtrusive pomps and noisy bustle of this visible world. The greater the necessity, therefore, for the believer and unbeliever both to reflect much on it. It has a glory that transcends all earthly things; and this is manifest in three particulars: its likeness, its origin, and its results. It bears the divine image, it springs from divine power and blood, it secures the highest blessedness.

§. I. Its glory.

It is the real image of God. Life, even in its lowest forms, is a mysterious thing. Vegetable life, as it develops itself from the tiny germ, and expands by the force of some unseen power into that same complicated system that first produced it, of trunk, and branches, and foliage, and flowers, and fruit, with all their secret vessels and circulating juices, is an object of deep interest. Animal life, with its still more complicated forms, and higher functions; and intellectual life, with its yet far loftier powers of thought and feeling, in all their inscrutable operations, are still deeper mysteries. No human penetration has ever been able to unfold this hidden mystery of life in any of its forms; while yet its existence, its laws, and operations constitute the chief glory of God's creation. What would all creation be without it, but the unbroken stillness and sameness of a

§. 1. Image of God.

creation of death? The child and the philosopher are alike interested in it, and alike baffled in the attempt to penetrate its secrets.

But the life of a new-born soul, the spiritual life, is something far higher than the highest of these. It is as much more excellent and glorious than they, as the very image of God, His moral image, is more glorious than the material work of His hands. This is its very essence. With all the scepticism of men who limit their views to the forms of life which this world alone presents, we really know more of the nature of this highest life than we do, perhaps, of life in any of its lower forms. It is the impress of God's moral perfections stamped by His own almighty power on the intelligent soul. These moral perfections are His chief glory. Holiness is but the sum of these. This gives to every other perfection its brightest radiance. When God promised to Moses that wonderful vision of His glory on the mount, it was in these words, "I will make all My goodness pass before thee," where goodness is but another word for all moral excellence, *the good*. Take away the justice, truth and love in which this consists, and immediately boundless power and knowledge, instead of being objects of admiring love, if conceivable at all, would be inconceivably monstrous and horrible. Without it man becomes a moral monster. His high intelligence is only a ruin, a mighty force without control, blind and destructive. "Wandering stars," the apostle calls such, "to whom is reserved the blackness of darkness for ever." Like some one of the heavenly bodies, broken away from its central sun and prescribed orbit, and sweeping on farther and still farther into the unknown regions of darkness and death, with the same force that would have borne it for ever onward in its original path of light, is a soul destitute of spiritual life. It is an anomaly in God's creation, just such as the devils are. Without this life of holiness, man, with all his powers, his immortal, intelligent nature, is, in the fullest and most dreadful sense, dead, morally and spiritually dead, insensible to, and incapable of, being influenced by that which is God's chief glory, and his own highest end and only happiness. And yet such may the reader of these pages be. Such certainly are we all by nature. "Dead in trespasses and sins," "alienated from the life of God,"[1] is the expressive language of the Holy Spirit. Now the life that can triumph in man over this moral death, and which alone can guide, control and bless his intelligent and immortal nature, and make it like God, must transcend all other life in glory, as much as this mysterious symbol transcends all living creatures.

2. Accordingly, this life has its origin in a new creation. One kind of life cannot originate another. Vegetable life cannot intensify itself into, or work out, animal life; and brute force cannot generate intellectual power. Hence, this life has its commencement in the soul, in what the Scriptures call a new birth, a regeneration, a resurrection. "We are His workmanship, created in Christ Jesus;" "quickened together with Christ." "Ye must be born again." It is this which adds so much to the mystery of this life and its interest. It is something superadded to our fallen nature. It is the recovery of a life once entirely lost; the restoration of a nature totally ruined. It is that same wandering, dark, frozen, and ruined orb that had burst away from its place, and was sweeping on to a still more frightful ruin, seized in its helpless course by the same mighty hand that formed it first, and by that brought back to its true orbit, under the light and power of its redeeming God. The marks of its past ruin are on it, and must remain there for ever, but will remain only as a testimony to the mighty power that seized and restored it; and will

§. 2. Its origin.

---

[1] Eph. 2 : 1.   4 : 14.

make it among all its living sister orbs for ever the most attractive and illustrious object of them all. And this for the simple reason that it is a new creation. In all the universe, no object has gathered upon it so much of the glory of creating power and love as a redeemed soul. Not only is this new life as much God's work as the natural life, it is the brightest display of His creating love. Its dependence, too, on the secret, constant influences of the Holy Spirit is just as complete as that of the natural life on God's providence. What could so adequately picture to our view such a "new creature," such a restored life, as these new and strange creatures of surpassing powers, unlike all other creatures of God?

This, however, is not the full view of its origin. The mystery and glory of this life, in this respect, are still further shown in the great truth of revelation, that it not only requires God's almighty power to create and sustain it, but required His redeeming blood to procure and justify the exercise of that power. God the Son must become incarnate, suffer, and die, that God the Spirit might descend to work this life in the soul. That precious blood must extinguish the curse, before this new creating power could extend the priceless blessing. This life, then, has its highest actual origin, its procuring cause, in redeeming love. It is constantly represented as the result of union with Christ, our risen Redeemer and Surety, who, by His death, abolished death for His people: so that His life is ours; He lives in us; we are one with Him, by His Spirit dwelling in us, as the branches are one with the vine, and sharers of the same life. The glorified humanity of the Son of God becomes thus the ever living source of this life, and, therefore, also the divine pattern, according to which the Spirit is forming it in His people. "Your life is hid with Christ in God." Hence, its symbol bears the image of divinity, as far as a creature can, and has its proper place in the throne and with the Lamb, in the dwelling-place of Divine sovereignty and redeeming love. There in Christ it stands, the highest monument of creating power and atoning blood.

3. In its *results* upon our poor, ruined nature, this life cannot but exhibit its matchless glory.

§. 3. Results.

It is the very consummation in the soul of the mighty work of redemption, by which is presented to the universe the brightest display of the glory of God. Its first faint throbbings of repentance and faith are the blessed beginnings of salvation from sin and from death. Even in its feeblest state, it has eyes to see the glory of God everywhere, and to admire the beauty of holiness; and wings of love to make obedience to God its easy and spontaneous movement, no longer the forced service of an unwilling heart. Its prevalence and power in the church on earth will be the destruction of all the outward forms of error and delusion, which, in beautiful symbolic harmony with this vision of the life, are in this book represented in strong contrast to these living creatures, as wild beasts of monstrous and dragon-like forms, devouring the church of God, and ruling over the helpless nations. Its complete perfection in the soul will be perfectly to know and to do the will of God, as the angels do in heaven. Its full consummation in each believer requires and secures the redemption of the body also from the power of death. For "if the Spirit of Him that raised up Christ from the dead dwell in you, He that raised up Christ from the dead shall also *quicken your mortal bodies by His Spirit that dwelleth in you.*" Its complete realization cannot be until the body, redeemed from the grave, and reunited to the glorified Spirit, and both made like unto the glorified Redeemer, shall, in all the ages to come, show forth "the exceeding riches of His grace, in His kindness toward us through Christ Jesus." Its full manifestation, therefore, will be at that most glorious epoch, for which a whole creation is represented as longing, and groaning, and travailing in pain together until now, "the manifestation of the sons of God:" when "the creature itself shall be delivered from the bondage of corruption, unto the glorious liberty of the sons of God." Then, as the death glanced from man himself upon all the earth, and creatures subject to him, so this life shall pour its indirect blessings and glories all over and through a renovated world.

Such are the unspeakably glorious results of this life. They are results in glory and magnitude worthy of its origin in almighty power and redeeming blood, and consonant to its glorious nature: the life of God in the soul. Of such a life only such living creatures as this divine symbol presents to us could furnish any adequate representation; and in all the wide universe there is no other real object that so combines mere human and creature with truly divine properties, as to make it truly answer to the apparently inconsistent and impossible properties of these living creatures. The new life of God in the soul does this fully. Make yourself, then, believer, familiar with these strange symbols. They will help to impress upon you the glory of this life, and to transform you into it. Their very strangeness will keep you in mind how widely this life differs from the mere life of nature. But its practical bearing will be more fully unfolded still in our other topic.

II. *The claims and privileges* of this new and heavenly life. These are here vividly pictured. This symbol sets before us with special definiteness the holy perfections which we are most strenuously to cultivate in our daily walk, and also the abundant spiritual power provided for their cultivation.

§. II. Claims and privileges.

1. It helps to remove any obscurity that may rest on the idea of true holiness in minds so filled and blinded by earthly things. It does this by presenting, in a definite and impressive form, the

§. 1. Holiness.

indispensable features of this life of holiness, few but complete. It shows it under four distinct manifestations, represented under the four entirely distinct forms of this living creature. We have already briefly explained these. We recall attention to them here, in order to impress the practical lesson taught. We have here a perfect and practical analysis of creature holiness. And each one of these four leading virtues or graces, in which it consists, is presented as a distinct and separate form, while they together form one symbol, as if to show that each of these must receive a distinct and separate attention, a decisive manifestation in the character, and hence a distinct cultivation, in order that the life of holiness may be complete.

In one aspect of it, holiness, like these living creatures, is all boldness and triumph; in another, it is all meekness and submission; in another, it is all benevolence; and in a fourth, it is all communion with God. These involve every emotion of the new-born soul, every aspect of the renewed nature; and according to the circumstances and relations of the soul, each for the time seems to absorb and control all its energies. This is the holiness which every child of the kingdom must possess, and cultivate, and finally be perfected in. In regard to sin and temptation, it is determined resistance and triumph; in regard to rights, and duties, and trials, it is meekness, humility, and submission; in regard to the creature and to man, it is kingly dominion, and a brother's love; toward God it rises in heavenly communion.

2. But who is sufficient for these things? In order to the attainment of these graces in their full harmony and power, there is required the highest spiritual understanding and strength, whereas we feel ourselves to be blind and weak. But this spiritual life bestowed in the kingdom of God, is provided with every faculty of spiritual knowledge and power. Eyes and wings being the most perfect faculties of knowledge

§. 2. Knowledge.

and action, and these living ones being full of these, teach us that the new life wrought by the Spirit is, in its whole nature, perfectly endowed for perceiving and for doing whatever is implied in this holy triumph, humility, love, and devotion. See set forth in this symbol the fulness and extent of your spiritual privileges, the unsearchable riches of grace provided, as well as the degree and nature of the holiness required. It is indeed true, that, while here, you are not freed from the old nature; you groan, being burdened. But we are everywhere taught the precious truth, which this symbol, all full of eyes and wings, so strikingly represents, that in this struggle we are not left to the powers of mere nature for wisdom and strength. Such passages as the following might be written under this symbol, as its best exposition practically, at least of this feature of it, full of eyes and wings: "*Be ye filled with the Spirit.*" "That ye might be filled with the knowledge of His will, in all wisdom and spiritual understanding;" "strengthened with all might according to His glorious power, unto all patience and long suffering with joyfulness." "That the God of our Lord Jesus Christ, the Father of glory, may give unto you the spirit of wisdom and revelation in the knowledge of Him: the eyes of your understanding being enlightened; that ye may know what is the hope of His calling, and what the riches of the glory of His inheritance in the saints, and what is the exceeding greatness of His power to us-ward who believe, according to the working of His mighty power, which He wrought in Christ, when He raised Him from the dead, and set Him at His own right hand in the heavenly places." And thus "hath He quickened us together with Christ, and hath raised us up together, and made us sit together in heavenly places in Christ Jesus." "That He would grant you, according to the riches of His glory, to be strengthened with might by His Spirit in the inner man; that Christ may dwell in your hearts by faith; that ye, being rooted and grounded in love, may be able to comprehend with all saints what is the breadth, and length, and depth, and height; and to know the love of Christ, which passeth knowledge, that ye might be filled with all the fulness of God."

Are these, indeed, the very words of God addressed to all His believing people, even while struggling here, where the currents of this divine life are so obstructed? Are these the unspeakable privileges of the saints? Is this the Spirit's own description of the life of a new-born soul?

Rise, then, oh! rise, believer in Jesus, to the true conception and enjoyment of this divine life in your soul. You are not straitened in God, but in yourself. It is because you regard these high attainments of holiness as beyond your reach, because you set such narrow limits to the grace of God, because, by confining your view so much to your own native helplessness and ignorance, you lose sight of the infinite resources of God's Spirit freely bestowed, that you fail so greatly to manifest the spiritual knowledge, activity, and holiness of these living ones. All the light of the Spirit is yours; all the might of the Spirit is yours. The command is, "Be filled with the Spirit." What more could you receive? You can receive it only by faith, by an exclusive reliance on the finished work of your Surety, and only as you believe yourself welcome to it, and actually venture upon it in the walk and work of holy obedience. "They that wait upon the Lord shall renew their strength; they shall mount up on wings as eagles; they shall run and not be weary; they shall walk and not faint." Let these living creatures in and around the throne of covenant grace and redeeming love be ever before your mind, holding up before you, in their unspeakably glorious forms, the surpassing glory, the holy nature, and the high powers and privileges of that spiritual life which you possess in Christ.

1. See how the Spirit of God employs every possible variety and form of instruction, in conveying to us the knowledge of spiritual things, and impressing them on our dull and sluggish hearts, and praise Him for the boundless treasures of His holy word.

§. 1. Riches of Scripture.

2. How vain, how contemptible the things of earth! In view of the glory and blessedness of this hidden life, how mean this bustling, boasting world appears! We who profess to have felt its power, and tasted its blessedness, shall we, can we, live for earthly good? To perfect this life in our own souls, to exhibit its beauty and power to a dying world, this is the design of our high calling. Shall it not be our daily effort, our unceasing prayer?

§. 2. Vanity of earth.

3. Here, too, is comfort in all our afflictions. It is "while we look not at the things that are seen, but at the things that are not seen, that these light afflictions work out for us a far more exceeding and eternal weight of glory," by perfecting this divine life in us. "For we know that if our earthly house of this tabernacle were dissolved, we have"—by virtue of this life—"a building of God, a house not made with hands, eternal in the heavens. For we that are in this tabernacle do groan, being burdened, not for that we would be unclothed, but clothed upon, *that mortality might be swallowed up of life.*"

§. 3. Comfort.

4. Mere nature here may learn its utter helplessness. Dead in trespasses and sins. Nothing less than almighty power can impart this heavenly life. It is a work of sovereign grace. God is under no obligation to bestow it on any. Multitudes venturing on day by day without it, are perishing in their sins. While God is under no obligation to bestow it, He declares that they who neglect it shall perish. "How shall we escape, if we neglect so great

§. 4. Man's helplessness.

salvation?" And directly from the very midst of these living ones—from the immediate presence of Him that sits upon the throne—from the lips of the Lamb Himself, comes the voice of that most gracious invitation found at the end of this book: "The Spirit and the bride say, Come. And let him that heareth say, Come. And let him that is athirst, Come. And whosoever will, let him take THE WATER OF LIFE FREELY." "For God so loved the world, that He gave His only-begotten Son, that whosoever believeth in Him might not perish, but have EVERLASTING LIFE."

LECTURE XIV.

THE WORSHIP OF THE KINGDOM.

Rev., Chap. iv: 8-11.

"And they rest not day and night, saying, Holy, holy, holy, Lord God Almighty, which was, and is, and is to come. And when those living creatures give glory, and honour, and thanks to Him that sat on the throne, who liveth for ever and ever, the four and twenty elders fall down before Him that sat on the throne, and worship Him that liveth for ever and ever, and cast their crowns before the throne, saying: Thou art worthy, O Lord, to receive glory, and honour, and power; for Thou hast created all things, and for Thy pleasure they are, and were created."

WE are not yet quite done with this chapter of wonderful things. We have seen that it represents the spiritual kingdom of God, the true invisible church of the Redeemer. In a single view it presents its covenant God, its redeemed people in their kingly and priestly dignity, its spiritual light and purifying influences, and its new and exalted life. This last and crowning blessing we have seen brought out into a most striking visible reality, in the living creatures, with their numerous eyes and wings, and four most perfect creature forms, showing a life combining the most perfect powers of knowing and doing whatever is implied in every form of holy action, whether successful resistance to sin, profound humility, intelligent love, or eagle-winged devotion.

Now this is the church which, throughout this book, is represented as in continual conflict with the powers of earth and hell; not that worldly, polluted, mongrel, deformed thing by which it is visibly represented, and which, therefore, receives its name, and which, though including nearly all the moral excellence of earth, has sadly obscured and degraded it by worldly conformity. It is not any external organization; all these have in them so much of human error, pride, and weakness, as to place much that belongs to them on the side of the opposition to the pure and spiritual church of God. Hence, in the course of the great conflict, it must often be that what in human eyes has been identified with the real church or kingdom of God, seems itself to be the object of the same sweeping judgments that desolate the nations, and not only comes into fearful peril, but is laid prostrate in utter confusion and shame. This for a time not only strengthens unbelief, and brings upon the truth and kingdom of Christ the sneer of the world, but tries and shakes the faith of God's own people. Hence the importance of carefully distinguishing between the real spiritual kingdom of God, and all of our imperfect organizations that represent it, and that need most thorough and radical changes before they can represent it adequately. It is with the whole church as with the individual believer; as each believer is a very imperfect representative of the spiritual life, so the visible church is, as we have previously seen, a very imperfect manifestation of the spiritual kingdom: and as the afflictions and the seeming desertions of the believer for a time are only in order to perfect this life in Him, so the apparent reverses and defeats of the visible church are only because it has in it so much of the world, and in order to perfect the spiritual kingdom, and bring it out at last into a distinct, separate, and glorious realization. Hence it is that, in contrast with the imperfections of the visible church, as previously presented in "the seven churches," the Spirit of God is so careful here to set before us, in the very beginning, the real nature and character of that invisible church, or spiritual kingdom, whose struggles and triumphs He is about to depict for the instruction and comfort of her suffering people.

To accomplish this, the Spirit saw that it was not enough to present the mere symbols of the objects which constitute it, its indwelling God, its redeemed people, and its heavenly blessings of light, and purity, and life. He sets before us the workings of this life, the secret springs of its spiritual activities and bliss, so as effectually to distinguish it from all counterfeits and admixtures. This is done with an ease, a simplicity, and a perfectness in the verses before us, which show the very signature of the Holy Ghost, and cause the mind that once clearly perceives them to stand awe struck as it reads. It is done by setting all the living activities of this kingdom in motion in the act of holy worship. By this one thing, the worship of the living creatures and the elders, the true workings of the spiritual life, and the true character and principles of the spiritual service of the true church, is presented in strong contrast to all that impure, perverted, self-righteous service which, in the name of religion and the church, has been presented to a holy God.

§. Activities of this new life.

This worship begins with the living creatures, by their unceasing adoration of the divine holiness. "They rest not day and night saying, Holy, holy, holy is the Lord God Almighty, which was, and is, and is to come." And it is "when" they thus adore, that the four and twenty elders, as by some essential and living sympathy, fall down before Him that sits on the throne, and worship Him, casting their crowns before the throne, and in a chorus of praise acknowledge His right to universal homage, and His will and pleasure as the creature's only law and end.

We are taught here that all spiritual worship and service proceeds from a renewed heart, and consists in adoration of the divine holiness, and consecration to the divine service.

1. All true worship must proceed from a renewed heart. In the scene before us, the worship begins with the living creatures. It is only when they adore that the elders fall down and worship. So that were it not for them, all would be silent and motionless. In the next chapter, also, they are represented as leading the service of the elders. Worship is an exercise of the new life, a work of the new creature. The unrenewed sinner is dead in trespasses and sins; and you might as well expect a lifeless corpse to move and speak, as such a soul to have the first emotion of true and acceptable worship. Whatever prayers he may offer, whatever solemn hymns of praise he may unite in, however he may sit in the place, and assume the posture of a true worshipper, there is no true worship in it. No influences from without, however impressive and powerful, can awaken, in a soul spiritually dead, one single emotion of true worship. You cannot galvanize a dead soul into life. No power of music can give hearing to the deaf, or a tongue to the dumb. Influences that stir the renewed heart to its depths fall powerless upon the natural man. The worship of God is the most spiritual act of which a creature is capable, and can, therefore, only proceed from a spiritual nature, a nature renewed by the Holy Ghost. "Except a man be born again, he cannot see the kingdom of God." He cannot, therefore, have any capacity to unite in its holy services and joys, either here or hereafter.

§. 1. Worship, the work of a new heart.

This becomes still more manifest when we consider the two essential elements of all true worship as here set forth.

2. Observe, then, secondly, that one, the first essential element in all true worship is adoration of the character of God, especially of His holiness. This is represented as the unremitting employment of these living creatures. "They

§. 2. Consists in (1) Adoration.

rest not day and night saying, Holy, holy, holy, Lord God Almighty, which was, and is, and is to come." "*They rest not;*" they have no intermission. It is their very nature to do this. The language teaches that it is the very nature of the new life to adore the divine perfections, and delight in them. This adoration belongs to the very essence, and must thoroughly pervade all true prayer, and every other act of communion with God. It

"* * is the Christian's vital breath,
  The Christian's native air."

The sovereignty, self-existence, eternity, unchangeableness, and omnipotence, which are essential to any true idea of God, and which fill the soul with awe, and present Him as the all-sufficient object of our trust, are all included in these few comprehensive words of the living creatures; but it is the holiness which characterizes and directs all these other attributes, which is the immediate object of their praise. On this the new creature delights to gaze and meditate; and in making fresh discoveries of its beauty and glory it finds its highest bliss. The moral perfections of a God of boundless power and knowledge, unfolding themselves with ever increasing brightness, is that which fills all heaven with its purest joys and highest praises. The delight of a soul here, as it discovers some new truth, or some important application of truth, is often most exquisite. But this is a discovery among merely His lower works. In all the universe there can be nothing in glory like the God that made it. What, then, must be the rapture of a soul that has discovered something of the glory of the infinite Jehovah Himself, and especially of His united moral perfections?

But in all the displays of these in creation and providence, there is nothing to compare with redemption. It is as these living creatures gaze upon that throne encircled by the rainbow of covenant mercy, and surrounded by the other symbols of redeeming love, that they obtain these rapturous views of the holiness of God; so in all the manifestations of the divine character, there is nothing like the holiness that beams so gloriously in the cross, to awaken the rapturous praise of a renewed heart. That amazing combination of unrelaxing justice and unfathomable love that brought the Son of God Himself from the throne to the cross, to suffer the penalty of the law, in order to the sinner's pardon; and that infinite purity that shines in the completed results of this amazing scheme, utterly destroying sin in every pardoned sinner, and causing such, from being the vilest, to become the most illustrious of God's creatures, and the most closely united to the divine nature itself, this especially must ever call forth the praise of the regenerate soul.

Observe, too, that it is not merely His goodness and mercy, in addition to His wisdom and power, that calls forth this adoring praise. These all men can, in some degree, appreciate. But it is His holiness, arraying all the perfections of His nature in eternal hostility to all sin and sinners as such. In this only the renewed soul can see any real beauty, so as to admire it. This is a feature in which false religion is specially distinguished from the true, and the fervours of a spurious worship from the rapturous praises of a renewed heart.

Listen to the utterances of the saints in Scripture. Read the Psalms. How the souls of these holy men of old delighted in God, and in devout meditation on His holy character. A large portion of the book of Psalms is but an expansion of the language of adoration uttered by these living creatures. This appears there as the leading principle of the spiritual life, its very breath. It lives in the contemplation of the holiness of God, as shown in all His dealings, and expressed in His word. It "rests not day and night" from this. Even when thwarted by the power of indwelling sin in struggling saints here, it could give rise to such language as this: "Oh, how love I Thy law! it is my meditation all the day." "In His law doth he meditate day and night."

Is this the character of our devotional exercises? Are the perfections of God the object of our delighted study? Do we love to gaze upon His holiness, till the soul melts and rejoices under its power? Since adoration is the nature of this spiritual life, so that it can no more cease to adore than a living man to breathe, we may by this judge of its vigour in our own hearts. We may thus discover also a secret cause of our own spiritual weakness. For as this is the essential nature of true religion, the habitual direction of the soul to this great object in meditation, and prayer, and praise is absolutely necessary to preserve a vigorous Christian life.

While self-inspection is essential to this divine life—these living creatures had eyes "*within*,"

§. A practical error.

as well as without—it can be properly conducted only in the light of the divine holiness in the plan of redemption. Many believers, it is to be feared, occupy their devotional hours in looking too exclusively into themselves, contemplating their own wants, and sins, and sorrows, and infirmities, instead of opening their hearts to the light and heat of this glorious sun. They carry into the dark chambers the light of the broken and avenging law, instead of throwing open the windows also to the brightness and melting warmth of the gospel of God's grace. Look upon that throne of covenant grace; bring your soul more and more face to face with a holy God in His infinite excellence and majesty, as displayed in His kingdom of grace, that thus the emotions of these living creatures may be made to fill it; and then inbred corruptions and other objects, whether of joy or sorrow, will soon lose their power.

3. The other essential element in true worship, as here set before us, is *consecration*. This is beautifully symbolized in the service of the twenty-four elders, which immediately follows the adoration of the living creatures.

§. 3. In (2) Consecration.

It might at first sight appear to some to be an objection to our exposition, that one of these principles of true worship is an act of the living creatures, and the other of the twenty-four elders, as if they were by different agents. A little closer attention to it will, we think, produce the conviction that in this we have one of the strongest proofs of its correctness, and of its perfect symbolic consistency. This apparently different agency was necessary to give a correct view of the spiritual reality. It is thus in perfect consistency with those passages of Scripture which represent this spiritual life as something distinct from, and additional to, the personality of the believer, though having existence only in it. It is the new man, in distinction from the old man; it is a new creature. We have this language: "The flesh lusteth against the Spirit, and the Spirit against the flesh, so that ye cannot do the things that ye would." "Ye are dead, and your life is hid with Christ in God." "I live, yet not I, but Christ liveth in me." So here, by this spiritual life being represented separately from the persons of the redeemed, it is shown, as it could not otherwise have been, as one of the blessings provided and laid up in Christ for them; and so, too, only could its infinite fulness and perfection be set forth. But this is not all. By this adoration being the act of these living ones, we are taught that this power to see, feel, and adore the holy perfections of God is the exclusive act of the new heart, the life wrought and sustained by the indwelling Spirit, and no mere enlargement of natural capacities. And by its at once bringing the elders from their seats, prostrate before the throne, is shown the perfect unity of feeling and action between them, how completely the emotions of this new life control the persons of the redeemed, even the whole spiritual church; and by the consecration being represented as theirs, and not the act of the living creatures, but prompted by them, we are taught that this consecration is the act of the whole being, of the whole person redeemed, carrying with it all he is and has; and that this is so just when, and to the degree, that this new life in Christ imparts to him adoring views of God.

Three things appear to be clearly taught us by this worship of the twenty-four elders, as to the nature of this consecration.

1. They fall down before the throne, and thus teach us that *profound and cordial submission to all the dispensations* of that throne is the very first principle of Christian consecration.

§. Three things: 1. Submission.

There can be no proper setting apart of ourselves to God and His service, except as we recognize His perfect right to dispose of us as He pleases, and regard it as our duty and happiness to yield ourselves up entirely to His disposal. In reference to all dark dispensations, it is saying, "Even so, Father, for so it seemeth good in Thy sight;" in reference to all afflictions and sorrows, it is saying, "It is the Lord, let Him do as seemeth Him good;" and in reference to duty, its single inquiry is, "What wilt Thou have me to do?" There is no reserve. Such a prostration before the throne intimates that all is His, body, and soul, and property, and time, and influence. It implies that the redeemed have renounced all right in and to themselves, and all other disposal of themselves, than this yielding of themselves to be used by Him, in His own way, for His own glory.

2. This consecration implies, secondly, the sweet obligation imposed by His grace. These elders cast their crowns before the throne in acknowledgment that these crowns

§. 2. Grateful obligation.

were from God, His free and undeserved gift. The redeemed are never tired of ascribing all their distinctions to free and sovereign grace. As they look around upon a world lying in wickedness, dead in sins, and resting under the curse, and realize the vast elevation to which, as sons of God, they have been raised, and the high honours and dignities conferred on them as spiritual kings and priests, do they feel a single throb of self-complacency or pride as the special favourites of heaven? Nothing could be more abhorrent to their nature; nothing more inconsistent with the ground on which they have received these blessings, and the tenure on which they hold them. So far from this, the feeling that grace alone has made them to differ humbles them in the dust, and leads them to lay all their honours and dignities at the feet of their redeeming God. The obligation to use these gifts and distinctions entirely in promoting the glory of the Giver, is felt pressing on their souls with all the force of the vast magnitude and weight of redeeming love and sovereign mercy. The grace received is itself consecrated and used for God; it is not regarded as a gift merely for their own personal benefit and comfort, but as an additional precious trust, by which to show forth the grace and glory of a covenant God. "Ye are a chosen generation, a royal priesthood, a holy nation, a peculiar people, that ye should show forth the praises of Him who hath called you out of darkness into His marvellous light."

3. Thirdly, this consecration recognizes God as the sole rule and end of the creature. This is very fully and forcibly expressed in the doxology of these elders. "Thou art worthy, O Lord, to receive glory, and honour, and power; for Thou hast created all things, and *for Thy pleasure they are*, and were created." The same sentiment is expressed by Paul thus: "Of Him, and through Him, and *to Him* are all things; to whom be glory for ever and ever,

§. 3. God our sole end.

Amen." "All things were created by Him, and *for Him*." All things are for God, because all are by Him. This single idea, so simple, so evident, and yet so grand, and so vast in the extent over which it sweeps, had it only been embraced in its full meaning, would have ended half the errors, and scattered the difficulties and perplexities that have obscured the great first principles of truth and duty. MAN IS FOR GOD, NOT GOD FOR MAN; the creation is for the Creator, not the Creator for His creation. And yet a very large portion of the reasonings in regard to the claims of God, and the duty of man, have gone upon the false and rotten principle that the good of the creature is the great test of truth and virtue. Hence the false theories as to the standard of virtue and duty. The proper application of this simple statement, "We are for God, not God for us," settles the whole business of duty, and decides every doubt and difficulty. On the other hand, however, we too often talk and act as if we had each some special, separate, independent interests of our own, for which we must secure God's patronage; and we think of God, and His service and worship, as the means to advance our petty interests, instead of ourselves, our country, and our race, and all other orders of being, as together means to advance His glory by doing His will. This becomes very manifest in times of great anxiety, when high earthly interests are in peril, such especially as a country's welfare and safety. In such cases men are everywhere ready to fast and pray, and to turn to the church, to get its intercessions with God, not in real acknowledgment of their sins, and true repentance, humiliation, and submission, but to secure Him to be on their side, and to blast the projects of their enemies. Then, too, if He refuse to favour their views of right, and utterly disappoint their cherished hopes, they are very apt to treat God very much as the heathen does his idol, they virtually dethrone Him, by denying His universal and sovereign providence.

The creature, on the other hand, has nothing whatever to say about rights and claims in relation to His Creator. He is but clay in the hands of the potter, to be formed as He pleases unto honour or dishonour. His private views of his own good, or his rights in reference to his fellow creatures, are not the test of what the Creator ought to do, or the standard by which he is to measure his own duty, or his expectations. There is but one standard, the will of God; but one end, the glory of God. "For Thy pleasure all things are, and were created."

Let us once enthrone this simple principle in our souls, that we are for God, and not God for us, and we shall soon find that most, if not all the difficulties that have enveloped some of the high doctrines of revelation, as God's sovereignty, and election, and predestination, and eternal misery, will vanish as mists before the rising sun; and all the mysteries that darken the providence of God, instead of troubling us, would only awaken profounder reverence and adoration. There is nothing higher than God, by which as a standard we may test His claims and dealings. He himself, His will and pleasure, on the other hand, is the only rule by which to test all doctrines, and measure all duties. Not until this truth is fully and cordially received, and bears practical rule in the heart, is the consecration of ourselves to God complete. We shall never fall prostrate before His throne, and cast our crowns at His feet, renouncing all right and claim to ourselves and His gifts for ever, until we joyfully feel that we and everything else exist for Him, and, therefore, that it is only in living for Him that our substantial happiness is infallibly secured.

Such is the divine pattern of the consecration required in every member of the spiritual kingdom. These three things are essential to it: cordial submission to the will, a sense of complete obligation to the grace, and entire devotion to the glory of God. In this, and the adoration of the divine character from which it springs, consists all spiritual worship.

This vision of the worship of the spiritual kingdom teaches us—

1. First, what must be the nature, and what is the true test of all acceptable external worship.

§. Inf. 1. What is true worship? It must be such as shall *express* adoration of God, and consecration to Him, and shall tend to *excite* these. These must be the origin and end of every act of worship, or it is worthless. No mere fervency of petition, no supposed ardour of grateful feeling, as we enjoy abundantly the blessings of a kind Providence, or experience some great deliverance, nor any excitement of emotion under the force of conscience, or the belief of pardon, distinctively marks genuine worship. All these may exist in connection with the purest selfishness, without any right views of the holiness of God, or His claims upon us.

Nor can it consist in, or be tested by, any outward forms or services. There are, indeed, certain outward acts, and bodily postures, which are universally regarded as natural expressions of trust, humiliation, reverence, and praise. These, however, are few and simple: the audible voice in prayer and praise, and witnessing to the truth; the publican's downcast eye; and standing, kneeling, and prostration, according to the circumstances. Even these, too, inseparable as they are in certain times and places from the genuine feeling of worship, if not the result of such feeling, or if regarded as possessing a distinct value in themselves, become positively offensive.

But when forms and ceremonies, which are not natural expressions of spiritual worship, are introduced by mere human will into the external worship of God, for the sake of their beauty, impressiveness, or solemnity, so far from being acts of worship, they vitiate it. Such influence can never touch the spiritual life but to benumb it. They divert the mind from the only object of spiritual worship. The impressions they make are dangerously deceptive, just in proportion to their power over the emotional nature. By a skilful manipulation of the emotional and sensational nature of man, in the use of language, music, and ceremonies, individuals and assemblies may be galvanized into the highest excitement of feeling, which may be readily mistaken by the subject of it for the fervours of true worship. Instead of awakening profound and humbling views of the holiness and glory of God, they intoxicate the soul with a dizzy whirl of undefined emotions, of which *self* is the centre and the end.

On the other hand, where these adoring views of God lead to a spirit of hearty consecration, the whole life becomes an act of worship. Hence, the completest test of its genuineness, is its expression in a life of grateful love and obedience. Without this, forms and professions are only hypocrisy. This is the Scripture test and standard. It takes the very words which distinctively express external and ceremonial worship, and applies them to true holiness of life, declaring that the true ritual, the outward form of worship, the only acceptable ceremonial of this spiritual church, under this dispensation, is a holy life. In James 1: 26, 27, the words "religious" and "religion" are words denoting strictly in the original the outward form of worship. The meaning, therefore, is, "If any man among you seem to be a worshipper, and bridleth not his tongue, but deceiveth his own heart, that man's worship is vain. Pure worship and undefiled before God and the Father is this, to visit the fatherless and widows in their affliction, and to keep himself unspotted from the world." So in the stirring exhortation of the apostle in Rom. 12: 1, where the word "service" is properly "*worship*," and is applied elsewhere to the Jewish ritual service, the whole extent of Christian consecration is included in it: "I beseech you, therefore, brethren, by the mercies of God, that ye present your bodies a living sacrifice, holy, acceptable unto God, which is your reasonable service," or *worship*.

2. How the Spirit pours contempt on all outward shows and pomps of worship, in unfolding thus the transcendent glory of this spiritual service. The seer here carries us entirely out of sight of all the pomps of external worship, with which men in their folly have marred the true worship of the church, in order to commend it to the senses of those who could not appreciate any thing else, and introduces to a scene far more grand, and simple as it is grand. It finds its corresponding spiritual reality, not merely in the state of glory, but in measure here on earth. There is here a temple nobler far than any vaulted pile that human art ever constructed, though filled with crowds of kneeling worshippers, and reverberating with anthems of loftiest praise: a regenerate human heart. Jehovah declares expressly, that He prefers this to all the glories of His own material creation. "Thus saith the Lord, Heaven is My throne, and the earth is My footstool, * * * where is the place of My rest? For all those things hath Mine hand made, * * * saith the Lord; but to this man will I look, even to him that is poor, and of a contrite spirit, and trembleth at My word." "I dwell in the high and holy place, with him also that is of a contrite and humble spirit." It is the worship of such a living soul, with its indwelling God, and its spiritual glory, which is here set before us in its true nature. Or rather, perhaps, the worship of the whole church of redeemed and regenerate souls, as this is ever passing before the all-seeing eye of God, all of them uniting in the same holy service, and under the power of the same spiritual life. The Holy Ghost, in these verses, seems to brush away the vail that conceals the deep and mysterious workings of a soul in its intercourse with God,

and lets us see the movements of its hidden life. He shows us the throbbings of this life at its heart—the secret springs of all holy action. As if some one would enable the physiologist to look within the heart of a living man, and to see those secret workings by which, at each successive moment, the tide of life is propelled through all the physical frame, so is this vision to the believer. The light which that would throw upon the mysteries of the natural life, this throws upon the deeper mysteries of the spiritual life. Let us earnestly and gratefully consider what the Spirit so elaborately and strikingly teaches.

3. Do we not here discover also one cause, certainly a clear mark, of the low piety of a large part of the church? Is it not in the neglect of the perfections of God, as objects of devout meditation and adoration? In our acts of devotion, public and private, do we sufficiently set the Lord Himself before us, in the majesty and holiness of His character? Is there not a very grievous, wide spread, and deep seated defect in the religious experience of the church, just in this particular?

§. Inf. 3. One cause, and correction of low piety.

The corrective is evident. Study the perfections of God. Make His holy character your meditation by day and by night. The vision of God's glory in the mount caused Moses' face to shine, so that Israel could not look upon it; such is the transforming power of devout meditation on His glory now. "Beholding as in a glass the glory of the Lord, we are changed into the same image from glory to glory, as by the Spirit of the Lord." Nothing else can do it. Nothing else will ever secure this hearty consecration to His service. This will bring your soul prostrate in joyful submission at the footstool of His throne. This will cause you, as you realize the amazing privileges to which, by adopting love, you are advanced, to pluck your undeserved honours from your own brow, and lay them at the feet of your crucified

King. The rights and claims of God will be acknowledged, just in proportion as the perfections of His character are known and cherished. What higher, grander, more elevating theme can be proposed to a creature's thoughts?

Finally. We may not dismiss this subject without calling to mind what a deep impression it gives of the dreadful depravity of the human heart, and the guilt of impenitence, that a creature, endowed and blessed as man is, should prefer every other object of thought to the character of his Creator, and every other view of His character to His holiness, which is its chief glory! "A son honoureth his father, and a servant his master; if then I be a father, where is Mine honour? and if I be a master, where is My fear? saith the Lord of Hosts unto you that despise My name." It is here that we see the dreadful enormity of sin, and the extent and heinousness of our apostacy from God.

PART IV.

THE MEDIATOR KING, AND HIS REIGN.

Rev., Chap. 5—Chap. 8 : 1.

Lecture XV. Its Administration Undertaken by the Slain Lamb.
" XVI. His Investiture and Praises.
" XVII. His Reign and its Results.
" XVIII. The Great Revolution Involved.

LECTURE XV.

THE ADMINISTRATION OF THE KINGDOM.

REV., CHAP. V: 1-7.

" And I saw in the right hand of Him that sat on the throne a book written within and on the back side, sealed with seven seals. And I saw a strong angel proclaiming with a loud voice, Who is worthy to open the book, and to loose the seals thereof? And no man in heaven, nor in earth, neither under the earth, was able to open the book. neither to look thereon. [Lit.—to see it, *i. e.*, its contents.] And I wept much, because no man was found worthy to open and to read the book, neither to look thereon: [to see therein.] And one of the elders saith unto me, Weep not : behold, the Lion of the tribe of Juda, the Root of David, hath prevailed to open the book, and to loose the seven seals thereof. And I beheld, and lo, in the midst of the throne, and of the four living creatures, and in the midst of the elders, stood a Lamb as it had been slain, having seven horns, and seven eyes, which are the seven spirits of God sent forth into all the earth. And He came and took the book out of the right hand of Him that sat upon the throne."

WE are taught to seek first the kingdom of God. We are taught daily to pray, Thy kingdom come. But this kingdom cometh not with observation. Like all greatest things, it is unseen and spiritual. Many, therefore, disregard its claims, and ignore its existence. Even those in whose souls it has already come have generally very imperfect conceptions of it. Yet if we ever pray and labour aright that ourselves and others may be brought to share its bliss and glory, we must have some true idea of its heavenly nature, and of the necessity of an interest in it. To give us this we have seen to be the design of the symbolic vision of it in the fourth chapter. We have there seen the preciousness and magnitude of its blessings represented in symbols of surpassing grandeur and sublimity; the God of glory in its midst as its covenanted God, the royal priesthood of its redeemed people, and the divine light, the purifying influences, and the spiritual and eternal life provided at the throne for them. Its joyous and sublime worship is there presented in similar stirring and appropriate symbols, teaching us the essential nature of all acceptable worship, the only true service of a holy heart.

Blessed, indeed, would this world be, if the secret, silent, invisible influences of this kingdom pervaded the hearts of men. To few, however, have its blessings yet come. By most they are repelled. But this shall not always be. It must and shall prevail. Our assurance of this, and our highest encouragement to pray and labour for it, is found in the administration of this kingdom by a divine Mediator. This is the subject of the present chapter, and appropriately follows and perfects this sublime and striking view of this spiritual kingdom, and introduces the graphic picture of the Mediatorial reign, which occupies the three succeeding chapters.

Four leading things present themselves in this chapter, the consideration of which will involve the explanation and improvement of every thing else: the book in the hands of Him that sat on the throne, the proclamation of the angel in regard to it, the Lamb receiving it, and the homage of the universe thereupon, spontaneously presented to Him. In this lecture we shall consider the first three of these.

I. First, the *book*, or roll, in the hand of Him that sat upon the throne. This can represent nothing else than the gracious purposes of God in reference to His church, or kingdom of grace. It is the divine plan of the administration of this kingdom, in conformity with that covenant, the symbol of which encircles His throne. It is written and sealed up, indicating the fixed unchangeable nature of these divine purposes; nothing can be added, nothing altered, nothing taken away. The whole course of future events, the whole arrangements of the ages to come, are all definitely determined. This wisdom is infinite, His knowledge admits of no addition, His foreordained arrangements, therefore, must be perfect, incapable of improvement. In His government, nothing is left to chance, to Him nothing is uncertain, no unforeseen contingency can arise, no exigency be unprovided for. To Omniscience nothing can be new. "Known unto God are all His works from the foundation of the world." "I know that whatsoever God doeth, it shall be for ever; nothing can be put to it, nor any thing taken from it." "I am God, and there is none else; I am God, and there is none like Me, declaring the end from the beginning, and from ancient times the things that are not yet done, saying, My counsel shall stand, and I will do all My pleasure."[1] In Eph. 3 : 11, the apostle declares that the whole unfolding of His providences to and for His church, are "according to the eternal purpose which He purposed in Christ Jesus our Lord;" and in Eph. 1: 9, 11, that the blessings of redemption are bestowed "according to His good pleasure, which He hath purposed in Himself;" "according to the purpose of Him who worketh all things after the counsel of His own will."

This roll is, therefore, represented as written "within and on the back side:" on both sides. In this it was unlike most rolls, which were written only on one side. Every part of it was written on; there was no where in it any empty space. So in the pre-arranged providences of God, there are no empty spaces left to be filled up by chance, or by some other independent agency or instrumentality not included in that providence. This book of His purposes is full, embracing every particular, not only

---

[1] Acts 15 : 18. Eccl. 3 : 14. Is 46 : 9, 10.

all the results, but all the means and instrumentalities, even to the minutest particular, by which they are brought about. All the varied and complicated processes of human thought and action, in all their freedom, stand out as fully and definitely to His eye, and in His plan, as though they were past. As the roll is unfolded in the progress of the ages, there will not be found space for a single word or letter to be entered anew by angel, man, or devil. The sparrow's fall is noticed, and the very hairs of your head are numbered.

Its being sealed denotes not only the fixedness, but the secrecy of these purposes. They are hidden from created eyes, until these seals are broken, and the roll unfolded by Him who alone has the power to do this. And He does it not by the mere prophetic declaration of these purposes, but by their development in history, in His actual dealings with His church and the world. God's plans can only be known and understood as they are accomplished. Accordingly, when the Lamb breaks these seals, each stage of the process is marked, not by enabling the apostle to read the book, to see the unfulfilled purpose, but by the acting out before his eyes of the scenes which he describes, the symbols of the actual fulfilment of the contents of the book.

This book, or roll, is sealed with seven seals. These are successive, evidently, each sealing up a portion, so that when the seventh is broken the whole is revealed. This indicates that the course of events included in these purposes of God extends over the whole administration of this kingdom, its entire progress and final consummation. It is not a partial record, extending over only a portion of the future, but perfect and complete, embracing all the successive steps in the providential plan, until all the engagements of that great covenant of redemption which caused the establishment of this kingdom shall be fulfilled, and the mystery of God be finished. Or, in the words of Paul, until, "in the dispensation of the fulness of times, He" shall "gather together in one all things in Christ, both which are in heaven, and which are on earth." It is the whole of that period of the divine administration during which the powers of redemption are in conflict with sin, till the last enemy is destroyed, and the end cometh, "when He shall have delivered up the kingdom to God, even the Father; when He shall have put down all rule, and all authority, and power," "that God may be all in all."

II. In the second place, we have the proclamation of the mighty angel in regard to this book. This is intended to show the immense difficulties of this administration, and the folly of dependence on any created power to advance the interests of this kingdom. This proclamation is uttered by a mighty angel, with a loud voice, so that every thing in the whole range of created being might hear it, and the utter incompetency of all for the mighty task be made manifest and acknowledged. "Who is worthy to open the book, and to loose the seals thereof?" Who has the right and the power to execute these purposes of God's covenant mercy; to carry forward to their full accomplishment the manifold agencies and processes, by which the blessings of redemption are to be applied to a fallen race, the covenant of God fulfilled, and this spiritual kingdom made to possess the earth? It is as if He would say, "Here is a kingdom of God already established, for bringing to a guilty world heaven's choicest blessings; here are thrones, and crowns, and robes of purity for those who now are slaves to Satan and sin; here is the light of divine truth and joy, as flowing directly from the Holy Spirit; here is an exhaustless sea of purifying influences in the blood of atonement; here is spiritual and eternal life, with all its powers of holy perception and action; here, too, is the divine decree, and the all-perfect plan, clearly and fully defined, even to its minutest arrangements, by which this kingdom of light, and purity, and life, is to triumph over the reign of darkness, and sin, and death; nothing more is now wanted but an agent able to execute the plan, to administer the kingdom, and convey its blessings to those for whom they were provided."

In vain is this call made. The whole universe is silent; it seems to stand appalled at the very idea of such a work being committed to creature hands. "No one in heaven, nor in earth, neither under the earth, was able to open and to read the book, neither to see in it." The highest created wisdom cannot even read the deep purposes of God, or comprehend the mystery of His vast plan; its keenest vision cannot see into it so as to discover a single letter from which it may learn what to do, or how to do it, much less is any created power able to execute the mysterious plan.

No merely didactic language could ever express with such impressive force as this scene does, the utter impossibility of advancing the spiritual kingdom of God by mere creature wisdom or might; and the extreme folly of depending on any human power or wisdom to secure this. "Not by might, nor by power." "Vain is the help of man."

But notwithstanding this impressive scene, many are ever turning with new expectations to some mere earthly influence or power to carry forward the schemes of God's salvation. All such expectations are destined to utter and advancing bitter disappointment. If our hope of success in the interests of the church were from creature resources, whether of power, or wealth, or wisdom, or eloquence, or any thing else, human or angelic, we should be doomed to weeping for ever, as John here was for the time in which only the creature's impotence appeared. "I wept much," says the waiting and anxious apostle, because no one was found worthy to open the book, or to see in it."

Just so far as our expectations are directed to creature power, to carry on the interests of the spiritual church, are we doomed to weep over the folly of them. All the despondency of the believer, on account either of the slow progress of the church, or of the extent and power of the opposition, or of his utter incapacity to conceive how the mighty work of a world's deliverance and restoration is to be accomplished, arises from the same misdirected expectations. John wept no longer when he saw the Lamb undertake the work. Though all the political powers, and the accumulated wisdom of the world, all its wealth and influence of every kind should combine to advance these spiritual interests, they could of themselves accomplish nothing more than the weak, and foolish, and despised things of the world. It is hard for men to be persuaded of this. Yet nothing can be more certain.

What can creature power do toward removing the real hindrances to the gospel, as found in the natural corruption of the human heart? This kingdom, though spiritual and invisible, yet comes in contact with men in all their relations and pursuits, in all their external life, as well as their feelings; and wherever it touches them it meets with opposition. The very blessings it brings they regard as burdens, and despise. Every passion, appetite, desire, and emotion of the natural heart bars it against the entrance of this kingdom; and all the habits of thought and action, all the forces that control and move the social and political energies of the world, are leagued in stern opposition to it. Even this is not all. All the principalities and powers of the kingdom of darkness, those unseen and powerful spirits of evil which the word of God reveals to us, banded together under their mighty leader, are exerting every energy to exclude from every heart all the influences of this kingdom of holiness. Against such difficulties, it is as great folly to marshal the resources of created wisdom, skill, and power, as it would be to attempt to control and cure the idiot or the maniac by the power of logic. All these combined cannot change the moral nature of a single human soul, or purify it from any of its foul corruptions, much less bring it in the power of a new life to adoring delight in God, and consecration to His will.

To open this book, according to which these blessings of the kingdom are to be applied to a lost world, requires ability to penetrate, comprehend, and unfold the secret mysteries of all the vast plan of God, both in providence and grace, ability to direct and govern at His pleasure all the multitudinous agencies of the universe, physical, intellectual, and spiritual, and to control, restrain, and infallibly to shape to His own ends all the actions and purposes of free agents, without affecting their freedom and responsibility. All this is a work requiring divine wisdom and power. Yet, vast as it is, the scheme of redemption has provided one, in our nature, who has both the power and the right to do it.

III. He is next introduced to the apostle. "And one of the elders saith unto me, Weep not: behold the Lion of the tribe of Juda, the Root of David, hath prevailed to open the book, and to loose the seven seals thereof." This announcement is very appropriately made by one of the representatives of the redeemed church in the actual enjoyment of its spiritual honours. The redeemed soul, as it sits in heavenly places in Christ Jesus, reposing on the riches of His grace, and rejoicing in the hope of His glory, can never doubt its Redeemer's power, and is always ready to comfort the desponding with assurances of His all-sufficiency.

Immediately on this announcement, the prophet sees in the midst of the throne, and of the four living creatures, and in the midst of the elders, "a Lamb, as it had been slain." This is the well known symbol of the crucified and risen Jesus. He is the Lamb of God to whom all the Jewish sacrifices pointed, and in whom they found their true meaning and fulfilment. He here and now appears as the very central object of the whole of this glorious vision. His incomprehensible nature, and especially His perfect power and wisdom, are represented by His "having seven horns and seven eyes." These are immediately explained as meaning "the seven spirits of God, sent forth into all the earth:" the manifold and perfect operations of the Holy Ghost. How beautifully and forcibly does this set forth the truth, that the Spirit is not given by measure unto Him, that the fulness of the Godhead dwells in Him, as a "fulness of grace and truth." It is by the omnipotent and omniscient spiritual influences sent forth from Him into all the earth, that He infallibly secures the interests of His spiritual kingdom. Pentecost is the great prominent example of the precious reality here represented, and the words of Peter its best brief exposition: "Being by the right hand of God exalted, and having received of the Father the promise of the Holy Ghost, He hath shed forth this which ye now see and hear."

Advancing to Him that sat upon the throne, the mysterious scroll containing the hidden destinies of men and of nations is committed to His hands. "He came and took the book out of the right hand of Him that sat upon the throne." What is this but the visible and more impressive picture of that blessed truth elsewhere so fully stated in words, that Christ Jesus is made "Head over all things to the church?" The following passages at once explain it, and are explained by it: "The Father loveth the Son, and hath given all things into His hand," "and sheweth Him all things that Himself doeth." "The Father judgeth [*i. e.*, ruleth,] no man, but hath committed all judgment [*i. e.*, ruling power,] unto the Son, that all men should honour the Son, even as they honour the Father." "Thou hast given Him power over all flesh, that He should give eternal life to as many as Thou hast given Him." "All things are delivered unto Me of My Father, and no man knoweth the Son, but the Father; neither knoweth any man the Father save the Son, and he to whomsoever the Son will reveal him."[1]

This scene vividly pictures to the church that great transaction to which our Saviour refers in those words of the great commission, uttered when He was about to enter upon the actual administration of this kingdom, and was establishing its agencies, and on which He there rests the grand promise of this whole dispensation—that of His continual presence. "All power is given unto Me in heaven and in earth. Go ye, therefore, and teach all nations, baptizing them in the name of the Father, and of the Son, and of the Holy Ghost; teaching them to observe all things whatsoever I have commanded you; and lo, I am with you alway, even unto the end of the world."

This act of the Lamb, taking the book, introduces the last scene in this particular vision: the whole universe uniting in the rapturous praises of the Lamb that was slain—a scene that, for grandeur and sublimity, is unsurpassed even in the Bible. Its comprehensive character, and richness in truth, requires for it distinct and special consideration. May we, every one, as we read these things, and gaze upon the slain Lamb, catch more and more of its spirit of joyful adoration, and learn to unite in its new song of praise even here on earth.

Meanwhile, let every troubled and afflicted believer listen to the cheering words of the elder to the apostle, and from them, and the infinitely glorious fact on which they are based, gather comfort and strength. "Weep not."

"Weep not" in view of the vast difficulties in working out your own salvation. Your strength is small, indeed,

---

[1] Eph. 1: 22. John 3: 35. 5: 20, 22, 23. 17: 2. Matt. 11: 27.

yea, it is nothing; your enemies are mighty; your corruptions are strong, and you may seem to be making little or no progress; so that, perhaps, in the fierce assaults of temptation, and the conscious instability of your own heart, you may sometimes be tempted to regard the issue of the conflict as doubtful. But the question is not one of the comparative strength of yourself and your enemies; it is only whether you are in Christ, and so resting solely on His blood, and righteousness, and Spirit. If you have committed your poor helpless soul to Him, then remember that in that roll the whole conduct of your case is put into His hands, is entrusted to the Lion of the tribe of Judah. He is not your helper, but your *Saviour*. He is able to keep that which you have committed to Him. He will be faithful to the trust reposed in Him. "Cast not away, therefore, your confidence, which hath great recompense of reward."

"Weep not" in comfortless, heart-broken sorrow under the afflictions which may be pressing so heavily upon you. These are all in the covenant; every one of them is recorded in that book in the right hand of Him that sitteth on the throne, as part of the process needed for your purification; and every one of them is administered by the Lamb that was slain for you. The same hand that was nailed to the cross unfolds your whole life's daily history, and does it with unerring wisdom, so as to secure the result promised in the everlasting covenant.

"Weep not" in view of the church's sad imperfections, impurities, and backslidings, or of her calamities, and the power and hostility of the world, and the darkness of those dispensations of Providence which seem to remove far distant the period of anticipated triumph. All these apostacies and calamities, all opposition and conflicts, are written in that sealed book; they are, as the succeeding revelations fully prove, part of that vast and wonderful plan which He has chosen, in order to show to all the universe the dreadful malignity of sin, and the infinite glory of redemption in triumphing over it, and saving the church. The power and love of the slain Lamb presides over the whole.

Not only "weep not," because no created power can be found to give success to the gospel, but rejoice that it is according to the divine plan, in carrying forward this kingdom, to make instrumentalities, contemptible in human eyes, mighty to the pulling down of strong holds. In the confidence of this, go forward daily, in humble, earnest, ceaseless efforts to advance its interests. Let us remember that it is the power of those seven spirits sent forth into all the earth, the almighty, and all-wise, exhaustless influences of the Holy Ghost, which the ascended Redeemer is always sending forth into all the earth to carry on His work, and that their chosen channel is the weak and despised things of the world. How very often that power has made the feeblest efforts produce mighty and glorious spiritual results, when put forth in humble dependence on it alone, the whole history of the church testifies.

Weep not, fear not, faint not. The slain Lamb governs the world. The days of your mortal life are prolonged, your daily food is given you, and each sun rises that you may do His work, and offer yourself, in all your helplessness as the glad instrument of His divine power, in extending the boundaries and blessings of His kingdom. Pervert not His gifts by idleness, or self-indulgence. If you have but one talent, use it in His strength, and with a cordial, earnest consecration to His service in this spiritual kingdom, and blessed results will follow, and a glorious reward.

Finally, how futile all the opposition of earth and of hell to the church of Christ! And how constantly this truth thrusts itself in these sacred pages upon our attention and our faith! It is one of those golden threads of heavenly truth that runs through and shines in all this book. Like the maddened Jews when they crucified Jesus, men and devils can only do with their wicked hands that which His hand and counsel determined before to be done. How deep must be the guilt, and how fearful the ruin of all who refuse to bow to this Saviour! How obstinate and wicked the unbelief that withholds from Him the heart's trust, and the life's obedience. Christ Jesus is king. He will rule. Every enemy shall be put down. Having offered Himself as the slain Lamb to redeem the world, "God hath highly exalted Him, and given Him a name that is above every name, that at the name of Jesus every knee should bow, and every tongue confess that He is Lord, to the glory of God the Father."

LECTURE XVI.

THE INVESTITURE AND PRAISES OF THE SLAIN LAMB.

Rev., Chap. v: 8–14.

"And when He had taken the book, the four living creatures, and four and twenty elders, fell down before the Lamb, having every one of them harps, and golden vials full of odours, which are the prayers of saints. And they sung a new song, saying, Thou art worthy to take the book, and to open the seals thereof: for Thou wast slain, and hast redeemed us to God by Thy blood, out of every kindred, and tongue, and people, and nation; and hast made us unto our God kings and priests: and we shall reign on the earth.

"And I beheld, and I heard the voice of many angels round about the throne, and the living creatures, and the elders; and the number of them was ten thousand times ten thousand, and thousands of thousands; saying, with a loud voice, Worthy is the Lamb that was slain to receive power, and riches, and wisdom, and strength, and honour, and glory, and blessing. And every creature which is in heaven, and on the earth, and under the earth, and such as are in the sea, and all that are in them, heard I saying, Blessing, and honour, and glory, and power, be unto Him that sitteth upon the throne, and unto the Lamb for ever and ever. And the four living creatures said, Amen. And the four and twenty elders fell down and worshipped Him that liveth for ever and ever."

IN comparison with this scene, all the vaunted glories, and splendid pageantries of earth become contemptible. Even in the great transactions of the spiritual and unseen world, where God displays His brighter glories, nothing equal to this has been revealed to us. It is the investiture of the slain Lamb with universal dominion; His rapturous welcome to the mediatorial throne by the whole witnessing creation. The universe is represented as uniting in joyous adoration of Him as He undertakes the administration of the spiritual kingdom. In taking the roll out of the right hand of Him that sat upon the throne, He engaged to carry into full execution all the gracious and still hidden purposes of God in reference to this kingdom, and by its perfect triumph over sin, and death, and hell, to bring back the lost bliss of Paradise, and man's forfeited dominion over the earth, and the manifested presence and glory of God.

If, when Paradise was lost,

> "Earth felt the wound, and nature from her seat,
> Sighing thro' all her works, gave signs of woe
> That all was lost,"

and if ever since, "the whole creation has been groaning and travailing in pain together until now," we might well expect just such a universal burst of grateful adoration from that creation, when One who has the right and the power appears, and actually undertakes the work of restoring these ruins, and bringing back the lost inheritance to Adam's fallen race, and a holy harmony to a disordered creation. The restoration may well be regarded as virtually accomplished. The triumph, though but anticipated, is sure, and may well become the theme of universal praise. And as every one of us has tasted the bitterness of the curse, as we have all united our groans with those of a suffering creation around us, have we not all the deepest possible personal interest in the theme of these songs? Can we help, even now, amidst all the imperfections of our present state, uniting with those worshipping hosts, and yielding the glad homage of our hearts to the world's Saviour?

> "Joy to the world, the Lord is come,
> Let earth receive her King;
> Let every heart prepare Him room,
> And heaven and nature sing.
>
> Joy to the earth, the Saviour reigns,
> Let men their songs employ;
> While fields and floods, rocks, hills, and plains,
> Repeat the sounding joy."

1. The NEW *song*. The first to offer their praises are of course the redeemed themselves, being those most immediately interested, and most directly benefitted. With this new song of theirs, every idea in the whole passage, and every voice of praise in all the creation, inseparably connects itself. The redeemed are here again represented by the four living creatures, and the four and twenty elders; and the perfect union of both these in praising the Lamb for their redemption, out of all the nations of the earth, is proof that they together are required fully to represent the redeemed church in its divine spiritual life, and its royal and priestly privileges, at least until that life that is as yet laid up in Christ for the church is actually possessed and fully enjoyed. Each of these elders is represented with a harp, the symbol of joy and praise; and with a goblet of incense, which in the text itself is explained as meaning "the prayers of saints."

This shows in what the priestly character of these elders consisted. They are not furnished with any symbols of sacrificial offerings; it is not with expiatory sacrifices, but only with these spiritual offerings of prayer and praise, that these priests, and the church they represent, draw near to God, and exercise their spiritual functions. So the apostle says, "By him, therefore, let us offer the sacrifice of praise continually; that is, the fruit of our lips giving thanks unto His name." "Praying always with all prayer and supplication for all saints."[1]

Their song is called a *new* song. This is evidently with reference to the song which the apostle had just before heard these same elders singing before the throne, and which he gives in the last verse of the previous chapter. That was addressed to Him that sat on the throne, to Jehovah, as the self-existent, unchangeable, and omnipotent Creator and disposer of all things; and it consisted in

---

[1] Heb. 13: 15. Eph. 6: 18.

the ascription of universal sovereignty to Him as the end of creation, because its author, to whose will and pleasure, therefore, it behooved all creatures to dedicate themselves. This is addressed to the Lamb, and is an act of praise to Him as the only one in all the universe able to secure to Him that sits upon the throne this rightful homage of a revolted world. It addresses Him as having the sole right and power to open the book, and carry into execution the secret purposes of the Eternal God in reference to this kingdom of grace, because by His blood He had redeemed them—the subjects of this kingdom—from their guilty alienation from God; by His power he had brought them back, and consecrated them to Him in the nearest and most honourable relations, and had thus enabled them to fulfill the original end of their creation, the pleasure and glory of God their Creator. It is, therefore, a new song, both in its object—the Lamb, and in its subject—redemption; but in both it is in perfect consistency, and, indeed, subordination to the former, since the end of redemption is the glory of God. Redemption is the restoration to God of that glory from His creation, of which sin had sought to rob Him; it is the securing to Him those eternal rights in His creatures which sin denied, yet so as to save the sinner.

The song was new, also, as to the occasion of it. This was the actual investiture of the slain Lamb with supreme dominion over all things to the church. It is a song of praise to Him as having already been slain, and having taken the book, and been invested with all power. The reality of this praise could not be sung until Christ's elevation to the Father's right hand. Before His ascension to glory, the affairs of this kingdom were, it is true, administered by Him, but only in His divine nature, and in virtue of His engagements as Mediator to fulfill in the flesh the conditions of the everlasting covenant by which it was founded. But now, in this vision, in accordance with the actual facts, the conditions are represented as fulfilled: the Lamb has been slain, the price of redemption has just been paid, and that human nature in which He endured the curse is itself glorified and borne to the throne. Then for the first time this song was sung, either on earth or in heaven, for then first had the event taken place which forms its special subject: "*Thou wast slain.*" Redeeming love, indeed, had been sung ever since the first *promise* of redemption was first embraced by a believing heart; but not a crucified, and risen, and exalted Saviour. Not until, with the scars of the terrible conflict upon Him, He ascended from the midst of His gazing disciples on Olivet; not until He approached the open portals of heaven, and its gazing and expectant throng, beholding the ascending conqueror, cried out, "Lift up your heads, O ye gates, and be ye lift up, ye everlasting doors, and the King of glory shall come in;" not until then, advancing to the throne, He took His seat at the Father's right hand, "angels, and authorities, and powers being made subject unto Him," could this song be sung. Since then, however, it has never ceased. It never can cease. Its strains swell with secret joy the heart of every struggling believer here, and its unmingled and rapturous praises must for ever be the theme of those whose conflicts are ended, who have received their immortal crowns, and been admitted to the presence of the Lamb.

Every gospel offer invites us to join in it. What joys like these? What joys will there soon be, without these? If we would sing this song in heaven and eternity, we must learn it here, and now. The way to learn it, prescribed by grace itself, is no laborious, pains-taking effort under the goadings of a troubled conscience, no mysterious process of self-purification, but this plain and simple direction, perfectly adapted to our utter helplessness, "Repent and believe, then sing." Repent and believe, and you cannot help singing. "Though now ye see Him not, yet believing," in Jesus Christ, "ye rejoice with joy unspeakable and full of glory."[1]

In this new song, and the others that follow it, and take from it their key-note, there are four principal points that should receive our frequent and devout meditation, if we would be able to unite heartily and habitually in it. They are, first, the right of the Lamb to this dominion; secondly, the assurance given to the redeemed by His administration; thirdly, the interest of the whole creation in it; and fourthly, the evidence it presents of His complete divinity.

II. We, therefore, next notice His right to administer this kingdom, to bestow its blessings upon a guilty world, and to secure the fulfilment of all the purposes of God's covenant mercy. No where in the Bible is this more forcibly and affectingly stated than here. "Thou art worthy to take the book, and to open the seals thereof, for Thou wast slain, and hast redeemed us to God by Thy blood." His cross secures His right to the crown. By that cross He removed the greatest of all obstacles to man's salvation—that interposed by the justice of a holy God. The question, "How can God be just, and justify the ungodly," seemed to be unanswerable, until the atonement of Jesus solved it. With man, to justify one justly condemned is an impossibility and a contradiction. But He, as the Lamb of God, standing in the sinner's place, and as the sinner's substitute, endured the penalty of the divine law, and, by doing so, removed the curse, and opened a free channel for the exercise of eternal mercy. "Christ hath redeemed us from the curse of the law, being made a curse for us."[2] This satisfaction being of infinite value, secures the right to offer its blessings to every sinner of our fallen race; and this accordingly is the very first act of the Redeemer in administering this kingdom. "Go ye into all the world, and preach the gospel to every

---

[1] 1 Pet. 1: 8.   [2] Gal. 3 : 13.

creature." "And let him that is athirst, come. And whosoever will, let him take the water of life freely."

But His death did more than this. It actually redeemed a people unto God. It did not merely secure an offer of deliverance; it secured the deliverance itself, and this offer as merely one of the means by which it is actually effected. "Thou wast slain, and *hast redeemed us to God.*" *That* is no mere *offer* of deliverance. The price has been paid; the prisoners, therefore, must be released and given over to Him. The curse cannot hold them, for He has already borne it; the law cannot hold them, for He has already satisfied it; death and hell cannot hold them, for these derived their claim from that violated law, and that claim is for ever cancelled. Having paid the price of their redemption in His own life's blood, they are His property: and since He cannot be deprived of His blood-bought right, sin, that by nature reigns in them, must be dethroned and destroyed, and the world, that holds them captive, conquered. The almighty influences of the Holy Spirit, by which alone this can be done, must be sent forth to subdue their hearts to Himself, and to put them in actual and complete possession of that spiritual and eternal life purchased for them.

That same death, moreover, which secured the right to minister all spiritual influences, necessarily secured the right to make all providential agencies of every kind and degree, from the fall of a sparrow to that of an empire, work together for their good. Nothing in earth or hell, in animate or inanimate creation, can be suffered to deprive Him in the minutest degree of the purchase of His redeeming blood, the complete salvation of every one of His people, whom the Father had given Him. All things, therefore, are committed to His hand, to be used for this great end.

For it will be observed, that they who sing this song ascribe to Him the praise of having not only redeemed them effectually from every enemy, but of having conferred upon them the highest dignities and privileges of this kingdom. "Thou hast made us kings and priests unto God." "*Thou hast done it.*" The death He died had already made all this sure. Whatever, then, was necessary to put them into actual possession of all implied by this royal priesthood, was His, and must be ministered to them by Him. The subjects of this kingdom themselves, and all its blessings provided for them, are equally and solely the purchase of His blood. Both, therefore, belong to Him, and in Him alone must be vested the eternal right to administer these, His blood-bought blessings, to these His blood-bought subjects, for whom He bought them. Thus, "we see Jesus, who was made a little lower than the angels for the suffering of death, crowned with glory and honour."

III. The church's and the believer's assurance of final triumph, founded on this redemption, is the next great theme of this song. "Thou hast redeemed us," "Thou hast made us kings and priests," and therefore, "Thou art worthy to take the book, and to open its seals;" it is Thine to use all the powers of the divine government in securing the triumph of the mighty scheme. There can be no doubt about the issue.

In regard to the salvation of each individual believer, there can be no doubt. Their *first* ground of security is in their Redeemer's *right*. Their salvation, as we have just seen, is His right. Their ruin would be injustice to Him. The justice of God now stands bound to the Redeemer, to throw around them its eternal protection, and so renders their salvation sure. A *second* ground of their security is His *power*. All the power of His arm will be exerted to defend those for whom He shed the blood of His heart.

Nor is there any doubt of the issue in regard to the triumph of the church here on earth over all opposing influences and powers. This is the point here more directly stated, because it is the main subject of this whole book. And it completely includes the former. "And we shall reign on the earth." The evident meaning of this is, that this spiritual kingdom, this redeemed church, shall even here on earth triumph over the world, and sin, and Satan; its true conception, in all its glory and perfectness, shall be fully realized, and shall take the place of that imperfect representation of it now presented in the visible church. In some way or other—whether we can tell precisely how, matters not—every influence of evil that now pervades human character, and human society, and human governments, polluting and blighting every earthly interest, and arraying even the very powers of nature often in opposition to man's happiness, all these shall be utterly swept away, and the dominion that Adam lost shall be regained by man redeemed. This is the result which this book toward its close depicts in such glowing language; and it is the unfolding of the various, and complicated, and wonderful agencies and processes of mercy and judgment by which this result is reached, which forms the subject of its successive visions.

In the book of Daniel, too, this same result is represented as following the same investiture of the Son with universal sovereignty. "One like the Son of man came with the clouds of heaven, and came to the Ancient of days, and they brought Him near before Him.[1] And there was given Him dominion, and glory, and a kingdom, that all people, nations, and languages should serve Him." The words of the interpreting angel describe the manner in which this vision shall be fulfilled, thus: "The saints

---

[1] Dan. 7: 13. "*The* Son of man;" literally, "*a* Son of man;" *i. e.*, one in human nature, and so distinguished from the symbols of the previous reigning powers; but yet one in His origin from above—from heaven—indicating His divine nature and person. See *Fairbairn on Prophecy*, p. 311, &c.

of the Most High shall take the kingdom, and possess the kingdom for ever, even for ever and ever." "And the kingdom, and dominion, and the greatness of the kingdom under the whole heaven, shall be given to the people of the saints of the Most High, whose kingdom is an everlasting kingdom, and all dominions shall serve and obey Him."[1]

When God created man, He gave Him dominion over the earth. When man sinned, he lost it, and Satan became, by usurpation, the prince of this world. Man, however, is God's king, and man must reign. God, therefore, becomes man, destroys Satan and his works, and in human nature takes the lost kingdom and bestows it on the saints, His redeemed. "We shall reign on the earth."

IV. We cannot wonder, therefore, at the next thing in this vision: the interest manifested by the whole creation in this administration of the Lamb. Immediately after the redeemed have sung their new song, an innumerable company of angels, who are His ministering servants in carrying on this work, are heard uniting with the redeemed themselves in the ascription of supreme and universal sovereignty to the Lamb that was slain. "And I beheld, and I heard the voice of many angels round about the throne, and the beasts, and the elders; and the number of them was ten thousand times ten thousand, and thousands of thousands, saying, with a loud voice, Worthy is the Lamb that was slain to receive power, and riches, and wisdom, and strength, and honour, and glory, and blessing."

But these high praises end not even here. The whole of this lower creation next joins in a sublime chorus, in which the Lamb is united with Him that sits upon the throne, in equal honours, implying that the result of this administration of the Lamb is to secure, not merely to the

[1] Dan. 7: 18, 27.

Redeemer as such, everlasting praise, but to the triune God, from all His creation, the glory due to Him as the Creator and disposer of all things. "And every creature which is in heaven, and on the earth, and under the earth, and such as are in the sea, and all that are in them, heard I saying, Blessing, and honour, and glory, and power be unto Him that sitteth upon the throne, and unto the Lamb for ever and ever." To this ascription of homage from a whole renovated earth, in all its extent, and parts, and processes, the symbol of the spiritual life of the redeemed first responds with a joyful "Amen;" and then, under this impulse of their new nature, the whole redeemed church prostrate themselves in an act of worship. The harmony which sin had marred so sadly is again restored. In it every creature's voice unites. This mediatorial administration secures every possible end required by the glory of the Creator and Redeemer, and all that a world blighted by the curse of sin longs after.

What a delightful consummation does this present of our blessed Saviour's redeeming work! If this scene does not represent the perfect deliverance of the redeemed from every evil, and that, too, on the earth, the whole creation delivered from the curse, it seems to us no language and no symbols could do it. "We shall reign *on the earth.*" All creatures in heaven, earth, and sea, and under the earth, join in the ascription of glory. This by no means implies the universal salvation of all men and devils, which is expressly contradicted by the repeated declarations of the whole Bible, and especially of this book, as it details the manner in which the result here indicated is finally secured. This perfect deliverance of a redeemed people and creation is not only perfectly consistent with, but is to be finally effected by, the eternal separation from them of Satan and his hosts, and of all his human followers, their eternal deprivation of all power to harm the feeblest creature, and their being made an eternal monument to the universe of the malignity of sin, and its direful consequences. For, just as we hear the words uttered from the throne: "Behold, I make all things new," and as we see the new Jerusalem descending out of heaven in unimaginable glory, to fill the earth with its light, and to receive into it the "glory and honour of the nations;" we hear the same awful voice declaring: "But the fearful, and unbelieving, and the abominable, and murderers, and whoremongers, and sorcerers, and idolaters, and all liars, shall have their part in the lake which burneth with fire and brimstone, which is the second death."[1]

But it does imply a church of redeemed sinners made perfect in glory and bliss, and reigning on the earth; and it does imply the deliverance of that earth from every vestige of the curse. We see no longer a feeble, struggling church, hidden, and almost overwhelmed beneath the thousand influences and hostile powers with which she is contending, in a world, all whose agencies and influences, whether mental, moral, or material, are either serving sin, or cursed by it; but a church purified from every internal defect and pollution, delivered from every enemy, whose spiritual power and glory penetrates every activity, and perfectly subordinates the whole inferior creation, so long prostituted to evil, and pours its blessings far as the curse is now found.

Not a few glimpses of this glorious renovation are found in the old prophets. "He will swallow up death in victory; and the Lord God will wipe away tears from off all faces; and the rebuke of His people shall He take away from off all the earth, for the Lord hath spoken it." "And the ransomed of the Lord shall return, and come to Zion with songs, and everlasting joy upon their heads; they shall obtain joy and gladness, and sorrow and sighing shall flee away."[2] In the New Testament, it is called

---

[1] Rev. 21: 8.   [2] Is. 25: 8.   35: 10.

"the times of the restitution of all things, which God hath spoken by the mouth of all His holy prophets since the world began." Christ calls it "the regeneration"—the thorough renovation—"when the Son of man shall sit in the throne of His glory."¹ But compare especially the clear and familiar words of Paul, in the 8th of Romans. He expressly teaches there, by the clear distinction being made between the creature, or creation, and the sons of God, that the full consummation of the life of God's redeemed carries with it the entire regeneration of all this lower world. In unfolding the greatness of the saint's future glory, he represents the whole creation groaning and travailing in pain together as the result of man's sin; and therefore, by a most expressive figure, looking forward with eager expectation of deliverance to *his* complete redemption. "For I reckon that the sufferings of this present time are not worthy to be compared with the glory which shall be revealed in us. For the earnest expectation of the creature waiteth for the manifestation of the sons of God. For the creature was made subject to vanity, not willingly"—*i. e.*, of its own accord—"but by reason of Him who hath subjected the same in hope; because the creature itself also shall be delivered from the bondage of corruption into the glorious liberty of the children of God. For we know that the whole creation groaneth and travaileth in pain together until now."²

By the mediatorial reign—the administration of the Lamb—therefore, this whole creation, of which man was made the head, and which was so blasted by his sin, shall not be carried with the lost into perdition, but shall again recover the beauty and the bliss of Paradise. Death itself shall die. The grave shall be no longer. Mortality shall be swallowed up of life. There shall be "a new heaven and a new earth." "I heard," says John, "a great voice

---

[1] Acts 3: 21.   Matt. 19: 28.   [2] Rom. 8: 18-22.

from heaven, saying, Behold, the tabernacle of God is with men, and He will dwell with them, and they shall be His people, and God Himself shall be their God. And God shall wipe away all tears from their eyes; and there shall be no more death, neither sorrow, nor crying, neither shall there be any more pain; for the former things are passed away. And He that sat upon the throne said, Behold, I make all things new."[2]

Such is the end toward which all things are tending. It must come, as certainly as that the Lamb was slain, and now reigns. In the dazzling brightness of that blessed future—how near or how remote is known only to God—the glories of heaven and the restored earth seem at last to meet and mingle, we can hardly tell how. Much must be unknown till then; but the fact is sure, and that is enough. Much, however, of the struggles through which that result is to be reached is revealed, and all for our completer comfort, guidance, and confirmation in faith. Let us look to the sure and glorious result, and in whatever is revealed of the path to it, learn our duty, never forgetting the terms so expressly laid down, "To him that overcometh," and to him only.

V. Finally, what a mass of overwhelming evidence is here again presented to us of the divinity of Jesus! It is as the slain Lamb, as He who had suffered on the cross; it is in His character of Atoner and constituted Mediator, that He is here advanced to the supreme government of the universe. It is as the Lamb that He is adored by all the redeemed church, by all the angelic throngs, and by a whole worshipping creation; and that with precisely the same homage, the same ascription of universal sovereignty, which they offer to Him that sitteth on the throne. As we hear their songs, and with them behold His ability to look into the secret counsels of God, and to execute

[2] Rev. 21: 1-5.

those counsels in unfolding the mighty scheme of Providence and Redemption, let us joyfully unite in their homage, prostrating ourselves before His throne in hearty consecration to His service, and hailing Him as our Lord and our God.

Yes, believer, that Saviour who died for you is the mighty God, and is able to keep your immortal soul, and even your mortal body, safe in life, in death, and through eternity. That heart of His is full of human sympathies, but they are the sympathies of a God, and not powerless, like the tears of a mere man. Where Jesus weeps, death itself lets go its grasp, and Lazarus comes forth. He loves you with all the tenderness, and gentleness, and warm affection of His human heart, but with all the force of that divinity to which it belongs. Trust Him implicitly, love Him fervently, live for Him entirely, as redeemed unto God by His blood.

LECTURE XVII.

THE REIGN OF THE LAMB: ITS AGENCIES AND RESULTS.

Rev., Chaps. vi., vii., and viii. : 1.

OPENING OF THE SEVEN SEALS.

ANALYSIS.

Seal 1. Chap. 6 : 1, 2.—Christ in His *gospel conquering*.
" 2. " 6 : 3, 4.⎱ ⎧ By *War and Discord*, in its so-
                 ⎰An opposing⎱   cial happiness.
" 3. " 6 : 5, 6.⎰ world smitten⎰ By *Want*, in its life supports.
" 4. " 6 : 7, 8.⎱ ⎩ By *Death*, in its life itself.
" 5. " 6 : 9–11.—The spiritual *church, bleeding, praying and waiting*.
" 6. " 6 : 12 ; 7 : 17.—The *triumph*, in three parts:
    (1.) Chap. 6 : 12–17.—The powers of the world overthrown and revolutionized, and all enemies destroyed.
    (2.) Chap. 7 : 1–8.—The saints, during all this delay, prepared by the Spirit's sealing.
    (3.) Chap. 7 : 9–17.—Their bliss and glory perfected.
" 7. Chap. 8 : 1.—The *end* of all conflict. The Eternal Sabbath begins.

IT had just been shown that all things were committed into the hands of the Mediator. The sealed book He had taken out of the right hand of Him who sat upon the throne. In all the universe He alone had the right and the power to unfold and execute these purposes of covenant mercy. His undertaking this, and His investiture with supreme dominion, calls forth from the redeemed church the thanksgiving of the new song, imparts to her the assurance that she shall reign on the earth, and fills angels that minister for her, and a whole renovated creation, with joy. It only remained to show Him exercising this supreme dominion, unsealing the book, and executing its hidden purposes; and thus to reveal the general nature of those instrumentalities and processes by which the Lamb was to vindicate His claims, and secure to His own redeemed the sovereignty of the earth, having " put down all rule, and all authority and power."

This is done by the Lamb's actually breaking successively each of the seals, and each broken seal introducing the symbolic accomplishment of a certain portion of these secret purposes, until all are broken, and the whole mystery of God is unfolded. It may not be amiss to repeat the remark, that the uniform and well-established meaning of the number seven in all symbolical representations, and occurring frequently in this book, being completeness in all covenant matters, renders it certain that this book, being a seven-sealed book, implies that it contains, not a part, but the whole perfect scheme of God's providence in regard to His church. The breaking of the seven seals, therefore, must be the unfolding of the whole plan of God, even to the end, when the Mediator shall deliver up the kingdom to the Father, all enemies having been put under His feet, and all the objects of His mediatorial reign having been accomplished. Hence, the symbols introduced under these seven seals, or rather by the opening of them, must give us a general view of the whole future course of God's providence in grace, of the whole of the reign of the Lamb, down to the final consummation.

Other series of revelations, indeed, follow these, especially the seven trumpets, and the seven vials, and, in connection with these, the dragon, the beasts, and the woman, before the New Jerusalem descends. But we regard the view as fully and satisfactorily established, by the later and ablest writers on this book, that these seven seals, trumpets, and vials denote, not successive periods in the divine administration, but each presents the whole under different aspects, all of which are necessary to give a complete idea of its true nature. This is very clearly indicated by these leading symbols themselves, the seals, the trumpets, and the vials. There is no such difference as these would indicate in the different periods of the mediatorial administration. The first, that of opening the seals, is the Lamb reigning, exercising supreme dominion over all temporal and spiritual agencies, and thus securing the salvation of His people, and the world's deliverance; the second, the *trumpets*, represents this reign as one of *conflict*, depicting the great conflicting agencies, and disciplinary and corrective judgments, which the trumpet summons of God in the gospel calls forth, until the seventh announces that the kingdoms of this world are become the kingdom of our Lord and His Christ; the third, the *vials*, represents the acts of divine wrath and vengeance, which characterize this kingdom, in some degree, in all its stages—those last plagues which descend on individuals and nations when God's long suffering is exhausted, and which, by their last visitation, shall utterly exterminate all opposition, so that, when the seventh is poured out, the voice from heaven declares, "It is done." Now, it is evident, that the Lamb ruling, the conflict raging, the judgments of God's wrath descending, are not distinctions of chronological periods in the history of the church and the world, but the three great, parallel, and harmonious aspects of the mediatorial kingdom, presenting themselves in every period of its progress.

In these two chapters, then, we have a summary view of the whole mediatorial administration, as the Lamb opens the seven seals. A rapid view of all these together will best enable us to understand them, and to perceive their beautiful and striking relation to each other, and to the grand result.

1. When the Lamb opens the first seal, one of the four living creatures, with a voice of thunder, cries, Come.[1]

---

[1] In all the later editions of the Greek Testament the words καὶ βλεπε "and see," are expunged, as being no part of the original text.

This is a summons to the agency just about to be introduced, and it appropriately comes from the first of those living ones which symbolize the spiritual life of the church, implying that these agencies come forth for the church's sake, and to perfect her life—that her life demands them; and it is in a voice of thunder, implying the vast magnitude of the agency demanded. The voice of the church's life is thus shown to be in perfect harmony with the dispensations of her King. Both the agencies of mercy and wrath which He employs are such as she calls for.

At this call, there comes forth a royal rider on a white horse, armed with a bow, and to whom a crown is given, indicating His sovereign dominion. Some would make this a symbol of earthly conquest and dominion merely, all of which Christ employs as a subordinate agency in advancing His kingdom. But this would make it hardly distinguishable from the symbol of war that immediately follows. It will be hard to convince the Bible student, who regards the Holy Spirit as His own best interpreter, that this can refer to any other than that glorious Personage addressed by the Psalmist in the forty-fifth Psalm. "Gird Thy sword upon Thy thigh, O most Mighty, with Thy glory and Thy majesty. And in Thy majesty ride prosperously, because of truth, and meekness, and righteousness; and Thy right hand shall teach Thee terrible things. Thine arrows are sharp in the hearts of the King's enemies, whereby the people fall under Thee." It is the conquering power of Christ in His church, and her visible ordinances. The symbol lifts up the vail that covers these, and shows a secret divine agency at work, that gives to the church her conquering power. It represents, not indeed the actual person of Christ, but His spiritual living presence, in and with those agencies and instrumentalities by which He subdues a rebellious world to Himself, imparting to them all their efficacy. "Conquering and to conquer," or literally, "in order that He may conquer:" this is His only mission. He knows no defeat. Victory is His work, His sole work, the end for which He has constituted His church, and sends forth the gospel of the kingdom. This gospel is "the power of God unto salvation." "The weapons of our warfare are not carnal, but mighty through God to the pulling down of strong holds." "My word shall not return unto Me void, but it shall accomplish that which I please, and it shall prosper in the thing whereto I sent it." The ministry and ordinances of His church, and the active energies and holy example of her people, are the grand visible agency, and the word of the gospel the all-sufficient instrumentality of this spiritual conquest. This horse and his rider is represented here merely as *going forth;* the long train of His victories, the brightening path of His spiritual conquests, increasing from age to age, could not here be brought to view. Not till the nineteenth chapter does He again appear, and then it is with His many crowns, and followed by the immense multitudes of His conquered and willing followers, on white horses, and in white robes, conquerors themselves through Him. But He is still abroad in power and great grace. "Lo! I am with you alway," said Christ to His disciples, "even to the end of the world." Daily His call is ringing in our ears: "Take My yoke upon you."

Happy had it been for the earth, had it only heard at once the summons of its crucified King, and yielded to Him its homage. But the prey was not to be so easily wrested from the grasp of the mighty. It was also God's purpose to demonstrate the terrible malignity of sin before all the universe, by showing what love and what wrath it could resist, and through what long ages, too. The world did not recognize her Saviour, any more than did the Jews their King. Hence, one after another the world's own powers are turned against her, and war, and want, and death are made to contribute to the triumphs of the great conqueror.

2. The second seal is now opened, and the second living creature cries, "Come;" and immediately the rider on the red horse, armed with the great sword, comes forth, to whom it is given "to take peace from the earth," to set men on the work of mutual destruction. This symbol represents, evidently, all those agencies that spread discord, and division, and murderous hate through families and nations. War, with all the passions and furies that produce and follow it, with all its fearful and bloody desolations of nations, homes, and hearts; and the whole variety and multitude of inferior conflicts that divide and distract mankind, and make even the church a scene of bitter strife, so far as she is pervaded by the worldly spirit, are the terrible results of a rejected gospel of peace. Well and fearfully do they vindicate the claims of Jesus Christ as the only peacemaker, and punish the world for rejecting Him. "There is no peace, saith my God, to the wicked." "I came not to send peace, but a sword," said Jesus. By this scourge, all the sources of social happiness in the whole earthly sphere are smitten.

3. The third seal is now opened, and a call from a third of the living creatures summons another agent to the conflict. It is the rider of the black horse, with all the insignia of want and famine, bread given by weight, high prices, and deep solicitude for the preservation of the fruits of the earth. The scales show scarcity; a measure, or *chœnix*, about a quart, was the daily ration of bread of a Roman soldier, and a penny, or denarius, was a day's wages of a labouring man, and was, some say, twenty times, others eight times, the usual price of this measure of wheat. Even the last would indicate great want, as it would imply that a bushel of wheat cost about seven dollars, when a day's labour was but fifteen cents. Barley was then only one-third the price of wheat. These symbols,

therefore, express the greatest scarcity, as the colour of the horse indicates the deepest sorrow. Famine, with all its terrors, is another of the King's servants, employed to scourge a rebellious earth.

But as the physical and material is always the figure of the spiritual and moral, and as in this case especially, the very same language is applied to both, as famine and bread have their familiar spiritual sense, as well as material, the only proper symbol of a spiritual famine and its causes, is that which represents the physical. This symbol, in its full significance, includes, therefore, the still more awful curse of a famine of the bread of life, and of the agencies which produce it; the withholding of the showers of grace, and the desolations of ecclesiastical ambition and selfishness, which operate in this higher sphere, just as drought and oppression in the natural sphere. By this scourge, all the supports of the earthly life, and all the comforts, and hopes, and joys, which sustain and cheer the heart under the burden of its cares and anxieties, and which the gospel alone can impart, are smitten—all that truly feeds either body or soul. It is a famine that consumes the whole man.

4. The fourth seal is then opened, and the fourth and last of the living creatures summons the last and most terrible of these agents, the rider on the pale horse, Death, with hell, or the grave, following him. These destroy the fourth part of men, forcibly representing the great, though but partial destruction with which death sweeps into the grave the beauty, worth, and loveliness of earth in each and every age. In this he employs every possible instrumentality—not only the instruments of the former two horsemen, the sword and hunger, but in addition, pestilence and all diseases—(this being the meaning of *death*, in distinction from dying by violence,)—and the beasts of the earth, even, which last multiply and devastate in the desolations caused by war

and famine. It is evident that this clause is a description of the nature, and power, and design of the symbol just presented, and becomes in part an explanation of it, additional to the name that was given to the rider and his attendant. It is not what John saw, but an explanation of its design.

This scourge strikes the seat of the world's life; it strikes the life itself. It consummates the effects of the previous scourges. It completes the terrible agencies by which a world, rejecting its Saviour king, is punished. All these together are the iron rod of His wrath, with which He smites the rebellious nations.

Death here may not be limited to the body, any more than famine in the previous symbol. It must be taken in its entire scriptural meaning, as the wages of sin. The rider on the pale horse, with his undescribed follower, is the terrific symbol, not only of physical death and the grave—that which destroys and consumes the body—but especially of that which destroys and consumes eternally the soul, and which is the fearful and final result of rejecting the gospel of the slain Lamb. So by disease or pestilence, and the beasts of the earth, as well as by the sword and hunger, spiritual plagues are indicated; the pestilence of error, that poisons the soul, and those earthly powers, political, ecclesiastical, and philosophical—falsely so called—which, in the latter portion of this book, are represented as wild beasts of horrid shapes and destructive power. All diseases of the body, and pestilential errors of the soul; all the monstrous forms that worldly power, worldly wisdom, and corrupt religion have assumed, are included in the instruments by which this final scourge of death to both body and soul is inflicted upon the earth, to vindicate the claims of Jesus and His church to rule over it and in it.

Now, it is evident, that under these four symbols are embraced all the agencies of the church and the providence of God, which are employed in the conquest of the earth. There is nothing else that can be called in. The first introduces all the agencies of the gospel, as it goes forth with its piercing truths, and in the power of its crucified and glorified Author; the second smites the opposing worldly interest, in all the social relations; the third, in all the supports of the world's life; and the fourth, in its very life, burying all earthly good in the darkness and rottenness of the grave. All earthly powers and joys are under the control of the Lamb, and all the influences which smite them go forth at His bidding.

Thus, at the call of these living creatures, the church has gone forth with her word and ordinances in the power of her unseen King; and all providential agencies have followed to scourge and subdue her foes. Accordingly, after this there are no more voices from these living ones, and no more of these messengers from the throne. All the spiritual and providential agencies necessary to perfect this new and divine life in man, and to prepare him to rule over a regenerated earth, have already gone forth in the train of the conqueror. Henceforward these living creatures, that represent it, await in silent expectation the sure result which, along with the elders, they express in the new song, "We shall reign on the earth."

These few simple and striking symbols show us beautifully the light in which we are to view all those providences that fill individuals and nations with terror. They appear not as opposers, not as emissaries of hell. The last three riders, let it be observed, are sent forth *from* the symbolical heaven, and *by* the slain Lamb, and *in answer to* the cry of the church's inmost life, just the same as the first one, which represented the church itself in her spiritual mission and power. They are summoned there, not as enemies, but as helpers. They are not, indeed, the agents by which the bloodless and spiritual victories of truth, and peace, and righteousness are won over human hearts, but those by which all who reject the sceptre of His grace are either chastened, humbled, and deprived of their earthly supports, and so made sensible of their folly; or else, if incorrigible, by which they are punished, their opposition rendered futile and crushed out, and the spiritual kingdom prepared for the occupancy of the earth.

Widely and fiercely have all these three riders been sweeping over the nations for eighteen hundred years, executing their high commission. Terribly has the God of providence smitten all the sources of the world's happiness, and made these very things, as turned into bitterness and death, to demonstrate its folly and madness in rejecting the gospel of His Son. Still the world seems not to recognize the true reason of its miseries. "Lord," says the prophet,[1] "when Thy hand is lifted up they will not see; but they shall see." Still, therefore, these terrible riders are abroad. Still the red, and the black, and the pale horse are careering all around us, and among us, entering our very homes, and sweeping away every joy and confidence that opposes the gospel of the slain Lamb, and submission to His claims. No country, no family, no individual can escape them, except as each bows in entire submission and cordial consecration to the rider on the white horse, and enters the train of his white-robed followers.

The attempt of interpreters to make a *specific* application—an exclusively specific application—of these symbols to the wars, famines, pestilences, and beasts of prey that desolated the Roman Empire during the first three centuries, while the first great struggle between Christianity and Paganism was in progress, is entirely arbitrary; and still more so, the exclusive application of it to the desolations of Judea just before the fall of Jerusalem: to the

---

[1] Is. 26: 11.

great struggle between Christianity and Judaism. These are fair and forcible illustrations of the wrong principles of interpretation that have been applied to this book. We regard them as arbitrary, because there is no such limitation of time in the text, and nothing whatever to imply it; nor is there any limitation of any kind in the symbols themselves; they represent a conquering gospel, and war, and want, and death, and nothing more, and nothing less. These have all been just as busy since, as then. There is nothing whatever here to indicate that the gospel, and wars, and want, and death in those ages were designed, any more than all that in the ages since have been desolating or blessing the nations, and to which the symbols are just as appropriate. If it be possible for symbols to characterize the whole dispensation, and to be so presented as to show this to be their design, it is done here. War, and want, and death, natural and spiritual, have been busy in every age, and must be, until the triumphs of the cross are complete.

While these four seals unfold all the great visible agencies employed by the Lamb in accomplishing the purposes of His mediatorial reign, much yet remains hidden beneath the three remaining seals.

5. The fifth seal is now broken, and a scene altogether new and startling breaks upon the view. From the souls of those "slain for the word of God, and for the testimony which they held," there arises the martyr cry, "How long, O Lord, holy and true, dost Thou not judge and avenge our blood on them that dwell on the earth?" They who dwell on the earth here are opposed to those who sit in the heavenly places in Christ Jesus, who belong to the kingdom of heaven, and must therefore mean, not of course all mankind in the flesh, but those who are in the interest of the world, who live only in the earthly sphere, and under earthly influences, and so form the opposition to the spiritual kingdom. These "souls" or

"lives," are seen under, or at the foot of the altar, as if slain on account of their adherence to it, and to the great cardinal doctrine of atonement, of which it is the standing symbol; and their blood, "which is the life," is thus represented, like the blood of righteous Abel, as crying for vengeance, and that in language showing that retribution had already been long delayed, long beyond the church's expectations. This is not the language of revenge, any more than the cry of Abel's blood was an expression of Abel's desire of revenge; it was the cry of outraged justice, and of compassion and sympathy for a still suffering church, and of longing desire for her deliverance and triumph.

To those whose blood thus cried unto God were given white robes, representing their own immediate and complete acceptance. The answer, that they must wait yet a season, until the whole number of their fellow-servants that should suffer be filled up, teaches that the whole period of the church's conflict here is one in which the martyr spirit will be required, and martyrs' blood be shed, and a divinely sustained patience demanded. It is implied that then, when the last martyr shall have bled, and not before, shall the long expected consummation come. Thus graphically was it portrayed, that the church's path of conquest, as indicated by the first royal horseman going forth conquering and to conquer, was to be stained, deeply stained, by her own blood, shed in defence of her own testimony, and that as a testimony to the infinite efficacy of her Lord's atoning blood, and to the supremacy of His kingly claims founded upon it. As it is expressed in chap 12: 11, "They overcame by the blood of the Lamb, and the word of their testimony; and they loved not their lives unto the death."

In addition, then, to the agencies to be employed, we have here revealed the long, long delay during which they are to be in conflict, the cries of a suffering, waiting church, and the promise of a coming deliverance. It is called "a little season," in comparison with the endless glory that shall follow, and as it lies in the divine plan. "One day is with the Lord as a thousand years, and a thousand years as one day."

6. The sixth opening seal, accordingly, unfolds, (1.) the long-delayed and prayed for vengeance. In symbols of most expressive force and well-established meaning, is portrayed the utter, complete, and awful overthrow of all earthly powers, and influences, and systems: revolutions and convulsions as destructive and universal in the whole social and moral world, the whole constitution of human society, as would be produced by a universal earthquake, by which the mountains would be swallowed up, and the valleys heaved above them, and the whole system utterly dislocated; and as if the whole of the world's lights were to be removed, the sun darkened, the moon turned to blood, the stars fallen from heaven, and the heavens themselves departing as a scroll rolled together. In the midst of this total confounding of all the old systems of the world as opposed to the Lamb, this universal ruin of the earthly and opposing power, and in order to show the utter hopelessness of all who resist His reign and neglect His grace, they are represented, from the highest of them to the lowest, from the kings to the slaves, as all alike affrighted, paralyzed with terror, and crying out, in the agony of despair, to the mountains and to the rocks, "Fall on us, and hide us from the face of Him that sitteth on the throne, and from the wrath of the Lamb; for the great day of His wrath is come, and who shall be able to stand?"

How long the catastrophe here symbolized shall occupy, whether it shall be sudden, or protracted through generations, or what special forms the agencies of ruin may assume at the last, we are not here told. What we have here is the consummation of that glorious revolution in all earthly things, which has been in progress ever since the church of Christ started forth on her mission of conquest. All the vast revolutions in human society and governments, all of which were heathen and idolatrous, produced by the spread of the gospel, and all the judgments with which so often already God has avenged the injuries done to His cause, and all the wrath and terror that forced from dying sinners the cry of despair, may fairly be included, indeed, in this, just as each soul's conversion is a contribution to the final triumph of the saints. But the final stroke of vengeance shall at last descend and end the strife. No language, no figures could more impressively depict the awful, total, hopeless ruin and despair of all the earthly power and interest. Such must be the end of all opposition to this kingdom, and such the despair of all who reject the mercy offered, and refuse the obedience required by the slain Lamb, as He is now gathering and perfecting His spiritual kingdom. That great day of His wrath must come; it is coming; all things are combining with the prayers of suffering saints to hasten it on.

So far, this seal makes the result, in regard to the opposition to the kingdom, all clear and certain; the earth is cleared of all opposition, and prepared for a reigning church; but where is that church? This is only one side of the triumph; the other, and positive side, is still more important. How has the church herself been preserved and gathered during all this long and bloody struggle, and prepared to reign? The only things yet revealed in this series of God's unfolded purposes, in regard to her, is the rider on the white horse conquering, and the martyrs bleeding.

Hence, to complete this view, and give the other side of this grand scheme, there is added in the next chapter two other scenes, in which the church herself is brought more fully in sight. These do not follow the former in chronological succession, even as the realities symbolized do not so follow each other but in part. It seems evident, from the very nature of the symbols here used, and their necessary meaning, that they must cover, partly at least, the same ground. Having traced the conflict with the world's opposition to its close in the world's overthrow, the Spirit now goes back to unfold, by a few equally simple pictures, the secret of the church's growth, and gathering and consummated bliss. May it not also be thus intimated, that it is only when the battle has ended, and the smoke of the conflict cleared away, that we shall be able fully to understand the wisdom and love that bound together in one harmonious whole the spiritual processes and the providential agencies of this kingdom?

(2.) Four angels are seen holding the four winds. The four winds are, of course, all the winds. Winds here ($ανεμοι$) mean not the gentle and refreshing breezes, but the hurricanes that sweep all before them with ruin, and spread complete desolation in their path. They thus represent all the violent and resistless powers and influences which, when let loose, are to sweep over the earth, and involve it in the ruin just depicted in the previous scene. These unseen forces are represented during all this long period as held back by the forbearance of God, until the redeemed are all secured. The long suffering of God restrains the thunderbolts of His wrath, and provides the providential agencies by which the selfish and malignant passions of a fallen race are prevented from working out their natural and ruinous results, until His saints are gathered in. This process is beautifully pictured by a mighty angel, having the seal of the living God, ascending from the east—the source of light and life—whence the Sun of Righteousness arises, with healing in His wings, over a dark and ruined world; and after charging the angels of the winds to hold them back till His work is done, He proceeds to affix the seal of the living God on all His servants. That angel is a mere instrumental agent, and, as such, can be a symbol of nothing else than the active agencies of the gospel itself, pervaded and accompanied by the Spirit's power. That seal is the divine impress of the truth fixed by the Spirit upon the soul of the believer and his character. Other passages make this plain. "Ye were sealed with the Holy Spirit of promise;" "whereby ye are sealed unto the day of redemption;" "God hath sealed us, and given the earnest of the Spirit in our hearts." The Spirit thus explains His own symbol, and it is one that in a word unfolds the whole process of grace. The seal stamps them as His; it certifies them to be His; it preserves them as His; and it does this by forming and perfecting the image of Christ in them. "The foundation of God standeth sure, having this seal: the Lord knoweth them that are His. And let every one that nameth the name of Christ depart from iniquity."

The number of these sealed ones is definitely stated. Known unto God are all His redeemed. However uncertain men may be, there is no uncertainty in the mind of Him who causes the seal to be affixed. That number is a perfect number, and so formed as to aptly symbolize the whole church, or spiritual kingdom of Christ, as it exists on earth, in each and every generation and age. Twelve being the number of the chosen tribes of God's people, it came very naturally to be the established numerical symbol of completeness in regard to the church, or any chosen body representing it, as the twelve apostles, the twice twelve elders, the twelve gates of the heavenly city, with their twelve angels. "Thousands," were the prominent and technical divisions of each of the tribes.[1] So here, twelve of these thousands are sealed from each of the tribes of Israel. Israel is the established symbol of the

---

[1] Ex. 18: 25. Num. 1: 16.

whole church; and in its twelve tribes, of the visible church in its organized capacity, and in all its divisions, in every age. The sealed are not the whole, only a part, and that the smaller part, of each tribe. And are we not taught that the spiritually sealed are an election within an election, in every age; that not all who are called to enjoy the privileges of the visible kingdom, but only an election out of them, are the true servants of God, stamped with His likeness? "Many are called, but few are chosen." "Not every one that saith unto Me, Lord, Lord, shall enter into the kingdom of heaven." "They are not all Israel, which are of Israel." Most strikingly, thus, do these sealed ones, *out of* all the tribes of a people, chosen *out of* the world, represent the whole of God's elect people, as they are gathered out of every nation and kindred of the earth into His visible church, there to be trained and disciplined, and thence gathered to Himself by His almighty and transforming grace in every age.

Until these are *all* sealed, the catastrophe described in the last chapter has been ordered to be delayed; when the sealing is completed, therefore, that takes place. There are then left, as the only occupants of the scene, the whole assembly of the redeemed, a great multitude, which no man could number, of all nations, and kindreds, and people, and tongues. They stand "before the throne and before the Lamb, clothed with white robes, and palms in their hands," crying "with a loud voice, Salvation to our God, which sitteth upon the throne, and unto the Lamb." The eternal praises of the triumphant church will ascribe the salvation of every soul to God and to the Lamb only, to free, sovereign, and unmerited grace. In its origin, its execution, its application, its progress, and its final consummation, salvation is of God. It is God's *to save;* it is man's only *to be saved.* The sinner has nothing to do in the whole process, but to receive, and use, and enjoy the free and matchless *grace.*

The next verses describe still further the perfected bliss and glory of this spiritual kingdom, with all its thousands of ministering servants—the angelic hosts—in terms that scarcely need a word of explanation, but are only enfeebled by any comment; and that have fed the faith and hopes of suffering saints in all ages; from which, too, the whole church has derived much of those conceptions of future bliss which have become thoroughly incorporated with all her thinking and feeling. For the comfort of the struggling believer, the whole of these overwhelming glories are brought into striking contrast with the tribulations through which they have passed, and by which they have been prepared for it, thus uniting in one the sorrowing and the triumphant church. The wonderful process, too, of their purification is described in language which bears the unmistakable stamp of divinity upon it: "they washed their robes, and made them *white* in the blood of the Lamb." Mysterious, but glorious process of almighty love and power! "Oh! the depth!"

"Therefore are they before the throne of God, and serve Him day and night in His temple; and He that sitteth on the throne shall dwell among them. They shall hunger no more, neither thirst any more, neither shall the sun light on them, nor any heat. For the Lamb, which is in the midst of the throne, shall feed them, and shall lead them unto living fountains of waters; and God shall wipe away all tears from their eyes."

7. Now, at length, the seventh and last seal is opened. But the opening brings to view no fresh actors or scenes. There is silence in heaven. No more lightnings, and thunderings, and voices out of the throne. The Eternal Sabbath has begun.[1] The new creation, the work of re-

---

[1] "*About the space of half an hour.*" To the above interpretation of the seventh seal, we see but one plausible objection, that arising from the specification of time. How could a half-hour's silence be emblematic of an eternal rest? The answer is, that it is not the length of the

deeming love, is completed. The Lamb has fulfilled all the purposes of redeeming love. He has gathered to Him all His blood-bought people, and filled them with bliss and glory. His work is done. His honour is vindicated. Satan is dethroned. All enemies destroyed. The world itself renovated. Paradise restored. The saints reign. God is glorified. All sounds of conflict are hushed for ever.

silence that makes it the symbol of this rest; but the silence itself being the only result of the opening of this seal, and this seal being the last, nothing more being left after this of God's plan in perfecting His kingdom to be unfolded, makes it necessarily a symbol of the simple fact that there was nothing more to be done—that all was completed; and if this was so, then of course the rest must be eternal.

But, then, why this specification of time? This seemed necessary, in order to show that it was not a mere momentary silence, introductory to new revelations in the same series, and that it should be long enough to show a complete separation between the opening of the seventh seal and any succeeding visions. The time is a designation evidently of the length of this silence in its relation to the sensible apprehensions of the seer, and is no more itself a symbol than the words "I saw," and "I heard," are symbols, or than the few hours of that Sabbath occupied by all these visions are symbols. It is a designation of the period this vision of silence occupied, as there was no other possible way to describe its importance, there being no actions of any kind to measure the time. A half hour's silence in a series of visions, the whole of which could have occupied but a few hours at the most, was quite enough to separate entirely the first series, this opening of the seals from what followed, and to produce the impression that the contents of the seven-sealed book were all unfolded.

LECTURE XVIII.

THE GREAT REVOLUTION.

REV., CHAP. VI: 12–17.

"And I beheld, when He had opened the sixth seal, and lo! there was a great earthquake, and the sun became black as sackcloth of hair, and the moon became as blood. And the stars of heaven fell unto the earth, even as a fig tree casteth her untimely figs when she is shaken of a mighty wind. And the heaven departed as a scroll when it is rolled together, and every mountain and island were moved out of their places. And the kings of the earth, and the great men, and the rich men, and the chief captains, and the mighty men, and every bondman, and every freeman, hid themselves in the dens, and in the rocks of the mountains, and said to the mountains and rocks, Fall on us, and hide us from the face of Him that sitteth on the throne, and from the wrath of the Lamb; for the great day of His wrath is come, and who shall be able to stand?"

WE have already given the general meaning of this grand and terrific scene. We desire further to confirm that view, and to make some further practical use of it. We regard it as a description of the utter overthrow of all the world's powers and organizations, in order to the eternal triumph of this spiritual kingdom. Such a triumph as that here described involves the completest possible revolution in all earthly things, the utter demolition of the whole frame work of society, certainly in all its moral aspects and tendencies, from the highest pinnacles of its power and splendour, to its deepest foundations, and its obscurest recesses. It involves just such a revolution in the social and moral world as geologists say took place at some former period in the physical.

Untold ages ago, they tell us, our whole planet, then filled with those huge vegetable growths, and those mammoth and monstrous animal forms, whose remains still preserve, in their deep beds, their mysterious history, was shaken by the most fearful convulsions, and its whole surface shattered to pieces, and submerged, upheaved in chaos and darkness, in floods and fire, and contorted into entirely new forms and systems, making it, not only in these respects, but in all its productions, too, a new world. Now, it is here and elsewhere in Scripture clearly revealed, that a revolution equally complete in the whole moral condition of human affairs, and in every thing affected by this, is to be produced by the triumph of the church of Christ, resulting in an order of things as different from the present administration of human governments, the spirit and working of social institutions, the habits of social intercourse, and especially the whole relations of man toward God, as that which some great geologic change would produce on the earth's physical surface and productions. That such is the certain result of the triumph of the spiritual kingdom on the earth, is the strongest conceivable evidence that all these things, in their whole spirit, and aims, and instrumentalities, and arrangements, are inconsistent with the gospel of the kingdom, and opposed to the reign of Christ so entirely as to require a complete overthrow and transformation. This is indeed making out a bold and broad indictment against the world; and if it can be made good, it must stamp with the guilt of apostasy, or hypocrisy, or rebellion, those who, professing to be Christ's followers, conform themselves to its maxims, habits, and pursuits; and must prove the folly of those who are looking to the power and the wisdom of the world, in any of its forms, for substantial help in advancing the interests of Christ's kingdom. It is made good, however, if our interpretation of this passage is correct.

Our first object, therefore, will be to confirm this interpretation by a fuller view of parallel passages of Scripture than could be given in the last lecture. To prevent misconception, however, and to give distinctness and precision to our design, it may be not amiss to observe in the beginning, that the question whether this revolution does, or does not, involve corresponding great physical changes on the earth is not here raised at all; it may be, or it may not be; that would involve a distinct and separate inquiry, to be settled, if indeed it can be, by a careful comparison of the Scriptures bearing on it. It is a question far less practical, and its decision does not materially affect the fact that this revolution produced by the triumph of the spiritual kingdom, is one that pervades the whole social and moral interests of the race and our world. If it be that even physical changes are also required to bring the world into harmony with the perfect triumph of the church; if it be true that, while corruption remains in human hearts, there can be no such radical revolution in human society; if it be true that this involves an entire change in the whole dispensation of God's mercy, beyond all that the universal prevalence of true religion reigning in regenerated, but partially sanctified hearts, could effect, it only makes our case the stronger. The more complete the change necessary to the triumph of the kingdom of God, the more total the opposition of the world as it now is to that kingdom.

Nor do we now raise the question of instrumentalities, or how this triumph is to be fully effected; how much will be due to the word and Spirit, and how much to providences and judgments accompanying these; how near an approach shall be made to the perfect triumph, by the gradual extension of gospel agencies and influences among the nations, and how long and universally the sealing process of the next chapter may continue and extend, and how much will be left for the last stroke of the iron sceptre, for the last shock of the mighty earthquake, when death itself shall be swallowed up in victory. It does appear to us, that on these points there has been a great deal too much dogmatism—a great deal too much effort to state these things more definitely and distinctly than the wide generalities of prophetic words or symbols will warrant. We can find nothing here that gives any definite answers to questions on this point; while on the great and important fact that all these agencies will be employed, and multiply the triumphs of the cross, producing changes the same in kind, and less or greater in degree, until the end, the response is perfectly clear and definite.

I. What, then, is the proper, natural and necessary meaning of this language? Is it to be taken literally, as indicating just such a convulsion of nature: just such affrighted multitudes congregated together in mountain recesses, and uttering these words of terror to the mountains and the rocks, as they fly from the descending throne, and from the wrath of the Lamb, when He appears in His bodily presence and in vengeance? This is impossible. The literal events here described cannot take place in nature.

Let it be remembered, that this is a plain, simple description by the apostle of what he saw when the sixth seal was opened, in the same way that he saw the white, red, black, and pale horses going forth, and the souls under the altar; and that, like those, this awful sight of what appeared a world in its last throes of convulsive agony, was a symbol of some great truths or facts in regard to the administration of this spiritual kingdom of God. These could be nothing else than that which is described in this language of Paul to the Hebrews, "The removing of those things that are shaken, as of things that are made, that the things which cannot be shaken may remain: the kingdom which cannot be moved."

Now, it has been so ordered, that every peculiarity in the language used here—every one of these symbols—is employed by the old prophets in predicting great changes that have already taken place, in whole or in part, in reference to particular governments and systems opposed to God's people. The difference is, that they are all collected here into one awful scene, and applied, not to any one government or system, but to the whole of the earthly opposition to the spiritual kingdom, to the utter overthrow of everything opposed to the reign of the slain Lamb, and of His saints on the earth. If this description does not indicate perfect universality, no symbols can do it. There is here, as no where else in this whole series of seals, no limitation of time or place. All such are added by interpreters. What these symbols therefore mean in the prophets, in their application to *particular* kingdoms and *visible* systems of organized opposition to God's *visible* kingdom, they mean here in regard to the *whole* of the power of *earth and hell*—the whole kingdom of the prince of this world—the whole opposition to the *spiritual* kingdom of Christ.

Even the last and most characteristic part of this description, which depicts so graphically the terror and ruin of the wicked, has its counterpart there. Isaiah, describing the coming judgments of God upon the Jews, says, chap. 2: 19, "And they shall go into the holes of the rocks, and into the caves of the earth, for fear of the Lord, and for the glory of His Majesty, when He ariseth to shake terribly the earth." Hosea, predicting the wrath about to be poured out on the apostate kingdom of Israel, uses these words, "They shall say to the mountains, Cover us; and to the hills, Fall on us;" words with which he concludes the threatening, "The high places of Aven, the sin of Israel, shall be destroyed; the thorn and the thistle shall come up on their altars."

In illustration of this whole scene, and the meaning of

its symbols, the passages which might be quoted are very numerous. It will be sufficient to direct our special attention to only four others.

(1.) The first is in the thirteenth chapter of Isaiah. The whole chapter is expressly styled the burden of Babylon. In it we read thus: "Behold the day of the Lord cometh, cruel both with wrath and fierce anger, to lay the land desolate; and He shall destroy the sinners out of it. For the stars shall fall from heaven, and the constellations thereof shall not give their light; the sun shall be darkened in his going forth, and the moon shall not cause her light to shine. * * * I will shake the heavens, and the earth shall remove out of her place, in the wrath of the Lord of hosts, and in the day of His fierce anger." As the cause of all the changes thus described, he adds, a few verses after, "Behold I will stir up the Medes against them." By this falling and obscuration of the lights of heaven, therefore, was predicted the utter destruction of the Babylonish power, with all its dependencies, and in all its extent, from the throne of its monarch to the humblest officer employed by it in ruling the nations. In all this there is nothing high-wrought or extravagant. It is not merely the warm imagination of the east that expresses itself thus; it is in perfect accordance with the feelings of all nations who have known what it is to live under powerful governments which controlled the destinies of millions of people. The analogy between the sun, moon, and stars—the heavenly bodies—in their relation to, and their influence upon our world, and human governments as to their high and subordinate offices in their influence on the masses of the people, has been always seen and felt. No other is so striking, or so universally expressed. Nothing is more natural in times of overwhelming national calamity, when the whole framework of social order is heaving and rocking to and fro, and all the interests bound up in one's country and its institutions are threatened with ruin, to speak of it as the great earthquake throes of revolution, to talk of the deep gloom as if the very sun was darkened, and the moon and stars had withdrawn their shining. How often just such language was used during the last few years in this country; and there were times and regions in which men felt as if even this language was not strong enough to express the intensity of their feelings—their perception of the magnitude and misery of the changes passing over them, or dreaded.

(2.) Again, in Is. 34: 4, we have language almost identical with the strongest of that in the text, and there applied particularly to Idumea, though the connection shows that Idumea was regarded as the representative of all the enemies of Zion. Having called the world's attention to the predicted slaughter of the nations, he adds, "And all the host of heaven shall be dissolved, and the heavens shall be rolled together as a scroll, and all their host shall fall down, as the leaf falleth off from the vine, and as a falling fig from a fig tree. For My sword shall be bathed in heaven; behold it shall come down upon Idumea, and upon the people of My curse to judgment." Here, this dissolution and falling of the heavenly host can only describe great revolutions, such as shall utterly overthrow the whole political, social, and idolatrous systems of the nations meant. This is evident from what follows; for afterwards, as the immediate result of this overthrow, we have a picture of universal peace, prosperity, and triumph, beginning with the coming of the Messiah, and ending in a consummation very similar to that described in the next chapter of this book by the symbols of the ransomed throngs around the throne. "The wilderness and the solitary place shall be glad for them, and the desert shall rejoice, and blossom as the rose. * * * They shall see the glory of the Lord, and the excellency of our God. * * * A highway shall be there, and a way, and it shall be called, The way of Holiness; the unclean shall not pass over it; but it shall be for those [the holy]; the travellers in it, though fools, shall not err. No lion shall be there, nor any ravenous beast shall go up thereon; it shall not be found there; but the redeemed shall walk there; and the ransomed of the Lord shall return, and come to Zion with songs and everlasting joy upon their heads; they shall obtain joy and gladness, and sorrow and sighing shall flee away."[1]

No one can carefully read and compare that whole passage in Isaiah, with this before us, to the end of the seventh chapter, without perceiving such a wonderful and close analogy between them, notwithstanding the great difference in form, as compels to a common application to at least providential and gracious changes of the same nature, and tending to the same blessed result. There are very few stronger confirmations of the Christian's faith, and more silencing rebukes to infidelity, than such striking agreement in far-reaching predictions between writers separated by hundreds of years, and totally different circumstances, and in long and complicated passages, so very dissimilar in their whole composition, and connection, and occasions, and yet both of them finding their only complete explanation in that which brings them into perfect harmony. The explanation, too, which does this, receives in it the strongest testimony of its correctness.

(3.) The third passage is that in Joel 2: 28-32: "And it shall come to pass afterward, that I will pour out My Spirit upon all flesh; and your sons and your daughters shall prophesy, your old men shall dream dreams, your young men shall see visions; and also upon the servants and upon the handmaids in those days will I pour out My Spirit. And I will show wonders in the heavens and in the earth, blood, and fire, and pillars of smoke. The sun

---

[1] Is. 35: 1, 2, 8, 9, 10.

shall be turned into darkness, and the moon into blood, before the great and terrible day of the Lord come. And it shall come to pass, that whosoever shall call on the name of the Lord shall be delivered; for in Mount Zion and in Jerusalem shall be deliverance, as the Lord hath said, and in the remnant whom the Lord shall call." Here, again, it will be observed, the two processes of the sealing of the Spirit, and the judgments that blot out all the lights of heaven, are brought together, and in the same relation to each other, and to the triumph of Messiah's kingdom, and the salvation of His people.

This passage is specially interesting, as being that quoted by the apostle Peter on the day of Pentecost, and finding then an incipient fulfilment in the outpouring of the Spirit, and the convulsions that swept away the old economy. Peter makes this express application of it. "This which ye now see and hear," he tells them, "is that which was spoken by the prophet Joel;" this is the beginning of the great revolution the prophet here describes. It must be, therefore, a description of those processes of judgment and mercy which were to characterize the whole administration of the Messiah in the establishment of His kingdom, by which the day of its triumph, a day great and terrible beyond all others to its adversaries, was to be brought about. It is really the very same thing as the Lamb's opening the seven seals—the concentrated view of His whole mediatorial reign and conquests, as seen from the greater distance of the old prophet. "The sun being turned into darkness, and the moon into blood," expresses the utter ruin of all the powers of the world that oppose that day of His triumph; and although it began to be fulfilled in the utter destruction of the Jewish State and church, it can only find the end of its fulfilment when the last of these powers shall in like manner fall before the might of a reigning Saviour.

(4.) The only other passage of the old prophets to which

we refer, is in the second chapter of Haggai. We quote only a few verses. "Thus saith the Lord of hosts, Yet once, it is a little while, and I will shake the heavens, and the earth, and the sea, and the dry land; and I will shake all nations, and the desire," or, more literally, "the desirable things of all nations shall come, and I will fill this house with glory, saith the Lord of hosts." * * * "I will shake the heavens and the earth, and I will overthrow the throne of the kingdoms, and I will destroy the strength of the kingdoms of the heathen." Here, again, the same figures of shaking the heavens and the earth are used to express the convulsions and overturnings in the political, social, and moral world which were to precede and introduce, as well as also to complete the gospel dispensation.

No where is such language used to describe a destruction of the visible framework of nature. The words of Peter, in his second epistle, do indeed describe a destruction of the world by fire, like that by water in the days of Noah; it is, however, in very different terms, and in order to a renovation, to a new heavens and a new earth. That may accompany this; but this is a destruction and a renovation as much superior, and more terrible and glorious than that, as immortal men are greater than the material world in which they dwell. That world will always be adapted to them; it will be made to punish them, if enemies to the Creator and Redeemer; and it will be so ordered and moulded as to be a source of bliss, and in harmony with the songs of the redeemed, when all enemies are destroyed. But neither in any of these passages, nor in this revelation of the sixth seal, are any such changes in material things the objects on which our eyes and thoughts are fixed, but the mightier and far more radical change in the whole intelligent and spiritual world.

The last passage has also a special interest and force, arising from the use made of it in the epistle to the Hebrews, and which shows the fulness of its meaning, and something of the extent of its application. It will be an appropriate close and application, not only of this, but of all the other passages; and is itself a forcible exposition and application of the scene of the sixth seal. " Whose voice"—the voice of Christ at the giving of the law— "then shook the earth; but now He hath promised, saying, Yet once more I shake not the earth only, but also heaven. And this word, Yet once more"—that is, this whole prophetic declaration—"signifieth the removing of those things that are shaken, as of things that are made, that those things which cannot be shaken may remain. Wherefore, we receiving a kingdom which cannot be moved, let us have grace, whereby we may serve God acceptably, with reverence and godly fear; for our God is a consuming fire."

It is impossible, then, in consistency with Scripture teaching, to apply these symbols to any thing else, or any thing less than the total destruction of all the systems and influences of worldly power and wisdom, whether in church, or State, or social life, which are inconsistent with a pure, a spiritual, a reigning Christianity, with universal and joyful submission to the reign of the Lamb. The universality of this revolution, and the entire change which these symbols represent, as produced by it in all earthly things, implies that the whole of these are inconsistent with it, except as they have already yielded to it, or been transformed by it.

II. But the question will at once be raised here, has not Christianity already done this in regard to those nations where she has established her sway? Has she not utterly swept away the old systems of heathenism, and introduced an entirely new order of things? How immense the difference between heathendom and Christendom! At least in those nations where she has triumphed, so as to change governments, laws, and social order, is there anything more to be expected in the way of such radical changes in the whole constitution of government and society?

If the past establishment of Christianity in the nations could in any single case satisfy the terms, and meet the evident design of this one great group of symbols to mark the utter destruction of all—at least of all open and apparent—opposition, then certainly we might feel that in that case this great revolution was past, and no other such day of terrors to be looked for; and also that there the world and the church were no longer at variance, but in entire harmony.

But this cannot begin to satisfy the meaning of these symbols, which require the destruction of all power and authority, and all systems and influences that are not in harmony with the design of the slain Lamb, and do not yield entire submission to His government; such an overthrow of the worldliness of the world, in both high stations and low, in the church and the State, as shall leave this spiritual kingdom in sole possession of the earth, and entire control of all its powers and agencies, to employ the whole to the praise and glory of the Lamb. It is, of course, true, that every overthrow of the heathen powers in the first establishment of Christianity, and of heathen and infidel governments and influences ever since, by preparing and contributing to the great result, is necessarily included in this revolution of the world's ruling powers; but these are only the partial shocks of the great earthquake, the premonitions of the coming overthrow.

The idea that the Christian world is pretty well Christianized, is a grand mistake. The notion that the ameliorating and elevating influences of the gospel have already so remodelled and renovated the forms of government, and the influences of social life, as to bring them so far into conformity with the claims of Christ, that only a *little* more gradual leavening of the mass is necessary to secure its entire conformity, shows an extremely low and erroneous idea of His claims, and the nature of spiritual religion. The Christian world, with all its splendid civilization, its science, its arts, and its multiform literature, is little more than a Christianized Paganism. Even in regard to the great multitude of professed believers in Christianity, it is but the worship of the world under Christian forms. The change, indeed, from Paganism to the present Christian civilization is very great; great beyond the power of all mere human influences, proclaiming the presence of a divine power. An element there is present, in some degree, almost every where, on which appears the evident stamp of the spiritual kingdom in its purity, its singularity, and its power, and perhaps more widely diffused now than ever before. This change ought not to be underrated; but neither ought it to be overrated, or overestimated. Great as it is, the change required to bring this godless civilization, this polished kingdom of the devil, to be thoroughly pervaded by a pure spiritual Christianity, is still greater, far greater; and can only be brought about by an overturning such as the text sets forth. Its language is not a whit too strong to set forth the deep, wide, transforming change required to bring, not a mere worldly, proud and corrupt church into the ascendant; that would be easy enough—that is so now in many cases—but a pure, spiritual religion, a religion that breathes the spirit of holy love to man and consecration to God, to bring this into the ascendant, so as to mould political, social, and intellectual influences, and to subordinate the material powers and wealth of the world.

How is it with the politics and governments of the very best nations? Are they controlled by Christian principles and aims? Are the honour and authority of the King of kings regarded in their council chambers and halls of legislation? Is it in the spirit of humble prayer, of a desire and determination to glorify Christ, to further the supreme ends of the kingdom of God in their own peculiar and legitimate sphere, that their plans are devised and matured? The very question almost provokes a smile. To think of the members of Congress, or Parliament, or cabinet ministers, engaging in their political duties with the same spirit, temper, and motives that govern a praying saint at the communion table!

More than this: what are the professed principles which they adopt? For example, is it not so generally regarded as an axiom in politics, that the principles of Christian morality in regard to injuries and forgiveness can have no relation to the intercourse of governments, and are not binding at all on men in their public relations, that to dispute it would be almost worth a man's reputation for sober sense in some quarters, and he would be set down by a large portion of even the Christian world, as a hair-brained enthusiast? But the wise man has yet to arise, that can show how men associated together in the high places of the world's governments, and in their discharge of the duties involved in the relations of whole nations, may indulge tempers and motives, and perform acts involving them, which are acknowledged in private relations to be wrong. Is not Jesus Christ the King of the nations? Does He not require His law to be supreme in the hearts of all rulers and legislators, as well as everybody else, and in all their relations? Does not His law embrace in its grasp all the relations in which man can be placed? Shall the highest and most important of them all, as regards this world, be exempted from the grasp of those precepts which are especially directed to the regulation of human intercourse, and especially characteristic of the peaceful religion of Jesus?

This is a very different thing from saying that the functions of civil government include the defence, or the propagation, or the support of the gospel, or involve any declaration of religious truth; it is only saying that every man called to exercise such functions is bound, in the performance of his duties, to act on the principles of the gospel of Christ, which govern him in every other relation. It is very different, too, from saying that a government may not perform acts which would be wrong in individuals; which is evident, since every relation and position has its peculiar duties. Government is for the punishment of evil doers, and for the praise of them that do well; and this very end, the protection of the people, and all the interests of justice and truth necessary to the existence of social order, may require it not only to punish the individual criminal, but even to wage a defensive war.

But after all these necessary limitations, this case may serve to illustrate the immense extent of the revolution required in all the so-called Christian governments of the world, to conform them to the law of the kingdom. It is said, to conduct a government on such principles is utterly impracticable: it cannot be done. Well, let this be granted; suppose, what may be true, that it is impracticable. It can be so for no other reason than the wickedness of man; and it is this very impracticability that proves the world's deep ungodliness: that it is impossible to conduct the high affairs of civil government on the principles of the religion of Christ, of love, forgiveness, and peace. How vast the change required to make it not only practicable, but universal! For as certainly as the Lamb is unfolding the seven-sealed book, it shall be universal. "We shall reign on the earth," sing the white-robed elders.

This, also, renders necessary a continual repetition of those wars, and revolutions, and upheavings of the masses of society, which have been always desolating the world, until the nations are transformed, society renovated, and the old systems utterly wiped out. Nothing less, and nothing else, can secure to the spiritual church that ascendancy in all human affairs here predicted. While such a state of things exists as now does in every nation of the earth, it is vain to hope for settled peace, and the steady, onward progress of truth and righteousness, like a gently flowing stream of rapidly increasing width, and depth, and blessing. Nothing but successive shocks of this earthquake, heavier strokes of that iron rod, can ever shake out from the earth its earthliness, and enthrone the spiritual kingdom.

Were we to drag out to the light the prevailing habits of social and business life, we should find them equally destitute of the pure and controlling principles of a spiritual Christianity, a holy consecration. In buying and selling, in sleeping, and eating, and drinking, and especially in dressing—in the vanity displayed in it, and the interest, importance, and time given to it; in all these the ingrafted habits of fashionable society are as opposed to spiritual consecration to Christ as darkness is to light. Still more in the pleasures pursued, not only in the public pleasures, as of the theatre and the ball-room, but the more private ones of the home circle, and the parlour, and the social gathering, and the wretched literature that disgraces often the tables of professing Christians, is this total alienation of the world's heart from God manifest, even in so-called Christian society. Let a child of God, after being brought to live for a time in close communion with Him, either through the discipline of affliction, or through some special outpouring of spiritual influences on himself and those around him, go out into the social intercourse of even church-going people and professing Christians, and he will find, as many will testify, that it is like breathing the atmosphere of a charnel house. Everything, every conversation, and pleasure, and labour, stinks of the earth; there is not a single odour of heaven.

In the whole business of education, with all the efforts made in that direction for generations past, it is a matter of real doubt whether, along with its extension and outward baptism, it has not, among Christian people, been imbued with a more godless spirit, a spirit more at variance with the claims of Jesus Christ, than ever before. An increase in breadth of influence may very well consist with great decrease in depth and purity. The almost entire divorce of religion from education, in the prevailing public systems of education, and in other schools, except that outward respect for its language and forms which society deems indispensable, is one of the most deplorable signs of the times. The whole general training of children in the family, as well as the school, under the very eaves of the church itself, is so defective in Biblical character and spiritual power, as to make us almost despair of any higher attainments in the church, or any greater power of spiritual Christianity, except by some earthquake shock that shall almost entirely dislocate society, accompanied by mighty spiritual outpourings that shall reconstruct it on the principle of Paul, "To me to live is Christ."

Another particular, in which the truth we are pressing rises to view most manifestly, is in regard to the Christian Sabbath. This is, in one aspect, the most distinctive badge of Christianity. But where is the Christian Sabbath, in the fulness of its privileges, to be found and enjoyed? In what Christian parlour even, where Christian friends have casually met, can you find it? Even the way to and from the house of God is too often an occasion of Sabbath desecration, at least a proof of the utter destitution of the Sabbath spirit. "Keeping the Sabbath *holy*," is a thing extremely rare Even where the open and public desecration of it is restrained by law, business and pleasure very generally only change their forms. Now the change required in the moral state of Christendom, and of the church itself, to secure a universal holy observance of the Sabbath, would involve the most radical changes in the whole habits of the civilized world. If it is ever effected, will any thing less than a great moral earthquake do it?

An examination of the visible church itself, and a comparison of it with the primitive model, which was not without its own imperfections, and with the requirements laid down in the messages to the seven churches of Asia, would show that the spirit and principles of the world have, to such a degree, perverted and degraded its holy action and its spiritual energy, that a revolution of the most thorough and radical nature is necessary to deliver it from the earthliness that every where pervades it, and that mars and enfeebles the working of all its organizations and institutions, and obscures and confuses, and almost silences the voice of a heavenly testimony in all its worship and discipline. It would almost seem that nothing less than such a revolution as that afterwards implied in the slaying of these, her witnesses for God, and their speedy resurrection by the power of the life-giving Spirit, could bring her back to her primitive purity and power. What, then, must be required to make her the instrument of spiritual triumph over all the earth? How great the revolution that shall fill the earth with the glory and purity of this spiritual kingdom, instead of with such a sadly defective and corrupt thing as this visible representative of it now is?

But enough has been said for our present purpose; enough to show that no symbol whatever, drawn from the material world, whence all symbols must be drawn, short of such a universal earthquake and dissolution of the whole visible system of nature, could ever adequately represent the all-pervading moral change which must yet take place, even in Christendom, in order that Christ may reign, and the principles of the spiritual kingdom triumph.

Let all, therefore, who love the world, and live for the world, and have nothing but what is in the world, see here how the world of their idolatry is doomed! All that bears not on it the mark of the blood of the slain Lamb, must in that doom of wrath go down to a hopeless perdition. How much of all that men now admire; how much of the power, and wealth, and art, and literature, and fashion, and social life; of the pomp, and glitter, and pleasure, and other things that now move the world's heart, and stir the waves of human agitation, that impel the wheels of business, or the sails of commerce, how much will survive if all must go down, except what bears on it the blood of the Lamb, and is consecrated to His service? How much will be left of what each of *us* are living for? And where shall we ourselves be? Before that coming doom overtake *you*, flee from the world, as Lot from Sodom. Escape for your life. Live no longer for interests that in the fixed purpose of God are doomed to utter perdition, and which are daily receiving in part their doom, as war, and want, and death, on the red, and black, and pale horses, are never resting in their work of vengeance. The great day of His wrath is coming. The unbeliever has not to wait till the end of the world, if that be far off, for the terrific scenes of the text. The day of the wrath of the Lamb, is to him when the day of grace ends. That wrath there is no escaping; and how can it be endured! The wrath of the Lamb is a thought that defies conception. When love itself, bleeding love, is turned to wrath, as it must be with very many if much longer slighted, nothing is left but a despair, a hopeless, endless, unintermitting agony, which the Spirit describes as the worm that never dies, and the fire that is never quenched. The text declares that even to be crushed beneath the ruins of a crumbling world on fire, would be an infinite mercy, if it could only hide from the wrath of the Lamb.

This, too, is the world, and these are the things of the world, which are so often interfering with the holy claims of Jesus on His followers. All that allures, or threatens, or tempts your feet in any way from the narrow path, from the footsteps of the Lamb, no matter how lovely, how desirable, how mighty, or how apparently needful now, is in the same condemnation, is set apart for this doom of wrath. Will you then listen to the siren's song? Will you conform to its maxims, and fashions, and opinions, and spend the energies of body and soul, which have been consecrated to the Lamb, in striving for its accursed objects? Oh! what amazing force and depth of meaning does this put into those words so often quoted, but so little felt and appreciated, "Come out from the world, and be ye separate, and touch not the unclean thing." "What communion hath light with darkness? And what concord hath Christ with Belial?" "The friendship of the world is enmity with God. Whosoever, therefore, will be a friend of the world, is the enemy of God." "Flee ye out of the midst of it; deliver every man his soul; be not cut off in its iniquity."

PART V.

ITS CONFLICTS AND TRIUMPH.

Rev., Chap. 8 : 2—Chap. 11 : 18.

Lecture XIX. The Prayers of the Saints.
" XX. The Earthly Good Smitten.
" XXI. The Soul Smitten; the Curse of Error Resulting in a Spiritual Despotism.
" XXII. The Reaction of the Worldly Power and Wisdom.
" XXIII. The Divine Agency and the Human Instrumentality.
" XXIV. The True Church and the Subjects of Her Testimony.
" XXV. The Power of the World in and Over the Church.
" XXVI. The Power of a Witnessing Church During the Abounding Corruptions.
" XXVII. The Vitality and Triumph of a Pure Spiritual Testimony.
" XXVIII. The Final Triumph.

LECTURE XIX.

THE PRAYERS OF THE SAINTS.

Rev., Chap. viii: 2-6.

"And I saw the seven angels which stood before God; and to them were given seven trumpets. And another angel came and stood at the altar, having a golden censer; and there was given unto him much incense, that he should offer it with the prayers of all saints upon the golden altar which was before the throne. And the smoke of the incense, which came with the prayers of the saints, ascended up before God out of the angel's hand. And the angel took the censer, and filled it with fire of the altar, and cast [it] into the earth; and there were voices, and thunderings, and lightnings, and an earthquake; and the seven angels, which had the seven trumpets, prepared themselves to sound."

WE have seen the Lamb taking the book of God's secret purposes in regard to His spiritual kingdom, and opening its seven seals. He has unfolded and executed all these purposes. *Jesus Christ reigns*, is the grand lesson of the seven-sealed book; reigns in all gospel agencies; in war, in want, in death, and in the sufferings of the martyrs; and is in all these only overturning the world, sealing His chosen, and so gathering His redeemed around His throne.

This great truth lies at the foundation of His people's faith and hope, and of all correct views of the government of God, both in providence and grace. It is, therefore, the first presented, and that so fully, and in relation to all kinds of events, as to show all the leading principles of His administration of the spiritual kingdom in the most brief and impressive form. Having thus presented the cardinal doctrine of the sovereignty and triumph of the slain Lamb, the Spirit next unfolds more particularly the working of the human agencies employed, and the conflicts through which this kingdom must pass, and the influences by which it shall triumph.

We have already given reasons for believing that the visions of the seven trumpets cover the same ground as those of the seals. If the view just given of the seals be correct, this must be so. And a careful inspection of this next series will, we think, go far to produce the same conviction. For it begins with a succession of symbols of destructive judgments designed to subdue a world, all of which appears in bitter and determined opposition—an opposition not entirely crushed till the very last, when the seventh angel sounds, and the same consequences follow as those that followed the opening of the sixth seal. Great voices proclaim in heaven, "The kingdoms of this world are become our Lord's and His Christ's;" and the time is come to destroy all them which destroy the earth. These cannot possibly follow the events symbolized under the sixth seal, which, on any natural interpretation of the symbols, represent all opposition already overthrown, and the saints already redeemed from all tribulation.

This whole series is divided into seven distinct visions, each introduced by the sounding of an angel's trumpet. Here, again, the symbolic sense of the number seven, which is so manifest all through this book, must not be overlooked. These seven angels, with their seven trumpets, teach that the events they herald cover the complete history of the kingdom in the aspect in which it is here viewed down to its consummation. This series is introduced by a very different vision, that of the angel with the incense, and one of very deep interest, intended to show as a distinct characteristic of all these visions of conflict, and confusion, and judgment, that they are in answer to prayer, as well as means of triumph.

The exposition and application of three leading symbols will sufficiently unfold the teaching of this passage: the meaning of "angels," used as symbols; of the offering of the incense; and of the fire cast upon the earth.

"I saw the seven angels which stand before God, and to them were given seven trumpets."

§. 1. The angelic agency.

These cannot be, as some have supposed, the seven spirits that are spoken of in chap. 5: 6, which are sent into all the earth; for those are the seven horns and the seven eyes of the Lamb; and in chap. 4: 5, they are symbolized by the seven lamps burning before the throne; and in chap. 1: 4, they are united with the Father and the Son, as the joint authors of grace and peace to the church, and can, therefore, mean nothing less than the Holy Spirit in His manifold and all perfect operations, which these seven angels cannot possibly do.

What, then, do these angels represent? As angelic agency is used throughout this whole book as a symbol, and as it is often regarded by readers and interpreters as not a symbol at all, but as representing actual angels, it may be as well here at once to give a more general answer to this question, and, if we can, learn what is meant by the symbolic agency of angels. It seems most natural to find this answer, not by hunting for some special analogy in each case first, but by answering the plain questions, What are angels, and what is their office? This will at once show what their symbolic significance is. These questions are explicitly answered by the Bible itself. "Are they not all ministering spirits sent forth to minister for them who shall be heirs of salvation?" Their very name expresses their office: it means simply "*messenger*," and is the common word used to denote this. In Ps. 104: 4, the name is applied even to inanimate things employed by God as instruments of executing His will. "Who maketh His angels, spirits; His ministers, a flaming fire." The meaning of this, as all agree, must be, the original word in Hebrew, as indeed in most languages, being the same for both "winds" and "spirits," "who useth as His angels, the winds; as His ministers, the lightnings." The application of the name is thus justified to any instrumental agency He employs. Of all such instruments and agents sent forth by Him to accomplish His purposes, the particular order of spiritual beings so-called are the highest and most perfect. In nature, in character, in their willing obedience, and perfect qualifications to do His will, nothing is wanting. All that is revealed to us of them is comprised in the fact, that all their powers are given that they may be "messengers of God," and employed as such. They are, therefore, the most natural and perfect symbols which the universe affords of that perfect, but invisible instrumentality which God employs in carrying on His providential government. That instrumental agency is often very complicated and deeply concealed, so that even when the results have been wrought out, it is impossible to define accurately the causes or agencies that produced them. A vast multitude and variety of influences and agencies are constantly at work among men, controlling their conduct and shaping their destiny, which it is impossible for us to penetrate, but the evidence of which we see continually in the great and often unexpected changes that pass over us and around us. Nothing, therefore, could be more appropriate than when it was designed to show that those mighty changes and sore calamities which were to befall the nations and the church were not fortuitous, nor of mere human or satanic origin, but the result of influences commissioned by the great Head of the Church Himself, to represent these by an angel. This symbolic angel may be so definitely described as clearly to point out the particular agency or messenger designed; He may be represented with such functions and attributes as to clearly point Him out as the great angel of the covenant, the Messiah Himself. Here the seven angels are evidently the symbols of a power or influence issuing from the throne, and going forth in the various agencies of His providence on errands of covenant love, to lead and marshal the hosts of the church and the nations in the conflict of ages, and thus to bring about the triumph of the spiritual kingdom. Accordingly, each of them is furnished with a trumpet, by whose stirring notes the actors in these events were to be called out, and both the church and the world warned.

Thus, again, the precious and consolatory truth is forced upon us, that not only does God overrule all events—wars, revolutions, convulsions, and persecutions even—for good, but that He orders them; that they come upon the church and the nations at His bidding, by a mighty influence sent forth by Him to do His work, both of judgment and mercy, and all in fulfilment of His covenant. By that influence, the united product of the various agencies He uses, He moulds and directs the free agency of man, and summons to its appointed work, at its appointed time, all the actors and instruments by which a rebellious world and an apostate church are scourged and subdued. "The Lord reigneth, let the earth rejoice; let the multitudes of the isles be glad thereof." "The floods have lifted up, O Lord, the floods have lifted up their voice; the floods lift up their waves. The Lord on high is mightier than the noise of many waters; yea, than the mighty waves of the sea." "The Lord sitteth upon the flood; yea, the Lord sitteth King for ever."

§. 2. The incense and the prayers.

Before these angelic messengers can go forth on their errand, a preparatory scene is presented, to show the real nature and design of all their ministry. Another angel appears with a golden censer, standing at the golden altar—the altar of incense inside of the tabernacle—to whom is given much incense, which he offers up with the prayers of the saints. The language in the original is peculiar and expressive. "There was given unto him much incense, that he should give it to the prayers of all saints upon the golden altar," that thus upon it they might ascend unto God. "And the smoke of the incense," thus added "to the prayers of the saints," carrying them with it, "ascended up before God out of the angel's hand." The prayers are heard. The answer follows. The same angel takes the censer, and fills it with living coals from the great altar of atonement, and casts them —not the censer—into the earth; and immediately, as the result, "there were voices, and thunderings, and lightnings, and an earthquake." These voices, and thunderings, and lightnings come out of the throne, which is still prominent in the scene before him;[1] the earthquake is their effect upon the earth and earthly things; and together they represent overwhelming divine judgments, confounding human plans and purposes, and overthrowing the earthly and God-opposing power. These are the same things which are afterwards successively presented, as each of the seven angels sounds his trumpet. Having thus shown that these convulsions are the result of the prayers of the saints and the fire of the altar, the seven angels, who had during this time been waiting, prepare themselves to sound.

The angel here cannot be Christ, for the incense which was given him are Christ's own intercessions, and can only represent that instrumental agency, whatever it be, by which the prayers of the saints are gathered, united, and made to rest on the intercessions of Christ alone for acceptance, and so carried up to the throne. It is the same instrumental agency that, bearing the same censer,

---

[1] Chap. 4: 6.

casts with it the fire of the altar upon the earth, throws out among men, and scatters abroad the great doctrine of atonement which this represents. It is the agency sent forth in and through His church, by which His people are taught to pray through Christ alone, and by which the great truths of Christ crucified are brought into contact with the earthly heart of man.

We are thus taught that all the judgments of God upon a guilty world, and an unfaithful church, are in answer to the prayers of the saints.

§. All judgments in answer to prayer.

This is too often lost sight of, even by God's own people, and to it the world is utterly blind. God here teaches us that true prayer is not a mere exercise of holy affection, and an expression of dependence, and a means of preparation for receiving a blessing, as some would teach, but is a real and a mighty power in the world. It is made so by Him who bestows on all means, and agencies, and creatures, whatever of power they may possess. It is mighty, not only to bring down the gentle rains and dews of the Spirit's gracious influences, and the daily blessings of our Father's providence, but equally so in calling down the judgments of heaven. It is in answer to prayer that the nations are desolated by war and pestilence, that the foundations of society are shaken, and the proudest monuments of human pride and wisdom laid prostrate. Though the angels stand waiting before the throne, though their trumpets are given to them, though an omnipotent God has ready prepared all needful agencies and instruments for His work; yet before a single angel can summon to the work of judgment a single agency of wrath, the incense of the church's prayers must ascend before God. "By terrible things in righteousness wilt Thou answer us, O God of our salvation, who art the confidence of all the ends of the earth, and of them that are afar off upon the sea; * * * which stilleth the noise of the seas, the noise of their waves, and the tumult of the people." "Yea, we have waited for Thee, O Lord, in the way of Thy judgments."[1]

Mark, too, and mark it well, that there is no such thing as unanswered prayer, if it be indeed true prayer. The much incense given to the angel was to be given to the prayers of *"all saints;"* the cry of the feeblest and humblest one of all the praying hosts is as fully heard, rises up before God as surely, as that of the strongest and most honoured leader of the host, and exerts the same influence in shaking the thrones of iniquity, and overturning the powers of the world.

But mark, further, that such prayers go not up by themselves. They can only be carried up by the incense offered upon the golden altar, and kindled by the fire from the altar of atonement. The prayers of the saints can ascend only as embodied in the intercessions of their great High Priest, and resting on the merits of His atoning sacrifice. This is the secret of their power. They are the cry of His redeemed; His redeemed are one with Him; He makes their wants His own; they are His body; what they cry for, He demands; and the fire of His atoning sacrifice carries the demand before the throne, and secures to its accomplishment all the power of that throne.

Again, observe that the prayers of saints are not answered according to their form, but their design; not in giving the precise things asked, and in the precise way, but by accomplishing the end desired by the holy heart that offers them in a far different way often, and by bestowing other and very different things. These prayers did not ask for the thunderings, and lightnings, and earthquake; but for deliverance and salvation for themselves and for the nations. The church cries not for vengeance, but for salvation for men, and glory to God. But salva-

---

[1] Ps. 65: 5. Is. 26: 8.

tion involves vengeance on all that oppose it, and sore trials—"much tribulation"—to all who shall share it.

> "Terrors attend the wondrous way
> That brings His blessing down."

The church in this land asked for faith, and patience, and conformity to the divine will, and greater consecration to God and His service. Many hoped to secure all this in some degree by securing Southern independence; God answered these prayers of Southern Christians by disappointing all worldly hopes, and drying up the sources of earthly prosperity, compelling the true saint to turn away from the idols he was unconsciously worshipping, and to seek in God and in the spiritual kingdom the good he was foolishly seeking elsewhere. Often, very often, is the praying soul compelled to say, in the words of good John Newton,

> "I asked the Lord that I might grow
> In faith, and love, and every grace;
> Might more of His salvation know,
> And seek more earnestly His face.

> "'Twas He who taught me thus to pray,
> And He, I trust, has answered prayer;
> But it has been in such a way,
> As almost drove me to despair.

> "Yea more; with His own hand He seemed
> Intent to aggravate my woe;
> Crossed all the fair designs I schemed,
> Blasted my gourds, and laid me low."

As the prayers of the saints in this way often bring down sore chastisements upon themselves, these being the best and only means to secure the good they seek, so their intercessions for sinners, and for a guilty world and nations, are answered, not merely by withholding judgments, but by sometimes pouring them out in seven-fold fury. They are always thus answered in regard to the incorrigible powers of the world, and all who adhere to the world as their chief good and their god. The church of Christ can triumph, and the saints obtain complete possession of the earth, only by the destruction of every thing that opposes spiritual religion. In no other way can the world itself be rescued from the curse. To the impenitent sinner, therefore, the prayers offered for him by his wife, or parent, or sister, or other loving friend, and by all the church of God, are no matters of indifference. As they rise up before God, they are daily gathering upon his soul fresh mercy or wrath. If they are not answered in his conversion, they will be answered in his deeper everlasting condemnation; for the ultimate design of every praying soul is, that God may be glorified in all His creatures. If this is not done by their taking refuge in His offered mercy, it must be by their becoming the monuments of His eternal justice. It is a fearful thing to be the subject of many prayers, and yet not the subject of converting grace. Do not dare to depend on the prayers of others for you, while you yourself reject the grace they seek for you, and which Jesus offers.

The rulers of the earth, too, as they sit in its high places of law and of power, may, as they very generally do, ignore the prayers of the saints as having any influence on the course of political events, the safety or the ruin of parties, or of commonwealths, except when, under the pressure of overwhelming calamities, they feel driven to ask her intercessions. These prayers, however, as they rise from the thousands of God's faithful ones, who are longing to have Him glorified in His own world, are none the less effective in secretly shaping the influences that sweep before them all human affairs. And as with individuals, so with nations. The prayers of the saints are not a thing to be trifled with, a thing which, if they do no good, will bring no evil. If a whole people, in the agony of their trial, or in apprehensions of danger, cry unto the people of God to pray for them, and their rulers assume the attitude of suppliants to the church of God, while yet they have no other ends in view than their own selfishness dictates, and are daily trampling on His laws to secure those ends, those very prayers can only bring down upon them a fiercer wrath, as they are the occasion of more daring guilt.

We are further taught here, that these results are produced by the doctrines of the cross coming in contact with human corruption. The immediate result of these prayers ascending before God was, that the angel took the same censer in which they had been offered, and filling it with coals from the altar, cast them into the earth, and by these were these terrible commotions produced. This fire, taken from the altar of atonement, can represent only the truth of Christ's sacrifice, the doctrine of the cross, elsewhere compared to fire, which purifies the pure gold and consumes the dross. The immediate answer to the church's prayers is the proclamation and diffusion of this truth in an ungodly world, attended with searching, purifying, consuming power. It is the censer of prayer that receives and scatters the burning coals of truth. Are we not here taught that Christ crucified, whether proclaimed from the pulpit or the press, or by the private Christian in the social circle, must come forth from a heart and lips consecrated and steeped already with the burning incense and prayers kindled by the same coals of the atoning sacrifice? It must do so, if, with burning power, it is to fall upon the world's heart. Is not here one reason why this great truth of Christ crucified is so often preached with little or no effect, and why the church in holding it and defending it exerts so little power? Such truths cannot live in cold and prayerless hearts; their glow is soon gone, and they become as dead coals. Equally cold, powerless,

§. 3. The fire of the altar. Truth and the world in contact.

and formal are all gospel truths, when uttered by lips, and coming from hearts, that are prayerless.

But when the truth does thus come in its warmth, all alive, and from hearts, and lips, and tongues of fire, it has a power that compels the world to confess and bow before it. It may be hated, it may be opposed most bitterly and furiously, but it cannot be ignored; it must be felt. In the heart of the sinner, the doctrine of Christ's offering Himself a sacrifice for man's sins, and thus making atonement, when it enters and comes in contact with the corruptions and lusts that nestle and reign there, creates often fearful commotions, and deadly struggles, and fierce conflicts, a very earthquake of the soul, before the power of sin is destroyed, and the peace of God reigns undisturbed. So, also, it is in the world. As the doctrine of the cross comes in contact with the wickedness of men, with their proud, self-righteous and ambitious schemes and systems, it meets with stern and determined opposition. Hence all these commotions. Hatred to the true doctrine of the cross has caused all the perversions of Christianity, and all those various forms of fanaticism that in its name have withstood it, and sweeping over the world, have kindled its fiercest wars, and desolated its fairest portions. History is full of illustrations. The crusades for the recovery of the Holy Sepulchre; the wars of Simon de Montfort, in the south of France, or, as they are commonly called, the Albigensian crusades; the wars of the Reformation, the French Revolution, are all familiar examples. And is not our own recent fierce and bloody struggle in this land another? The world is thus made to punish itself; and it is thus that the cross will eventually triumph. All these are the necessary result of truth and error meeting; of the cross of Christ and His claims coming in contact with human pride and lusts. They are as inevitable as that these burning coals scattered among the combustibles of earth will produce a furious conflagration. They are also fully foretold as the destined path of the church, and the destined fate of the world's opposition; and foretold, too, in language beautifully harmonizing with the symbols here used.

"Is not My word like a fire? saith the Lord; and like a hammer that breaketh the rock in pieces?" Christ himself says, "I am come to send fire on the earth, and what will I if it be already kindled? * * * Suppose ye that I am come to give peace on the earth? I tell you, Nay, but rather division." The prophets describe the effects of this heavenly and peaceful religion in such language as the following: "In those days," says Jehovah, by the prophet Joel, "I will pour out My Spirit, and I will show wonders in the heavens and in the earth, blood, and fire, and pillars of smoke." The coming and progress of Christ's kingdom is thus described by the prophet Malachi: "The Lord, whom ye seek, shall suddenly come to His temple, even the Messenger of the covenant, whom ye delight in: behold, He shall come, saith the Lord of Hosts. But who may abide the day of His coming? And who shall stand when He appeareth? For He is like refiner's fire, and like fuller's soap." "For, behold, the day cometh that shall burn as an oven; and all the proud, yea, and all that do wickedly, shall be stubble; and the day that cometh shall burn them up, saith the Lord of Hosts." But that day, terrible as it shall be, is necessary to the consummation of the church's hopes, the answer of all her prayers, and the triumph of the kingdom of God; for the prophet immediately adds, "But unto you that fear My name shall the Sun of righteousness arise with healing in His wings. And ye shall tread down the wicked; for they shall be ashes under the soles of your feet in the day that I shall do this, saith the Lord of Hosts." Let the saints, then, never faint in prayer; let the church not only hold fast the truth, but with hearts warmed by close communion with God, declare it to others; and especially let her ministers, glowing with a devotion kindled at the golden altar, go forth to the world with burning heart and lips, knowing nothing, and declaring nothing but Christ and Him crucified, the wisdom and power of God unto salvation.

LECTURE XX.

THE FIRST FOUR TRUMPETS. THE EARTHLY GOOD SMITTEN.

Rev., Chap. viii: 7–13.

" The first angel sounded, and there followed hail and fire mingled with blood, and they were cast upon the earth; and the third part of trees was burnt up, and all green grass was burnt up. And the second angel sounded, and as it were a great mountain burning with fire was cast into the sea; and the third part of the sea became blood; and the third part of the creatures which were in the sea, and had life, died; and the third part of the ships were destroyed. And the third angel sounded, and there fell a great star from heaven, burning as it were a lamp, and it fell upon the third part of the rivers, and upon the fountains of waters; and the name of the star is called Wormwood; and the third part of the waters became wormwood; and many men died of the waters, because they were made bitter. And the fourth angel sounded, and the third part of the sun was smitten, and the third part of the moon, and the third part of the stars; so as the third part of them was darkened, and the day shone not for a third part of it, and the night likewise. And I beheld, and heard an angel flying through the midst of heaven, saying with a loud voice, Wo, wo, wo to the inhabiters of the earth, by reason of the other voices of the trumpet of the three angels which are yet to sound!"

IN the opening vision of this series, we have the prayers of all saints carried up in the smoke of the incense of a Saviour's intercessions before the throne of God. These are the cries of a suffering, struggling church for the consummation of the triumph promised, and of which the administration of the slain Lamb gave her the confident assurance expressed in her new song of praise, "We shall reign on the earth." For this the saints are elsewhere represented as groaning within themselves, and waiting in longing expectation. Prominent among these prayers is the martyr-cry heard on the opening of the fifth seal, "How long, O Lord, holy and true, dost thou not judge and avenge our blood on them that dwell on the earth?" In answer, the fire of the atoning sacrifice is cast down into the earth. The holy power of Christ's cross and crown coming in contact with all that is in the world, the lusts of the flesh, and the lusts of the eye, and the pride of life, fearful commotions are the result.

But let not the church in her trials be alarmed. Messengers from His throne preside over all the apparent confusion. Immediately the seven angels, which the apostle had seen standing before God, waiting His commands, prepare themselves to sound the trumpets given them. These messengers of God for the heirs of salvation fitly represent the mighty influences which are sent out from the divine throne, to preside over and direct the great spiritual conflict; to proclaim the world's great jubilee, liberty for the captives, and the opening of the prison to them that are bound; to summon the powers that so long had tyrannized over humanity to submission; to warn the praying church of her perils, and to marshal on the field all the special agencies to be employed. The general language of these trumpets is, "Come, behold the works of the Lord, what desolations He hath made in the earth." "The heathen raged, the kingdoms were moved: He uttered His voice, the earth melted." "The Lord sitteth upon the flood; yea, the Lord sitteth King for ever. The Lord will give strength unto His people; the Lord will bless His people with peace."

These angel trumpets have, therefore, a voice for each of you. No more solemn call was ever uttered from heaven to a world of sinners. To every sinner they say, Repent, or be lost; to every suffering saint they say, "Rejoice in the Lord;" "Be faithful unto death, and I will give thee a crown of life."

You will observe that these whole seven angels are prepared from the beginning. They all stand together before the throne, all are presented to the eye of the seer at the same moment; all at once make ready to sound their trumpets. "Known unto God are all His works from the beginning of the world." All the influences needed to give to the spiritual church a complete triumph, have been made ready from the beginning. Does it not also intimate that they are all in perfect harmony, and also, that though successively called into action, and following each other in a certain *necessary* order, as we shall see, yet that they may all be operating in the world at the same time, after they are all once sent forth? Even the seventh and the last, which ushers in the last woe and the triumph, has its partial application to the repeated and partial triumphs of the cause which have at different times followed the previous course of divine judgments, and which have indeed been but parts of this great and final triumph, and have in fact secured it. It is perfectly consistent with this view, as also with all human history, that each of these agencies or influences should in successive periods rise above all the others, and taking a world-wide sweep, for a time challenge the whole field to itself, pervading the world and the church; just as it is only at the last, when each and all the others have done their best and their worst, that the triumph, the complete and universal triumph, indicated by the trumpet of the seventh angel, can be consummated, however long before it was begun.

1. It is to the first four of these that we direct attention in this lecture. These four are entirely distinct from the last three. They differ in their character, their objects, and their results. They are distinctly marked in the visions themselves as two classes. The last three are specially designated as woes; and are separately introduced in verse 13 by an angel flying through mid-heaven,

and crying aloud, "Woe, woe, woe to the inhabiters of the earth, by reason of the other voices of the trumpet of the three angels which are yet to sound." The more closely, too, that we inspect each of these two divisions, the more marked will appear the difference between them, and the more evident that symbols differing so very widely must refer to entirely different kinds of agencies.

These four form a kind of whole in themselves as regards the objects of the judgments. The first smites the earth; the second, the sea; the third, the rivers and fountains of water; the fourth, the sun, moon, and stars; and in each case to the extent of one-third only. In the region of visible nature, these include every thing. They thus cover the whole of the world's system, of the mere earthly good. Nothing is left. Every thing in the world's interest and service is thus made to feel the divine displeasure; yet so that great mercy mingles with the judgment, yea, predominates in it, for in each case only a third part is smitten

The reader of this book must never forget that by "*earth*" and "*heaven*" we are to understand not two places, but the whole system of earthly things and influences, and that of heavenly things. The symbolical use of earth is two-fold, just as the literal use of it is, which applies it to the whole world, and to the land in distinction from the sea. When used as a symbol in opposition to the sea, it means, of course, consolidated society, in opposition to the nations in a tumultuous and unsettled state, so often in the Bible compared to the sea. But when the whole earthly system, the world, is the thing meant in the symbol itself, the idea intended is the "*world,*" in the sense fixed in the Bible, the aggregate of all mere earthly interests as opposed to spiritual things; the world as opposed to the spiritual kingdom; which last accordingly is always represented as occupying a higher sphere, a heavenly position, corresponding with its true character. It is just the distinction between earthly and spiritual; the latter is as high in moral elevation above the former as heaven above earth. The whole groundwork of these visions is the visible realization of the vast moral elevation of the true spiritual kingdom of Christ above the ungodly world, an idea elsewhere wrought into the whole texture of Scripture thought and language. Now the objects of infliction under these four trumpets, make up the whole connected and mutually dependent system of the world's good. And the instruments employed are the world's own, also; the sources of these judgments are the same as its blessings; its blessings are turned to chastisements by its own wickedness.

2. Consider, now, what these instruments are, and their effects. They are different under each trumpet, just as the class of objects smitten differs. When the first angel sounds, there follows a horrid storm of hail and fire, mingled with blood, and it falls upon the earth, the land: established, consolidated society under organized government; and the third part of the trees, and *all green* grass, are burned up. These are the productions of the earth; and hence can represent only the benefits growing out of such a state of consolidated social order, as the regular administration of laws by civil rulers; and the security, wealth, and thousand enjoyments of social life and civilization. Of the higher and loftier of these a third part is destroyed; and all the minor blessings of social and political order are withered, if not destroyed: the *greenness*, the joy, is all gone.

When the second trumpet sounds, a volcanic mountain, in a state of eruption, is cast into the sea, and a third part of its waters become blood, and a third part of all living things in it, and on it, perish. As the sea is always a symbol of the nations in an unsettled and tumultuous state, which are like "the sea and the waves roaring," and restless, it well represents the condition of society produced by the previous infliction; and this new infliction represents the anarchy, and carnage, and wide-spread desolation produced by whatever this overturned volcanic mountain represents.

When the third angel sounds his trumpet, an altogether new phenomenon presents itself; a great star is seen falling from heaven, burning like a lamp, embittering and poisoning the third part of the rivers and fountains, its very name being Wormwood, a name obtained in its fall, making it as the very source of the intensest bitterness, so that many died of the poisoned waters. The rivers and fountains include all the living waters of the earth, on which depends its fertility and habitableness; and these must symbolize, of course, all the springs of earthly happiness, family influences, and public instructions, together with the social affections, the kindly impulses, the moral feelings and principles, and the mutual confidence, that refresh the heart, and give life to the energies of men, and success to their pursuits. A third of all these are poisoned by whatever this fallen star represents.

When the fourth angel sounds, it is to be observed that no new agency or instrumentality is represented as producing the obscuration of the sun, moon, and stars, and darkening them for a third part of the time, which is the infliction here visited, and which is manifestly just the withdrawal of a third part of the world's light, the light of truth shining upon all subjects pertaining to human happiness. The sun, moon, and stars here are regarded only as the world's lights, not as a part of the heavenly system; they are the world's sun, moon, and stars. The fact that in smiting the world's light, no new instrumentality is employed, implies that none was needed. The effects produced by the first three trumpets were quite enough to secure this further and last result of comparative darkness.

Now to make these three agencies, the storm of hail,

and fire, and blood, the burning mountain and the falling star, smiting each a different class of objects, to make these all symbols of the very same kind of inflictions as those do who regard them as referring to the successive incursions of the hordes of Northern barbarians, the Goths under Alaric, the Huns under Attilla, and the Vandals under Genseric, all calamities of the same nature, and producing very much the same consequences, is in the highest degree arbitrary. It would never have been thought of, had it not first been assumed that these trumpets were intended to give a chronological history of the events by which the Roman empire was to be destroyed. In other words, they could never have been drawn out of the text here, had they not first been put into it.

3. We are now prepared to understand the meaning of each of these symbols, and to what class of events they are each to be applied.

All those incursions of Northern barbarians to which we have alluded, as also all similar events since, by which God has punished the nations favoured with His gospel, are well represented by the storm of hail, fire, and blood, destroying the third part of the trees and the green grass of the earth. These barbarian hordes, like successive tempests, swept over the whole face of the Christian world, so called, then included within the Roman empire, spreading every where the most fearful desolations. With terrific and resistless violence they swept over the loveliest regions of the earth, unsettling all order, disorganizing the local governments, revolutionizing many of the tribes and nations composing that great empire, and so blasting all the prosperity produced by such a stable order of things as had always been to a considerable extent secured by Roman rule. Thus was produced that unsettled and tumultuous condition of the nations, which is represented as the object of the next destructive agency introduced by the second trumpet, and thus, too, indeed, that very agency itself, the burning mountain.

A mountain, in the figurative language of Scripture, always represents an established government, and that, too, most appropriately, because of its elevation in power and conspicuity, and its stability. A volcanic mountain cast into the sea, is a government, therefore, that, instead of giving protection and security to the people under it, has become a source of misery and ruin, and so, by its own internal fires of corruption, and misrule, and furious dissensions, is itself overturned, and falls a mass of fiery ruin in the very midst of the nations already in a state of commotion, producing all the horrors of wide-spread anarchy and bloody desolation, well symbolized by the third of the waters becoming blood, and the death of a third of all that lived in them, or sailed on them.

The symbol finds, then, its first striking verification, on the largest scale, in precisely that event that followed the incursions of these barbarian hordes, the fall of the Roman empire, and its utter dismemberment, together with all the fearful calamities that accompanied and followed, by which the worldly interest was so fearfully scourged. This empire had such relations to God's plan and kingdom, that it had already found a place in prophecy; its rise and progress had been pointed out by Daniel; and its mighty agency in preparing the world for the gospel, and producing that wide community of nations that gave an open door to the apostles and their successors for generations, and so secured the establishment of Christianity, is well known. Being the last and fullest form of the *world's* power seeking universal empire, its decline and fall could not fail to find a most striking place in some of these symbols that indicated the overthrow of the ungodly world. Its work had been done, and now its dismemberment and ruin becomes an instrument for chastising that worldly power and interest that had at this time almost covered up out of sight the pure spiritual kingdom of Jesus Christ.

Nearly simultaneous with the decline and fall of the empire, was that of the spiritual power of the church. Accordingly, this is the next agency of divine chastisement. The star, Wormwood, falling from heaven upon the living waters, and poisoning them, finds its only proper and distinctive meaning in an ecclesiastical power falling from the heavenly sphere, where it had been wont to shine with mild and cheering rays, and blazing like a lamp, with a smoky and an earthly glare, instead of a heavenly light, smiting the very fountains of human happiness, and poisoning the springs of life. Nothing could more forcibly represent the immediate effects of degeneracy in a church upon the social happiness of men, the terrible embittering of all the springs of earthly joy in all the relations and pursuits of life, by the moral principles becoming debased, the affections embittered, confidence destroyed, bitter dissensions and animosities awakened. Only let the authority and influence of the church descend from the high sphere of the spiritual to mere earthly matters, let it from being a spiritual, become a political and earthly power, and it infuses a deadly bitterness into every fountain of earthly happiness; it becomes a blazing lamp instead of a star, wormwood instead of light, and infuses only misery where it ought to have spread the light of heavenly hope. The infliction is indeed limited to the one-third; all spiritual light is not turned to wormwood, and all the good is not embittered, but to have such a portion as this poisoned indicates a calamity of fearful extent.

And now, when the fourth angel sounds his trumpet, no other *agency* is needed to produce the darkness that follows. The necessary result of the overthrow of civil governments, and the prostitution of church power, is to smite the lights of the world, when the more immediate consequences do not lead to repentance. Truth speedily becomes obscured. Selfishness, passion and worldly lusts rule the heart, and ignorance settles down upon the nations, or on any portion of them thus visited. Every one, even the mere schoolboy who has read the history of those ages, knows how the civil commotions, and the prostitution of church power to political purposes, and to serve a personal ambition, darkened all the lights of the civilized world. The holy light of the gospel, the blessed news and claims of the kingdom of Christ shone too brightly and purely for eyes of the world to bear; the judgments that smote them in their material enjoyments, their political confidences, and their springs of social and individual happiness, failed to correct their intense worldliness. They turned away from it still; and thus the world, in the dust and fogs raised by its own commotions and by its pretended wisdom, obscured its own lights. Upon every department of really useful knowledge, as well as upon that of religion, increasing darkness gathered, till a full third of all the world's own lights, of which it boasted, and in which it trusted, had gone out.

Such are the visitations called forth upon a rebellious world by these first four angel trumpeters. It is smitten in its solid continents, its troubled oceans, its springs of life, and its sources of light. And though this is allowed to proceed only to the third part, though the judgments are restrained and limited, and still a very large portion of the earthly good is left, the nations are not suffered to sink down into utter barbarism; yet the fact that the sweep of these calamities is so universal in its objects, and so great in its degree, so that there is no telling where it will end, might well excite the most fearful apprehensions. It would seem impossible that, having gone so far, they should stop there, and not beget still greater calamities, that should sweep their devastating woes over the earth, till not a third, but the whole, of its boasted good should be destroyed.

This is just what the next symbol most strikingly expresses, by an angel flying through mid-heaven, and saying with a loud voice, "Woe, woe, woe to the inhabiters of the earth, by reason of the voices of the trumpet of the three angels which are yet to sound." The inhabiters of the earth are those who dwell in the earthly sphere, who live for the world, and under the influence of worldly things, in distinction from the heavenly minded, who live for spiritual and heavenly things, and under their influence, and who, therefore, are always represented as sitting in the heavenly places. Over such the increasing judgments of God must roll with crushing power, until the prayers of a waiting, suffering church are answered, and the kingdoms of the earth are given to the saints, and the crowns of them all placed upon the brow of their redeeming Saviour.

We have illustrated the meaning of each of these symbols by a brief reference to the history of the church as a whole, and the united power of the world, when they had their fullest and most general development. We now observe,

4. In conclusion, that they apply to similar calamities in all succeeding ages. The symbol is given in its most general form. No special application is made or indicated. We have no right to limit its application, except to the kind and class of agencies and events to which, by its own nature, it is limited. In every age like causes produce like effects. Like sins bring like judgments, and these follow always and everywhere in the same order, except where the testimony of the truth, and Spirit accompanying, makes them means of repentance.

Warlike invasions of Christian lands, whenever and wherever made, have the same place and design in the great comprehensive scheme of divine Providence that those had by which the Roman empire was visited, and the worldliness and ambition that then resisted and perverted the gospel so severely scourged. These storms of hail, and fire, and blood, have been oft repeated, and their desolating effects experienced by an ungodly world, and an unfaithful church. The voice of the first angel's trumpet still spreads its warning echoes through the disobedient nations, and summons these storms to their work of devastation. Look abroad over our own fair land. Is not the third part of the trees, of the loftiest and noblest of the earthly and material good we gloried in, burned up, and *all the green* grass. The beauty, the loveliness, where is it? Where, in all our Southern land, is there one green spot left untouched by the storm of fire and blood?

So, also, the symbol of the burning mountain cast into the sea has had its verification in every age, in the overturning of thrones and governments. Almost every nation of the civilized world has realized something of its awful meaning. The propriety and force of the symbol, we in this part of this land cannot but feel, when we remember with what a fearful crash our Southern government, which, though so young, many looked to as a mountain of strength, fell a burning ruin right in the midst of the people that trusted in it, spreading its blazing fragments all around, over all the alarmed, confounded, and excited multitudes; "the sea and the waves roaring, and men's hearts failing them for fear, and for looking after those things which are coming on the earth." This terrible agency, then, for chastising the ungodliness of men, God is still employing; the nations that resist our King may still tremble at the voice of the second angel's trumpet. Even now the volcanic roll, and the internal fires, show that this great mountain of ours, that to many seems to stand so strong, may at any time pour forth a desolating flood of fire, and fall a blazing ruin like old Rome. And it must do so, and every other too, unless the authority of the King of kings is acknowledged, and the gospel of *His* kingdom, received by the people, become the "stability of our times, and strength of salvation."

The symbols of the other two trumpets find also many realizations in the history of God's dealings. Whenever the church, in any community or land, has come down from its high vocation, and sought to become a political power, meddling in these purely worldly matters, either by way of direct authority or dependence, it has embittered, just to the degree it has done so, the very fountains of human happiness, and sadly obscured the light of truth. This found a striking illustration in the sad history of the Protestant church of France, and, indeed, in a greater or less degree, of all the established churches of Europe. Is it not finding another illustration, on a smaller scale, at this very time, in those portions of the church in our own country, that have been legislating in regard to political questions and issues? While the church may never dare to withhold her faithful testimony against *sin* in every human relation and official position, drawing that testimony solely from the word of God, we cannot labour too carefully, or pray too fervently, that she may be kept from meddling with, depending upon, or becoming in any way a party in mere political and earthly things. She shines to bless and to save men only as she keeps herself in the heavenly sphere; when she descends to the world's low level, she is the worst, the most bitter and poisonous of all influences. The best things, when prostituted, become always the vilest. Nothing can preserve a church made up of sinful men, holding all kinds of worldly relations, and subject to all worldly influences, from this, but the power of the Holy Spirit shed down upon her ministry and people in abundant measure. This, too, is the only thing that can prevent the worldly element from pervading the church in other ways, and obliterating, more or less, the marks of consecration, and so bringing down upon her people all these judgments of her divine Head in proportion to her worldly conformity.

For upon all the inhabiters of the earth, upon all the worldly minded, the three-fold woe denounced by the warning angel is sure to fall. To live in the world, and for the world, to have your whole heart and your treasures in it, and your objects of pursuit, is to be living always exposed to woes that are irresistible and irreversible. "Be not deceived, God is not mocked; for whatsoever a man soweth, that shall he also reap. For he that soweth to his flesh, shall of the flesh reap corruption." It is only he who "soweth to the Spirit," that, in the midst of abounding judgments and sweeping desolations, "shall of the Spirit reap life everlasting."

LECTURE XXI.

THE FIFTH TRUMPET. THE SOUL ITSELF SMITTEN.

Rev., Chap. ix : 1-11.

" And the fifth angel sounded, and I saw a star fall from heaven unto the earth; and to him was given the key of the bottomless pit. And he opened the bottomless pit; and there arose a smoke out of the pit, as the smoke of a great furnace; and the sun and the air were darkened by reason of the smoke of the pit. And there came out of the smoke locusts upon the earth; and unto them was given power, as the scorpions of the earth have power. And it was commanded them that they should not hurt the grass of the earth, neither any green thing, neither any tree; but only those men which have not the seal of God in their foreheads. And to them it was given that they should not kill them, but that they should be tormented five months: and their torment was as the torment of a scorpion, when he striketh a man. And in those days shall men seek death, and shall not find it; and shall desire to die, and death shall flee from them. And the shapes of the locusts were like unto horses prepared unto battle; and on their heads were as it were crowns like gold, and their faces were as the faces of men. And they had hair as the hair of women, and their teeth were as the teeth of lions. And they had breast-plates, as it were breast-plates of iron; and the sound of their wings was as the sound of chariots of many horses running to battle. And they had tails like unto scorpions, and there were stings in their tails; and their power was to hurt men five months. And they had a king over them, which is the angel of the bottomless pit, whose name in the Hebrew tongue is Abaddon, but in the Greek tongue hath his name Apollyon."

UNDER the first four trumpets every earthly good is so far smitten as to show that a curse is on it, and that in it men can never find a satisfying portion. Do they rejoice in their social privileges, the honours, wealth, and refinement of a high civilization? The fierce storm of war sweeps over all, and leaves a blackened ruin. Do they boast of the stability of their governments, that, like the solid and lofty mountains, seem to defy all attempts to shake them? Internal fires are kindled, that burn more and more fiercely, until they fall, a crushing, fiery ruin, in the midst of the agitated masses. Do they glory in mere external religious privileges, and, like the Laodicean church, say they are rich, and increased with goods, and have need of nothing, making their boast in the church's power, and wealth, and learning, and splendour? The very object in which they glory is thus corrupted, and becomes a source of bitterness, poisoning the very springs of influence and happiness: the pulpit, the press, and even the affections and conscience. Do they glory in the lights of advancing science and art, and spreading knowledge? Even this, by being severed from God's truth and claims, soon loses its brilliancy, and becomes degenerate and delusive.

In the whole course of His providence, God has written on all that is earthly, even in its best forms, when regarded as in itself a satisfying portion, "vanity and vexation of spirit." But men will still cling to it. So strong is the love of the world, that men will live in it, and for it, very much as if they had no souls, no spiritual interests to care for, and no heavenly interests to seek. It is so with many of you. God has chastised you in every possible way. By war with all its desolations, by political ruin and its wide-spread results, by embittering your springs of joy, and darkening your light; by many a private sorrow, as well as public calamity, He has, as by repeated trumpet notes, called you to turn away from earth, and to seek in heavenly things a better portion. But I see you still clinging to the world, some of you more eagerly than ever. Be warned in time of the fatal delusion; invite not upon yourselves still heavier afflictions, those emphatically called woes.

This worldliness of many of you is but a special

instance of that which invoked the judgments of the seven trumpets. The heart of man is the same in every age; and while, in the course of societies and nations, it works out from time to time combined results of great magnitude, and thus necessitates judgments of vast sweep and power, such as the symbols of these chapters specially indicate, it is also working out, in individual cases and more limited spheres, like results, and bringing down like judgments. In the fact that the earthly good is always the object of the world's idolatry, there is sufficient ground for the universal application of these symbols and their startling warnings. If, then, after all God's dealings with you, you are still clinging to the world as your portion, you have a deep, personal interest in that warning voice that introduced the last three trumpets, that voice which proclaimed, "Woe, woe, woe to the inhabiters of the earth," to those who, after all these inflictions, are still earthly minded, by reason of the heavier judgments yet coming.

What are these? After the whole circle of earthly good has been smitten, what comes next? What but something that smites the very soul?

Accordingly, when the fifth angel sounds, a still more terrific plague appears, distinct both in origin and effects from all before, arising not from any mere earthly source, nor directed against any mere worldly good, but issuing from hell itself, and directed against the souls of the unsanctified. It is an army of scorpion locusts, of monstrous and unearthly forms and power, and can find its full and distinctive realization only *in those swarms of hell-begotten heresies, and soul-destroying doctrines, that sting and poison the souls that reject the gospel of the kingdom.* Their *origin*, their *form*, their *king*, their *commission*, and its *limitation*, all agree in proving this.

1. Their origin. They are seen to come out of the dense smoke that arises out of the bottomless pit; and

that pit is opened by one who appears as a star that had fallen (Gr. πεπτωκοτα) from heaven. To him was given the key of it, and when he opens it, the very sun itself, and the air, are darkened by the smoke that issues from its mouth, and generates these locust hordes. The original author of this plague, therefore, is one represented as a star already fallen from heaven, an ecclesiastical or spiritual power that had already descended from its heavenly sphere, and become a mere earthly power, the appropriate agent to introduce into the earth the smoke of hell, a dense cloud of unholy, polluting, fleshly influences, darkening the sun, and burdening the very air, so that men's souls may neither see clearly, nor breathe freely. From such a dark and thickened atmosphere as this, what but the most soul-destroying errors and delusions, doctrines of devils, could proceed?

Christ gave to His apostles the keys of the kingdom of heaven. " I will give unto thee," He says to Peter, and substantially the same elsewhere to the other apostles, "the keys of the kingdom of heaven; and whatsoever thou shalt bind on earth shall be bound in heaven, and whatsoever thou shalt loose on earth shall be loosed in heaven." This power, as committed through them to the church itself, consisted in the possession and teaching of the truth of salvation by a crucified Redeemer. When the church apostatized from this truth, and instead of the sufficiency of *Christ's* blood, and righteousness, and intercessions, proclaimed the efficacy of human merits and saintly intercessions, she lost the keys of the kingdom of heaven, and took up instead the keys of hell, and became Satan's chief instrument in darkening, deluding, and tormenting the nations.

2. Their strange and unearthly forms are in keeping with their origin, and graphically describe just such an agency. The length and particularity of the description here directs special attention to it. The agency intended

was so unique in its character, and so monstrous too, so utterly at variance with all the laws and symmetry of God's visible creation, that nothing in the whole round of created being, even among the most destructive of reptiles, could supply an analogy that would fully set it forth. In form, therefore, these locusts are unlike any thing in nature, and, indeed, inconceivable as material beings. They had "*the shape of horses prepared for battle,*" representing a belligerent and powerful agency; "*on their heads were as it were crowns of gold,*" making pretensions to the kingly authority and honour of the crowned elders; "*their faces were as the faces of men,*" making plausible professions of humanity and benevolence; "*they had hair as the hair of women*" indicating an agency voluptuous, licentious, and alluring; yet "*their teeth were as the teeth of lions,*" showing a nature cruel and devouring; "*and they had breastplates as it were breastplates of iron,*" impervious to all the weapons of adversaries, to the arrows of truth, or the appeals of their suffering victims; "*and the sound of their wings was as the sound of chariots of many horses rushing to battle,*" making a great noise in the world, the confused noise of tumultuous strife, fomenting strifes and wars; "*and they had tails like unto scorpions, and there were stings in their tails,*" showing their essentially venomous, deceitful, and malicious nature. These secret stings in their tails, inflicting a sudden and poisonous wound, not in the attitude of open attack, but when they seemed about to depart, were the instruments of their power, for *power was given unto them as the scorpions of the earth have power,*" "*and their* torment was as the torment of a scorpion when he striketh a man." They indicated an agency, therefore, whose power consisted in their inflicting, unexpectedly, a small but inflammatory and poisonous wound, whence the virus would spread through all the moral system.

Where, in all the records of our race, is there a picture

at once so true, so comprehensive, and so graphic, of the doctrines of devils and their teachers; of those emissaries of Satan going forth to deceive the nations with high pretensions to divine authority, and professions of great philanthropy, yet essentially licentious, bloody, unpitying, deceitful and venomous, and filling the whole world with the confused noise of their daring and restless legions? Has not the Spirit here thrown upon the canvass as it were the very descriptions of these destructive influences given by Paul and Peter? "Now the Spirit speaketh expressly," says Paul in 1 Tim. 4: 1, 2, "that in the latter times some shall depart from the faith, giving heed to seducing spirits and doctrines of devils; speaking lies in hypocrisy; having their conscience seared with a hot iron; forbidding to marry, and commanding to abstain from meats." And says Peter, in his 2d Epistle, chap. 2, "There shall be false teachers among you, who privily shall bring in damnable heresies, even denying the Lord that bought them, and bring upon themselves swift destruction;" who "walk after the flesh, and despise government. Presumptuous are they, self-willed; * * * as natural brute beasts, made to be taken and destroyed, they speak evil of the things they understand not; beguiling unstable souls. * * * For when they speak great swelling words of vanity, they allure through the lusts of the flesh, through much wantonness, those who were clean escaped from them who live in error." Who can doubt the identity of these false teachers, and damnable heresies, with these crowned scorpion locusts ?

3. Their king. " The locusts have no king," says Solomon; but these locusts have, and he is no other than the angel of the bottomless pit, named Abaddon in Hebrew, and in Greek Apollyon, both meaning *" the Destroyer,"* the destroyer and murderer of souls. While all the forms of evil may be said to be under him, there is no agency that can with any propriety be singled out as distinctively

and peculiarly his emissaries, but the teachers and influences by which soul-destroying errors are propagated. These are all most perfectly united in producing the one result, that of poisoning unbelieving souls; but in nothing else do they agree, except this devilish and soul-destroying nature. They are so numerous, so various, so contradictory often in their character, that it is impossible for them to unite under any other head than Satan himself. The use of this agency is his characteristic work. It is by the powerful, subtile, deadly poison of error in doctrine and practice that he effects the ruin of souls. By his first great lie in Eden he poisoned all the race, and it is as the father of lies that he still murders the souls of men. As so again, in perfect harmony with the symbol here, the apostle declares that the great apostacy "*is after the working of Satan with all power, and signs, and lying wonders.*"

4. Their commission is peculiar, and is strictly applicable only to these soul-destroying heresies. "It was commanded them that they should not hurt the grass of the earth, neither any green thing, neither any tree, but only those men which have not the seal of God in their foreheads." Recollecting the description a few verses before (chap. 8: 7) of the judgment introduced by the first trumpet, that it was directed especially against the trees and the green grass of the earth, we cannot fail to see that this marks a very characteristic distinction between the effects intended to be produced by *this* infliction and that. This was not to affect the products of mere earthly good; it was not to punish men in their wealth, or social privileges, or other blessings of an earthly civilization: these locusts, unlike their natural prototypes, were not to touch at all the mere earthly good, but to torment only the ungodly. This is true of no external inflictions; these come alike to all. Their torments, therefore, must be of a purely spiritual nature; their scorpion wounds are inflicted on the soul, and spread their fiery

poison through all the spiritual system. They might even, as has often been the case, seem to advance the worldly interests, as was partially the case with the corrupt church of the middle ages, in restraining lawless violence, and preserving the remnants of a former civilization. Or, they might produce external evils, and fearful social and political miseries, as the whole annals of religious tyranny show they have done; and these external sufferings would often be inflicted upon God's own sealed ones. But such sufferings are not "torments." No external evils that man or devil can inflict upon the child of God are ever any thing else than a fatherly discipline, and never could be classed with the torments these locusts were commissioned to inflict upon those who rejected Christ as their King, and refused the Spirit's mark of grace and love. So that, even when in times of the bitterest persecution, and in the dark cells of the Inquisition, the bodies of the saints were tortured even unto death, these locusts had no power to sting them. The faith of the patient sufferers was a heavenly, an impenetrable armour, on which their scorpion stings had no power. In all their bodily agonies, there was the peace that passeth all understanding; the martyr's joy, and his song of triumph, no power of the persecutor could deprive them of. It was the dark and gloomy soul of the inquisitor, or persecutor himself, that this venomous sting pierced; and the souls of those who, not having the seal of God to secure them, were terrified by his threats, and, afraid of bodily suffering or worldly losses, rejected or renounced the truth of God.

But to make the nature and results of this torment still more evident, it is added, that "*it was given to them that they should not kill them, but that they should be tormented*" for a limited period. This *whole class* of the unsealed were given up to their torments, but not to be destroyed, or brought to an end by them. Consistency of interpretation requires that this should be understood neither of killing the body, nor of the spiritual ruin of the soul, which last, as the followers of Apollyon, it is their special province to effect, but that they should not put an end to this unsealed, unbelieving race. The apparent incongruity between their character as tormentors and destroyers, and their want of power to kill, is thus not only removed, but the two brought into perfect harmony. The torments of the soul that they produce are such as at once destroy the soul, and perpetuate the existence of this unsealed and unbelieving class of men in the earth. To kill them would be to rid the world of them; but the effect of all superstition, fanaticism, and error, is just the opposite.

Could any thing more effectually limit the complete application of this symbol to spiritual and soul-destroying delusions of the devil? Of what other infliction is it true, that its torments reach only the unrenewed soul, and yet have no power or tendency to cure its unbelief, but only aggravate it, develope more fully its enmity to God, and so make its helplessness and misery more apparent?

How terrible such a curse! How appropriate the symbol! The scourge of these delusions, that under the garb of truth, deceive, and poison, and destroy the soul, is well worthy of being called a woe, in comparison with those milder judgments that blast our earthly joys, and hopes, and lights, as exhibited under the previous trumpets. Such afflictions might seem to have some tendency to loosen the heart from its earthly idols, and induce it to seek a better portion; but these delusions only bind around the poor, infatuated soul more tightly than ever the chains of a ruinous and horrid slavery, increasing both its misery and helplessness at every turn, though all the time promising liberty and peace.

Let those who have not received God's renewing and sealing Spirit take warning. All such are at every moment exposed to the sting of these scorpion locusts of error.

And they inflict their torments by insidiously, and most effectually shutting out all the true and rich consolations of the gospel and its heavenly hopes, substituting for them a miserable counterfeit in false grounds of confidence, and the hope of the hypocrite that shall perish. While increasing the feverish thirst of the soul, they lure it on by false promises, deceptive as the fiery illusions of the desert, till at last, disappointed, fainting and despairing, the famished soul sinks down in the agony of utter helplessness.

The terrible nature of this woe is still further shown by these torments being represented as *unendurable*. "Men shall desire to die, and death shall flee from them." Escape is impossible. The full meaning of this we shall see in considering some special applications of the symbol. But it is to be observed here that the victims of superstitious, fanatical, and soul-destroying errors are doomed to torments, at once unendurable and unavoidable. "There is no peace, saith my God, to the wicked." And of all classes of wicked men, the victims of such superstition and fanaticism as follow a perverted gospel and a deluded conscience, or of such errors as constitute apostacy from God, are the furthest from peace. It is true, that these delusions are often embraced to quiet the conscience, and that they produce often utter searedness of conscience and hardness of heart; but this result is only reached after long and terrible torments of soul; and when reached, is the most fearful of all curses, and the prelude to the torments of the undying worm. In all cases they utterly exclude, as we said before, the sweet peace of God's forgiving love. Their poison inflames the passions and lusts, aggravates instead of relieving all the moral disorders of the soul, and makes it still more a prey to unsatisfied desires, and torturing fears.

5. But lastly. This terrible infliction, as well as those preceding it, is limited, and the *limitation* is in beautiful and striking consistency with the symbol, and the reality

too. In the former inflictions, under the first four trumpets, the limitations are indicated by the judgments being confined to a third part of each class of objects visited. Here, however, the whole of the obnoxious class are visited, all who have not the seal of God in their foreheads; and hence the limitation is indicated by confining the time of its operation to "*five months.*" These five months are the period assigned to the ravages of these symbolical locusts, and must themselves be symbolical. The life and ravages of the locust are measured neither by years nor by days, but by months; and five months of the year is the period to which they are limited. This period represents the whole time of the devastations in the power of the symbol to effect, and so, of course, it must represent the natural limitation to the agency symbolized by it. As God does not give up the natural world to be utterly destroyed by permitting the ravages of such a plague to be continued through all the year, but by the very constitution of its nature has limited it to the smaller portion of it, just so has he limited, in the very constitution of things, the reigning power of these delusions. Like the locust, they run their course, they live their natural life, and die. They, indeed, leave terrible effects behind them, and give rise to other woes, but in doing so they exhaust themselves. The existence of error consists in its power to deceive. When it ceases to deceive, it ceases to be. But no deception can last. All delusions, in the very nature of things, must in due time discover themselves. However they may reign for a time, truth is mighty, and will prevail. God has not withdrawn His truth; He has not given over a truth-hating world even, entirely to the power of those lies of hell that it so willingly often receives. They run their course, and thousands fall victims to them; but by the effects they produce, the miseries that ever flow from them, they are sure to discover their real origin and nature. It is indeed true, that as the locust renews itself in successive seasons, so these locusts of the pit are renewed in successive generations and ages; and men, ever ready to be deceived, as they turn away from the truth, become again their victims; again, however, to prove their false and ruinous character, by showing, in the times of man's greatest need, in temptation, in sorrow, and in death, their utter inability to help, and their power to torment. The fact that time always surely unmasks these hell-born delusions, has saved the world from the awful ruin with which they would otherwise have swept it, if unchecked and unrestrained.

The reign of these crowned and venomous locusts, however often they reappear, is limited in their very nature. They die by the desolation they produce. When they have poisoned the soul's powers, and destroyed its joys, and crushed its hopes, they are discovered, and perish, either in the agony of the soul aroused to see how miserably it has been deluded and ruined, or in the power of revived reason and truth. Though fulfilling their mission of woe in every age, and terribly as they have ruled and tormented an unbelieving world, they have thus always been checked in their career of desolation. Their mission is one of chastisement and discipline, not of utter ruin; it is to show the misery of forsaking the truth, and so to exhibit more clearly the heavenly nature and power of

---

1 It seems more natural to interpret this five months in its relation to the locusts, of whose ravages it is the limit, than by its independent symbolic meaning, as half of ten, the symbol of *earthly* completeness in general. The sense resulting would be nearly the same; for this would represent them as stopped in the very midst of their ravages, when they had reached only half of the fearful results which, unchecked, they would have produced. To those who have observed the symbolic significance of numbers pervading this whole book, and, indeed, all the Jewish symbolism, it is gratifying to see how, even here, when the number indicates a literal relation of time in reference to the symbolic agent, by which the limitation of the agency represented is indicated as fixed in its very nature, the symbolic sense of the *number* itself indicates the very same thing.

truth, and not to triumph over it, and subject the world to Satan.

Such is the interpretation of this very remarkable and very important woe, as drawn from the meaning of the inspired words themselves, with nothing but other Scripture truth as our guide. And it is one that shows it to be full of solemn warning, of important instruction, and of rich encouragement to the church and the world in every age, and in none more than the present.

On the whole of it we remark:

1. That it sets forth most impressively one of the great principles of God's moral government, especially in its relation to the administration of Christ's kingdom, and its triumph. *The sin of unbelief brings the curse of error.* God first smites men in all their earthly good, and their external religious advantages and comforts flowing from them. This is the lesson of the first four trumpets; unbelief brings a curse upon all the worldly good and all external privileges. But when this fails to bring to repentance, the work of judgment proceeds till unbelief becomes positive and earnest belief of a lie. Thus the prevalence of unbelief brings on the reign of superstition and fanaticism in doctrine and practice. A fallen church is given over to the reign of the crowned locusts instead of the crowned elders. An apostate church is the "mother of abominations." This is, indeed, only one of the operations of that still more general law, that men must "eat of the fruit of their own way, and be filled with their own devices. The turning away of the simple shall slay them."

Thus God dealt with Israel of old. "They made a calf in those days, and offered sacrifice unto the idol, and rejoiced in the work of their own hands. Then God turned, and gave them up to worship the host of heaven." (Acts 7: 41, 42.) "They had despised," says God by the prophet Ezekiel, (chap. 20: 24,) "My statutes, and had polluted My Sabbaths, and their eyes were after their fathers' idols. Wherefore I gave them also statutes that were not good, and judgments whereby they should not live; [*i. e.*, I gave them up to the government of the heathen, whose gods they sought after;] and polluted them in their own gifts, in that they caused to pass through the fire all that openeth the womb, that I might make them desolate, to the end that they might know that I am the Lord."

2. But, secondly, in all the history of the world there never has been so awful an exemplification of this law, and on so vast a scale, as in the apostacy of the Christian church that introduced the middle ages, and during them tormented an unbelieving world, apparently forsaken of the Spirit of God. Mohammedan and Papal delusions are both alike included under these scorpion locusts, both being the results, though in a somewhat different degree and manner, of church apostacy. Both classes of delusions were begotten of hell, and the dark smoke of the pit whence they issued was let forth upon the world by an apostate church. Almost the whole of the visible church, east and west, had fallen from the truth, and become the propagators of devilish error, and of corrupt and corrupting practices. It did really seem as if the church had become the very porter of hell, and had let loose upon the earth a whole host of incarnate fiends. By the doctrines of the celibacy of the clergy, of auricular confession, of saintly intercessions, and human merits, and purgatory, and especially of the power, and almost divine authority, of the Pope and bishops in the western church, and the similar claim of the eastern bishops, the door of the pit was fully opened, and there burst forth an almost infinite number and variety of poisonous errors, and superstitious and fanatical practices, and foul and loathsome corruptions, that culminated in and formed the substance of that great spiritual despotism that held the nations in bondage for ages, and that still spreads its darkening pall and its spiritual torments over deceived and degraded

millions. The agency which opened the bottomless pit, was the agency or power in whose service these locust hordes spread abroad, under their king Apollyon, and whose full and complete establishment they effected. By them the peace of men was destroyed, and the torments of conscience made often insupportable. Under their pressure men were driven to endure the most cruel penances, and to inflict upon themselves all kinds of tortures. The watchings, and fastings, and hair shirts, and exposures, and flagellations, and fights with fiends—the fruit of a crazed mind—and the horrid impurities, and black and bloody crimes perpetrated in the very name of religion, were such as no summary notice, or even much reading, can give any adequate idea of, and are well represented by the torments of these scorpion locusts and their venomous stings. The self-inflicted tortures of the Hindoo devotee are often horrible enough; but they are comparatively isolated cases: in those times this misery seemed to pervade all society. These doctrines and practices had a visible personification in the immense multitudes of priests, and the numerous monkish orders, each of whom was an emissary of, and a part of, this immense despotism. They literally swarmed like locusts everywhere, and everywhere poisoned the souls of men. Some idea of their immense number and power may be formed from the fact, that in England, at the time when Henry VIII. suppressed the monasteries, there were, in addition to the numerous secular clergy, connected with these houses, of all kinds, about fifty thousand persons, and that in a population of probably less than five millions.

The spiritual oppression of which these were both the victims and the instruments, the wretchedness they produced, and the utter hopelessness often, could find no fitter expression than in the language of the passage before us. "In those days men shall seek death, and shall not find it; and shall desire to die, and death shall flee from them." There was no escape from the torment. In *this* world, by all their spiritual teachers and rulers, instead of being directed to the comforts of the gospel of peace and love, they were directed to exhausting and degrading toils, or to renounce all the endearments and charities of domestic life, to perform painful and protracted penances, that left the heart as dark, and the conscience as full of tormenting fears as ever. And when they looked to the *next* world, and to death, as if in that there might be a relief from the torments here endured, what met their gaze but the still more dreadful horrors of purgatorial fires, where they might have to burn whole ages, unless they were so happy as to leave the wealth behind them to purchase masses and prayers for their more speedy deliverance. In no other case was it ever so true that men desired to die, and death fled from them. Under such teachings there could be no such death-bed scenes as it is now our privilege often to witness; no such heavenly consolations as now cheer the hearts of weeping friends in the chamber of sickness and death, and around the graves of their dead; none of that peace and triumph that now often enables the suffering saint, amidst bodily agonies and other crushing afflictions, to *wait* in *patience* his appointed time, and to welcome death then with gladness. Then there was no comforter. Above, around, below, in the church and out of it, living, dying, and dead, it was torment. Such was the misery of a world and a church, so-called, that rejected the gospel of Jesus, and especially the grand doctrine of atonement represented by the fire of the altar cast upon the earth.

It is only necessary to repeat the apostle Paul's prophetic sketch of the rise of this monstrous system of delusion, in 2 Thess. 2: 3-12, to show how perfectly it harmonizes with this view of these scorpion locusts, and this application of the symbol, and confirms both. "There shall come a falling away, and that man of sin" shall " be revealed, the son of perdition, who opposeth and exalteth himself above all that is called God, or that is worshipped. * * * For the mystery of iniquity doth already work; only he who now letteth will let, until he be taken out of the way." That hindrance was removed by the judgments of the previous trumpets, in the overthrow of the political power of Rome, and the degeneracy of the ecclesiastical power. "And then shall that wicked be revealed, * * * even him whose coming is after the working of Satan, with all power, and signs, and lying wonders, and with all deceivableness of unrighteousness in them that perish; because they received not the love of the truth that they might be saved. And for this cause God gave them up to strong delusions, that they should believe a lie, that they all might be damned who believe not the truth, but had pleasure in unrighteousness."

3. How fearful, then, the consequences of undervaluing the truth of God. This opens the door to every perversion of its saving doctrines, and then to these "strong delusions." This truth is to us the very waters of life, the bread of heaven, the only remedy for human woe. To poison these waters, this bread, this only remedy, is a crime, the enormity of which language has no power to express; nor can it express the terrible results to human souls. But the horrible thing has been done; it is still done: the world is full of these delusions; souls are ever perishing by them; and every man and woman that turns away from the Bible, and neglects its holy teachings, is in imminent danger of falling a victim to some of these delusions, if indeed he has not already done so, and bringing on his soul its torments. Here only do these waters of life flow with perfect purity; here only are you sure of getting the bread of heaven unadulterated; here only do you find this remedy in its simplest, purest state, and most fitting form, to apply to your soul's woes. As, then, you would escape the deep-laid snares of the devil, and secure

eternal life, search the Scriptures diligently, and obey them earnestly. Let the church contend earnestly for the faith once delivered to the saints, especially for the cross and crown of Jesus. Let her remember the praise of the church of Ephesus, and the keen censures of the churches of Pergamos and Thyatira. Nothing could show more impressively than this subject, the unspeakable value of a pure gospel, and an earnest, faithful church, holding it fast, acting it out, and defending it even unto the death.

4. Finally, remember that the only security against the insidious and fatal sting of error, is in the sealing of the Spirit. Only when these truths are sealed upon your heart by the Holy Ghost are you safe. A frigid orthodoxy can no more save you than a fierce heresy. The greatest heresy of all, as one has well said, is the want of love: love to Christ, to His cross, His crown, and the souls He died to save. It is only as that Spirit dwells within you, and teaches you, and fills your heart with the sweet experience of the power and grace of your redeeming God, that you can resist the assaults of error. Taught by this Spirit, and bearing, in a holy life, the seal of the living God on your foreheads, you may defy all its artifices. Hence, says this same apostle, when speaking in his first Epistle of the antichrists that were then abroad, " But ye have an unction from the Holy One, and know all things." " The anointing which ye have received of Him abideth in you; and ye need not that any man teach you, but as the same anointing teacheth you of all things, and is truth, and is no lie, even as it hath taught you, ye shall abide in Him." "Many false prophets have gone out into the world. * * * Ye are of God, little children, and have overcome them, because greater is He that is in you than he that is in the world. * * * Whatsoever is born of God, overcometh the world; and this is the victory that overcometh the world, even our faith."

LECTURE XXII.

THE REACTION OF THE WORLD'S POWER AND WISDOM.

REV., CHAP. IX: 12-21.

" One woe is past, and behold there come two woes more hereafter. And the sixth angel sounded, and I heard a [lit. one] voice from the four horns of the golden altar which is before God, saying to the sixth angel which had the trumpet, Loose the four angels which are bound in [upon] the great river Euphrates. And the four angels were loosed, which were prepared for an [Gr. unto the] hour, and day, and month, and year, for to slay the third part of men. And the number of the army of the horsemen were two hundred thousand thousand, [twice ten thousand times ten thousand]: and I heard the number of them. And thus I saw the horses in the vision, and them that sat on them, having breastplates of fire, and of jacinth, and brimstone, [fiery, hyacinthine or purplish blue, and sulphurous]: and the heads of the horses were as the heads of lions; and out of their mouths issued fire, and smoke, and brimstone. By these three was the third part of men killed, by the fire, and by the smoke, and by the brimstone, which issued out of their mouths. For their power is in their mouth, and in their tails; for their tails were like unto serpents, and had heads, and with them they do hurt. And the rest of the men which were not killed by these plagues, yet repented not of the works of their hands, that they should not worship devils, and idols of gold, and silver, and brass, and stone, and of wood, which neither can see, nor hear, nor walk, neither repented they of their murders, nor of their sorceries, nor of their fornication, nor of their thefts."

"ONE woe is past." What has just been detailed in the previous verses, of the vision of the scorpion locusts, is the whole of the first woe. Its being past does not imply that it occurs once for all in the whole history of the church and the world; but that this is the complete course of the evil thus described, and whenever, in any case or at any time, it has proceeded thus far, it has then and there done all it can do, and disappears in the effects which it produces. " Behold there come two woes more hereafter." These two follow the first, not merely in the order of time, but as, in part at least, results. This is especially true of this second woe. Though essentially different in its nature and working, it is the necessary effect of the first. The cause must exist before the effect; but it does not follow that the cause ceases to operate when the effect appears, nor that the same cause may not repeat itself again and again, producing the same results. How long, therefore, this first woe may continue its inflictions; how long these five months' locusts will continue to re-appear and torment the unsealed, we are not told; but we would naturally infer that it would be as long as there were any unsealed to be tormented, or until these torments had produced upon them their full results. As the red and the black horses of the second and third seals do not cease their work when the pale horse of death appears, nor this cease its work when the martyr-cry from under the altar is heard; and as the judgments of the first four trumpets do not cease to fall upon an ungodly world, smiting the whole circle of its earthly blessings, when the fifth brings upon it the curse of error, so it is with these woes. Before the second woe can appear at all, the first must do its peculiar work; and the first, still operating, produces continually the same recurring results; but the two are perfectly distinct and consecutive.

The first of these woes, heralded by the trumpet of the fifth angel, is, as we have seen, the awful scourge of fanatical and soul-destroying error, bringing on the reign of spiritual despotism. Under it the mere worldly power, and the worldly wisdom, is subjected to the power of an apostate Christianity. It is not, however, the church in its external organizations, or the working of these, which is here described, but the origin, character, and operation of the devilish doctrines that make up this apostacy, and especially the torments which they inflict upon the soul itself. The world, too, in this view, is presented, not in its outward political or secular organizations, as having a distinct and separate form from the church, but in its elements of unsealed souls, souls devoted to the mere earthly interest, and in whom this whole earthliness of affection is subjected to the power of fanatical delusions.

By a beautiful propriety of order, the Spirit, before presenting to the vision of the seer these organized forms of the evil against which the spiritual kingdom would be called to contend, as developed in their political and ecclesiastical combinations—which he does in the twelfth and succeeding chapters—presents the constituting principles of evil which developed into these. The complicated working of these principles, and their abominable and hellish character and consequences, are the things here set forth more particularly. By a few wonderful touches of the pencil of inspiration, we have here traced a picture of the very deepest working of the perverted religious principle under the control of Satanic delusions, and then of the result of all this when the delusion is discovered, and the mere selfish and earth-loving principle rises up and casts off the reign of this spiritual tyranny, trampling every thing sacred with it in the dust.

This last is the first thing brought forth by the sounding of the sixth angel's trumpet, and described in the rest of this chapter. It is the first part of the woe of the sixth trumpet, the whole of which is brought to light, by the announcements of the mighty angel concerning the slaying of the witnesses, in the eleventh chapter, and in the earthquake which follows.

§. 1. It comes at the call of the great Intercessor.

This woe is represented as coming forth at the summons of the great Intercessor Himself, and in answer to all the prayers of all God's people. As soon as the sixth angel sounds his trumpet, a voice, a single voice from all the four horns of the golden altar, the altar of incense, is heard. This origin of the voice intimates that the command is in answer to the prayers that thence ascend through the merits of our Saviour's intercessions. That it is a single voice—the expression in the original is very emphatic—though coming from all the four horns of the altar, intimates that all the prayers of all the church unite in now letting loose this last result of a world's rebellion upon itself. The altar of incense represents the intercession of Christ, through which the prayers of the saints find access and acceptance. This voice may, therefore, be regarded as not merely the united cry of God's people, but as the voice of the great Intercessor Himself, who, having received and presented the cries of His suffering people during their long trials and conflicts with the soul-destroying errors, which, like locust hordes, had been spreading such desolation, now gives the command which is to bring signal vengeance on their enemies, and remove the last obstruction to the triumph of the kingdom.

Secondly, this infliction comes from those very powers that had been tormented by this spiritual despotism. The command is, "Loose the four angels which are bound in the great river Euphrates." It seems strange, and it certainly violates all consistency of interpretation, that by so many the Euphrates here should be regarded as meaning the real river in the realities represented, instead of its being the symbol of something analogous to it in the conflicts of the church. We might just as well regard the angels as indicating literal angels, or the city of Babylon, afterwards introduced, as indicating that material city, or the empire of which it was the capital. The river Euphrates was that on which Babylon was built; its waters were at once the source of its wealth and security. Hence the prophet Jeremiah, addressing Babylon, and threatening her total ruin, uses this language, "O thou that dwellest upon many waters, abundant in riches, thine end is come." Babylon,

§. 2. The agencies of this woe.

by its history, becomes the appropriate symbol of the world's power triumphing over the church, by leading her into captivity, and so bringing about the reign of spiritual despotism, a Satanic compound of worldly power and spiritual and fanatical delusions. The Euphrates, therefore, must represent that on which this spiritual Babylon was founded, and from which she derived her prosperity and security. "Waters" are the familiar symbol of nations and multitudes. Accordingly, in chap. 17: 15, we are expressly told that these waters on which "the whore sitteth," the corrupt church whose name is "Babylon the great," are "peoples, and multitudes, and nations, and tongues."[1] The four angels bound on these waters are, therefore, the sum of all those influences and powers in these nations and multitudes, which, by the mighty providence of God, had hitherto been restrained from bursting forth on their work of destruction. It is implied in this, and is fully brought out in the succeeding verses, that these agencies were of a violent and destructive nature. They were now to be loosed, and to go forth on their mission of vengeance. The number *four* is the symbol of totality in regard to earthly things, as the four corners of the earth, the four winds, the whole four sides of a thing. This is doubtless its force here. But it is also true, and worthy of remembrance, that the forces here indicated as having been so long restrained, and now let loose, most naturally fall into a fourfold classification, the lust of wealth, of political power, of sensual indulgence, and of worldly knowledge. These seem to be exhaustive. These principles, which give rise to so much of personal activity and national energy, and which, when under right government, produce so much of the mere earthly good which men enjoy, and when uncontrolled, so many of the convulsions that shake the whole framework of society and revol-

---

[1] Compare Is. 17: 12, 13.

utionize nations—these, it will be observed, are the very points in which the spiritual despotism of a perverted Christianity had come into direct contact with the souls of unsanctified men. In misdirecting, controlling, and tyrannizing over these natural principles of human activity—the love of wealth, and power, and sensual pleasure, and knowledge—instead of properly training them, and subjecting them to the claims and service of Christ, the reign of error always so stimulates or violates them as to continually torment men. It is in these especially that the scorpion locusts inflict their inflammatory and poisonous stings. By these errors of devilish origin and fanatical nature, a corrupt spiritual power lays hold on men's wealth, absorbing it into the so-called church, deprives them of all real political rights, and torments them by bodily penances and ascetic ordinances, and by innumerable and tyrannical restraints on the freedom of thought and the pursuit of knowledge. Under the power of spiritual delusion, all this may be long submitted to, and thus all these principles subsidized to the support of a corrupt church. But as it becomes by degrees apparent that these torments which they endure, these restraints imposed, this continual interference with their property, their liberty, their pleasures, and their very thinking, is a tyrannical and cruel thing, and really brings them nothing of the unseen good which it promised, and which they sought, they are ready to burst their bonds, and turn in vengeance on the very power to which hitherto all their support had been given. It is the working of these principles that brings about the catastrophe described in chapter 17: 16; the ten horns, representing the world's powers, turning upon and destroying the harlot church, that had been riding the beast to which they belonged, and tyrannizing over it for her own ends. This violent reaction of these principles, especially in communities and nations, could not, however, have any thing in it of a truly healing or saving character. Being essentially selfish and ungodly, it could be only violent and destructive; but as such was a most fitting judgment upon the powers which had so corrupted the church, and poisoned the fountains of human happiness, and opened the door of the pit for its scorpion locusts to come forth. In it the world has been made to eat of the fruit of its own doings, and is still made to do so.

These terrible forces are for a time restrained by the delusions that tyrannize over them. Such is the law of God's providential government, that the very influences that are stimulating these forces to this violent reaction, also restrain them until the very moment arrives for which they are prepared. This last idea is, no doubt, the true meaning of the phrase, "prepared for an hour, and a day, and a month, and a year." In the original, the *definite* article is used, and, literally translated, it is "prepared *unto the*[1] hour and day, and month, and year." The words cannot express, as they are often made to do, the period of time during which these forces were to operate, but the point of time *at* which they were to be developed and burst forth. They are made ready in these arrangements of God to be let loose at the precise moment fixed for the accomplishment of the divine purpose. Some of them may take longer, some shorter, periods in which to develope themselves; but however various, their times are all appointed, and nothing can either precipitate or delay them. Not only the year, but the month, and the day, even the very hour is fixed. The instant these restraints, which are thrown around these worldly forces, can no longer contribute to the progress of the kingdom, the whole apparent line of divine judgments shall be reversed, and these same forces that before seemed quiet

§. 3. The restraints by which they are bound.

---

[1] Gr. εις την.

and harmless as the sleeping infant, shall burst forth with all the ferocity of the tiger. So wonderfully has God wrapped up in the constitution of human nature and society those forces and restraints, by which human wickedness, under the control of Satanic delusions, is made to develope, to limit, and then to punish itself.

The truth, thus symbolically and forcibly stated, finds an appropriate illustration in those facts of history which, by different writers, have been presented in entirely opposite characters, and with contrary tendencies. Because many Protestant writers have represented the corrupt church of the middle ages as the real "mother of abominations," and the torment of the world, and the source of its darkness, others, looking at the same events in a different aspect, have charged them with prejudice and misrepresentation, and held up that same church as the only restraining and light-giving power that kept the world from sinking under the terrible inroads of barbarian power and brute violence. Now, each of these classes is, to a certain extent, right; the one in its positive views of the evil, and the other in its positive views of the good; but neither are right in the denial of the other. It was the defection of the church, her corruption in doctrine and practice, that brought on the darkness of those ages; it was this that enfeebled and divided the nations, and made them an easy prey to invading hordes sent to scourge them. A healthy and vigorous Christianity would have produced far different results. It, indeed, possessed light, and gave some light to a dark world; but it is just as certain that it also restrained and covered up more of the pure light of truth than it gave, by its attempts to bind freedom of thought, and limit the circulation of the Scriptures. At the same time, it was this very church, corrupt as it was, that, by its power over the minds of men, restrained the violence of barbarian hordes, and often of

§. Historical illustration.

lawless rulers and half civilized nations. It held in check those very forces that it tyrannized over, from bursting forth into a general anarchy, which could have spread nothing but utter desolation over the earth, without a single accompanying benefit. The good things of God, even though most terribly abused and perverted, when compared with the unmixed principles of depravity, retain something to bless and to restrain, and so to prove their original excellence. But it is no great praise to a corrupt church, that it restrains from outbursting violence evils which itself had produced, and which it is the commission and prerogative of every pure church to prevent. There was still a little light shining, a little truth was known, the Bible was still possessed; and this very light, of which the great ecclesiastical power of those ages was the keeper, but which she withheld from the oppressed nations, could not but occasionally break forth on the darkness around, and spread through her own dark chambers of imagery, enlightening a soul here and there, and bringing to view enormities hidden for ages. And so it went on, until the powers of the world discovered, more or less, how grievously they had been tormented by the emissaries of Satan coming as angels of light, until they found out that those faces of men, with their golden crowns, were only a deception, and that the realities were scorpion locusts from the pit. Then it is that the command comes from the place where prayer is heard and answered, "Loose the four angels," these hitherto restrained forces. "Let an oppressed and down-trodden world rise up and take vengeance on a corrupt church. Let the violence, and ambition, and infidelity hitherto restrained, rush forth in their work of devastation, and trample in the dust an unfaithful church. Let them throw off the restraints imposed by these delusions of Satan, by which these delusions made them subserve their own ends." Thus only can the way of truth be prepared.

We have next the vast multitudes under the control of these four agencies or influences. The loosing of the four angels brings forth upon the scene immense armies of horse. These, therefore, are the immediate product of these unrestrained forces. Their number is particularly proclaimed in the apostle's hearing, in such a way as to claim special attention. It is the enormous one of two hundred millions. The idea first and necessarily conveyed by this is that of the inconceivable vastness of the multitude under the power of these destructive agencies; and this seems clearly designed to intimate that these forces have an almost universal extent, pervading in some degree the whole of the children of this world. The expression in the original is far better adapted to convey this symbolical meaning than our more definite translation of it here; it is literally "two myriads of myriads." Myriad is the Greek word, but slightly changed, meaning, when definite, "ten thousand," but very often used indefinitely, as it always is, in English. The expression is the same as that in chap. 5: 11, describing the number of angels round about the throne, without the limiting addition "two," there translated "ten thousand times ten thousand," more exactly "ten thousands of ten thousands," or "myriads of myriads."

§. 4. Extent of their influence.

But why this peculiarly definite limitation "*two*," to an expression evidently designed to convey the idea of an immense and indefinite number? Let it be remembered, that this number is not introduced incidentally, but that in the vision itself it was made a matter of special and distinct revelation, and the seer gives it special prominence in his account of the vision. After stating their number, he adds, "and I heard the number of them." In interpreting such a passage, it is mere trifling to pass it by with the remark that it is a definite put for an indefinite number, as a sufficient explanation. The question is, why such peculiar definiteness is here combined with such vastness and indefiniteness? If the latter were the only idea to be conveyed, why not have said, as was said in regard to the angels, "myriads of myriads?" There must be a meaning in this limiting "*two*," and at least its general sense of a definite bound being fixed to these multitudinous hordes of the armies of hell, is both precious in itself, and in this connection very important. Widely as these forces of evil seem to sweep over the masses of men, and to pervade the nations, interminable as this living stream of fiery monsters seems to be, as they pour forth with volcanic fury from their pent-up prison, their limit is definitely and unchangeably fixed. They are not like the messengers who minister for the heirs of salvation, an indefinite and unlimited number of myriads of myriads; but though indeed "myriad of myriads," they are but *two*. As, therefore, the suffering and waiting church of God looks out from the chambers where she has taken refuge, upon the wide prevalence of monstrous and destructive influences and agencies, of polities and error, which, like successive blasts of a desert simoon, sweep over the face of society, and pervade its most secure retreats, spreading desolation and death, and which, instead of exhausting themselves in the progress of ages and of civilization, seem only to multiply as they spread themselves, let her remember, that in the words by which the Spirit of God describes this terrific extent of these hellish influences, a limit is affixed to them, and that the narrowest possible, consistent with the full exposure of their vile and Satanic nature.

But why should this limitation be "*two?*" May we not see a manifest reason for this in the fact, that all these forces must always manifest themselves in a two-fold manner, or in one of two ways? It has been already noticed that the forces let loose by the unbinding of the four angels, naturally fall into four classes, the love of wealth, of pleasure, of power, and of knowledge. Now it is also true, that all of these, and all the human activities called forth by them, when a loose rein is given them to resist and cast off the tyranny of a false church and corrupt doctrines, manifest themselves in the two forms of outward violence or force, and of infidelity. So, afterwards, in the thirteenth chapter, all the resources of the kingdom of Satan are developed into the two beasts; the one of seven heads and ten horns, representing the outward or political power of the world, and the one with two horns like a lamb, working miracles, and supporting the former, representing the world's wisdom. These made war upon the church, prevailed over her, until she mounted the former, and, as a bloody harlot, rode it, until at length its ten horns turned upon her and destroyed her, the same thing here taught. The same forces that corrupt the true church take vengeance on that church corrupted by them. It would seem especially appropriate that this duality in the form of action of these forces should be indicated in their number, since it is this that accounts for the vastness of their number, the world's wisdom and force combining. The nature of these two things declares also the degree of limitation before spoken of; numerous and powerful as the multitudes of people and of influences which they control may be, they can only go as far as worldly wisdom and mere force can carry them. What can these accomplish against the spiritual kingdom? Scourge and ruin a corrupt and worldly church they may; for this they are the divinely prepared and adapted instruments; but they can do nothing more. Then let them do their worst; they are only preparing the way of the kingdom.

§. *Their true character.* The character of these forces is set forth very vividly and unmistakably in the horrid and hellish forms of these horses and horsemen. They might well be called "the cavalry of hell." The horsemen are described as having breast plates, not as in our version, "made of fire, and jacinth or hyacinth, and brimstone," but "*fiery, hyacinthine or purplish blue, and sulphurous,*" words expressing their appearance as flashing forth in their armour the flames, and emitting the odours of the bottomless pit. These are the very symbols elsewhere used for hell and its torments. Such are the riders. But it is especially the horses themselves that represent these forces of evil, and by which the work of vengeance is accomplished; their riders, while they seem to guide them, being borne onward by them furiously to deeds of violence, and the extremes of infidelity. "Their heads were as the heads of lions, and out of their mouths issued fire, and smoke, and brimstone. By these three was the third part of men killed, by the fire, and by the smoke, and by the brimstone, which issued out of their mouths." Their lion-like heads indicate an agency of brutal violence and power; and the fire, and smoke, and brimstone issuing out of their mouths, as the instruments of this deadly violence, indicate most clearly the very inspiration and instrumentality of hell. They mark the nature, and expose in its true light the hidden character, of many of those great movements of the world's powers on behalf of "liberty and equality," and "human rights," and "general progress," and even "the diffusion of knowledge:" mere disguises, under which the selfishness and ungodliness of the world has concealed the true character of those movements to which it has been driven by the tyranny and torments of a spiritual despotism, of a corrupt and corrupting church, and of the fanatical errors it has propagated.

By this violent and devilish agency a third part of men are slain; the worldly interest is ruined to the extent of one-third of it. The world's own mightiest agencies are thus made to inflict a severe, and to a certain extent, a ruinous blow upon itself, especially upon its power in and over the church.

But, combined with this, these horses have another instrument of inflicting injury still more unnatural and hellish. "Their tails were like unto serpents, and had heads, and with them they do hurt," "for their power is" not only "in their mouths," but "in their tails." This, let it be observed, is no part of the instrumentality by which they kill the one-third of men, or ruin the one-third of the earthly interest; but an additional power by which they inflict a deadly, poisonous wound, in a concealed and stealthy manner. It very well expresses the world's wisdom, as arrayed in opposition to God and the spiritual kingdom, stealthily inflicting upon men wounds of a most poisonous and deadly character, and combining with, and inseparable from, the worldly power. In explanation and confirmation of this view of the symbol we may compare the words of the prophet, speaking of Israel, "The ancient and honourable, He is the head; and the prophet that teacheth lies, he is the tail."[1] This kind of agency has no tendency to lessen the worldly interest, but exactly the opposite; while at the same time its secret poison inflicts upon all in that interest a fearful injury, the injury of a deep and insidious infidelity professedly basing itself upon the inductions of science and philosophy, and adorning itself in all the fascinations of art.

We have here, then, in the few words describing this symbolic scene, a graphic and even minute picture of those great movements of the world's forces, in their reaction against the corruptions of a false Christianity, of which history is full, and which we see going on even now in the nations, the combination of the worldly power and the worldly wisdom to throw off the tyranny of spiritual delusions; and, while thus scourging the worldly interest, as allied with spiritual delusions, their spreading at the same time the poison of a deep, insidious, and professedly

[1] Is. 9 : 15.

philanthropic infidelity, and thus apparently strengthening it. This is the scourge summoned to the field by the sixth angel's trumpet.

The attempt to locate this woe upon any particular event in history is almost preposterous. Yet very able and learned interpreters have done it, and so done it, that the interpretation has appeared very plausible. But it has been only by slurring over some of the characteristic features of the vision, or the symbols, and mixing up a literal interpretation with a purely symbolical, in a way to set at defiance all consistent rules of interpretation. Such is the widely received exposition of this and the previous woe, as referring to the Turkish and Saracenic conquests. On the other hand, whenever and wherever a perverted Christianity has tormented the soul, it has developed this reaction. The locusts of the pit have prepared the way for these monster horsemen. And the whole history of the church and the world, from the time that any part of the visible church became a spiritual despotism in any part of it, is inwrought with the working of this principle. Especially during the latter period of the middle ages, in Germany, in France, and, indeed, almost everywhere thoughout Europe, this rising up of the world's powers to avenge themselves on their ecclesiastical oppressors, the oft-repeated, violent, and fierce attempts to throw off the yoke of Rome, and the miseries thus brought about, together with the enfeebling of the earthly power, both in and out of the visible church, in its opposition to the spiritual kingdom; these form a large portion of the staple of the history of those times. Immediately before and during the Reformation this reaction began to develope itself more fully than ever before. The whole history of Henry VIII., of England, considered apart from the gospel influences that were operating at the same time, was one of its developments. The numerous insurrections of the peasantry for generations before

Luther, the noted "war of the peasants," and the Anabaptist commotions during the Reformation, were marked cases of the same. The most striking in still later times, though neither the last, nor alone, is doubtless the French Revolution, with its untold horrors, which, manifestly to all, was a hellish combination of the worldly power and wisdom against a corrupt and apostate church. It was one Satanic agency turning itself in fury upon another, and working out the gracious purposes of God in reference to His spiritual kingdom.

Finally, in the last verses we are taught the utter inefficacy of this agency, and of all that went before it, to cure the world of its ungodliness and unrighteousness. "And the rest of men which were not killed by these plagues, yet repented not of the works of their hands, that they should not worship devils, and idols of gold, and silver, and brass, and stone, and of wood, which neither can see, nor hear, nor walk; neither repented they of their murders, nor of their sorceries, nor of their fornication, nor of their thefts." Even after these plagues had killed the one-third, the rest were none the better. They still clung to their abominable idolatries and immoralities. These two classes comprehend all the sins enumerated, which are evidently those which brought down these judgments. Those sins are named, not as they appear to human eyes, but according to the uniform and natural method in inspired and prophetic descriptions, as they appear unto God, as they are in reality. The terms used represent the real character of those sins that constitute apostacy from God, and especially as they developed themselves in the great apostacy, and, indeed, which, in all times and places, oppose the progress of the spiritual kingdom.

§. 6. Their utter inefficacy to save.

The belief of soul-destroying errors, and practical submission to their power, may well be styled the worship of devils, as the doctrines themselves are called the doctrines of devils; and the honours given to Popes and priests, to the Virgin, and to canonized saints, and to images, and relics of all kinds, which were due to God alone, together with the far more general and earnest devotion given by others to idols of the soul, as real as those of wood, and stone, and gold, and silver, and as helpless, could not be better described as to their true nature, than the worship of idols. These two things, then, the worship of devils and of idols, is at once a comprehensive and definite description of this earthliness in its aspect toward God. The whole of the worldly system, whether baptized or unbaptized, is essentially demonology and idolatry in its relation to God, and God will so deal with it, and always has so dealt with it.

In its aspect towards man, this earthly system is essentially murderous, bewitching, foul seduction, and lust, and glaring dishonesty and robbery; and these in relation both to this world and the next. Whatever be its pretensions to philanthropy, and these are very loud, it is here characterized, therefore, most fitly as it appears to God, " murders," and " sorceries," and " fornication," and " thefts." When men make the world their god, and still more, when they give themselves up to spiritual delusions, they murder each other's souls, bewitch one another into the most unreasonable notions and practices, seduce to the foulest lusts, and rob of the most precious possessions and rights.

From this deep-rooted, ungodly, and foul immorality, no judgments of heaven will ever turn men. Even after the whole quiver of God's judgments has been exhausted, and every part of the world's good been smitten, and the soul itself smitten with torments of error, and then these delusions exploded in a fierce and resistless reaction, the world, all that remains of it, is the world still, the same ungodly and wicked thing it was before. It may fret, and rage, and blaspheme; it will writhe in its agony, but it will never repent under this treatment. And yet this is the precise treatment that is most just, the treatment which is the natural result, the necessary fruit, of its own doings. The world, left to itself, and under the working of those judgments which God has, by the very constitution of man, rendered inevitable on its forsaking Him, can never become better. "Evil men and seducers wax worse and worse, deceiving and being deceived." Only as the "little book" of the gospel of Jesus is brought to bear by a witnessing church upon this festering mass of moral corruption, can its progress be arrested, and any sinners saved out of it, and the world be ready for the triumph of the seventh angel's trumpet.

Do we not see and feel in these verses the very presence of the divine Spirit? Are these strange symbols, and their wonderful and perfect adaptation to picture forth the deepest and most complicated workings of that mysterious thing, a depraved human heart, in all its relations, fitting as they do with a divine precision, into all the facts of history, are these within the inventive power of the mightiest human genius? In this single chapter, and these symbols of the monster locusts and horsemen, we have set before us at a glance all the wonderful complication of causes and influences that, working secretly and powerfully, shaped the events of ages, and are still shaping much of human history. We have here the deep truths which have wrought out the history of ages in its relation to the kingdom of God, and which are taught by it; all, therefore, that is truly valuable in it. With this clue, a clue which the mere world-historian, in all his researches, never clearly saw, the strange mazes of history during the dark ages assume the simplicity of two all-pervading principles, the perversion of God's truth leading to spiritual despotism, and the resistance and reaction of man's selfish

§. Inf. 1. Divine authorship.

nature against such despotism. It is thus made to illustrate the wisdom and justice of God, and the enormity of man's sin, as nothing else could do. Such a condensed account of the abstrusest workings of the human heart in its relations to God and to society, as unfolds the true nature of all the great movements of the world for ages, and penetrates with its light the darkest and most mysterious portions of their history, and harmonizes the whole into one grand onward movement on behalf of the spiritual kingdom of God, and does this, not in the form of abstract propositions and philosophical reasonings, but in a few simple pictures, such as fix themselves indelibly in the imagination of the simplest reader, proves itself to be the direct work of God, and cannot but awaken in every believing heart the most profound awe and adoration.

How inveterate the depravity of the human heart!

§. 2. Inveteracy of human depravity. Though ground to powder under the successive and crushing judgments of the Almighty, its nature remains unchanged. Ungodliness pervades every fibre of its being; it prefers the service of the devil to that of God; it persists in adoring the creature rather than the Creator, and in the folly of fixing its hopes and dependence on what it knows to be false and vain as the dumb idol of the most stupid idolater. "Madness is in the heart of men while they live, and after that, they go to the dead." "Though thou shouldest bray a fool in a mortar among wheat, with a pestle, yet will not his foolishness depart from him." Terrible, indeed, is it to be thus left to the crushing power of unsanctified affliction. "The bellows are burned, the lead is consumed in the fire; reprobate silver shall men call them, because the Lord hath rejected them." Oh, reader, if the hand of God has been laid heavily upon you, if you are now smarting under the strokes of His rod, it becomes you, with an agony of earnestness, to cry unto

God without ceasing, not for a removal of the stroke, but for the grace which alone can make it a blessing, or prevent it from hardening for the heavier stroke of final wrath, when the last trumpet shall sound, and the mystery of God be finished.

LECTURE XXIII.

THE DIVINE AND GRACIOUS AGENCY, AND THE HUMAN INSTRUMENTALITY IT PROVIDES.

Rev., Chap. x.

"And I saw another mighty angel come down from heaven, clothed with a cloud; and a rainbow was upon his head, and His face was as it were the sun, and his feet as pillars of fire; and he had in his hand a little book open; and he set his right foot upon the sea, and his left foot on the earth, And cried with a loud voice, as when a lion roareth; and when he had cried, seven thunders uttered their voices. And when the seven thunders had uttered their voices, I was about to write; and I heard a voice from heaven saying unto me, Seal up those things which the seven thunders uttered, and write them not. And the angel which I saw stand upon the sea and upon the earth, lifted up his hand to heaven, and sware by him that liveth for ever and ever, who created heaven, and the things that therein are, and the earth, and the things that therein are, and the sea, and the things which are therein, that there should be time no longer; but in the days of the voice of the seventh angel, when he shall begin to sound, the mystery of God should be finished, as He hath declared to His servants the prophets. And the voice which I heard from heaven spake unto me again, and said, Go and take the little book which is open in the hand of the angel which standeth upon the sea and upon the earth. And I went unto the angel, and said unto him, Give me the little book. And he said unto me, Take it, and eat it up; and it shall make thy belly bitter, but it shall be in thy mouth sweet as honey. And I took the little book out of the angel's hand, and ate it up; and it was in my mouth sweet as honey; and as soon as I had eaten it my belly was bitter. And he said unto me, Thou must prophesy again before many peoples, and nations, and tongues, and kings."

THE whole course of the world's opposition to the cross and crown of Jesus has been portrayed. The entire succession of the judgments it invoked, and the woes it engendered, has also been unfolded, except, of course, the last, by which it is to be crushed out entirely. It has been shown how that worldliness which rejected the offered mercy of atonement,[1] had at first been smitten in the objects of earthly good;[2] that then, instead of turning to heavenly things, it had corrupted the church itself, had turned its saving truths into the doctrines of devils, and thus brought upon itself a horrid spiritual despotism;[3] and finally, how the torments of this had driven men to desperation, and caused the wisdom and power of the world to unite in its destruction, by movements involving wide-spread and ruinous calamities.[4] The descriptions apply equally to the individual and social development of these evils. Terribly thus had the world's hatred to the kingdom of God been made to scourge itself. The whole working and effects of the opposition, under the judgments which itself produced, was now complete. Its ripest fruit had been brought forth. It could do no more.

And what had it done? It had wrought no deliverance for itself. It had demonstrated its own folly and madness, its incurable depravity, even under the most sweeping judgments, and its utter helplessness. It groaned in its agony. It cursed God in its rage. It shed not a single tear of repentance, even when surrounded by the wreck which its folly and ungodliness had wrought. In the very midst of the desolations caused by its service of devils and idols, and its lusts of all kinds, it still clung to them.[5]

The necessity, therefore, of another and very different agency is demonstrated. That agency is now presented to the view of the seer. It is introduced, you will observe also, as the necessary preparation for the seventh angel's trumpet. Six angels had already sounded. Only one

---

[1] Chap. 8: 5.   [2] 8: 7–12.   [3] 9: 1–11.   [4] 9: 13–21.
[5] 9: 20, 21.

remained. That was to sound final woe, and the eternal triumph.[1] But was this triumph to be one of vengeance only on an impenitent world? This would not have been a triumph at all of the spiritual kingdom. This would have been no proper answer to those prayers of all saints, that had gone up in the incense of a Saviour's intercessions, and in answer to which the seven angels with their trumpets had gone forth from before the throne. Hence, before the seventh angel is permitted to sound, (11: 15), another and far different series of visions, different in their whole nature and tendency, is presented. These are designed to exhibit the true and real influences by which that triumph is to be secured; influences which had been all this time working quietly, yet powerfully, in the witnessing of a chosen few to the saving truth of the gospel of the kingdom. These visions, by which the positive and saving influences of the kingdom are brought to view, include every thing from the beginning of the tenth, to the fourteenth verse of the eleventh chapter.

Four prominent symbols give character to this whole passage, and decide its meaning: the mighty angel, his little book, his ordered measurement of holy things, and his two witnesses. The first two of these will occupy this lecture. In the exposition they must be taken together. Together they represent the divine agency in the church; and the use made of the little book shows the human instrumentality it employs.

I. THE DIVINE AGENCY.

This mighty angel, by the grandeur of his description, arrests every reader's attention. He is seen descending from heaven, clothed with a cloud, as it is promised Christ should come on His visible return to earth. "A rainbow was upon His head,"

§. The mighty angel.

[1] Chap. 11: 15.

the symbol of the covenant; " and his face was as it were the sun, and his feet as pillars of fire:" the same glorious appearance that distinguished the Son of Man as He appeared to John at first. Clothed thus with the symbols of the glory of a risen and ascended Redeemer, he must represent, not indeed His visible presence, but the real, glorious, and mighty agency of the great Messenger of the covenant, and Head of the church. Though in His human nature He is now only in heaven, yet He is there on the throne, and as a divine person, administering thence the affairs of the spiritual kingdom. There are ever descending from that throne those agencies of covenant light, and glory, and power, which manifest His real spiritual presence as fully as did the rainbow, that face like the sun, and the feet as pillars of fire manifest His glory and authority to John in vision. Working in and by these agencies, and by the almighty Spirit dwelling in the hearts of His people, and accompanying His word, He is ever present in the midst of His churches. This is no mere figurative presence, no presence by a substitute, but an actual personal presence, present in His divine person, which still retains its union with the human nature in heaven. " Lo, I am with you alway, even unto the end of the world," is the promise with which He accompanies the great commission, "Go ye into all the world, and preach the gospel to every creature."

But He is not always manifesting equally His presence and His power. He is represented as hiding His face. To the apprehensions even of His own people, He seems to have withdrawn himself. The world and the devil seem to have every thing their own way. The fearful and faint-hearted are ready to despair. The selfish and worldly among His professed servants, when injustice triumphs, and their prayers are rejected, renounce His service and their faith altogether. Hence the divinely recorded prayers of God's people take such forms as these: "Arise, O Lord, * * * lift up Thyself because of the rage of mine enemies." "Return, O Lord, deliver my soul." "Thou that dwellest between the cherubims, shine forth." "O God, to whom vengeance belongeth, show Thyself." The language of unbelieving hearts is: "The Lord hath forsaken the earth; the Lord seeth not." When, therefore, He delivers His people; when, either in His providence, or by His Spirit, He displays His presence and fulfils His promises, He is said to come down from heaven, to visit them, to break the silence which their prayers had long encountered. "He uttered His voice; the earth melted." "The Lord hath visited His people." Now the symbols of this passage are in perfect accordance with this common scriptural conception, by which He who is always with His people is represented as coming forth from time to time during their long struggle, to strengthen them, and check their foes by special displays of His power, in His providence and grace; and when these foes shall have reached their greatest triumph, and the malignity of sin most fully developed itself, and the inefficacy of all judgments to correct it been shown, to display the mighty power of His gospel to humble, convert, and save.

This is always the agency of His power. The gospel is "the wisdom and power of God unto salvation." Accordingly, the angel had in his hand a little book open, beautifully symbolizing this very gospel. The book is open; the truth is no longer shut up in types, or shut out from the nations, but fully revealed, and freely offered to all the world. It is "little," like the grain of mustard seed, a feeble agency to human vision. Holding it in his hand as the instrument of his power, he places "his right foot on the sea, and his left on the land," asserting thus his dominion over all, "and cried with a loud voice as when a lion roareth." Of the meaning of this, Scripture usage

§. *The gospel of His power.*

leaves us in no doubt. "The Lord shall roar out of Zion, and utter His voice from Jerusalem."[1] "Like as the lion, and the young lion roaring on his prey, when a multitude of shepherds is called forth against him, he will not be afraid of their voice, nor abase himself for the noise of them; so shall the Lord of Hosts come down to fight for Mount Zion."[2] This heavenly messenger comes, then, in the very character of the "Lion of the tribe of Judah." We are thus reminded of the power with which the gospel is armed. It spreads terror to the foes of Jesus, while it assures His people of a speedy and complete triumph. To the poor sinner, trembling under a sense of his guilt, and struggling with the burden of his corruptions, it is sweeter than the mother's voice of love; but to him who turns from His offered grace, it is the roar of a lion presaging a wrath of fearful import. "Consider this, ye that forget God, lest I tear you in pieces, and there be none to deliver." Let it never be forgotten that the gospel is not a mere voice of invitation, but of divine authority, and of resistless power, either for salvation or ruin. It is a savour of "death unto death," if not of "life unto life." "How shall we escape, if we neglect so great salvation?"

The very fact that there is nothing noted here but the voice itself, as a voice of majesty and power—no articulate utterances—only makes it symbolize more distinctly the power of that gospel which He brings to men and communicates to His church to proclaim to the world, and the nature of that power: this power of it in distinction from its matter. It is the voice of an almighty Saviour. It is the word of God. It "is quick and powerful, and sharper than any two-edged sword, piercing even to the dividing asunder of soul and spirit, and of the joints and marrow, and is a discerner of the thoughts and intents of the heart."[3] This is that sword of the Spirit which is to

[1] Joel 3: 16.   [2] Is. 31: 4.   [3] Heb. 4: 12.

slay the opposition to the kingdom. The gospel is the power of God unto salvation, because it is the word of Christ; not the dead, printed word of a dead and departed Christ; but the living word of a living and present Christ. And it always will be found, as it always has been found, that just as its announcements and claims are presented as the *voice* of the Son of God, in all their naked simplicity and authority, and not claiming assent because of the human philosophy and reasonings that too often presumptuously offer their proud support, will it prove mighty to the pulling down of strongholds.

But this does not yet fully represent the power of this gospel. Immediately responding to this voice of the mighty angel of the covenant, is another and more mysterious and awful voice still. "And when he cried, the seven thunders (the original is definite) uttered their voices." These "thunders," or "thunderings," as the same word is differently translated, are nowhere the symbols of human powers, but always set forth distinctively and emphatically the power of God. "The thunder of His power, who can understand?" "He thundereth with the voice of His excellency." "The voice of the Lord is upon the waters: the God of glory thundereth."[1] Thunder, thus, in Scripture language and conception, becomes the natural and unmistakable symbol of His displayed power. Hence, in the introductory picture of the spiritual kingdom, in the fourth chapter, these thunderings proceed from His throne. Their being *seven* indicate the perfection of that display of His power; there is no variety of its exercise which does not respond to the voice of the angel of the covenant. All the thunders of Omnipotence leap forth at the call of Judah's Lion. All the full powers of the eternal throne, all of which are pledged in the

§. The mystery of his power.

[1] Job. 26: 14.   37: 4.   Ps. 29; 3.

covenant of redeeming love, spring forth at once into their grandest and completest display, to give efficacy to the promises of that covenant when He calls for them. The word of the kingdom is attended by the powers of the throne. Hence Jesus said, "All power is given unto Me in heaven and on earth. Go ye, therefore, and teach all nations."

The utterance of these thunders was not a mere cry, but, as the words themselves imply,[1] it was an articulate utterance, a "speaking," which the apostle was about to write down, when a voice from heaven forbade him, saying, "Seal up those things which the seven thunders uttered, and write them not." He was commanded not to seal them up for a time, as Daniel was to seal up what he had written "till the time of the end," but not to write them at all, to seal them up entirely. They were matters not to be revealed at all to the church on earth. This precisely and forcibly describes the deep mystery that must for ever here shroud the working of the divine power, both in providence and grace. "Clouds and darkness are round about Him." "Thy way is in the sea, and Thy path in the great waters, and Thy footsteps are not known." "Verily Thou art a God that hidest Thyself, O God of Israel, the Saviour." It is, as this last passage intimates, in His character of Israel's God and Saviour, and the manner in which He accomplishes this salvation, that He hides Himself, often working out the blessed purposes of His mercy in ways so mysterious and incomprehensible, that He seems completely to conceal Himself and His mercy. So it was in the processes described under all the previous trumpets. That infinite power and love should have so permitted those powers of hell so long to have corrupted the church and tormented the world, and delayed for ages the accomplishment of the Redeemer's

[1] ελαλησεν.

glory and His church's triumph, seems to our shortsighted minds very inexplicable. While it is all important for the church ever to be deeply impressed with the assurance of the almightiness and all-sufficiency of the divine powers attending the gospel of the grace of God, and so to hear it with holy trembling as the word of His power, and to trust it with unhesitating confidence, as supported by all the agencies of the seen and unseen world, it is not possible nor needful for her to understand the articulate manner in which those mighty influences of His providence and Spirit work in and with the word, and upon the soul to secure the heart's submission, and the triumph of the kingdom. All this is a mystery we are incapable of understanding, and which we do not need to understand, even for our present comfort. Especially is this true in regard to the deepest mystery of the working of God's mighty power, that involved in the saving of a soul, its new-creation, and translation from the kingdom of darkness into the kingdom of God. It has never been written how the divine power works on the human will, and, in perfect accordance with its essentially free nature, sweetly leads it to bow in joyous submission to the grace of God, changing the very lion into a lamb, and enmity into love; how God "works in us to will and to do of His good pleasure." The blessed fact is revealed, and that is enough; enough to fill us with the most joyful confidence in working out our own salvation, and in working for the salvation of others, and for a world's deliverance. It would have been well for the church had she always remembered this, and not enfeebled her testimony by foolish speculations, efforts to be wise above what is written; had she remembered that this especially, the operation of new creating grace in the human soul, is one of the things sealed up and unwritten. For it is the mightiest display of that power of God which accompanies the gospel, of that power that answers from the throne to the voice of our redeeming Saviour, and as inscrutable as it is mighty. "The wind bloweth where it listeth, and thou hearest the sound thereof, but canst not tell whence it cometh, and whither it goeth; so is every one that is born of the Spirit." But we do know that "the preaching of the cross is unto us which are saved the power of God;" that it is "in demonstration of the Spirit and of power," "mighty through God;" and that its triumphs display a power as much beyond all human agency as the voice of the seven thunders is beyond the feeble utterances of man.

Having thus exhibited, in these expressive and comprehensive symbols, the divine agency by which the kingdom was to triumph, so totally different from the destructive agencies hitherto called forth by these trumpets, consisting in an open gospel in the hand of its almighty Author, whose own living and awful voice challenges the world's attention, and, accompanied by the mightiest demonstrations of divine power, the grand announcement is now made, with a sublimity of manner worthy of it, that there shall be delay no longer, that no more judgments are intervening, that the long suffering of God has waited long enough to develope the full enormity of human depravity; and it only remains for this word of life and salvation to be proclaimed in new power, and glory, and efficiency, in order to introduce the notes of triumph which the seventh angel's trumpet shall ring through the nations. The mighty angel of the covenant, standing upon the sea and the land, and claiming it all as His own inheritance, of which He is now about to take possession, "lifts up His hand to heaven, and swears by Him that liveth for ever and ever, who created heaven, and the things that therein are, and the earth, and the things that therein are, and the sea, and things that are therein, that there should be time no longer:" no more delay, as the words must mean; "but in

§. No more delay.

the days of the voice of the seventh angel, when he shall begin to sound, the mystery of God should be finished, as He hath spoken unto His servants the prophets."

That mystery was, of course, the unaccomplished plan of God's administration here on earth; its finishing was the fulfilment of the promise, "I will give Thee the nations for Thine inheritance, and the uttermost parts of the earth for Thy possession," the destruction of the last enemy, and the accomplishment of the anticipated joys, and triumph of a waiting and praying church. "We shall reign on the earth."

II. The Human Instrumentality.

In setting forth the gospel of a present Saviour, attended with almighty power, as the divine agency by which the kingdom was to be advanced, and to triumph, nothing had been said or exhibited in the symbols to show the human instrumentality to be employed. Important as it is to be ever deeply impressed with the fact, that all the power is of God, it is equally important to have a like deep impression of the fact, that this power works through a feeble human instrumentality. "We have this treasure in earthen vessels, that the excellency of the power may be of God, and not of us."

The little book in the hand of the angel of the covenant must be taken and eaten, received and incorporated into the very life of the church, and in that life give forth the testimony by which the power of God works. A voice from heaven, the same that before directed the apostle to leave unwritten the words of the seven thunders, the secret manner in which the power of God works with the word of Christ, now directs him, on the other hand, to the past, which he and the church he represented were required to take. That in this case the apostle himself becomes a symbol, a representative of something else, seems evident. He no longer gazes on the vision; he becomes a part of the scene passing before him; he takes himself a place among those forms of the Spirit's creation, these mere symbols of spiritual realities, and receives the symbol of the gospel, and, in doing so, must represent all those who do receive and appropriate it. Beautifully and strikingly, therefore, does this set forth the truth, that the church of God, to whom this revelation comes, is called upon, not merely to gaze upon the visions of glory presented, and to rejoice in the mighty power of a present, though unseen Saviour, and of His gospel now fully revealed, and in the hope of a speedy deliverance; but she must herself come forward, and present herself as the instrument of that power, as the necessary channel through which the blessed truths symbolized by the little book were to become the life of the world.

While, therefore, there were secret things with which he had nothing to do, except to tell the church there were such things which belonged to God alone; and while there were many other things he was to see, and hear, and record for the church, here was something he was to *do* for the church, in her name, and thus to show her what she must do, what she must be doing, even when seeing and hearing these things of the kingdom; yea, more, that the very design of her Lord in showing to her these things, these purposes of His mercy, was that she might take her place in their accomplishment. He was to take this book, not that he might read it, not that he might write down its contents here—that was not necessary— they were already sounded abroad over the earth; but that he might eat it. Such is the charge which he receives from the angel who gives the book; and in obeying it, he finds this book, as he was told he would, sweet at first, but afterwards producing much bitterness, great internal anguish. The further design of this is expressly stated in the next verse, by the charge which the same angel immediately gives him. "Thou must prophesy again before many peoples, and nations, and tongues, and kings."

If the previous account of this little book should have left a doubt upon the mind of any as to its meaning, these last verses surely must dispel it. This book, like that given to the prophet Ezekiel[1] in the same symbolical way, and with the same directions, contained the subject matter of his and the church's testimony or prophecy. It can be nothing else than that truth to which the true church is to bear witness in all ages, and among all nations; those precious facts and doctrines that cluster around the sufferings and kingdom of our glorified Redeemer. These, as received by faith, fill the soul with joy; they are sweeter than honey and the honey comb, precious beyond all comparison or conception. But in working them out in the life, in the midst of an ungodly world, in the earnest spiritual appropriation of them in our daily experience in the various relations of life, and in making the whole life a consistent testimony to them, many bitter experiences are to be passed through; trials, sufferings, persecutions, and often death itself to be endured. It has been so every where, and in all ages, though not in the same degree. It is involved in the whole nature of that personal, spiritual conflict through which every soul must pass into the kingdom, and by which it bears its testimony to the power of that gospel.

There is a bitterness of spiritual sorrow resulting from inwardly digesting the truths of the gospel, and bringing them thus into close contact with the secret maladies of the soul, that might very well be described by this bitterness produced by eating the little book. It is an invariable part of Christian experience. The secret and deep corruptions of the soul are never eradicated without many a secret pang, which wrings from it the cry, "O wretched man that I am, who shall deliver me from the body of

[1] Ezek. 3 : 1–3. See also Jer. 15, 16.

this death." All this, indeed, is necessary, in order that the life of the believer may be a clear testimony to the truth, and the church may shine as the light of the world, with the power of true holiness. But it seems more directly here to relate to the sufferings incurred in bearing this testimony before the world, in incorporating it into the visible life, though, really, the two are inseparable. It accordingly prepares the way for the representation, in the next chapter, of that testimony as it is actually borne by the church, as the prophesying of the two witnesses clothed in sackcloth.

"Thou must prophesy again." This "again," intimates that at that time this testimony had already been widely delivered, but that it was still to be repeated. The church had, even during the first century, carried the gospel to all portions of the civilized world. The apostles, and their immediate helpers, had caught the spirit of their Lord's commission, " Go ye into all the world." No difficulties, or dangers, or opposition, arrested their progress. They went forward in the strength of their glorified King, and conquered in His name. It might seem to some that this work was almost done. The story of the cross was every where made known. But no. The work must continue. Again must the word be borne by the church every where. Again, too, with the zeal, and energy, and devotion of primitive and apostolic times. From this work she must never rest. If weariness, or opposition, or want of success, tend to make her slacken her efforts, she must still hear the voice of her Lord calling, " Again," and so on from day to day, and age to age, repeat her story of love, and call the nations to bow at Jesus' feet. It is her one great mission, her never ceasing work; no matter how often repeated, still "Thou must prophesy again," until the mystery of God be finished, and the last peal of the seventh angel's trumpet announce her labours ended, and her glory complete.

Let us, in conclusion, get from this subject a deeper impression of what this prophesying, or witnessing of the church, is. It is very much more than a mere publishing the glad tidings from the pulpit and the press; very much more than the printing and distribution of Bibles, and sending forth missionaries, and defending the truth against the assaults of infidel learning, or corrupting heresy. All this is well, is indispensable. The testimony which is attended with the power of God, is one that sets forth the truth in its living power on the life, in cleansed lepers, and palsied souls made strong, and dead souls restored to life. It is such a testimony as none, therefore, can utter but such as have felt the power of Christ's death and resurrection, and tasted the infinite sweetness of pardoning mercy, and sanctifying grace, and adopting love. This alone can enable you to take part in this work of the church. You must go to Jesus, and take from Himself the words of eternal life, and feed upon them till their power invigorates your whole spiritual being, and till you are ready to bear the cross, and utterly renounce the world for Him, and shrink from no labour or suffering, to extend to others that are perishing the means of life and salvation.

This work of witnessing, as we have remarked already, involves suffering. It is an utter impossibility to be faithful, and not incur the world's displeasure and contempt, and often worse than this. How continually this thought is brought out in these revelations of God's will. If the world now does not imprison, or banish, or burn, for the testimony of Jesus—though this it still does in some places—it is only because it has put on new forms in these ages and these Protestant countries; and forms, too, which often render it a very difficult and bitter thing to hold fast our testimony in all its fulness and purity. Are you, then, ready to suffer? If we suffer, we shall also reign with Him; if we deny Him, He also will deny us. Have you tasted the sweetness of this gospel, and do you daily also experience something of the bitterness? If we know not the sweetness of this little book, we know nothing of the joys of pardoned sin, and heavenly hope, and communion with God; and if we know nothing of the bitterness it afterwards caused the apostle, it is because we have been unfaithful to our testimony, and denied our Lord by base and wicked conformity to the world.

LECTURE XXIV.

THE TRUE CHURCH, AND THE SUBJECTS OF HER TESTIMONY DEFINED.

Rev., Chap. xi., 1, 2.

"And there was given me a reed like unto a rod; [and the angel stood][1] saying, Rise, and measure the temple of God, and the altar, and them that worship therein. But the court which is without the temple leave out, and measure it not; for it is given unto the Gentiles; and the holy city shall they tread under foot forty and two months."

WE have seen the divine agency by which the triumphs of the spiritual kingdom are secured. We have seen, also, the human instrumentality through which it works. The word of a present and reigning Saviour, accompanied by the power of His Spirit and providence, is the first. The latter is that word received into a believing heart, and incorporated into the spiritual life, and expressing itself as a divine testimony in works of holy living and patient suffering, in confirmation of an unswerving confession of God's truth. "Thou must prophesy again before many peoples, and nations, and tongues, and kings."

But the inquiries at once arise, How is such an instrumentality to be secured? and, How is this prophetic work to be exercised, in the midst of an opposing world? Such inquiries must have forced themselves even on the apostle's mind, while the gospel was yet in its first fresh-

---

[1] These words are left out in all the later critical editions of the Greek Testament. The sense, however, is not thereby altered, as both the connection, and the words of verse 3, show that these are the words of the same mighty angel who had just been speaking.

ness, and while yet the powers of the invisible world, that at first attested its divinity, were still encircling it with their glory. How could it be otherwise, when he looked at the condition of the seven churches of Asia, to whom he had just before received such messages of solemn warning. Already, in most of them, had their testimony been impaired by foul errors in doctrine and practice; and in some the corruption was triumphant, leaving but a name that they lived, while they were dead, or so offensive to their Lord as to be almost rejected with loathing. And even the best of them were assaulted by the same foes, and called to contend for truth and purity at the peril of life. How was it possible for the church, in such a condition of things, to perform her prophetic office? And, if possible, how was it to be done? How was she to receive, digest, incorporate, and propagate the truths of that little book, so that they should win the victory? And how should her testimony be distinguished from that of false witnesses, with which, as with locust hordes, the world was to be filled?

That such an instrumentality should be preserved and perpetuated, would indeed be naturally inferred from the divine agency engaged. Such almighty power would always secure a willing people to receive the truth from its Author into glad hearts, and faithfully to hold it forth at every cost. But how? This, too, has been partially answered. The instrumentality is prepared by the word of the gospel being received into the heart, and wrought into the life of God's people; the little book *received* and *eaten*. Thus prepared, it is to hold forth this truth as a divine testimony. "Thou must again PROPHESY," is the last charge of the Angel of the covenant to His church. In the verses before us the rule and the subjects of this testimony are forcibly and graphically presented as a rod to measure with, and sacred things to be measured, while unmeasured things are to be rejected. The consideration of these symbols will help to impress upon our hearts much precious truth.

Consider, first, the act of measuring. This, as well as the result, is evidently symbolical. The prophet is, as we have seen, not a mere spectator of the vision he is recording, but himself becomes a part of it, as the representative of the church. The prominent and leading part he is required to take in this scene, by the rod given to him, and the call made upon him, must be designed to represent the duty of the church. Having received and appropriated the little book, and as the result of that, being commissioned to prophesy on behalf of the nations, he is now shown how this commission is to be fulfilled. A measuring rod is given to him, and he receives directions how to use it, and to what subjects to apply it. "Rise and measure the temple of God, and the altar, and them that worship therein." The prophetic function of the church is here presented as the application of a divinely furnished rule to certain specified sacred objects.

§. 1. The act and standard of measurement.

This measuring of sacred things well describes the first great duty of the church in regard to her testimony. She must first of all ascertain with precision the truth in regard to the things of God. She can only bear witness to what she knows, and in proportion to the certainty and the clearness of her knowledge. She must know, in regard to these sacred objects, their whole shape, and limits, and relations, else she can never deliver any clear and sure testimony concerning them. One great reason of the wavering and variable testimony of the churches, is the want of a definite and clear perception of the truth itself. Multitudes of the people of God have never measured these great objects of God's revelation; all their views concerning them are dim and hazy. They see them, indeed, as objects of acknowledged glory and value, but they see them from afar; like some lazy Israelite, who would have been satisfied with a distant view of the glories of the temple, its outer courts, its altar, and laver, and sacred shrine, with the smoke of the offerings, and the incense, and the crowd of worshippers, all mingled in one confused view, as a splendid but indistinct whole, instead of entering in, and closely examining each object, marking its distinct character, and place, and use. Worse than this, indeed; many are more like some Reubenite, who, staying at his home amid the luxuriant pastures and cities of Bashan, had been content with what knowledge he could get of the holy city, and the wonders of the temple and its services, from the reports of others who had seen it with their own eyes. "Rise and measure," is the command. Rest not in any dim and indistinct views of the great things of God's salvation. Rest not in the mere reports of others. If ever there were objects which it behooved each one to search, and see, and examine with the intensest solicitude, to know them fully, to leave no uncertainty hanging over any part of them, they are these, in which God reveals Himself and salvation. You can never be certain of these things, so as to find comfort to your own soul in them, or bear a testimony concerning them of any worth to other suffering and perishing souls, but by a personal, a heart acquaintance with them. No measurement of these great things can give any certainty, which does not ascertain your own share in them, producing the full assurance of faith. "Rise," then, "and measure." Be not satisfied with the general certainty that the gospel is true, that there is salvation for sinners in Christ; but rest not until you find all obscurity resting on its terms, and claims, and promises entirely dispelled, and see the broad and strong foundations laid in the everlasting covenant for man's faith and hope to rest upon. Rest not in any thing short of such a certainty as will enable you to say, "I know whom I have believed;" such as will enable you to rejoice with joy unspeakable and full of glory. This will give to your testimony a power that shall be far more resistless than logical demonstrations. This will make even the gainsayer feel the realities, and claims, and forces of the invisible kingdom as nothing else can. When such is the prevailing testimony of the church, when, in the full confidence and rejoicing of hope, produced by an actual, personal measurement of these divine things, the habitual language of her people is, "Come, and hear, all ye that fear God, and I will tell you what He hath done for my soul;" "I am my Beloved's, and He is mine;" then, and only then, is she fulfilling completely her great mission as a witness for God. "Restore unto me the joy of Thy salvation, and uphold me with Thy free spirit. Then will I teach transgressors Thy ways; and sinners shall be converted unto Thee."

But in no measurements can any diligence and earnestness secure correct results, unless the rule or standard be correct. In things affecting our relations to God, this is of infinite importance. Hence the seer is not left to measure by a standard of his own selection. The rule is divinely furnished before the command is given to measure. "*There was given to me a reed* like unto a rod." So the church can say, "We have a more sure word of prophecy."

§. The divine rule.

Christ has not left His church to a standard of her own devising. Divine things cannot be measured by a human standard. Here human opinions avail nothing; human reasonings, and supposed natural intuitions, decide nothing. It is not for the culprit at the bar to decide upon the law by which he is to be judged, or, if found guilty, upon the conditions of his pardon, or even whether pardon be at all possible. Man is the guilty culprit, his whole nature is depraved; can his reason and intuitions, so called, be trusted to tell him what his God requires, and whether He will pardon, and, if He will, how? That men, calling themselves philosophers, should have been found to teach, and others to believe, that a creature, the whole working of whose moral nature shows itself to be deeply depraved, could find in that nature itself a rule for his faith and practice, is one of the many proofs that men professing themselves to be wise become fools. But while man cannot make a rule of truth, nor find one by diving down into the depths of his own consciousness, he can receive and apply one. His Creator can give him such a rule; God can speak to His creatures in words and tones that will attest their own divinity, and he can look up, and hear, and receive.

That standard has been given. It is the written word. "All Scripture is given by inspiration of God, and is profitable for doctrine, for reproof, for correction, for instruction in righteousness, that the man of God may be perfect, thoroughly furnished unto all good works." "God, who at sundry times, and in divers manners, spake in time past unto the fathers, by the prophets, hath in these last days spoken unto us by His Son." These words He has caused to be committed to writing, that thus they might become a definite, fixed, and unchangeable rule for His church in all ages. In this form it is like the measuring rod of the angel, incapable of being stretched, or contracted. Unwritten traditions, on the other hand, could never have been a rule, because subject to endless variations themselves, by reason of the endlessly varying capacities and infirmities of those through whose minds they must pass. To preserve them pure would have required a constant inspiration, and constant miracles to prove it; in other words, it would not have been giving any rule at all to the church, for her to use in testing truth and duty; but keeping her always under the direct guidance of a divine inspiration in every age, like that of the apostolic age.

The BOOK, the BOOK, is the glory and safeguard of the church, the inestimably precious ascension gift of her Lord, without which she would be left like a vessel on a dark and stormy ocean without chart or compass. A cunning and hypocritical infidelity has affected to despise what it calls the *book worship* of the church, and, under pretence of a higher spiritualism, would call us away to some better revelations of the divine will, in the deep intuitions of the soul, the workings of a pure reason, or the direct operations of the unseen spirit upon each heart, without any other interpreter or judge than the heart itself: a standard about as definite as the dim ghosts of Ossian, or the shadowy forms of the heathen Elysium, and as variable as the clouds of heaven. There is no indefiniteness here. This book of God utters no ambiguous responses. It may be perverted by human ingenuity and depravity, as the words of Jesus were when He was on earth; as every thing good is; a thousand falsehoods may pretend to shelter under its authority; but to every sincere inquirer it gives one sure and clear response. When received as the word of God, it is of perfectly easy application. All real difficulties, and apparent diversities, arise from carrying to it a previous standard of our own, and a desire and effort to bribe or force it to speak according to our wishes. It makes even the simple wise.

It is, moreover, the standard which will be applied to all human hearts, and opinions, and actions, at the last day, and by which the eternal state of each will be decided. "The word that I have spoken," says Christ, "shall judge him at the last day." "In the day when God shall judge the secrets of men according to my gospel," says Paul.[1] By it, then, must we now ascertain what is truth in regard to all things pertaining to the kingdom of God, and our relations and duties to Him.

---

[1] John 12: 48. Rom. 2: 16.

But that it may be such a rule, we must hold fast to the doctrine of its perfect, plenary, verbal inspiration. This is the very anchor of the church's safety. Take away this doctrine, and we drift with the varying currents and conflicting winds of human opinion, without help or hope. Take away this, and the Bible ceases to be any rule at all; the fixed rod becomes an elastic line, that can be stretched over all irregularities, be made to embrace any additions, and to leave out any difficulties, according as the vanity, pride, and corrupt lust of man may desire.

It is not only because these thoughts are the thoughts of God, but because these words are the words of God, because the Holy Spirit so directed the sacred writers as to secure their choice of such words and expressions as would correctly convey His mind, that it becomes a perfect rule. "Holy men of God spake as they were moved by the Holy Ghost."

As, therefore, the seer with the commission of prophecy received the reed to measure those things which were to be the subject of this testimony, so the church, with her commission, has received the Bible as the rule defining the substance, the extent, and the manner of her testimony. With this, she can draw the line definitely and distinctly between what God receives and rejects, between salvation and damnation. With this she can go to all nations, and set up the kingdom of God, and speak with divine authority and power. "The Lord God hath spoken; who can but prophesy?"

Let every believer, then, lay up this rule in the secret places of the soul, keeping it pure from the perversions of a proud philosophy, or of worldly wisdom. It bears upon it the unmistakable marks of its heavenly origin. It has been tested by ages, and, by its touch, has detected and exposed the thousand deceptions of error, and pointed out the only sure foundations for human hope. Let it be to us what the Urim and Thummim was to the priests of old. Let us neither add to or diminish its record; but take it just as it is, and all of it. "Add thou not unto His words, lest He reprove thee, and thou be found a liar." Let no part of it be neglected as useless; "every word of God is pure." Away with all human opinions or reasonings, scientific demonstrations, as grounds for faith, or tests of truth in regard to spiritual objects, or standards of the church's testimony before the world. "To the law and to the testimony; if they speak not according to this word, it is because there is no light in them."

These are three, "the temple of God, the altar, and them that worship therein." In the spiritual kingdom there are three things answering precisely to these: God reconciled and dwelling among men, the blood of atonement by which this is secured, and a consecrated people offering spiritual sacrifices. The very same are distinctly mentioned by Jehovah in summing up the whole typical ordinances which He had appointed for Israel of old to set forth the nature of His spiritual kingdom. "I will sanctify the tabernacle of the congregation and the altar; I will sanctify also both Aaron and his sons, to minister to Me in the priest's office. And I will dwell among the children of Israel, and will be their God."[1] The symbolical antitype thus corresponds exactly to the ancient type, whose tabernacle, altar, and Aaronic priesthood, pointed to precisely the same great spiritual objects here symbolized by the temple, the altar, and the true worshippers, who together constitute God's spiritual priesthood. The great spiritual truth designed to be taught in those ancient types is precisely the same as that which the gospel proclaims and the spiritual church secures, the restoration of holy fellowship between God and man. Paul quotes the very language of that passage in stating to the

§. 2. The objects to be measured.

[1] Ex. 29: 44, 45.

gospel church the great sum of its privileges: "I will dwell in them, and walk in them, and I will be their God, and they shall be My people."[1]

§. 1. The temple.

"The temple" here is not the whole sacred enclosure, including the several courts that surrounded the central fane, and to which, in English, the name "temple" is also applied, but which in the original is expressed by an entirely different word. It here means the central building, the house composed of the holy place, and the most holy, where originally was the ark of the covenant, and the manifested glory of God. Both in the ancient type, and as a symbol here, it first of all clearly sets forth, as the spiritual reality corresponding to it, the person of Christ as Mediator, God manifest in the flesh, dwelling in human nature and among men, and restoring to man the means of access to God, and of fellowship with him. But not Christ, the God-man alone, but as the Head of a redeemed people, in covenant and in living union with Him. The *Christ*, the *Mediator*, the *Redeemer*, never stands alone; is not known, does not exist, apart from His redeemed people, whose place He took in the covenant of redemption, and in taking which He *became* the Christ, the Redeemer. Regarded solely as the eternal Son, the second person in the divine trinity, He is, and must be, conceived of as apart from, and existing independently of, His people; but as *the Christ*, He never has existed, and never can exist, without them, any more than we can conceive of the head as existing without the body, or the vine without any branches. The last analogy, used by our Saviour Himself, beautifully presents this fact, "I am the vine, ye are the branches." But are not the branches a part of the vine, and a part necessary to its perfection? Is it a perfect vine, is it any more than a naked trunk of one, without its branches, and their foli-

[1] 2 Cor. 6 : 16.

age, and fruit in their season? So, also, the church is called His body, the *fulness* of Him that filleth all in all.

Such is the scriptural idea of the temple of God, the mystical body of Christ, His redeemed, not as so many separate souls merely, each saved by some special exercise of His love and power, but as so chosen of God, and so saved by a living union with Him, as to form one organic whole, one body pervaded in all its members by His Spirit and life, one glorious building filled with the all-pervading presence and power of God, and every stone of which is formed according to the same divine pattern, polished into the same beauty of holiness, and reflecting His own glorious image. "To whom coming," says Peter, " as unto a living stone disallowed, indeed, of men, but chosen of God, and precious, ye also, as lively stones, are built up a spiritual house."[1] "In whom," says Paul, "ye also are builded together for a habitation of God through the Spirit."[2] " The temple of God is holy, which temple ye are."[3]

This idea of the unity of the church in Christ, its head and life, runs through the whole Bible, so that often, especially in the Psalms and in the prophecies of Isaiah, it is not easy to tell which, if indeed either, was principally intended, Christ or His people, the Spirit's language applying equally to both. Here again, too, the nature of that unity is presented. It is not a mere external thing; it cannot be, because the thing itself is not external; and it is idle to talk of a visible unity of an invisible thing—invisible in the materials that compose it—redeemed and regenerated souls; invisible in the bond which unites them together, the Spirit of Christ working in them faith upon Him; and invisible in their living Head Himself. Any other unity, as a mark of the true church or body of Christ, must be a mere figment, except, of course, the

---

[1] 1 Pet. 2: 4, 5.   [2] Eph. 2: 22.   [3] 1 Cor. 3: 17.

mutual love that binds to each other those who have the same Spirit, and unites them in faith and action in proportion to their measure of that Spirit, and to the sphere of service assigned to them. Above all, is any unity of visible organization, under one visible head, an impossibility; and the mere attempt to make this a test of the true church of God has been the source of untold disasters to the cause of truth and human happiness; it has, indeed, been one of the very things which have so often caused the obscuration and suppression of the testimony of God's witnesses.

Surely, then, the meaning of this symbol is evident. We have endeavoured to use the rod of the angel in so far measuring this spiritual temple as to make clear its character and limits. It is the true church of Christ, where God dwells in humanity, where He manifests His gracious presence and redeeming power; and it at once describes its divine and spiritual nature, and its true and blessed unity. It is God in Christ, and Christ in His redeemed, and they all one in Him.

This temple includes, of course, all those ordinances whereby God makes Himself known to His people, and in which He holds communion with them, as the ancient temple did their types. These are not specially designated here, because included in the temple itself, and secured and pointed out certainly where *it* is measured. But we must bear them in mind as an essential part of the idea, even as the ark, the golden altar, the candlesticks, and the shew bread were essential to the temple. The actual manifestation of God to His people, the indwelling of His Spirit, and His communion with them from off the mercy seat, in the forgiveness of their sins, the hearing of their prayers, the acceptance of their services, and filling them with light, are all here in Christ, and they are in Him only. In Christ the Immanuel, God with us, and in and through

§ The contents of the temple—in Christ.

no other, can we find God, or approach Him, or hear His pardoning voice, or offer an accepted prayer, or work of righteousness. "I am the way, the truth, and the life; no man cometh unto the Father but by Me."

Not only the whole form and dimensions, and even the materials of that ancient temple of God, were of His appointment, but also every article in it, and every form of service rendered there. The audacious priest that presumed to add to or alter the exact orderings of the God of the temple incurred His severest displeasure, and some were struck down at once by the fire of His wrath. No more may any mortal power now dare to prescribe any other conditions or means of access to God, and of communion with Him, than precisely those He has prescribed. The temple is God's. It is His house. In a man's house, for a stranger, or even a child, to assume authority, is an act of contempt toward its head. To prescribe the manner of God's worship in His house, the kind of prayers, and praises, and other service by which in it He is to be honoured, is to assume His prerogative. It is the prominent characteristic of the great apostacy, of that man of sin that was to be revealed, that "he as God sitteth in the temple of God, showing himself that he is God:" a blasphemous claim that has often been made in this very way, by assuming to legislate in the worship of God.

§. All human ordering excluded thence.

It is thus the temple is to be measured; every thing in and about His church must be regulated according to the same divine measure, the angel's rod, the word of inspiration. As God said to Moses in reference to the tabernacle, so now He says to all engaged in the work of this spiritual temple: "See thou make all things according to the pattern showed to thee in the mount." And, therefore, in ascertaining the true temple of God, the spiritual church, this same measure must be carefully applied.

§. 2. The altar.

The altar is the second thing to be measured. This, as the place of the divinely appointed sacrifices, together with these sacrifices themselves, was, as every Bible reader knows, the type of the grand central truth of the atonement of Christ. It becomes here, therefore, its appropriate symbol. As the altar was the first object in the sacred enclosure, as every other object, and every service in the whole of that typical picture of the work of salvation, had its particular place, and value, and very being there, by means of its relation to that, so in the great spiritual realities represented, the atonement of Christ—reconciliation by His blood alone—embodies the one grand truth around which all others cluster, and from which all others derive their place and importance, and which gives to a redeemed church its very existence. No other blood can procure pardon and peace for sinners. It is all-sufficient. "By one offering He hath perfected for ever them that are sanctified." It is "by His own blood that He," as our great High Priest, "has entered into the holy place, having obtained eternal redemption for us." Nothing but this, therefore, can "purge your consciences from dead works to serve the living God." To hope for pardon and acceptance by any other means or merits, to doubt the perfect sufficiency of this, to be adding to it any works of penances, prayers, or tears of our own, or of others, as the ground of the divine favour, is to undervalue its infinite worth, to insult a crucified Saviour, and to treat the whole work of redeeming mercy with dishonour. It is as if the priest of old had offered swine's flesh upon the altar, to compensate any defect in the sacrifice of God's appointment.

Such being the place held by this doctrine of the altar, how important that it be carefully measured, and ascertained by the divine rule. Thus, too, we see how fully that rule does define this ground of a sinner's pardon, the conditions of his approach to God, and union with Him in this spiritual temple. Nothing may be added, nothing taken away from the one sacrifice. Nothing but Christ's cross, and nothing less than all of it. All of Christ, and nothing but Christ. "I am the way." "None other name under heaven." The terms are divinely measured.

The only other object to which the seer is directed to apply the angel's measuring rod, is the worshippers, "*them that worship therein.*" To measure these, is to ascertain by the rule given who are God's true worshippers, and so to define clearly in what the character of a true worshipper consists. It is only those who worship in the sacred enclosure that are to be measured; outside worship is worthless. The temple proper, the sacred shrine, always carried with it the open space immediately around it, consecrated with it, where the altar stood, and where the priests performed most of their services. It was inseparable from it; and with it was separated from the courts around it. Only those, therefore, who worship in this sacred enclosure, at its altar, and in its holy place; that is, those who perform priestly service to Him, does He acknowledge as His. They are such as lay their hands on the head of the sacrifice, confessing over it their sins; such as are washed in the laver of regeneration; such as are sprinkled by the blood, and press in even to the holy places of secret communion with God, at the altar of incense and the mercy seat. They are consecrated ones, whose only service is to the Lord, whose only reliance is on the blood of atonement, and whose chief joy is in proclaiming the honour and authority of Christ as their king. The manifestation of this consecration is their worship. They thus have fellowship with Christ as their great High Priest in His holiness and nearness to the Father, and His union with Him, and as their King in His royal honours, and are therefore called a royal priesthood.

These accepted worshippers, then, are precisely those

§. 3. The worshippers.

who in real life answer to the pattern of the worship of the spiritual kingdom already laid down in the worship of the twenty-four elders, and the living creatures. That was, as we there saw, the result of adoring views of God's holiness, produced by a divine life in the soul, and consisting in making the will of God their rule, His grace their hope, and His glory their end. So here these worshippers begin with the altar of atonement, which stands at the very entrance, and by its blood they find a peaceful entrance into, and bow in joyful submission before, the mercy seat, the throne of a covenant God, which displays its glory in the extreme recesses of this spiritual temple, and beyond which mortal cannot go. Dependence on the cross of Jesus, and submission to His crown, is only another form of stating the character of these true worshippers. Such are the only worshippers that meet the requirements of this divine measurement, for they alone worship after the divine pattern; they only show the likeness of the four and twenty elders, or feel the power of a divine life; they only fall before the throne, and casting there their crowns, cry out, "Thou only art worthy."

In these measured objects, then, we have another picture of God's true church, so simply and clearly drawn as to fully distinguish it from all the corruptions that press upon it, that mingle in it, and that pollute its external ordinances, obscuring its glory, and defacing its beauty. To do this is the manifest special design of this vision of measuring. The very direction to measure these things implies that they would become so closely connected with the world, that the line of separation would be no longer distinctly visible, and there would be great difficulty in distinguishing the true from the false; so much so, indeed, that it could be done only by the careful application of a divinely furnished rule. But this vision, simple and brief as it is, makes this distinction perfectly definite, and gives us, in a word, all needful direction to enable every inquirer to ascertain it with certainty. By three simple, and perfectly defined objects, the true church is drawn out into bold relief and distinctness from the world and all spurious imitations; and its limits laid down so precisely, as to leave no uncertain or neutral space between, no border ground where corruptions and foul heresies may lurk in security. The temple of God, the altar, and the worshippers therein, one body of Christ; one habitation of God in Christ by His Spirit; one ground of acceptance, the blood of atonement; one spiritual worship of adoring trust and submission. How perfectly distinct its features! How easily recognized! How completely separate from, and contrary to, the world! How heavenly and holy in its nature, its origin, its character, its privileges, and its joys! How unlike many of the outward things and organizations that call themselves by its sacred name, that cry so loudly, "The temple of God, the temple of God are we." Even the churches we most boast of, and regard as nearest the pattern, how faintly do they correspond to the consecrated priesthood, and altar, and temple of this vision of the seer!

In thus clearly defining the limits of that which is distinctly God's own, the subjects of the church's testimony, and the rule by which alone she must regulate it, are briefly, but yet clearly laid down. The whole *matter* of her prophesying must be in regard to these three things; the *rule* of it must be the word of God only. She has no commission to teach concerning any thing but these; these she must carefully measure, that she may testify correctly concerning their nature and limits; and, therefore, concerning these, she has no authority to teach anything but what the word of inspiration directs. The law that governed the inspired apostle must be the law of the church, of her people, and her ministry: "For I determined not

§. The subjects of the church's testimony.

to know any thing among you SAVE JESUS CHRIST, AND HIM CRUCIFIED. * * * And my speech and my preaching was not with enticing words of man's wisdom, but in DEMONSTRATION OF THE SPIRIT AND OF POWER."

There is a still further significance in this measuring, which will appear more fully in considering the other part of this vision.

LECTURE XXV.

THE POWER OF THE WORLD IN THE VISIBLE CHURCH.

Rev., Chap. xi. : 2.

"But the court which is without the temple leave out, and measure it not; for it is given unto the Gentiles; and the holy city shall they tread under foot forty and two months."

WE have considered this symbol of *measuring* in its simplest and most natural signification, that of ascertaining carefully, by a divine rule, the precise shape and limits of the objects designated, that is, of the true and real church of God. The application of this measure to them alone evidently implies that they alone were acknowledged as God's, and within the limits of consecration to Him, and of His covenant care and protection. It was designed to mark them as His, appropriated and set apart to His service; not only that thus the testimony of the church to them, to the facts and truths of which she was to be the living representative, might be clear and definite, but that it might be clearly understood what, and what only, had a claim on the divine protection, and would infallibly enjoy it amidst all perils. This whole significance of this vision of measuring can only be seen when the remaining portion of it is considered, the unmeasured things which were to be rejected.

Connected with the sacred shrine of the temple proper, there were outer courts, which were necessary to it, through which it was to be approached, and by which it was, to a certain degree, separated visibly from the

§. 1. The externals of the church given over to the world.

unenclosed and common ground, and dwellings around it. These courts of right were for the service and protection of the temple proper, for the better accommodation of the worshippers, and where all the people might assemble to receive instruction in the mysteries of God. To them the Gentiles were admitted, not to rule, but to learn. The relation, therefore, of these outer courts to the inner temple, was similar to that which the outward forms and government of the visible church bears to the inward and spiritual worship and privileges of the true church—the spiritual kingdom. They were, therefore, the appropriate symbol of the external organizations, and form of government and order, thrown around the true church of God, both for her edification and protection, and for a way of access, through which the stranger might draw near, and learn the character and will of God. These outer courts were mere divisions of the enclosed area surrounding the temple, and are here spoken of as one; and this whole space is to be left unmeasured. "But the court which is without the temple leave out," or rather, for such is the exact rendering, as in the margin, "cast out:" exclude it from any share in the divine appropriation and protection which this measuring implies; exclude it, as without the pale of His covenant, and though in visible connection with the temple, and in the same enclosure, separated from the outside world, yet not acknowledged by its Lord, and essentially and only worldly.

It was thus indicated that it was a part of the all-wise purpose of God to suffer His visible church to be overcome by a false profession, to give up the exterior of this inner spiritual temple and visible worship to be to such an extent desecrated by an ungodly world, as no longer to bear any distinctive marks of being His. "Cast it out," says the angel, as unmeasured and disowned; and this is the reason: "For it is given unto the Gentiles; and the holy city shall they tread under foot forty and two months." "Gentiles" here are, of course, the appropriate symbol in this connection of all who do not belong to the true Israel or people of God, of all the spiritually uncircumcised. And "the holy city," as being the place and community in and among which God established His dwelling place, naturally represents the social and political relations and influences surrounding the visible church, and in the midst of which, and in connection with which, it existed. This expresses, then, most clearly and forcibly, that the outward business of the kingdom of God, the mere external affairs of the church, all that outside the limits of a pure, priestly, spiritual consecration, were to be given up to the dominance of a mere worldly power. The world, by its insidious and ensnaring influences, was to enter into the domain of the visible church, to occupy and control those places and influences which of right belonged to God's covenanted people, and to degrade and pollute, by their management, all the earthly conditions and relations of the church, so as to render them essentially a mere worldly thing. Though preserving a decided, and, indeed, a necessary relation to that spiritual temple and worship hidden within its most secret enclosures, and known only to the consecrated priesthood, it would be essentially Gentile in its whole spirit and character. Its high places of influence would be seized by the worldly minded, and turned to worldly ends; and in its crowded highways, and broad avenues, and palaces of renown, the spiritually minded would be regarded no longer as the native inhabitants, but as a strange and foreign people, frowned upon, maligned, and persecuted, and finding their only peace and freedom in the sacred enclosure of the altar and the temple, in communion with God, in faith in the cross, and in fealty to the crown of their divine Redeemer.

Hence the command is, "Cast it out," measure it not,

reject it. The line is thus distinctly drawn, showing how far God's temple extends, and how very much that was intended entirely for its use, and that ought to have been subject to its influence, and, for the comfort of its worshippers, should be given over to the mere worldly power. The court cast out, and the city trodden under foot, represents a condition of things in the outward affairs of the church, and its relations with the world, the very opposite of the divinely measured, appropriated and preserved temple, and altar, and worshippers. The wall of separation between these outer courts and the consecrated place is no imaginary or variable thing; it is as fixed and unchangeable as the character and perfections of God, so long as these courts are thus occupied. There is no real affinity between them; there can be no compromise.

§. Such mere externals rejected.

"Cast it out." Though ever so near, so lovely, so magnificent, so externally advantageous, or apparently necessary, yet if not consecrated and in communion with God, if the seal of the altar and temple, of the cross and crown of Jesus be not on it, it belongs to the world, and with the world must be its portion and its doom. There can be no fellowship between light and darkness, between Christ and Belial, between God's consecrated priesthood worshipping at His altar and in His temple, and the crowds that fill the outer courts, and tread the streets of the holy city, but never get any nearer to God's throne or altar. All who come no nearer to God than the outside courts can bring them; all who approach as near as they desire or think necessary, when they draw near enough to hear the voice of its sacred melodies, to gaze upon the glorious objects within, upon the smoking altar, and the blood of reconciliation, and the garments of priestly consecration, and the outside beauty of that mysterious spot where are realized the deep mysteries of communion with God, but who come not themselves to that altar, nor into that holy place, nor make the entire consecration to God which it implies, all these God rejects. All this mere outside religion and worship, "cast it out." It has no part in the blessings of the spiritual kingdom now; and hereafter this shall be made to appear to the shame and confusion of many that trusted in it. "Many shall say to Me in that day, Lord, Lord, have we not prophesied in Thy name, and in Thy name have cast out devils, and in Thy name have done many wonderful works? And then will I profess unto them, I never knew you; depart from Me, ye that work iniquity."

This part, then, of the vision expresses the result upon the visible church, in all its external forms and relations, and even its ordinances, of what has been, in this interesting and remarkable series of visions, already unfolded, in the ninth chapter. It is the effect of that opening of the bottomless pit by a fallen ecclesiastical power, and letting forth the locusts of error, producing the reign of spiritual despotism, and followed by the ravages of revived worldly power and wisdom. It is also the same thing which, in another relation of it, and for another purpose, in the latter portion of this book is clothed in the symbolical form of the woman, or corrupt church, riding the beast, or worldly power, itself having become entirely apostate, and resting for support on the world's powers, and persecuting the saints of God.

This secularizing of the external church, this employment of her sacred courts and streets, her ordinances, organizations, and political connections, by the world, and in opposition to a true spiritual religion, and so as to crowd the true worshippers into the most secret places of the church, out of the world's sight, has been manifest for ages. It was once far worse than now. Previous to the Reformation, the whole city seemed completely trodden under foot. All the organizations of the visible church, except such as were concealed in

§. Fulfilment.

the valleys of Piedmont, and some similar unknown places, perhaps, were given over to this Gentile power. The true children of the kingdom, driven from all its external privileges and honours, were to be found only in its most sacred places, where the world could not follow them; spiritual recesses, where the arm of external power could not reach; but where they could still find the blood of atonement, and enjoy sweet communion with their Lord at the mercy seat. In other words, the true saints of God were excluded from all management of the affairs of the kingdom, and confined in their Christian life to the exercise of faith in atoning blood, the exercises of a spiritual worship, and personal services, and works of holiness, in a life of retirement.

The reformation from Popery brought about a great change, as is well known. It was the first great act of purification. As far as it was received, it reinstated the spiritual power of God's true people, and reclaimed for them the control, in a greater or less degree, of the external church and its relations to the world, of the outer court and the holy city.

It was only partial, however. Even the churches of the Reformation were sadly polluted and enfeebled by the prevalence of the worldly power, and crippled in their political connections. Even now, after the continued struggle of three and a half centuries, there is in the very heart of Protestantism very much of this same tendency to overrun the courts of God's house with a Gentile influence. Even where all political power is professedly excluded, and all connection between the church and State renounced as injurious, there is a constant tendency of the worldly element to assume undue influence in managing the house of God, and a constant tendency in the church itself to allow worldly principles and motives to control her discipline and her enterprises. This prevalence of the worldly power and wisdom in the purest visible churches, and the most favoured and enlightened lands, is still enough to distress the earnest and spiritually minded, and to cause them to cry out, "How long, O Lord, how long?"

This desecration, the angel declares, shall be only for a limited period, designated here as forty and two months. It is the same period as that describing the prophesying of the witnesses in the third verse, in terms of days: a thousand two hundred and threescore days; and as that describing the flight of the woman into the wilderness, first in terms of days, and then in terms of years, or times: three and a half times;[1] and again, as that denoting the continuance of the power of the beast—the symbol of the *organized* power of the world—in the same terms as used here, forty and two months.[2] This expression of the same period by entirely different terms in describing it by different symbols, and in entirely different relations, has not been sufficiently noticed; and also the use of the same terms where the relations are similar, while the symbols differ, as the prophesying of the two witnesses in sackcloth, and the divinely prepared nourishment and refuge of the woman during her stay in the wilderness; and here the same terms of forty and two months applied to the trampling of the holy city by the Gentiles, and, in chapter 13:5, to the persecuting power of the beast. This renders the identification of these symbols comparatively easy and sure; showing that this desecration of the court and the city was not to be confined to the prevalence of private and individual influence, but to take the form of organized political power, and so rule over God's heritage under the inspiration of the dragon.

§. 2. The period of this desecration limited.

But this triumph of worldly power is limited. Whatever else this designation of a period of forty-two months may mean, it certainly means this; and this is the first,

[1] Chap. 12: 6-14. [2] Chap. 13: 5.

and, to us, the most comforting and important. This period of the church's depression is fixed and limited, and perfectly defined in the purpose and plan of God. He who rules the raging of the sea has said to this power also, "Thus far shalt thou go, and no farther." Its days are numbered; and it is not merely the fact that they are so, but that the number is so definite, and precise, and peculiar, that gives to this form of limitation its peculiar power and adaptedness to confirm the faith of God's waiting people.

This holy city, and these exterior courts, are the Lord's. This power of the world in them, and over them, is a foul usurpation. It is permitted, as was the tyranny of Jezebel in Israel, and the desecration of Jerusalem and the temple of old, in the time of Antiochus, foretold by the prophet Daniel in similar language, for the chastisement of an unfaithful church, and to demonstrate more fully than ever before, the malignity of sin, and man's dependence on God's simple truth and the Holy Spirit As soon as that end is accomplished, these courts shall be reclaimed and purified; and all the outward business of the house of God, and all the administration of church government and order be no longer under secular, but spiritual control. The worldly intruders shall be cast out, and God's own people rule in God's city and house.

As, therefore, the humble and earnest Christian now looks over the church, and marks her conformity to the world, how widely the influence of the world's power and wisdom has extended into the church, and perverted its organizations, and obscured its spirituality, and his heart is saddened, and his fears awakened, and despondency begins to enfeeble his efforts, let him remember that these sacred things are still the Lord's, and that the time is coming when He will sweep away from these sacred enclosures the whole of this worldly power, that again Christianity shall rule the church, the influences of the altar, and the temple, and a spiritual worship shall extend over all the courts and the city. Let him only the more earnestly persevere, assured that no effort directed toward this result shall be lost, however the complete triumph shall be delayed.

Such a designation of time specifying the duration of this symbol of the church's depression, was absolutely necessary to give to the church a correct view of its nature and design, and to sustain her faith. Otherwise it would have appeared without limitation, and the world's triumph perpetual. If there was nothing more, this would be a sufficient reason for such a designation. It is, indeed, the chief reason, whatever else more definite there may be in its meaning. This, however, would not account for the use of such a definite, and of this particular, number.

§. But why so specific a limitation?

There is no part of the book of Revelation, the interpretation of which has elicited more learning, ingenuity, and labour, than this period of forty-two months, or twelve hundred and sixty days; and there is none that has rendered less satisfactory results. The old and universal desire to know the times and the seasons has greatly stimulated this; but it has only proven, over and over again, what Jesus said to His disciples in answer to almost the same query that impels this inquiry, "Wilt Thou at this time restore the kingdom to Israel?" "It is not for you to know the times and the seasons, which the Father hath put in His own power." This declaration of Christ is so general, so sweeping, and so decisive, that one would think it ought to have led men, from the beginning, to hesitate, at least, before they adopted as the basis of their inquiries the principle that these periods were intended for any such purposes as to enable us to antedate any of the great events in the establishment of this kingdom.

But why, then, reveal them? And why these definite and peculiar numbers? They must have a meaning, and that meaning must be of use, else they would not have been here. They must, too, designate the duration of the things to the symbols of which they are applied. Of all this there is no doubt. But it does not follow that they have no meaning or use, unless we can tell the precise calendar years they indicate, when they begin, and when they end. They may have a very important design, and this be no part of it, and made to be impossible. And, indeed, they have, as we have just partly seen, such an important relation to the understanding of this whole series of visions as to be essential to it, without at all indicating the precise point in the world's history at which they begin or terminate, or even without their having any one precise point in reference to its history as a whole. It may at least be with these, as with all the other symbols that we have examined, which apply not to one precise event, occurring once only, but to whole classes of events.

§. *Their location in history impossible.*

Most interpreters have been agreed in regarding a day in these prophetic numbers, as standing for a year. The authority for this is found in the direction given to Ezekiel in his vision of the siege of Jerusalem, to lie upon his side a certain number of days, bearing the iniquity of Israel and Judah, "I have appointed thee each day for a year." Also in the prophecies of Daniel, the prophecy of the seventy weeks, and different periods of days there mentioned, which are taken by most as indicating necessarily years, are regarded as confirming this view. But these are by no means decisive; and by some this view is earnestly controverted, and it cannot be regarded as a settled point. But supposing it to be true, and that by these numbers a period of twelve hundred an sixty years is designated, who shall or can tell where to set this period in history? Who shall fix its commencement? When did the witnesses begin to prophesy in sackcloth? When were the courts and the city given up to the Gentiles? When did the woman begin to be nourished in the wilderness? Is it possible to fix the beginning of the state of things thus indicated, upon any event in history? Is it not one of those things whose actual commencement is invisible, whose progress is very gradual, and whose development, from its first to its completed manifestation, is such as to defy the skill of the mere chronicler?

It is, indeed, true, that the early history of the church was one of glorious triumphs over the powers of the world. Though persecuted and oppressed, still, by the power of truth and of the Spirit alone, she bade defiance to all the might and wisdom of the world, and trampled them under her feet. They fell before her. Her early history for a while certainly was not that of a fugitive woman, nor were her outer courts, or her external government and order, and her earthly relations, given up to the Gentiles. Her whole surroundings were spiritual.

But this state and position of purity was of short duration. Her prostitution to the power of the world commenced during the very period of her visible triumphs, but who can say when? Even in Paul's time, the mystery of iniquity had begun to work. But it was ages in developing itself; and who can say when this development was so complete as to give date to the commencement of this era of corruption, of mournful witnessing, and wilderness concealment? The date of A. D. 606, so often referred to as that of the Pope of Rome being proclaimed universal bishop, is not at all supported by historic evidence as marking any such fact; and even if the complimentary grant of "the first," or "chief," from the usurper Phocas, to the Roman bishop, conferring mere priority of rank, but no power, be accepted as true, it is a most arbitrary epoch and unimportant fact from which to date the commencement of a period described as this is. So, also, the date of 755, when the Pope was made a temporal prince, by the gift of the exarchate of Ravenna, an Italian province, and of 774, when this gift was confirmed by Charlemagne, is, if not equally arbitrary, at least but one among many distinct marks in the progress of the church's corruption by the power of the world, which is the precise thing here described, and whose commencement we are seeking. Had not the Papal, had not also the Eastern church, become, to all intents and purposes, worldly powers, in the true scriptural sense, long before? Were not the outer courts pretty effectually overrun, and the holy city trodden under foot, even in the time of Constantine?

Moreover, how can the state of things here described, a spiritual condition of the visible church, arising from her alliance with the world, and external servitude to it, have such a definite and fixed "setting in history" as has been sought for, when in every separate country and community it must have been different? How different the condition of the seven churches of Asia from each other? In some of those this very condition of things had already not only progressed, but had almost hidden the true church, as Pergamos, and Thyatira, and, still more, Sardis and Laodicea.

To the eye of God, indeed, the beginning of this sad defection was definitely marked. But in its very nature it must have been gradual. Even, therefore, when we regard the church as a whole, and her general aspect, and the progress of this defection from age to age, and regard this forty and two months as definitely describing its duration, it must be ever impossible for us to fix any other date of its beginning than the centuries during which this apostacy was forming, and of its end than the centuries during which it gradually wanes, until at last it is utterly destroyed.

But does this indefiniteness of location as to the exact place of this period in the world's history render this designation of time any the less useful or important? Assuredly not. On the other hand, we think this very indefiniteness, combined with the certainty of the fact of such a fixed limitation, fits it to be of especial service to the church in every age, and causes it to fall in with the whole analogy of prophecy in its relation to time, and thus effectually prevents the abuse to which it would otherwise be subject. It has its full value thus, both of affording comfort in the deepest darkness, and encouragement in view of the certainly approaching end. Without some designation of time, the revelation just given could not have been understood at all, and could never have ministered any comfort, or held forth any prospect but one of gloom, so long as there was a church on the earth. And what other designation than one perfectly exact and definite in itself, and yet entirely indefinite and uncertain in its position in history, could have been so well calculated to strengthen the faith of endurance, and to quicken the effort to revive and to regain the lost position, the spiritual elevation and character properly hers?

In addition to this view, that the days and months are symbolical of the *years* of the church's external depression, there is another question which has been little noticed by interpreters until recently: whether these *numbers* themselves, as well as the *days*, have not a symbolical significance? This we might naturally expect; indeed, any thing else would be strange and inconsistent with the use of all numbers throughout this book, especially of the number seven. Expositors, the most judicious and cautious, have remarked, and, indeed, every careful reader must have observed, that the number indicating this period is, in every case, "*three and a half*" years or times, or their equivalent in months and days; that is, just the half of the perfect "*seven*;" and also, that the only other definite period here mentioned is that of the slain witnesses, which is precisely the same number of *days*, three and a half. This is no mere coincidence: it has a

§. The numbers themselves symbolize the enemy's failure.

meaning. Shall we not, then, give to these numbers their proper symbolical significance, as thus tacitly, but forcibly, intimating, by the very term of the duration of the world's power, its utter abortiveness, the certainty of its never being able to go further than half way to the attainment of a complete development, that in the very midst of its progress it shall be crushed, and the covenant people delivered? And have we not in this a further reason for this particular specific limitation?

Again. This very period of three and a half years had already become an historic reality in the history of the old covenant, and in application to a precisely similar condition of things to that here predicted. The allusion in verses fifth and sixth of this chapter, to the character and works of Elijah, compel us to observe the first, the period of *the three and a half years' drought*, during which the power of the Gentile Jezebel was unbroken and unresisted, and which was ended by Elijah's triumphant testimony on Carmel, a glorious resurrection of truth, and the slaying of the prophets of Baal.

§. Their typical and historic use.

Again, in Daniel, the apostacy of Israel, and the triumph of the world's power in the reign of Antiochus, which is there described in terms so very similar to those used by the same prophet in describing the very same period here referred to by John, as to show that one was intended to be typical of the other, was literally, in its duration, the same period of three years and a half; that is, from the taking away of the daily sacrifice, until its restoration.[1] As literal years it there describes the duration of that old Gentile usurpation, and history shows it to have been literally and remarkably accomplished.[2] There, too, this same number is used enigmatically in the

---

[1] Dan. 11: 31. 12: 7-11.
[2] Prid. Con. Annis 168, 165, 164. Vol. ii., pp. 120, 133, 141.

seventh chapter to describe this usurpation, of which that of Antiochus Epiphanes was there made a type.

As, therefore, these most remarkable of the ancient usurpations of the rights and privileges of God's true people were literally of three years and a half's duration, so this, which is the final repetition of the same thing on a far wider scale, and in a higher sphere, is designated by the same number of years used symbolically; so that the literal and symbolic times bear the same proportion to each other that the literal or historic facts bear to the symbolic and predicted ones. Here, then, have we not another reason for these particular numbers?

There remains one other view of the value of these numbers, and that as important, if not more so, than either of those noticed. The period of the church's depression, and witnessing in sackcloth, is three and a half *years*, or forty and two months; next follows the period of her enemies' complete triumph, but that is the extremely brief one of three *days* and a half; and then, in the latter part of the book, the triumph that follows is designated as a thousand years. In this comparative value of these numbers, a value that no interpretation can deprive them of, have we not a truth revealed of vastly greater interest and glory, of vastly greater encouragement to faith, and hope, and earnest effort in the face of the world's opposition, than in any definite fixing of coming events? Of this last, even could we do it, the value would be doubtful; of this other, which is certain on any principles of interpretation, the truth conveyed is one that fills the soul with joy in the darkest hours of the church, and enables the believer even then, even when the shout of the nations over the slain witnesses is ringing in his ears, still to sing with the crowned elders, "We shall reign on the earth."

§. Their comparative value.

Let the church be faithful in her measurements, that she may be firm and clear in her testimony. Let us each apply the rule given to our own hearts and lives. Are you, reader, one of these interior worshippers, in daily communion with God through atoning blood, living at the altar and the throne; living a life of consecration and separation from the world? Are you one of that holy priesthood, offering up spiritual sacrifices acceptable to God through Jesus Christ? Or do you belong only to the outer courts, and the open streets and thoroughfares of the city of God, living in the places, and amidst the privileges of the church of Christ, but with the whole character, garb, and demeanour of a stranger to spiritual things? Are you a true worshipper, approved and preserved of God, or are you desecrating these sacred courts by a mere outward profession, with a heart and life devoted to the world, or acts and expressions of outward respect, while openly rejecting the authority of Christ, and the communion of His people?

LECTURE XXVI.

THE POWER OF A WITNESSING CHURCH DURING THESE ABOUNDING CORRUPTIONS, IN HER WORSHIP AND GOVERNMENT.

REV., CHAP. XI. : 3-10.

" And I will give power unto My two witnesses, and they shall prophesy a thousand two hundred and threescore days, clothed in sackcloth. These are the two olive trees, and the two candlesticks standing before the God of the earth. And if any man will hurt them, fire proceedeth out of their mouth, and devoureth their enemies; and if any man will hurt them, he must in this manner be killed. These have power to shut heaven, that it rain not in the days of their prophecy, and have power over waters to turn them to blood, and to smite the earth with all plagues, as often as they will. And when they shall have finished their testimony, the beast that ascendeth out of the bottomless pit shall make war against them, and shall overcome them, and kill them. And their dead bodies shall lie in the street of the great city, which spiritually is called Sodom and Egypt, where also our Lord was crucified. And they of the people, and kindreds, and tongues, and nations, shall see their dead bodies three days and an half, and shall not suffer their dead bodies to be put in graves. And they that dwell upon the earth shall rejoice over them, and make merry, and shall send gifts one to another, because these two prophets tormented them that dwelt on the earth."

THE first two verses of this chapter show not only the subjects of the church's testimony, but the condition and circumstances in which her two witnesses for God should be called to bear it. They teach us that it was to be in a visible church in which the true people of God were to be confined to the exercises of a purely spiritual service, while the chief management of its external ordinances and government should be controlled by the power and wisdom of the world. They describe a state of things in which the true Israel would be kept under forcible restraint, deprived of religious freedom, and in all the outward conditions of their religious life, and in their connections with the world, subject to its dictation. This would make it no easy thing to be faithful witnesses of the truth. This view of the corruption of the visible church, and the depression of the true people of God, prepares the way for the revelation which follows of the work of the true church in these circumstances, as comprehended in the testifying of two witnesses in sackcloth.

Let no one fail to observe that these verses—this whole account of the two witnesses—are not the words of John describing what he saw, but the words of the angel who was addressing him, and who had just before given him the little book, and the charge to prophesy. This is evident from the language of verse 3, "*My* two witnesses," showing the speaker to be him by whose authority these witnesses are sent, and to whose truth they testify. His words continue evidently to the end of the tenth verse, when the tense changes, and the seer describes what he saw, the things described becoming at that point visible. These revelations of the angel cover the same period that the visions of the six trumpets do, up to the end of the tenth chapter, unfolding the condition of the true church during that period, while these judgments were progressing. And, accordingly, when the revelations of the angel have reached that point in the condition of the church corresponding to the point in the conflict at which the curtain dropped upon the vision, at the end of the ninth chapter, when the world's power and wisdom seemed to be triumphant, and sweeping desolation over every thing, again the curtain rises upon a desolated earth and a scourged church, and the vision moves on with a change of symbols to the approaching triumph.

"And I will give unto My two witnesses, and they shall prophesy a thousand two hundred and threescore days, clothed in sackcloth." The months of the previous verse are here turned into days. Every day of these forty and two months of depression and corruption, these witnesses shall prophesy; the period is the same, but here in terms of days, to indicate the continuity of their testimony; it should be daily, constant, and unintermittent. "*Clothed in sackcloth.*" Their testimony would be in circumstances of trial and sorrow, of deep mourning, because of the prevalence of the worldly power, corrupting the church, and perverting her ordinances and influence. It would be like the prophesying of Elijah during the usurpation of Jezebel, or like that of Jeremiah during the dark days that preceded, and the darker still that followed, the triumphs of Babylon over the city and people of God.

On this point we are not left in any doubt. The divine revealer Himself explains the symbol by a reference to the ancient revelation here again, as so often elsewhere, in this book, connecting the two dispensations into one divine plan. "These," he says, "are the two olive trees, and the two candlesticks, standing before the God of the earth." We turn to the prophecy of Zechariah, which, of all the old prophecies, most resembles the Apocalypse, both in its manner and the vast field over which it sweeps, and to which reference is here made. There we learn that the golden candlestick which Zechariah saw, together with the two olive trees that supplied it, represented the church of God then existing, sustained as a light-bearer by the Spirit of God operating through certain appointed instrumentalities, and not by visible might or power.[1] There, too, we are taught the meaning of the two olive trees, or branches, that fed the golden lamps, by the angel's answer to the prophet's inquiry concerning it. "These are the two anointed ones that stand by the God of the whole

§. 1. Who are these witnesses?

---

[1] Zech. 4: 1–6.

earth."[1] A further examination of that context shows that these two anointed ones, or sons of oil, were the two great offices through which God's power and grace flowed into the church, and sustained its light, the priestly and kingly, the functions of which were then exercised by Joshua and Zerubbabel, who are here addressed by name as the chosen instruments by whom God would re-establish the theocracy. These two offices, indeed, are so essentially connected with the church's life, that they always have been, and always must be, the sole means through which it receives the divine influences.

In the vision of Zechariah there is but one candlestick, fed by the two olive trees; this duality of function does not extend into the church itself, but is confined to its rulers, the high priest and the prince. Here, however, the candlesticks are two, as well as the olive trees; this duality of official functions has a correspondent duality in the light-giving function of the whole church. The language here teaches that the symbol of witness here is not adequately represented by the olive tree alone, but that the olive tree and the candlestick must be taken as one symbol, and in their union, when doubled, equivalent to these two witnesses.

Adhering closely, therefore, to the Spirit's own interpretation, there can be no hesitation as to the meaning of these witnesses. They represent, first, the church as the light of the world, by its testimony for God, and as supported in that testimony by the Spirit; and then, secondly, that this testimony is borne by the exercise of these two functions or offices, the kingly and priestly, which now pervade the whole of God's people; that in the exercise of these consists her light-bearing, or witnessing power, hence beautifully symbolized as God's two witnesses. These priestly and kingly functions are in these latter days no

---

[1] Zech. 4: 11–14.

longer the mere means by which the church is sustained, and fed with spiritual influences; in that respect, and to that result, they are exercised by her divine Head, her great High Priest and King. Before His coming, these priestly functions and royal privileges were confined to her officers, as representatives and types of Him; now that He has come, and brought to light the way of access, and the bond of union that cements Him and His people into one, the whole church, in her capacity as a light-bearer, shares with her divine Head in the exercise of these two functions: these now are the two candlesticks, as well as olive trees; it is now the privilege of the whole church to say, "Thou hast made us kings and priests unto God." And as they exhibit to others their royal privileges and priestly character, do they give light to the world; by these two they bear witness: these are the two witnesses.

Now, when we come to examine more particularly *how* the church bears its testimony, by what agencies it ever has and must prophecy in the midst of an ungodly world, and of abounding corruptions, we find there are precisely these two, corresponding to her priestly and kingly character, a pure *worship* and *discipline*. These include every instrumentality of individuals or organizations, every duty and privilege by which the testimony for God is held forth to the world.

These words, *worship* and *discipline*, we use in their truest and widest sense, to express two well defined and frequently expressed scriptural ideas. *Worship*, in its true scripture sense, we have had occasion before to define as including every expression or manifestation of true homage and adoration of God, and consecration to His service; *discipline* we use as expressing all the Bible means by *ruling* in the church, the whole exercise of her government, as applied to its only legitimate purposes of securing her purity and holy efficiency. This idea of witnessing must never be restricted to the mere declaration and defence of the truth against the assaults of error, in her preaching, and pulpits, and books. The doctrines of the gospel must find their expression, not only in the preaching of her ministers, but in the praises, and the prayers, and the alms, and the sacrifices, and the holy living of her people; that is, in all her worship; and her discipline must employ the whole authority of her Head, and the means of His appointment, to secure this one great object, the holding forth of the word of life.

The worship of the church, therefore, and its discipline, are these two witnesses of God in His church: the two functions—the one priestly, the other kingly—by which she testifies, through all her members and enterprises, the character and salvation of God.

It is in and by these, and these only, that her testimony becomes clear, definite, united, and convincing. These make it not only audible, but visible. As said her Head, so the church in her measure can say, "The works that I do, they bear witness." In the one class of these works, her priestly duties and privileges shine forth; in the other, her fellowship with her King in the administration of His kingly office. It is by these two agencies of worship and discipline, as by two perfectly distinct, yet continually united witnesses, that she declares with power the whole counsel of God, that she testifies to the truths and powers of the spiritual kingdom. She has no other witnesses but these. When she has dared to employ others, as the political powers of earth, the influence of wealth, or the authority of worldly wisdom, to deliver and support her testimony, that testimony has only provoked the sneer of the world, and the scorn and joy of Satan. Such testimony, and its authors, have been treated by the powers of evil just as the seven sons of Sceva in Ephesus were in their appeal to the name of Jesus. "Jesus I know, and Paul I know, but who are ye?" was the spirit's response, as the demoniac leaped upon them, and they fled, naked and wounded. With like powerlessness and shame will every such worldly witnessing for God, such worldly attempts to exorcise the powers of evil by the name of Jesus, ever be visited.

But let the church be pure in her *worship;* let her worship be, not a ritualistic form, or a mere lip service, but the declaration of a real and hearty consecration of all she is and has to her Redeeming God. Let it be what Paul declares it ought to be, and beseeches us to render: "I beseech you, brethren, by the mercies of God, that ye present your bodies a living sacrifice, holy and acceptable to God, which is your reasonable service,", or, literally, "worship." Let it be what James defines it to be: "Pure religion"—literally, "worship"—"and undefiled, before God and the Father, is this: to visit the fatherless and widows in their affliction, and to keep himself unspotted from the world." Let it be this, and her testimony to the power of the cross and the priesthood of Christ would be perfect. Let also her discipline be purely spiritual, and exercised in all respects according to the laws of Christ, repudiating all other authority than His, and in entire dependence on His power and Spirit, and her testimony to His divine power and kingly rights would be complete. And these being complete, the whole counsel of God is declared, and the whole end of the church's testimony in the midst of the abounding corruption is secured. Let the cross of Christ and the crown of Christ be held forth, in all the fulness of their meaning, by the church, in the exercise of her priestly and kingly functions, and every error, both of doctrine and practice, that has ever polluted the church and ruined souls, receives its condemnation.

So few and simple are the principles necessary to preserve the truth amidst the assaults of error; so clear and definite, and easily and briefly summed up and understood, the testimony which is to be for ever rung in the unwilling ears of a wicked world and a corrupt church! The theologian may fill volumes with discussions of doctrines which are true and precious, and in tracing the relations and connections of revealed truth and duty, and very profitably; but, after all, the whole of his teachings is embraced in these two words, the Cross and the Crown of Jesus; and the degree in which every utterance bears the impress of these two things—the cross and the crown—decides its real worth. Every form and relation that truth can take finds its truest expression in the lives and prophesying of these two witnesses: the worship of a true and living church or believer, and the faithful discipline of such a church, or the submission of the believer to Christ's authority alone. And these two go together. They never can be separated. They have the same life. As long as one shall prophesy, the other will; and when one is slain, the other must be also.

These two witnesses for God are essential and characteristic elements of every true church. The possession of these make her a church; the want of these is proof of apostacy. We have, therefore, here only a fuller and more definite account of the church's mission, as set forth in the very beginning of this revelation to John, by the first object presented in the first vision which he saw, the golden candlesticks. We have it here as it was to be fulfilled during the period of the church's affliction, a prophesying in sackcloth.

The next thing presented is the power of these witnesses. "If any man will hurt them, fire proceedeth out of their mouth, and devoureth their enemies; and if any man will hurt them, he must in this manner be killed. These have power to shut heaven that it rain not in the days of their prophecy, and have power over waters to turn them to blood, and to smite the earth with all plagues as often as they will." That is, they shall be endued with a

§. 2. The power of these witnesses.

power equal to the mightiest of the prophets of old, and of which the recorded acts of these prophets are the appropriate symbols. Elijah, calling down fire from heaven on those who sought to take him, and shutting heaven that it rained not for the space of three years and a half—the very same period here assigned to this testimony in sackcloth—is but the symbol of the withholding of divine influences, and of that more fearful fire of God which the word of these witnesses brings down upon all that wilfully and maliciously reject their testimony and seek their destruction; and Moses, turning the waters of the river into blood, and smiting Egypt with all plagues, is but the symbol of the curse that would follow their rejected testimony, making the very gospel itself, which in its true nature is a savour of life unto life, to become a savour of death unto death, and smiting every earthly good, turning waters into blood and joys into spiritual plagues. Can these plagues be anything else than the same that were visited upon an unbelieving world, first on the whole round of temporal good, and then upon the soul itself and an apostate church, at the summons of the first six trumpets, to the end of the tenth chapter; all of them, too, it will be remembered, in answer to the prayers of the saints? Have we not here another evidence that these two things—the testimony of the witnesses and the judgments of those trumpets—cover the same ground, and run parallel with each other? Thus we are made to see the relation between those terrible inflictions, and the testimony of a suffering church. They are the effects of that despised and rejected and perverted testimony—of violence done to God's true witnesses.

Such is the awful power of a rejected gospel, as it comes to us even amidst all the prevailing worldliness of the visible church. So long as any true worship of God exists, and the authority of Christ is acknowledged, they are uttering their testimony; and it is such as leaves men without excuse for their neglect of the calls and claims of Christ. "He that despiseth, despiseth not man, but God." And God's word despised, His word of mingled authority and love—that word which unfolds the mysteries of Christ's cross, and the glories of His crown—must of necessity become a word of terrible condemnation, and must set in array against the sinner all the agencies and instrumentalities of God's creation. "How shall we escape if we neglect so great salvation?"

"If any man will hurt these witnesses, he must in this manner be killed:" that is, by the fire that proceedeth out of their mouths; by the rejected testimony turning to a fire of wrath, and the soul being thus given over to spiritual and eternal death. "*Hurt these witnesses.*" Let us be careful not to mix up the literal with the symbolical. These witnesses are not the saints of God in person—not the mere organizations of the visible church; but the true spiritual functions of these, as exercised in a life of holy consecration and unswerving obedience. If any man will hurt these—not merely will neglect them, but wishes and aims to injure or destroy the holy worship and discipline of God in His church, out of hatred and opposition, he must thus perish; he necessarily brings ruin upon himself. The symbol of fire here, to represent a rejected or resisted divine testimony, is also in accordance with the figures of the old prophets. God said to Jeremiah, "I will make My words in thy mouth fire, and this people wood, and it shall devour them." So He says still to every one of His ministers and people, who, in the midst of opposition and reproach, holds forth in his life a faithful testimony. How much more, then, must this result follow when the testimony resisted is the united testimony of these two great agencies, that comprise all the holy activities of the church? In its persecuting rage, an incensed world or an apostate church may torture and slay the saints, but this, so far from annulling the avenging power of their rejected testimony, shall only give it more terrible efficacy. The dying testimony of the martyrs has often consumed their persecutors in the fire which it kindled. *Slaying saints is not killing these witnesses.* The words of Latimer to his fellow martyr, Ridley, at the stake, forcibly express this: "Be of good comfort, brother; we shall this day light such a candle, by God's grace, in England, as I trust shall never be put out."

Let the world and Satan rage as they may, but let not the child of God be faint-hearted, or shrink from open and steady allegiance to his Lord, or entire consecration to His service. While he exemplifies in his life the character of these two witnesses, he is, even in all his outward weakness, clothed with their power. These witnesses are invulnerable. Every stroke aimed against their holy testimony, as that is uttered in his life, shall only rebound on the aggressor. That testimony is God's own truth, and involves the authority and honour of the King, and carries with it the power of the kingdom.

But, thirdly, notwithstanding their power, these witnesses are killed. Were we to confine our view to the mere symbol, this would appear to be utterly impossible; and equally so, if these witnesses represent the persons of God's people, or its external organizations. How could those out of whose mouth fire should proceed and devour every one who even sought to hurt them, ever be killed by their enemies? But what in the symbol, viewed as a reality, might seem to be impossible and contradictory, becomes perfectly consistent and natural when the spiritual realities are considered, and finds in the symbol its exactest representation. Thus we shall still further find that the symbol itself compels us to understand it of the church of God, not in its persons, its membership, but only in its great spiritual functions.

§. 3. The killing of these witnesses.

Whenever, in any case, it comes to this, that the visible church becomes pervaded by the spirit of the world, or the perversions of error, to such a degree that her worship and government no longer bear testimony to the cross and crown of Jesus, then these witnesses are dead; from such a worship and government the life has departed, and what remains is a mere form, a lifeless corpse. If the atoning blood and all-sufficient intercession of Jesus be not the very spring and life of worship, it is as worthless as the mummeries of heathenism; and if the authority of Jesus be not the spring and guide of discipline or government in all its acts, it is destitute of spiritual power, and as worthless as an Egyptian mummy.

Now, what is the enemy, and where, that can so destroy the life of these great agencies of the witnessing church, and hush their testimony? Can open violence do it? Can the direct assaults of individuals or nations, by the infliction of mere temporal pains and penalties, do it? Have the faggot and the stake, the dungeon and the rack, ever crushed out the testimony to God's truth? Is it not proverbial that the blood of the martyrs is the seed of the church? For how came they to be martyrs? Was it not their testimony that brought them to the stake? And did not the voice of that testimony ring more clearly and loudly in the fires that consumed their bodies, and so become a living power in other hearts, and a consuming fire to their adversaries? The whole history of the New Testament church, from the martyrdom of Stephen to the present moment, is one continued demonstration of the truth and meaning of the words, "If any man will hurt them,"—these witnesses—"he must in this manner be killed." He only secures his own destruction.

The very nature of these witnesses, as the two great functions of the church by which she utters her testimony, shows, not only what their death, and their lifeless, unburied forms must mean, but what the nature of the enemy must be that makes successful war upon them, and kills them. It must be something that destroys the very nature of spiritual worship and discipline. Nothing can kill these witnesses but some power that corrupts the spiritual character of the church, removing insidiously the blood of atonement as the sole ground of her faith and hope, and the authority of her King as the sole rule of her duty. When such a power obtains the ascendency, it destroys her priestly consecration, corrupts her loyalty to Christ, and obliterates her separation from the world, until at length neither her worship nor discipline utters a single testimony for Christ. The witnesses are slain.

This is precisely the meaning of the next verses. "The beast that ascendeth out of the bottomless pit shall make war against them, and shall overcome them, and kill them." Here again this account connects itself with the visions already described in the ninth chapter, under the fifth trumpet, showing that the two have reference to the same condition of things. The reference in these words of the angel is to the locust king, "the angel of the bottomless pit,"[1] the beastly leader of those hordes of errors with which he spread abroad a spiritual desolation, and established a great spiritual despotism. This same hellish power, in its more fully organized aspect, is described at still greater length afterwards in the thirteenth, and again in the seventeenth chapters.[2] It is the beast representing the worldly power, under the head that had received, in its pagan form, a deadly wound, but was healed by its satanic conversion into an ecclesiastical form, or assumption of an outward Christian character, and which in this form came forth from the bottomless pit, and to whom "there was given a mouth speaking great blasphemies; and power was given to him to continue forty and two months; and it was given unto him to make war with the

---

[1] Ch. 9: 2, 11.   [2] Ch. 13: 1-8.   17: 8.

saints, and to overcome them; and power was given him over all kindreds, and tongues, and nations."

It is impossible to doubt that this is the same war in which the witnesses here are killed. In it this beast, we learn, was supported by another: a lamb-horned and dragon-tongued beast,[1] representing the godless wisdom of the world, doing great wonders, and deceiving the earthly-minded by the miracles he did in the sight of the first beast. This is the spiritual and mighty enemy, the world's power, supported by the world's proud wisdom, which, entering into and controlling the visible church, corrupts its worship and prostitutes its government, until the church itself casts off its true character, and comes to be fitly represented by the harlot riding the beast. It is this that kills the witnesses, and it is thus it kills them.

When the spirit of holiness and life has departed from the church, and the world is no longer tormented by the faithful testimony of a pure worship and discipline, that world is very willing to retain their lifeless forms, for the gratification of its self-righteousness and ambition. A dead church is a favourite with worldly people, especially if it be rich, and fashionable, and powerful. Forms in which there is no spiritual life, and a government in which there is no Christ, just suit them. These corpses of the witnesses they will not suffer to be buried. They rejoice with mutual congratulations when the faithful testimony is silenced that disturbed their consciences, and rebuked their pride and selfishness, and obstructed their indulgences, and when the agencies that uttered it are turned into trophies of their power, and ministers to their pride.

§ 4. Their dead bodies: dead forms.

"Their dead bodies are in the street of the great city, which spiritually is called Sodom and Egypt; where, also, our Lord was crucified." That city can be no other

---

[1] Ch. 13: 11-14.

than the one just before mentioned, the holy city, once the city of God, but which had been given over to be trodden under foot of the Gentiles, till it became polluted as Sodom, and worldly and cruel as Egypt itself: and therefore receives these *spiritual* designations. In such an apostate church these external forms of worship and government are still preserved and displayed; but they are but the lifeless carcasses of what once were the witnesses of God. There they are seen and delighted in by a rejoicing world.

All this can take place only "when they shall have finished their testimony." This we shall leave to be considered in connection with their revival, all of which will be seen to be perfectly harmonious with the interpretation given, and will give to the truth it teaches additional force.

The principles here unfolded, in regard to the conflict of the church with a corrupting world, have been working themselves out through her whole history, whenever and wherever her outer courts have been trodden under foot, her external ordinances and relations controlled by worldly alliances. In some of the seven churches of Asia, especially in Sardis and Laodicea, the witnesses were even then almost silenced. And since then, the same process has been repeated in every church which has yielded to the encroachments of the worldly spirit, and modified her worship, and lowered her discipline, to make her more acceptable to the earthly-minded. In the very nature of the case, this is not a development that could occur but once, and that throughout all the church. As described so graphically by these symbols, it has been always repeating itself, though sometimes on a much larger scale. To this there has always been the same tendency. The cross is still an offence and a stumbling-block. To remove it by clothing her ordinances of worship, and all her services, with external attractions, the pomp of impressive forms, and entrancing music, and artistic skill; to gratify the eye and the imagination, and thrill the whole emotional nature, has ever been an object with the worldly-minded. To allure the world by lowering her standard of separation from it, and adopting many of its characteristic habits, and pleasures, and principles; to secure on her side the political powers of the world, and its wealth and its wise men, and so to invest her with that kind of greatness that strikes and attracts the natural heart, has seemed equally desirable to very many. Thus it has gone on, in both individuals and congregations, until the life of these witnesses for God, a spiritual worship and order, became extinct, and nothing remained but a name to live: a mere dead form.

What at first took place only in single congregations, at length pervaded the church generally. This mystery of iniquity, working age after age, seemed at last to have at one time almost destroyed the life of the whole church; and her entire system of government and discipline was converted into a great hierarchy for the gratification of human ambition, and into a spiritual despotism in which men lorded it over God's heritage. In a large part of the Christian world, wherever, indeed, its political power had wound its fatal hug around the church, the witnesses were killed, and the world rejoiced over them. But they were not everywhere killed; and in every case the triumph of the world was brief. All through the gloomy reign of the ages preceding the Reformation, even when the stillness of death seemed to rest upon the church, the voice of these witnesses would be again heard, clear and startling, tormenting the world. Instances of adherence to the cross of Christ, and unswerving fealty to His crown, were continually presenting themselves. This testimony burst upon the world with new power at the Reformation. But, great as that reviving was, it did not end the conflict. The same beast is still making war upon the same witnesses, and will be till he goes into perdition in the burning lake, for this is his very nature. Still there are the same partial triumphs of the world's power, and the same periods of death and revival.

The general impression is, that this passage indicates a simultaneous and universal silencing of this testimony, beyond what has yet occurred, when, perhaps, throughout the world the defection will become so great, the worship and labours and discipline of the church so pervaded by a regard to the worldly power and wisdom, that they shall cease to give any clear testimony. Whatever the text may indicate, it is very certain that such a tendency is manifest now in every church, all over the world. Formerly it was ignorance and power, culminating in spiritual despotism, in which a corrupt church enslaved the world; now it is the power and wisdom of the world culminating in an enslaved and lifeless church. Formerly it assaulted the people of God in their earthly rights and possessions, depriving them of liberty and property and life; now, on the other hand, it comes as the great defender and protector of earthly rights and privileges, with the watchword of liberty and equality, and the promise of a new era of social and material prosperity. And it works "great wonders," even apparent "miracles," effectually deceiving them that dwell on the earth, the earthly minded.[1] But it is still the same beastly power; and, even when it dissevers the disastrous union of the church with the state, it does it only the more effectually and insidiously to connect the church and the world, and enslave the former. This is the last, and the most deadly of its attacks: the most deadly because the most concealed, and assuming the mask of friendship, and often even boasted of by a deceived church itself as an evidence of the church's triumphs. When all this will end, God

[1] Ch. 13: 12–14.

only knows, and time only can reveal. The passage before us cannot enable us thus to antedate history. It clearly reveals the impending danger and the inevitable result, so far and so long as the cause is suffered to operate; but that is reserved among the secrets of God. It may be that the result, so often before brought about, of a partial killing of the witnesses, shall, by this more insidious form of attack, be so enlarged and extended as to become a universal prostration of the church's witnessing agencies, that the symbol shall find a simultaneous realization through all the church, leaving the external forms of worship and discipline entirely lifeless and powerless, and leaving the great work of witness-bearing entirely to the scattered individuals here and there who, like the few in Sardis, shall have kept themselves unspotted from the world. All this, too, may be—and, if it come at all, it will be—while the church imagines herself to be rich and increased with goods, and in need of nothing; while she is praised and honoured by the world, and boasting of the advanced civilization, and high refinement, and triumphs of science which she has secured, never dreaming that her riches and power and worldly glory are only the splendid funereal trappings with which her subtile foe has adorned the lifeless bodies of her once living and powerful witnesses.

But, however uncertain we may be as to the extent to which this defection of the visible church may be suffered to proceed at any one time, we are left in no doubt whatever that precisely this condition of things, symbolized by the killing of God's witnesses, has existed, does exist, and will exist, wherever conformity to the world controls the services and government of the church. Whether this shall ever be a simultaneous thing over all the visible church, it is not important for us to know; but it is of importance for us to remember that all this which we have described may take place here, and now, and that everywhere the tendency to this result is strong and manifest. It is not, indeed, unresisted by many a faithful servant of God; but it saddens the heart to observe how, notwithstanding the warning cry, and the earnest expostulations and example of humble saints, the great tide of worldliness rolls on and spreads, and the simplicity of a spiritual worship, and the holiness of an entire consecration to the work of the kingdom, is more and more driven into a corner. This war of the beast upon the witnesses was never waged more earnestly and insidiously than at the present moment, and that, too, everywhere. Every church and every heart is the theatre of its battles. In many the witnesses have been killed already, or are just dying; their voice is scarcely heard. Everywhere the world is aggressive, and mounts the highest places in the kingdom, at least modifying its worship and its discipline, if not entirely corrupting it, and threatening to extinguish their life. Never were the true children of the kingdom more loudly called on to be faithful to their high calling: to see well to it that their consecration is complete, and their lives lives of witness-bearing, lives of simple trust in the Lord Jesus, as their King as well as Priest, lest, by conformity to the world, they betray or deny Him. The practical lesson is for all times and ages, and for none more than ours. Let us heed it. Our encouragements are equal to our perils. It is declared that "when the enemy cometh in like a flood, the Spirit of the Lord shall raise up a standard against him;" and this is in immediate connection with the assurance, "So shall they fear the name of the Lord from the west, and His glory from the rising of the sun." Then let not the standard-bearers faint. Let not the feeblest child even, in the kingdom, regard his testimony as powerless. "Thou hast given a banner to them that fear Thee, that it may be displayed because of the truth."

LECTURE XXVII.

THE VITALITY OF GOD'S WITNESSES, AND THE TRIUMPH OF A PURELY SPIRITUAL TESTIMONY.

Rev., Chap. xi.: 11-14.

"And after three days and a half, the spirit of life from God entered into them, and they stood upon their feet, and great fear fell upon them which saw them. And they heard a great voice from heaven saying unto them, Come up hither. And they ascended up to heaven in a cloud, and their enemies beheld them. And the same hour there was a great earthquake, and the tenth part of the city fell, and in the earthquake were slain of men seven thousand, and the remnant were affrighted, and gave glory to the God of heaven. The second woe is past; and, behold, the third woe cometh quickly."

WE have seen that these two symbolical witnesses of God, as defined by the words of the angel himself, are the two great functions of the church, her worship and discipline, by which she testifies to the cross and crown of Christ. We have seen the power of that testimony, even in their sackcloth state, amidst the corruptions that pollute the city of God and the courts of His house, in the plagues it brings down upon an ungodly world, who reject and oppose it. We have seen that, in the war of the beast from the bottomless pit, of the world's power in a spiritual form, upon the saints, these two functions of the church become lifeless, dead forms, over which the world rejoices, while she carefully preserves them. The earlier history of these witnesses is thus one in which there is a strange mingling of mighty power with sackcloth and death and unburied corpses.

We come now to the glorious sequel of all this. The triumph of the beast is brief. The world's shouts over a prostrate church are premature, and shall soon give way to terror. The witnesses of God are indestructible, not indeed by virtue of any life in themselves, but by virtue of their relation to God. Their death is but temporary, and only in order to show to the church itself and to the world the true source of their life and power, and so secure their eternal triumph. This is the subject of the verses before us.

We first call attention to a passage in the previous verses not yet noticed. It is only "when they shall have finished their testimony,"—verse 7—that the beast obtains power to kill them.

§. 1. These witnesses safe while delivering their testimony.

As long as these agencies are delivering their testimony, they are safe. The exercise of their spiritual function is their defence. It is only when they cease to utter it, when their lips no longer move under the inspiration of God, and no longer utter a testimony for him, that they are killed. While the worship and discipline of the church deliver a clear spiritual testimony to the cross and crown of Jesus, they are indestructible. So that, according to the account here given, the cessation of their testimony is rather the cause of their death than merely its effect. The *death* of these witnesses is not the suppression of their testimony, but the extinction of the whole life of worship and spiritual government, which is the result of their ceasing to testify. This result, of course, renders all further testimony impossible. The faithfulness and constancy of the church, in employing these agencies in declaring a pure testimony for God, secures their spiritual life and power. They can only be killed by ceasing to testify for God.

But the language here used implies still further, that even this shall not be until their testimony is complete: all the truth clearly made known necessary for the salvation of a believing sinner and the condemnation of an unbelieving world. The church has a work to do by these witnessing agencies during the weeks of the world's trampling of its courts, which must be done. Every syllable of the testimony given to it shall be proclaimed, and that in every variety of form and manner necessary to meet every encroachment of error, and every art of the beastly power. Not until the Lord, who presides over this whole process, sees that this is done, that this testimony to His love, and blood, and power, is all-sufficient, does He, in just judgment upon an unbelieving world and a corrupt church, deliver over the latter to the world's deadly embrace, to such a degree that its worship and government are no longer living powers, but dead forms. How this bears upon the progress of the kingdom we can easily see. He thus shows to His church where her life and power lies; and by suffering her conformity to the world to work out its legitimate and fatal results, He shows the necessity of entire separation from the world, and of another testimony than this of the witnesses in sackcloth, of the worship and discipline of a church whose outward courts are overrun by the world; the necessity of a testimony to be uttered from a purely spiritual sphere, like that of Peter and the other apostles on the day of Pentecost. He thus, too, demonstrates the essential malignity of the world, and the fatal power of its friendship; how, even in its best forms—the best that modern civilization and refinement can give it—it is beastly in its nature, and from the bottomless pit, and fatal to the purity and life of the church, to all that makes her worship and discipline to mirror forth the cross and crown of her Redeemer. This triumph of the world, therefore, is only in order to the more complete overthrow of its power in and over the church, and to the deliverance of the church from it; and this slaying of these witnesses is only a predestined and necessary step to their entire deliverance from the power of the world, from their sackcloth state, and their sorrowing testimony.

Accordingly, they remain dead but three days and a half. This period of time, as literally applied to the symbol, was barely long enough to show that these bodies were certainly dead; thus teaching that this period of spiritual death shall only continue long enough to prove the dependence of these agencies of the church upon the Spirit of God; that without it they are hopelessly dead. The number three and a half, being the expressive symbol itself of imperfection—the half of the seven—is itself an intimation that this death can never be complete and perfect, so as to be beyond reviving. And when viewed comparatively with the three years and a half of their previous testimony, and the unlimited triumph afterwards, it forcibly represents the very great brevity of this period of death, compared with that even of their powerful testifying in sackcloth, much more with that of their succeeding triumph.

§. 2. Their speedy reviving.

Then "the spirit of life from God entered into them, and they stood upon their feet; and great fear fell upon them which saw them." Here, again, are the words of the seer, describing what he saw and heard, and not, as in the verses before, reporting the words of the angel making known the history of the witnesses during the period of the preceding trumpets, or rather the state of things revealed by them. This seems to follow from the change in the tense of the verbs; in the previous verses the future is used, and they are all the language of simple prediction; here the simple past is resumed, and the language is that of plain narrative, of the symbolic scene presented.

These words need no laboured exposition. Their meaning almost forces itself upon us. What could express more beautifully and forcibly than these symbols do, the truth which is the only hope of the suffering, struggling church of God, smothered and crushed under the power of the world, that in her extremity the life-giving Spirit of God shall reanimate her torpid frame, and, instead of the stiffness and ghastliness of spiritual death, shall infuse His own mighty energies, lifting up her prostrate agencies to their feet, and clothing them with the fresh and vigorous powers of a heavenly life? Is not such a resurrection of the dead the very scene presented by every revival of pure religion in a church previously sunk in formalism and death? When the spirit of life from God enters into the lifeless forms of her worship and government, how complete the transformation! Her songs of praise, her prayers, and her preaching, are no longer mere music, and vain repetitions, and powerless displays of intellect, eloquence, or fanaticism, nor her discipline an expression merely of human power; they are the awful, living communion of souls with a present God, and they display the power of a present God, and beholders are filled with awe. Before, they ridiculed; before, they rejoiced in the very powerlessness of these forms, as if religion itself were but a name; now, they fear and tremble, and confess that God is in her of a truth. So "fear came upon every soul" who beheld the wonders of spiritual power on Pentecost, and in the primitive church of Jerusalem.

But the transformation does not end here. These witnesses, thus revivified, hear "a great voice from heaven saying unto them, Come up hither. And they ascended up into heaven in a cloud; and their enemies beheld them." Here, again, the meaning is as evident as the truth is important and precious. No sooner are the worship and the government of the church revived by the Spirit of God entering into them, and animating all their forms, than they are called up out of the mere earthly sphere, and from under the earthly influences

§. 3. The spiritual elevation of these witnessing agencies.

before surrounding them, into the purely spiritual and heavenly sphere. Their ascension into this sphere is a thing that even their enemies are compelled to see. Even now, when reviving influences come upon a dead church, this spiritual elevation, this rising up on the cloud of heavenly influences, from the low level of the worldliness in which they before seemed to mingle, to sit in heavenly places, surrounded by the displays of heavenly powers and of the Divine presence, is seen, and acknowledged by all.

Now, it is this spirituality, this heavenliness of these agencies, this complete separation of them from all worldly connections and supports, whether political, social, or literary, so that they manifestly to all move and act in dependence on a higher power, and under its mighty, though secret, influence; it is this which is to secure to the church of Christ her victory. In whatever degree she has been victorious over human powers and hearts, this has ever been the means; her enemies have been made to perceive her spiritual nature and power. But this has been hitherto so limited and partial ever since apostolic times, that when the church, as a whole, is looked upon, these agencies of her's, her worship and discipline, though they testify for God, yet do it as if clothed in sackcloth, rather than raised on a cloud to heaven. The sackcloth testimony of these times of worldliness can never bring about such a triumph of truth and holiness as God has promised to His church. It is enough to condemn the world for its resistance to the kingdom, and it is made powerful to save an elect people even in the darkest times; but not till a new and mighty baptism of the Spirit shall descend upon the entire worship and government of the church, now so often dead and powerless, and call them up into the high places of the spiritual kingdom, and show them as agencies, not of an earthly, but a heavenly power, are we to expect the courts of the house of God to be cleansed, and the corruptions of the city of God cast down. This is the result which is next represented as following this resurrection and ascension of the witnesses.

"And the same hour was there a great earthquake; and the tenth part of the city fell, and in the earthquake were slain seven thousand names of men; and the remnant were affrighted, and gave glory to the God of heaven." The hour of a spiritual resurrection of the great witnessing agencies of the church, and their ascension into a purely spiritual and heavenly sphere before the world, is the hour of a great overthrow of the worldly powers opposed to the interests of God's spiritual kingdom, especially of such as had established themselves within His visible church. Of this the earthquake is the appropriate symbol, as we have already fully seen. The apparently solid foundations on which men have built their schemes and systems, and sought to introduce a golden age of earthly good, in which liberty, and science, and literature should heal all human woes, this heaves as the ocean waves, and prostrates all these godless superstructures. In this overthrow, the tenth part of the city, of that city which was given over to be trodden under foot of the Gentiles—verse 1—that is, of the visible church which had been corrupted by the world, falls. The tenth, or tithe, is the acknowledgment that all is held from God; the tenth part falling is the pledge and symbol of the deliverance of the whole from the power that had been treading it under foot so long, and implies the destruction of all their unauthorized additions. Such overthrow, confusion and ruin of the great and massive structures of these Babel-builders, shall fill them with shame and confusion. All their reputation and authority in the church shall utterly perish.

We here meet with a very unusual phrase, one which

§. 4. The effects of their revival and elevation.

could not have been chosen by the Spirit without design. It does not appear in the translation, but is given in the margin. There " were slain," not " seven thousand men," but " seven thousand names of men." Does not the expression, "names of men," in such a symbolical description, seem at once to suggest that the objects destroyed were the human influences, opinions, and forms of authority that by the thousand had been prevailing in the visible church? The number *seven* thousand implied the completeness of this destruction throughout the whole extent of the covenanted city of God, and in all covenant relations. These thousands of human opinions and authorities are the very things that have so trodden under foot the holy things of Zion; and these certainly must perish as soon as spiritual power invests and pervades the worship and discipline of the church.

In this overthrow of the proud structures and adornments with which a corrupting world has polluted the simplicity of the spiritual Zion, all human authority in the church shall die; all the thousands of names of men, of authorities of every earthly kind, so long appealed to, and so universally regarded, shall perish; and one name alone, the name of Jesus, be adored, and His authority only revered.

Then " the remnant," the rest that is of the city, all within the precincts of the visible church, all enjoying her privileges, and dwelling within her walls, " were filled with fear, and gave glory to the God of heaven." The state of things depicted in verse second of this chapter is thus brought to an end; the visible church is cleansed, and restored to her primitive simplicity and purity. All the proud schemes of men for advancing, and adorning, and enriching the external church being overthrown, all the hopes formed from worldly alliances being crushed, all shall be compelled to see that there is no hope for man but in the simple gospel of God's grace, as proclaimed by heavenly witnesses, and with the martyr spirit of unmixed and unwavering trust in God. That alone shall be felt to be the power and wisdom of God unto salvation. "They shall give glory" thus "to the God of heaven."

This completes the second woe, and the revelations of the sixth angel's trumpet. "The second woe is past, and behold the third woe cometh quickly."

It will help to a clearer apprehension of the meaning, the connection, and the unity of this whole portion of the book, and to a deeper and more correct impression of the great truths here taught, to glance at the disclosures of this sixth trumpet together, viewing them as one whole. It is in this aspect that they are here presented.

This trumpet, first, in answer to all the prayers of the saints, releases from the restraints by which they were bound, all the forces of the world controlled by its power and its wisdom; which immediately, as monster horsemen, with all the insignia of hell, spring forth in such numbers as to cover the earth, to their work of merciless violence and serpent cunning, inflicting deserved vengeance upon a corrupt and oppressive church, and producing most fearful and widespread calamities, but no repentance. This is an effect that judgments cannot produce; it requires a far different exercise of divine power. That is next, and immediately presented. The mighty Angel of the covenant appears, with the book of the divine testimony in His right hand—the gospel of His power—and laying claim to earth and sea, declares that there shall be no longer delay. This implied that the last development of the worldly and Satanic power had appeared; what had just been shown in the last vision, was the last species of judgment which the world should be made to inflict upon itself. But all the agencies and judgments hitherto presented were those of wrath, not of salvation; and yet salvation was the very design of the conflict, the end of the kingdom. It remained, therefore, to show how and by what means that end was to be secured, which the Angel declared to be at hand. In doing this He shows that, besides those agencies of wrath and destruction, there is all along another, a secret, and yet most mighty agency of mercy working out this very result in some degree; and that these very judgments were but the effects of that mercy abused and rejected. There were other and saving results which are wrought out during all this process; and the same agency by which these are wrought shall have its way prepared by those judgments to a final triumph of salvation, when "the mystery of God shall be finished, as He has declared unto His servants the prophets." This agency is represented by the "little book" given to the prophet, and the charge to prophesy before many people, the gospel of His grace committed to His church to be preached to all nations. It should preserve a true spiritual church, answering to the exactest measurements of the divine word, even while the external church should be trodden down by the earthly minded. Thus is represented the condition of the spiritual kingdom, and also of the visible church, its proper representative, during this whole period of the conflict. While the locusts of error, and the innumerable and monstrous influences of the worldly power and wisdom were desolating the visible church, and causing its sacred courts and external ordinances to be desecrated, as the temple and holy city trodden down by foreigners, the true church was still secure, and her voice was still to be heard uttering her simple and powerful testimony, by means of her two witnesses, her two great functions of worship and discipline. This testimony would be active and unceasing. But it would be in sackcloth. Instead of being for the most part joyful and triumphant, it would be largely that of a rejected gospel; and hence the very plagues that had already been described are made to appear as the result of rejecting these witnesses. While these witnesses testify, they are safe; but when they finish that, and cease to testify for God, their life is gone. Not until the beast from the bottomless pit, in the last development of his power and cunning, has so entered and controlled the church as to render its worship and government dead forms, can this ever occur. This is the last result of the world's power and wisdom, as represented in the monster horsemen; they not only cast off the chains and torments of the spiritual despotism, but subject the church, in all its external order, to their poisonous and deadening influence. Then there is no more delay. Then, in the very moment of the world's fancied victory, these dead forms are revived by the spirit of life from God entering into them, and ascend at the divine call into their proper spiritual and heavenly sphere, where, entirely untrammelled by, and independent of, all worldly influences, they are seen by all men to be of God, and their testimony exerts its divine power as when first delivered by the apostolic church. Then the powers of evil fall; the church, delivered from the embrace of the world, appears as a purely spiritual power; and the world, impervious to mere judgments, bows at the simple words of the gospel: great fear comes upon all beholders. This, and nothing else, and nothing less than this, this reviving of the witnessing of apostolic times, under the mighty outpouring of the spirit of life, is what must overcome the great obstacle to the church's victory, and makes ready the world for the triumphs of the seventh trumpet, the final destruction of all Satanic and earthly influences. This "third woe cometh quickly."

The whole of these varied and striking symbols, introduced under the sixth trumpet, are thus seen to relate to the one grand theme, the purification of the visible church, and the perfecting of her witnessing agencies, the instrument of her power. They show the utter overthrow of apostacy, and the restoration of the true church to her primitive purity and power. Fierce judgments shall sweep away the one; sore chastisements shall purify the other; and a new life from the Spirit shall pervade all her agencies, and fill them with the power of God.

Since, then, this ascension of the witnesses, and its effects, is a restoration to the church of the Pentecostal spirit and power, with which she first went forth conquering and to conquer, the scenes of that day will give us the clearest illustration of the glorious things which are here spoken of her. No where do the nature and power of a simple spiritual testimony so shine forth. Before that, even the apostles, though associated with Jesus for three years and a half, had learned but little of the testimony they were to deliver; they were still dark and silent, under the power of Jewish and sinful prejudices, until the Spirit of power descended, and transformed their whole natures. Then they seemed to have heard a voice saying, Come up hither, and at once they arose into a new sphere, in which the true glory and blessedness of the spiritual kingdom spread itself before them. They felt its mighty influences. All Jewish prejudices, and visions of earthly thrones and splendours, were fused and dissipated by the intense glow of that divine fire that burned in their newly enlightened souls. They then uttered, as the messengers of their crucified and glorified King, their simple but sublime testimony, announcing the efficacy of His blood, the power of His throne, the reality and glory of His personal reign, the extent of His claims, and the freeness of His grace. They were words of power. The strongholds of national pride, and carnal prejudices, and worldly attachments, fell as did the walls of Jericho before the trumpets of Israel's priests. Thousands of hearts were humbled in the dust. This spiritual power pervaded and moulded the whole infant church. She sprung into being full-armed and mighty. "They continued steadfastly in the apostle's doctrine, and in breaking of bread, and in prayers. And fear came upon every soul. * * * And they, continuing daily with one accord in the temple, and breaking bread from house to house, did eat their meat with gladness and singleness of heart, praising God, and having favour with all the people. And the Lord added to the church daily of such as should be saved." That, certainly, was no prophesying in sackcloth. Such gladness this world has seldom witnessed. Now it is precisely such a testimony as this, so purely spiritual, so completely separated from, and raised above, the earthly sphere, which must again be uttered by the church, and fill her with like scenes of joy and triumph, and a gazing world with wonder and awe.

Then, indeed, it seemed as if the mighty influence would sweep before it both Jew and Gentile. But the wisdom of God had ordered otherwise. "His way is in the sea, and His path in the great waters, and His footsteps are not known." Very soon the enemy was permitted to enter in. The mystery of iniquity began to work, and the witnesses no longer appeared in their native spiritual sphere; but being surrounded and oppressed by earthly encroachments and usurpations, they appeared clothed in sackcloth, and their testimony, though powerful to condemn the world, was comparatively weak to conquer and to save it.

But this state of depression and feebleness is not to last always, as indeed it never has been continuous and universal. It has again and again been relieved by the descent of the Spirit of God, filling all the ordinances of the church with the power of a new life. When the purposes of God in this are fully accomplished, these witnesses, whose lifeless forms have so often been the subject of the world's rejoicing, and are so even now to a deplorable degree, shall be reinvested with life by the Spirit of God, and every where the gospel shall reassert its power. The promises of God that the Spirit shall be copiously poured out on all flesh, have not been exhausted by the opening scenes at the establishment of the kingdom, and by the limited and partial revivings since. These last are, indeed, blessed intimations of the glorious things spoken of the city of our God, intimations given now to sustain the faith and hopes of the church, and gather in an elect people, during her fierce struggle with the beast, and while this beastly power pollutes her courts and external ordinances so widely. It needs only the same power that is now imparted to a dead church, like Sardis, by the spirit of life from God entering into it, and the voice from heaven calling it up, in the exercise of its great functions, from its earthly connections and dependencies, into its own "native heavenly and spiritual sphere;" it needs but this to descend upon the church generally, and to rest upon it permanently, in order to realize through all its extent, and in all its branches, the glorious vision of the text.

And it shall come. Blessed be God for this vision of the risen and ascended witnesses. Not always shall the worship and discipline of the church testify in sackcloth; not always shall their testimony fall so powerless upon a scoffing world and a corrupt church. Again shall the Spirit descend as a rushing mighty wind, filling the assemblies of the saints with evidences of the gracious presence and power of our ascended Lord, not less convincing than the tongues of fire and words of power that filled Jerusalem with wonder and joy on the first day of the kingdom's appearing. Let not the hearts of God's people, then, be filled with fear because of the apparent triumphs of the world. Let them remember that the world's highest triumph immediately precedes the highest triumph of the slain witnesses, the complete separation of the church in her worship and government from the world.

But have we nothing to do, or to hope for, in the mean time? By no means. Even during the wide prevalence of the power of worldliness in the church, the work of witnessing must go on; it is her only hope and defence.

Let every child of God keep near to the altar and the mercy seat, and separate from the world. Let every member and every officer of the church, and especially every minister, seek to infuse into all her forms and acts of worship, into all her enterprises and organizations, into all her government and discipline, the spirit of an entire consecration, the spirit of holiness and submission, that so the triumph of the beast may be as limited as possible; and though in many places it may kill these witnesses, yet that in many others their voice may be heard ringing clearer and louder in the world's ears the truth, both of salvation and perdition.

Not only so. We are here assured that this final triumph shall be brought about by the very same means and power that the church has in covenant possessed ever since the ascension of her Lord, and the first descent of the Spirit; the same that in individual churches, and for limited seasons, have repeated in their measure the scenes of the day of Pentecost. There is no new agent or element to be brought in; at least no intimation of any such is here given, where, if anywhere, it might be expected. In all these agencies of judgment and of grace, there is not one that has not already scourged and blessed the church and the world. These symbolic visions, sweeping as they do over the whole conflict, and purposely unfolding its nature and the means of triumph, must present to us all that it is right for us to depend upon or expect. The same testimony, the same agencies, the same life-giving Spirit that laid in Jerusalem the foundations of the church, are those which are to bring forth its "headstone" with shoutings of, Grace, grace unto it. These, be it remembered, are the constant heritage of the church. In her union with her divine Head she has an exhaustless fountain of spiritual influences. It is her own unfaithfulness that postpones her triumph, and delays the promised blessing. No other cause dare we give, with the Bible in our hands, whatever views we may entertain of the sovereignty of God in permitting it. And these influences and agencies can even now secure to the individual church and believer, the same victory that will then cover with its glory all the churches of Christ. If in any case now, the world has so entered the church as to make her worship and ordinances a dead form, cold and powerless, there stands on record the solemn charge to the church of Sardis, " Be watchful, and strengthen the things which remain, that are ready to die, * * * and repent;" and there stands also the gracious invitation to Laodicea, " Behold I stand at the door," the door even of such a church, " and knock; if any man," even a single member, " hear My voice, and open the door, I will come in to him, and will sup with him, and he with Me." There stands, also, as the chiefest of all the promises, diffusing its glory over every page of revelation, the promise of the Holy Spirit to every one who asks; let the church plead for it with believing earnestness, until, descending, it reanimate them with new life and power. That voice, too, " Come up hither," is but the constant voice of the Word calling the church and all her agencies away from all mere worldly dependencies and associations, to move amidst heavenly things, and under heavenly influences, to rise on the cloud of the divine presence to a spiritual elevation above the world, high as the heaven is above the earth. Let not the din of worldliness prevent our hearing, and joyful obedience.

LECTURE XXVIII.

THE TRIUMPH.

REV., CHAP. XI. : 15-18.

"And the seventh angel sounded, and there were great voices in heaven, saying, The kingdom of this world has become our Lord's and His Christ's, and He shall reign for ever and ever. And the four and twenty elders, which sat before God on their thrones, fell upon their faces, and worshipped God, saying: We give Thee thanks, O Lord God Almighty, which art, and wast, [and art to come,] because Thou hast taken to Thee Thy great power, and hast reigned. And the nations were angry, and Thy wrath came, and the time of the dead that they should be judged, and that Thou shouldest give reward unto Thy servants the prophets, and to the saints, and them that fear Thy name, small and great, and shouldest destroy them which destroy the earth."

THE seventh trumpet calls up only a grand vision of victory. Like the opening of the seventh seal, it shows that the conflict has ended, and reveals the blessed and eternal results. Nothing more was left to be revealed, according to the plan and design of this section of the book. That design was not to give a prophetic narrative of facts, but a comprehensive picture sketch of the whole history of the kingdom; to show the secret springs, and true nature and tendencies of all those events and changes which should attend the progress and spread of the church. It was intended to bring to light the world's hidden history, as seen from the Redeemer's throne, and working out His glory, and the church's salvation, and the earth's deliverance.

Now, the symbolic scenes evoked by these seven trumpets do this completely; and those of the six already considered leave not out a single feature of the great conflict. There is not a fact in the whole history of the Christian dispensation, the leading characteristics of which, in its relation to the kingdom of God, is not described in these visions. There is not a single trait in the social and corporate life of the church, nor a single principle of human nature, as influenced by the truths of the gospel and the devices of Satan, either unto life or unto death, that does not naturally and necessarily find its place, and a revelation of its true nature, under some one or more of these symbolic views. Every soul, and every church, as well as the whole kingdom of God, may find here an analysis of its spiritual history. When, therefore, the trumpet of the seventh angel sounds, it can reveal nothing but victory to the kingdom, and the last woe to all that have opposed it.

First, therefore, this triumph is presented here as a thing already accomplished by the agencies, and instrumentalities, and processes already made known. As soon as the seventh angel sounds, we hear great voices in heaven, the shout of the redeemed church, proclaiming, "The kingdom of this world is become the possession of our Lord, and of His Christ." This is not a prediction that the present political organizations of this world are Christianized, that all civil governments are administered by the saints, and according to the principles of the gospel; it is rather a declaration that these kingdoms are all swept away, as things adapted only to a fallen and depraved race, and that one kingdom, the kingdom of Christ, has taken possession of the whole field, and that the dominion and inheritance lost in the fall, and so long usurped by Satan, has been regained by Christ. This seems to be implied by all that follows; and if the reading of the text now universally adopted be correct, in which we have "the kingdom of the world," and not "the

§ 1. This triumph already completed.

kingdoms," it must be the meaning. But, on any interpretation, it asserts Christ's universal reign, as actually established and fully acknowledged over all the earth.

The victory, therefore, is presented in its full completeness, exactly as under the other trumpets; the various agencies of discipline and grace appear full grown and developed, in which state alone their true nature can be distinctly understood. But it includes, of necessity, all minor, previous, and subservient victories. Every triumph of truth and holiness over the power and wisdom of the world, the victory of each individual conqueror in that personal conflict, to whom, in the messages to the seven churches, the glories of the perfected kingdom are promised, has been a part of this victory, has contributed to the final result, and is therefore included.

§. 2. By no other agencies than those already revealed.

Now, the fact that, in order to this consummation, either in whole or in part, no other agencies than those previously described, are here introduced, and no further conflict indicated, shows that under the previous trumpets all these have been presented. This fell under our notice in the last lecture; but its full confirmation here, and its importance, justifies some additional exposition. All the means and agencies entering into this conflict, and securing this eternal triumph, must be found under the previous six trumpets. We have already found them there. That little book in the hand of the mighty angel, and its divine testimony, as proclaimed in the church by her two witnesses, first in their sackcloth estate, then as revived and elevated, and beheld by the world in their true spiritual sphere, are the only saving influences. The Spirit of God, pervading the worship and government of His church, and so giving power to her testimony, is the sole means of converting sinners and sanctifying believers. And to this is attributed, as we have seen, the overthrow and victory recorded in the thirteenth verse.

Whatever, therefore, is meant by this consummation of the kingdom must be the result of this, so far as any conflict is involved. We say, so far as any conflict is concerned, for of course it does not exclude the final stroke of almighty wrath and saving power which ends the conflict, by the final act of judgment, by which the dead are raised, and death and hell are cast into the burning lake, when Christ "shall judge the quick and dead at His appearing and His kingdom." That is the final act of the Great King himself, putting an end to all conflict, and to all these means and agencies, and awarding the final glory and the last woe. But the worship and government of a church filled with the life of the Spirit, and cut loose from the world, and moving in a purely spiritual sphere, is the sole agency of triumph in that spiritual conflict by which the saints are gathered, and the kingdom perfected in the number and character of its subjects: the sole agency till the end comes, and agencies and conflicts cease together.

It was announced by the mighty angel who stood on the sea and the land, that "delay should be no longer, but in the days of the voice of the seventh angel, when he shall begin to sound,"—literally, when he is about to sound,—" the mystery of God should be finished;" or, as now generally read, "whenever he is about to sound, the mystery of God is finished." This sounding accordingly brings to our ears the shouts of a victory already accomplished, without any other means than those before revealed. No other, therefore, is to be expected. By the very same means that every individual conqueror has been enabled to secure possession of those glories held out by the seven promises "to him that overcometh," by the same shall every future victory be secured, until the whole body of Christ's redeemed shall be completed. By the same weapons with which this kingdom has been always achieving its victories, weapons "not carnal, but mighty through God to the pulling down of strongholds," it shall achieve the last, subduing by the Word and Spirit the very last elect sinner. These weapons derive their power from Him who sits on the throne, and ministers the Spirit to His church, and to whom we look for those reviving influences which shall put life into even a dead church, and make it the joy and praise of all the earth. He is reigning. "He must reign till He hath put all enemies under His feet." This is the very design of the present mediatorial dispensation. "The Lord said unto my Lord, Sit Thou at My right hand until I make Thine enemies Thy footstool." "The Lord shall send the rod of Thy strength out of Zion; rule Thou in the midst of Thine enemies." "God hath highly exalted Him, and given Him a name which is above every name, that at the name of Jesus every knee should bow, of things in heaven and things in earth, and things under the earth; and that every tongue should confess that Jesus Christ is Lord, to the glory of God the Father." Till this design be accomplished this dispensation cannot end. It is the accomplishment of this which is here announced. Then the whole nature of the administration changes, and eternal triumph succeeds the long conflict.

The triumph here described, when complete, is the consummated end of redemption. This is the very idea of "the seventh." It perfects and completes.

§. 2. This triumph the consummation of redemption.

It is also expressly taught by its being the trumpet of "*the last woe.*" No others, therefore, can follow; so that this must be the final and irremediable destruction of all opposition to the kingdom. It is the final judgment that seals the ruin of every opposer, and leaves the kingdom in sole possession of the earth.

§. The last woe.

When the second woe was announced as past, it was said, "behold the third woe cometh quickly." It does not follow from this that this woe will be completed quickly, or rather that the whole of it will come at once, or immediately after the second; but the beginning of it, the first outpourings of it, follow quickly. That second woe was the judgments that crushed out the earthliness of the church, and in consequence she became filled with new life by the Spirit. Now, whenever and wherever this is done, the third and last woe is impending over every one who rejects her testimony. As triumph follows revival, so damnation treads upon the heels of a rejected gospel when accompanied with such demonstrations of the Spirit's power. This is a truth that pervades the whole history of the kingdom. This last woe began to descend when the first soul finally rejected the Spirit of God and the testimony of His grace; it has always been quickly following the second; but it will not be finished until the last sinner receives his doom, and the last trace of the reign of sin is burnt out from the earth.

No intimation, therefore, can be drawn from these words, "the third woe cometh quickly," of the length of time that is to pass between the resurrection of the witnesses and the complete consummation of the triumph, even if the former event, which is confined to no particular time or place, should at last find a general and universal fulfilment in a church revived and purified over all the earth. It will still be true that the third woe will quickly follow the second. The brighter the displays of spiritual power, the quicker the sinner fills up his cup of wrath, and every evil hastens to its final development and ruin. But before that woe is all exhausted, the conquests of the church may be multiplied, for aught we know, certainly for aught we are here told, through a thousand generations or ages. No mortal can say they will not. While it was not only important, but necessary, that some intimations of time should be given in connection with their church's tribulations, that their limited and comparatively brief duration might appear, it is sufficient to know that when the Spirit of life comes triumph follows, a triumph without any limitation; and though years and ages may intervene before the Spirit's work is done, and all of God's redeemed gathered in, and the triumphs symbolized by the seventh angel's trumpet completed, yet that, when they are completed, redemption is consummated, and also that till then, whenever and wherever the Spirit thus works with power, infusing new life into the agencies of the church, the end to each soul is at hand, whether it be one of salvation or damnation. The beginning of triumph, or the beginning of the last woe, cometh quickly. So in regard to the whole world: the completion of this last woe is the consummation of the triumph, the completion of the mediatorial work of redemption.

The whole, also, of the language of this shout of triumph, and song of the elders which follows, can fairly mean nothing else.

§. Not merely the expected millenium.

These, indeed, have been applied by some to the period popularly called the millenium, when, as is supposed, Christianity shall be extended over all the earth, and control all its governments, and pervade and mould all the social life of men, while yet men are living in the flesh, and born in sin, and subject necessarily to the spiritual conflict, and while, therefore, death still reigns. This would be just such a state of things as sometimes is witnessed, in a limited extent, during a great revival, when all opposition is borne down by a mighty effusion of the Spirit, and everybody is either seeking the Lord, or filled with wonder and awe. But this is the precise condition symbolized by the revival of the two witnesses and their ascension, the Spirit of life filling the worship and government of the church, and causing them to appear in their true heavenly character and relations. The universal prevalence of such Pentecostal times, and their long continuance, would constitute precisely that millennial glory. Now, beyond all doubt, all such spiritual triumphs, whether partial or universal, and continued through ages, are, as we have already said, included in the announcement of the seventh angel's trumpet; but only as every minor victory, during a long war, is included in the final triumph. It is included only as it is related to, and helps to, that triumph. If, indeed, the Spirit, like a rushing mighty wind, comes down on all the church, as He did on the little band in the upper room at Jerusalem, and sweeps over all the nations as over the thousands there and then, the church may then more fully than ever anticipate the final and glorious consummation, and may give expression to her joy in some of these strains uttered by the great voices in heaven and the crowned elders. But none of these, nor all of them together, can exhaust the meaning of the words here used. These words cannot be used till the *everlasting* kingdom of our Lord and Saviour shall take the place of His mediatorial reign; till the dead are raised and judged. This triumph, therefore, must include the end of this whole period of the mediatorial reign of conflict, and the glorious introduction of that everlasting kingdom of our Lord over His own redeemed upon a regenerated world, the times of the restitution of all things.

"The kingdom of this world is become our Lord's and His Christ's; and they shall reign for ever and ever." Two things are here most clearly taught. First, that this kingdom, or reign, is here on this world, and over it; and second, that of it there shall be no end. It is, then, nothing less than Christ's everlasting reign over the completed body of His redeemed, and that on the renovated earth. It cannot be His mediatorial reign, that same mediatorial reign which He is now exercising, and by which He is bringing back a lost world to God, for that ends

§. Christ's eternal reign on earth.

when its design is accomplished. It ends by a limitation in its own nature, when the last enemy is destroyed, and nothing more left for a mediatorial reign or work to accomplish. Hence the apostle says, "Then cometh the end, when He shall have delivered up the kingdom to God, even the Father; when He shall have put down all rule, and all authority and power. For He must reign till He hath put all enemies under His feet. The last enemy that shall be destroyed is death. * * * And when all things shall be subdued unto Him, then shall the Son also Himself be subject unto Him that put all things under Him, that God may be all in all."[1] But here we have a reign, a kingdom of Christ on earth, which shall be for ever and ever; and we have it, too, as the result of the great conflict of the mediatorial reign, by which all enemies are subdued. It can, therefore, be no other than that which follows His present mediatorial reign, and includes all its glorious and eternal results; when Christ, having completed His mediatorial work, shall enjoy the full reward, and reign with His people upon the renovated earth, and God Himself again dwell with them, and be their God. "He shall reign for ever and ever."

§. In harmony with other Scriptures.

This view of the triumph is in beautiful harmony with every other view of the end and results of redemption, and the glory promised and expected. It must be that "manifestation of the sons of God," "when glorified together" with Christ, at "the redemption of their bodies," until which, Paul represents the whole creation as groaning, and for which both it and the church are waiting as the period of their deliverance. "For the earnest expectation of the creature waiteth for the manifestation of the sons of God. * * * Because the creature itself also shall

[1] 1 Cor. 15: 24-28.

be delivered from the bondage of corruption into the glorious liberty of the children of God. For we know that the whole creation groaneth and travaileth in pain together until now. And not only they, but we ourselves groan within ourselves, waiting for the adoption, to wit, the redemption of our body."[1]

It must include, as the consummating act, Christ's second visible coming, when "He shall appear the second time, without sin, unto salvation;" when the Lord Himself shall descend from heaven with a shout, with the voice of the archangel and the trump of God; and the dead in Christ shall rise first; then we which are alive and remain shall be caught up together with them in the clouds, to meet the Lord in the air; and so shall we ever be with the Lord." Or, as the same apostle describes the same closing act of this administration in his second epistle to the same Thessalonian church, when God shall "recompense tribulation to them that trouble you; and to you who are troubled, rest with us, when the Lord Jesus shall be revealed from heaven, with His mighty angels, in flaming fire, taking vengeance on them that know not God, and that obey not the gospel of our Lord Jesus Christ; who shall be PUNISHED WITH EVERLASTING DESTRUCTION from the presence of the Lord, and from the glory of His power, when He shall come to be GLORIFIED IN HIS SAINTS, and to be admired in ALL THEM that believe."[2] That is the first act of vengeance; till that is done the last woe cannot be consummated; when that is done, there is nothing more for His ransomed to wait for.

That is the same day of which the apostle Peter says scoffers shall inquire, saying, "Where is the promise of His coming?" and in his description of which some other striking features are added, which complete this vision of triumph. It is, he teaches us, the day for which "the

---

[1] Rom. 8: 19-23.   [2] 1 Thess. 4: 16, 17.   2 Thess. 1: 7-10.

heavens and the earth that are now," in like manner as the old world, "being overflowed with water, perished," "by the same word are kept in store, reserved unto fire against the day of judgment and perdition of ungodly men;" which "will come as a thief in the night, in the which the heavens and earth shall pass away with a great noise, and the elements shall melt with fervent heat; the earth, also, and the works that are therein, shall be burned up. Nevertheless we, according to His promise, look for new heavens and a new earth, wherein dwelleth righteousness."[1] Nothing short of this can satisfy the comprehensive idea demanded by the words, "the kingdom of this world is become our Lord's, and His Christ's, and He shall reign for ever and ever:" an eternal reign on the earth and over it. This only can consummate the hopes of a groaning creation and church, and perfect for ever the triumph of the spiritual kingdom.

§. *The whole history of the kingdom points to this.* To this the whole history of our fallen world and of the kingdom of God, points as the kingdom here meant. When God created man He made him His king on earth. As His vicegerent he was to rule it, and, as its head, to be the intelligent channel through whom all its works and processes were to find a voice to praise their Creator. He fell, renounced his allegiance, and gave himself to Satan's service. Henceforth, Satan became "god of this world;" God gave it over to his power for its own sore punishment. But not wholly. The Son of God engaged to deliver it, to crush Satan's head, to destroy his kingdom, and restore to man redeemed all that Adam lost, and all, and more than all, that Adam could have gained had he preserved the kingdom as originally given. He has redeemed it by His blood. He is now vindicating His claim to it. The opening of the seven seals revealed Him doing this by

[1] See 2 Peter 3: 13.

His mediatorial reign. These angel trumpeters reveal the conflicts and instrumentalities by which He is preparing His redeemed, who are to constitute His eternal kingdom, for their final triumph. And this last trumpet represents Him as in possession of this kingdom, as having destroyed every enemy, having abolished death, and having swept away, by the consuming and purifying fires of His second coming, every vestige of the curse which had scathed with its wrath this whole beautiful creation of God. It represents Him as reigning visibly and gloriously in the midst of His risen and glorified people, who share in His reign, over a renovated and glorified earth, whose changed conditions and laws perfectly adapt it to their glorified nature and employments. Only in such a changed condition can such an eternal kingdom of Christ on earth be conceived of.

§. *The song of the elders here requires this.* This view is not only consistent with the thanksgiving song of the twenty-four elders which follows, but necessary to preserve to its language its full and natural meaning.

"And the four and twenty elders, which sat before God upon their thrones, fell upon their faces, and worshipped God." It may be observed here that the four living creatures, previously always associated with these elders, leading and sharing with them in the same praises, are for the first time wanting; and appropriately so, because the perfect life of God's redeemed, which they symbolized, is now fully realized by this triumph, in a glorified church and a renovated creation, and in actual possession, in all its completeness and glory, by the redeemed, and therefore here, as afterwards in the New Jerusalem, the symbol disappears. That life, as developed in their own persons, is no longer imperfect; their bodies are no longer under the power of death. Their life is no longer a merely hidden life with Christ in God; "for when Christ, who is our life, shall appear, then shall we also appear with Him in glory."

Now, these elders, the representatives of the redeemed, in full personal possession of their life, no longer sing in joyful and assured hope merely, "We shall reign on the earth;" they celebrate the complete fulfilment of that hope. "We give Thee thanks, O Lord God Almighty, which art, and wast, [and art to come,[1]] because Thou hast taken to Thee Thy great power, and hast reigned." It is no longer an administration by a mediator, to remedy the evils which sin had brought, and which had caused God to withdraw from the world the direct and glorious manifestations of His presence. Those evils have been remedied, and the triune God is addressed as reigning directly, and in love, over His reconciled creatures.

In the next words, the final judgments, by which this triumph was accomplished, are made the theme of thanksgiving. "And the nations were angry." So it has always been, as in the second Psalm it is said, "Wherefore do the heathen rage, and the people imagine a vain thing? The kings of the earth set themselves, and the rulers take counsel together against the Lord, and against His Anointed." "And Thy wrath is come,"—more correctly, "came,"—"and the time of the dead, that they should be judged, and that Thou shouldest give reward unto Thy servants the prophets, and to the saints, and them that fear Thy name, small and great, and shouldest destroy them which destroy the earth." Let us beware of adding to, or taking away from, these words. This we must do if we confine them to a partial resurrection, a partial judgment, and a partial binding or destruction of the earth's destroyers. Such a meaning is forced into the

---

[1] If the true text, as all the later editions of the Greek Testament seem to agree, omits these words, it is not because He is no longer "*the coming One*," He having already come in the fulness of His glory and the fulfilment of all covenant engagements.

language, not drawn out of it. The terms are without limitation. It is *the dead*, not some of the dead, not the holy dead, that are to be judged; it is the saints, the small and great, all of them, that then receive their reward. Most assuredly these words describe the final overthrow of all evil, and its utter extermination from the earth, and destruction of death, the last enemy. Nothing more is left to be done, but for the redeemed to sit down with Christ on His throne, as He is now seated on His Father's throne.

Thus the seventh trumpet has brought us to where the seventh seal left us, gazing into an eternity of glory. Under those seals were unfolded the almighty agency of the Mediator King, directing all the events of providence and grace to this glorious result; under these seven trumpets, the human agencies and instrumentalities, and their fierce and protracted conflict with earthly and Satanic powers, are traced, until the shout of triumph rings through the heavens, and the glory of God covers all the earth.

Here the curtain drops. The glories of that state are too bright for mortal gaze, or for human speech. Some conception, indeed, of their reality, magnitude and imperishable nature we may form, and a deep impression of these is necessary if we would ever share in them. Accordingly, after some further visions of these destroyers and of their destruction, ending in the burning lake, the infinite blessedness of that state is spread out, in the last two chapters, in language which glows all over with the very brightness of heaven, and which has cheered the struggling saints in all ages, and given a clearness, definiteness and vividness to their conceptions such as have greatly strengthened their faith and quickened their hopes. With a few verses of it we shall close this view of the triumph of the mediatorial kingdom, and the opening glories of the everlasting kingdom of Christ and His saints.

"And I saw a new heaven, and a new earth; for the first heaven and the first earth were passed away; and there was no more sea. And I, John, saw the holy city, new Jerusalem, coming down from God out of heaven, prepared as a bride adorned for her husband. And I heard a great voice out of heaven, saying, Behold, the tabernacle of God is with men, and He will dwell with them, and they shall be His people, and God Himself shall be with them, and be their God. And God shall wipe away all tears from their eyes; and there shall be no more death, neither sorrow, nor crying, neither shall there be any more pain; for the former things are passed away. And He that sat on the throne said, Behold, I make all things new. And He said unto me, Write, for these words are true and faithful. And He said unto me, It is done; I am Alpha and Omega, the beginning and the end. I will give unto him that is athirst of the fountain of the water of life freely. He that overcometh shall inherit all things; and I will be his God, and he shall be My son."